More Praise for

"Towards the end of the last century North American Lutheran church bodies went through a realignment over disputes over biblical authority and the ordination of women. Now slightly more than a generation later the largest Lutheran body in America and other Protestant denominations are facing disruption over whether homosexuality is an impediment for entering the church's ministry and over giving the marriage blessing to those in same gendered relationships. In his thoroughly researched and easy to read book, *Bearing Their Burden*, Lutheran pastor Tom Eckstein points out how biblical authority is again being replaced by cultural norms. He looks at the problem from biblical, historical and pastoral perspectives and provides sympathetic guidance for those who are confronting this issue in themselves and their families and congregations. It would be difficult to locate a more useful book on this subject."

Dr. David P. Scaer, Holder of the David P. Scaer Chair of Systematic and Biblical Theology and Chairman of Systematic Theology at Concordia Theological Seminary, Fort Wayne, Indiana. Dr. Scaer is the author of *James: The Apostle of Faith; Sermon on the Mount; Christology; Baptism; Law and Gospel and The Means of Grace.*

"With grace and clarity, Tom Eckstein has cleared away the confusion of the pro-gay revisionist arguments to show that the biblical ethic of sex between one man and one woman in the covenant of marriage is in force for every Christian - regardless of whether they are heterosexually or homosexually oriented. This book is not only a great resource to people in The Lutheran Church – Missouri Synod, but to anyone who wants to answer the pro-gay arguments in order to speak the truth in love to people with same-sex attractions."

Rev. Sean Maney, ordained pastor in the Presbyterian Church of America and Director of FirstLight Ministries, St. Louis, Missouri.

"Pastor Eckstein's book is passionate, personal and pastoral. In our day it is certainly provocative as well. The author persuasively engages those who object to the traditional Christian understanding of what Scripture teaches regarding homosexual conduct. At the same time, a 'care for souls' permeates the book in a manner which makes the title most appropriate."

Dr. Mike Middendorf, Professor of Theology at Concordia University, Irvine, California. Dr. Middendorf is the author of *The 'I' in the Storm: A Study of Romans 7* and also the upcoming *Romans* commentary in the Concordia Commentary series.

"Pastor Eckstein is a catechist par excellence. In this Christ-centered gift to the Church, Eckstein demonstrates how he can take the deepest, most complicated topics and teach them in a remarkably simple way. Eckstein has done a masterful job in dismantling secular homosexual arguments, and has done it with Gospel clarity and the use of God-given reason. While Eckstein displays his command of Biblical Hebrew and Greek, at the same time, this book is written with a pastoral heart of compassion, experience, and wisdom. *Bearing Their Burden* is a fine example of intersecting Biblical truths with the faith and life of the reader; which is apologetics at its finest!"

Rev. Dr. James A. Baneck, President of the North Dakota District of The Lutheran Church – Missouri Synod.

"This well-researched book is written in the spirit and tone of the Gospel of Jesus Christ and God's compassion for sinners. It is sensitive and understanding yet without compromising Scriptural teaching but speaking God's truth in love. The author places the questions on homosexuality in the context of the central message of the Bible. Every significant passage is carefully considered and the various interpretations are evaluated in the light of the Scriptures. This very informed, helpful, and Scripturally based book is also very practical as it engages real persons who bear this burden. I highly recommend it to pastors and lay persons."

Dr. Eugene Boe, Professor of Systematic and Historical Theology as well as Academic Dean, Lutheran Brethren Seminary, Fergus Falls, Minnesota. Dr. Boe is also an ordained pastor in The Church of the Lutheran Brethren.

Front Cover Picture

The picture on the front cover of this book was taken by me in the summer of 2007. It is a picture of the Badlands in western North Dakota. Why did I choose this picture for the front cover of my book?

The desolate nature of the Badlands brings to my imagination the Desert of Judea where Jesus fasted for forty days and was tempted by the devil. If Jesus is the Son of God, why did he endure this horrible burden? He did it for US!

You see, in the Garden of Eden where Adam and Eve were surrounded by food and where they had the certain hope of living in God's love forever – in that place the devil tempted them to reject God and decide for themselves what is good and what is evil. They rejected God and believed the devil's lie.

In contrast, in the Desert of Judea where Jesus was hungry after fasting forty days and where He meditated upon the suffering and death he would eventually endure upon the cross – in that place the devil tempted Jesus to reject His Father and live for Himself.

Jesus trusted His Father. Jesus rejected the devil's temptations. Jesus was victorious over temptation FOR US! We sinners who reject God in so many ways can come to the Father in repentance knowing that we are forgiven and holy in His sight because His Son's victory over temptation has been credited to us.

Through faith in Jesus God sees you as someone who is holy and who has never believed the devil's lies or fallen to temptation. This is Good News for ALL sinners – *including those who bear the burden of homosexual desire and behavior.*

Bearing Their Burden

(Galatians 6:1-2)

Speaking the Truth in Love to People Burdened by Homosexuality

by

Tom Eckstein

Published by Lulu, Inc.

ISBN: 978-0-557-79319-8

Thanks to all who have encouraged me and supported me over the years as I researched for and wrote this book. You know who you are!

I especially want to thank my wife, Andrea, and my three children - Birgitta, Joshua and Christianna – as well as my mother, Janice Eckstein, without whose love and patience I would never have finished this book.

This book is dedicated to my father, Robert Eckstein, whom the Lord called to Himself on April 1st of 2009. My father was a loving servant, and he taught me what it means to be a man of God:

"Husbands, love your wives, just as Christ loved the church and gave himself up for her..." – Ephesians 5:25

"Fathers, do not exasperate your children; instead, bring them up in the training and instruction of the Lord." – Ephesians 6:4

╬ TABLE OF CONTENTS ╬

╬ *INTRODUCTION* ╬

I'm so glad that you are about to read my book! I don't know *why* you are reading this book. However, before you read any further, if you are a man or woman who bears the burden of same-sex attraction, then I want you to know this: GOD LOVES YOU! As you will learn from this book, we are ALL sinners who deserve nothing from God. But He chooses to love us anyway! I'm no better than you are. Even though I don't bear the burden of homosexual desire and behavior, I DO know what it means to bear the burden of a multitude of other sinful desires and behaviors. I'm a fellow sinner, and I must rely completely and totally on the mercy of God that is ours through faith in Christ.

I wrote this book out of a desire to be faithful to the God who saved me and out of love for the many people who bear the burden of same-sex attraction. ***But maybe you don't think of your same-sex attraction as a burden. Maybe you don't think of your same-sex attraction as a sin. Maybe you're very offended when I say that you need to repent of your homosexual behavior and receive forgiveness in Christ.*** That's fine. I'm willing to meet you where you are at. All I ask is that you give this book a chance and allow me to speak God's truth in love to you.

This book will show what God's Word clearly teaches about same-sex desire and behavior. This book will also respond to various attempts to *reinterpret* what God's Word clearly teaches on this issue – *reinterpretations* that deceive people and keep them from seeing God's loving plan for their lives. **But most of all, this book will help you see how Scripture points us to JESUS:** *The eternal Son of God Who died for our sins and conquered death for us by His resurrection from the grave so that we poor sinners might become God's children and live in His love – now and for all eternity. With that said, please read on!*

The Apostle Paul writes: "Brothers, if someone is caught in a sin, you who are spiritual should restore him gently. But watch yourself, or you also may be tempted. Carry each other's burdens, and in this way you will fulfill the law of Christ." (Galatians 6:1-2)

The title for my book is *Bearing Their Burden.* In the Scripture text I quoted in the previous paragraph the Apostle Paul teaches that Christians should seek to restore any person who is burdened by any kind of sin. Paul describes sinful behavior as being "caught in a sin." This language gives us an image of a person being caught in a trap - enslaved and imprisoned by his or her own sinful desires and behaviors. As Jesus said: "I tell you the truth, everyone who sins is a slave to sin." (John 8:34) All people without exception bear this burden, as Paul says: "...all have sinned and fall short of the glory of God,..." (Romans 3:23) Why do we humans bear such a burden?

Scripture teaches that God created this world and all life "very good." The first humans, Adam and Eve, were created in God's image. They did not have the burden of sin. They were perfect and holy. They and all their descendants (YOU and I) were meant to live forever in a love relationship with God. But that all changed when the devil, a rebellious angel, tempted Adam and Eve to make the same evil choice he had made: REJECT GOD AND DECIDE FOR YOURSELVES WHAT IS GOOD AND WHAT IS EVIL! Sadly, they doubted God's Word and believed the devil's lie - and the rest is our tragic history.[1]

All people descended from Adam and Eve are burdened with a sinful nature that enslaves us and separates us from God and His loving plan for our lives. The Apostle Paul writes: "...sin entered the world through one man, and death through sin, and in this way death came to all men, because all sinned..." (Romans 5:12)[2] This burden of sin results not only in physical death but, even worse, also in ***spiritual*** death – which means that we are cut off from God and His love because <u>we</u> fail to love and trust in Him.

We have been conceived as sinners (Psalm 51:5) whose natural inclination is to rebel against God and His will for us. Concerning every human being descended from Adam, God Himself has said: "...every inclination of his heart is evil from childhood." (Genesis 8:21) The Apostle Paul affirms this when, by the Holy Spirit, he

---

[1] See Genesis 2:15-17 and 3:1-19. Also 2nd Corinthians 11:3.

[2] Also see Genesis 5:3-5, Romans 6:23a, 1st Corinthians 15:45-49 and Ephesians 2:1-3.

writes: "...the sinful mind is hostile to God. It does not submit to God's law, nor can it do so." (Romans 8:7)

We sinners can do nothing to set ourselves free from the burden of sin. King David writes about this: "My guilt has overwhelmed me like a burden too heavy to bear." (Psalm 38:4) However, the same King David also writes: "Praise be to the Lord, to God our Savior, who daily bears our burdens." (Psalm 68:19)

The good news is that God has provided a way for us sinners to be set free from sin – a burden that is unbearable for us. The good news is that Jesus, God's eternal Son, has taken the burden of our sin upon Himself! As the Apostle Peter writes: "He himself bore our sins in his body on the tree, so that we might die to sins and live for righteousness; by his wounds you have been healed." (1st Peter 2:24)

Through faith in Jesus and His death and resurrection for us, we sinners can be set free from the unbearable burden of sin which expresses itself in a multitude of evil desires, thoughts, words and behaviors. This freedom flows from the fact that God has forgiven our many sins because Jesus, His Son, suffered the punishment and damnation we deserve when He died on the cross.

Paul writes the following: "...[God] has rescued us from the dominion of darkness and brought us into the kingdom of the Son he loves ... Once you were alienated from God and were enemies in your minds because of your evil behavior. But now he has reconciled you by Christ's physical body through death to present you holy in his sight, without blemish and free from accusation..." (Colossians 1:13, 21-22)

Of course, this freedom from sin through faith in Jesus does not mean that we cease to be sinners who no longer have evil desires or who no longer engage in evil behaviors. The Apostle Paul himself grieved over the fact that he continued to struggle with various sins even after God brought him to repentance and faith in Jesus. The Apostle Paul writes about this burden with these words: "I know that nothing good lives in me, that is, in my sinful nature. For I have the desire to do what is good, but I cannot carry it out. For what I do is not the good I want to do; no, the evil I do not want to do – this I keep on doing. Now if I do what I do not want to do, it is no longer I who do it, but it is sin living in me that does it. So I find this law at work: When I want to do good, evil is right there with me." (Romans 7:18-21)

Please understand! Paul does not mean that those who trust in Christ NEVER do good works and ALWAYS give in to sinful desires and temptations. By the power of the Holy Spirit working in us, those who believe in Jesus are often able to resist sin and do many good works.[3] Nevertheless, those who trust in Christ and have received the freedom of his forgiveness still continue to struggle with their sinful nature which expresses itself in various evil desires and deeds that are opposed to God's loving plan for our lives.

Simply put, being a Christian does not mean that if you try really hard you can become less sinful and more holy over time – eventually reaching a state of sinless perfection this side of heaven. No! Instead, Scripture teaches that those who trust in Christ must struggle with their sinful nature every day – a sinful nature that will be with us until the day we die. Being a Christian does **not** mean that you never sin. Being a Christian **does** mean that you grieve over the sin in your life and trust in Jesus to provide freedom through His forgiveness and the strength to say "No" to sin and "Yes" to His loving plan for our lives.

Therefore, the Christian life is defined by daily repentance and faith in Jesus. As the Apostle John writes: "If we claim to be without sin, we deceive ourselves and the truth is not in us. If we confess our sins, he is faithful and just and will forgive us our sins and purify us from all unrighteousness … My dear children, I write this to you so that you will not sin. But if anybody does sin, we have one who speaks to the Father in our defense – Jesus Christ, the Righteous One. He is the atoning sacrifice for our sins, and not only for ours but also for the sins of the whole world." (1st John 1:8-9 and 2:1-2)

This takes us back to the title of my book: *Bearing Their Burden.* We all struggle with various sinful desires and behaviors – and one such sinful desire and behavior that has taken center stage in today's culture is what many call **"homosexuality."** Some people are sexually attracted to people of the same sex - and the result is that they have sexual desires for people of the same sex and some may even act on those desires and become involved in homosexual behavior.

In Galatians 6:1-2, God teaches that Christians should bear the sinful burdens of other people and thereby fulfill the law of Christ. In a spirit of love we are to proclaim repentance and forgiveness of sins in Jesus' Name. *My prayer is that this book will help fellow Christians to serve those who are burdened by homosexuality by "bearing their burden" with the Gospel of Jesus Christ.*

---

[3] See Ephesians 2:8-10, Colossians 3:1-17, Titus 2:11-14 and 1st Peter 5:6-11.

Why another book on homosexuality?

If you perform a book search on *Amazon.com* under the topic of homosexuality, you will find numerous books and articles dealing with this issue from sociological, psychological, biological, philosophical, political, historical and religious points of view – all having different presuppositions and conclusions about homosexuality. Many Christians have written books on the issue of homosexuality from various points of view. So, why am I adding yet another book into the mix?

First, I am writing this book as a man who is an ordained pastor in the Lutheran Church – Missouri Synod (LCMS).[4] As a pastor in the LCMS, I believe I have an important contribution to make in this area. In fact, you may or may not know this, but not all Lutheran denominations agree on the issue of homosexuality. For example, the Evangelical Lutheran Church in America (ELCA), as of their national convention in August of 2009, decided to affirm their congregations who choose to bless same-sex relationships that are publicly accountable, life-long and monogamous as well as deciding to ordain into the pastoral office individuals who practice homosexual behavior within the context of publicly accountable, life-long, monogamous relationships.[5]

---

[4] For more information about the LCMS, see the web page: www.lcms.org

[5] **There are many pastors and laypeople in the ELCA who are opposed to the decisions of the 2009 ELCA convention regarding homosexuality. Many in the ELCA are striving to give a faithful witness from Holy Scripture regarding this issue.** However, the official position of the ELCA is that we should respect the "bound conscience" of those who believe that Scripture teaches we should affirm people who are living in publicly accountable, life-long, monogamous, same-sex relationships. (See *A Social Statement on Human Sexuality: Gift and Trust* , which can be found on the ELCA official web page: www.elca.org) As this book will show from Holy Scripture, the "publicly accountable, life-long, monogamous" nature of some same-sex relationships does not remove such relationships from the category of being sin and rebellion against God's will for our sexual lives because God limits sexual activity to one man and one woman within marriage. In fact, the unrepentant nature of "publicly accountable, life-long, monogamous" same-sex relationships should concern us even more than a person who agrees with God that homosexual behavior is sin and yet may engage in such activity during times of weakness and temptation, only then to repent and seek forgiveness from Christ. However, those who deny what Scripture teaches about homosexuality and engage in such behavior without repentance are in great spiritual danger – a spiritual danger that can not be removed by their sexual relationship being "publicly accountable, life-long and monogamous."

Second, I also hope to contribute some helpful insights into the debate surrounding homosexuality – insights which I have gained through my own experience of ministry to individuals and families who bear the burden of homosexuality.

What is my story?

I remember the day well. It was 1977, and I was 13 years old. I was watching TV one night, and the show I was watching had a character who confessed to his friend that he was gay. I was confused. I didn't know what it meant for a person to be "gay." I did some research and discovered what the word "gay" meant. I must admit, at that point in my life the idea of same-sex attraction and activity had never entered my mind. I could not imagine how or why someone would engage in such activity. The idea of two men having sex especially confused me. "How would that work, exactly?" I thought to myself. Let's face it, I was innocent and naïve. But it wasn't that long before I would learn that the issue of homosexuality would be much more a part of my life than I ever conceived.

I recall my first year in high school. On several occasions I overheard fellow students talking about other fellow students who were, as they said, "fags" and "queers." In some cases these young men were given the labels "fag" and "queer" because of their effeminate demeanor. Whether or not these young men actually had same-sex desires or were involved in same-sex activity, I do not know. However, I do know that I felt sorry for them. I knew some of them. They tried so hard to fit in and be accepted. They wanted to be like one of the "regular guys." In fact, they admired the young men who were very athletic and very masculine – but these were the same young men who rejected and made fun of those few young men who did not choose to have an effeminate demeanor.

During my junior year in high school I developed close friendships with other Christians my age. My family was very active in our local LCMS congregation, and God had used an experience I had at a youth event during September of my sophomore year of high school to help me mature in my faith and give me the desire to become a pastor in the LCMS. By my junior year I was craving friendship and fellowship with other Christians my age, and God provided me with such friends. However, one of my close Christian friends would eventually share something with me about himself that he had told very few others. For the sake of anonymity, I will refer to this friend as "Sam."

One day I received a letter from Sam. "What is this about?" I wondered. I saw Sam at school every day, and we also spent time with each other at bible studies and other activities involving our mutual Christian friends. Sam and I talked often. Why did he need to write me a letter?

I opened the envelope and started reading his letter, and I soon discovered why he had written to me. He started out by saying that he had tried to tell me about his problem face to face, but he never felt comfortable doing so when the opportunity arose. He then shared with me what he called his shameful secret: He was gay. Sam explained how he had always been less masculine than most other guys his age. He also confessed that during puberty he started to experience sexual attraction for men. He said he felt comfortable around young women and even enjoyed their friendship, but he never had strong sexual feelings for them as he did for men.

Later on in his letter Sam said that he wasn't sure how his gay feelings fit into God's plan for his life. He wanted to do God's will and avoid sin. But did this mean denying his sexual feelings for men? What did the Scriptures say about homosexuality? If homosexuality was a sin, how would he deal with this issue in his life? Sam confided in me as a friend and he wanted me to help him.

I must confess, to this day I have feelings of guilt over the fact that I was not much help to my friend, Sam. He entrusted me with some personal information and asked for my guidance as a Christian friend, but I let him down.

First of all, at that point in my life I didn't know the Scriptures well enough to point out even one passage that spoke to the issue of homosexual desire and behavior. I had always assumed Scripture condemned it, but at that time in my life I would not have been able to quote you even one text of Scripture that addressed homosexuality. As a result, I wasn't able to give Sam the guidance he desired from Holy Scripture.[6] I could have gone to my pastor for help in this area, but I

---

[6] In fact, many Christians (laypeople and even some pastors) may be in the same situation. They assume that homosexuality is a sin, but they would not be able to give a clear teaching of what Holy Scripture teaches about the issue, much less be able to answer and refute many of the pro-gay arguments and revisionist biblical teaching coming from liberal sectors of Christianity. How can we help others seek God's will in their struggle with homosexual desire and behavior if we do not have a clear understanding of what God Himself teaches about this issue in Holy Scripture? I hope my book will help you in this area.

didn't. I wasn't comfortable talking with him about homosexuality. I now see how that was a mistake on my part. At that time I didn't have many resources to help me study what Holy Scripture taught about homosexuality, and so my biblical knowledge of this issue remained very limited until I studied Scripture's teaching regarding homosexuality more thoroughly during my seminary years.

Another way I let Sam down was that I quickly became uncomfortable discussing this issue with him. I could not relate to his homosexual orientation, and so I thought I had nothing to offer him. *I didn't understand that what he needed was an intimate, non-sexual relationship with another man. Sam needed to learn how to be friends with other men (especially Christian men) and learn from them what it means to live as a man.* Such non-sexual friendship with other men would not necessarily have erased his homosexual desires, but such friendships would have provided the non-sexual male intimacy he needed – the lack of which in his life being one of the driving forces behind his desire for sexual intimacy with men.

One other reason I was uncomfortable talking with Sam about his homosexuality is that I was not sure how he felt about me. Was Sam attracted to me? Would spending time with me send him the wrong message? What if he initiated some sort of sexual contact with me? These fears, legitimate though they were, kept me from being the kind of friend that Sam needed me to be at that time. I should have trusted God more to help me be a friend to Sam in spite of the fears I had about the outcome of such a friendship. He was willing to be honest with me, and I could have been honest with him about how I felt concerning our relationship as well as being willing to confront him in love if I concluded that some aspects of our relationship were becoming inappropriate. Sadly, I allowed my fears to keep me from giving Sam the help he needed – and the result is that our friendship grew more and more distant. I met him once a few years after high school while I was living in St. Paul, Minnesota. But our conversation was superficial and we did not even bring up the issue of his homosexuality. That was the last time I spoke with Sam. I lost contact with him after that. I haven't heard from him in over 24 years.

In September of 1981 I enrolled as a freshmen at Concordia College in St. Paul, Minnesota. During my 4 ½ years there I had the opportunity to meet more people (both men and women) who had homosexual desires and, in some cases, acted on them. These people were my fellow students at Concordia. They fell into one of two groups. Some of them were unrepentant concerning their homosexual desire and behavior. They either denied Holy Scripture altogether or they reinterpreted the pertinent texts in such a way as to conclude that God actually affirmed their homosexual desire and behavior. But not all of my fellow students with a homosexual orientation were like this. Some of them agreed with Holy Scripture that homosexual lust and behavior are condemned by God as sinful. They had guilt over their struggle with homosexuality, and they trusted in Jesus for forgiveness and the strength to live a pure life.

I especially remember one of my fellow students at Concordia who came to me one night in our dorm while I was reading for one of my classes. For the sake of anonymity, I will call this man "Nick." Our conversation began with superficial discussion about the weather, classes, Christian music and sports. But then suddenly our conversation took a very serious turn. Nick asked if he could share some very personal information with me because he respected me and wanted my advice. I agreed. Nick then opened up to me about his struggle with unwanted same-sex desires. He confessed to me that he had recently given in to temptation and willingly engaged in a "one night stand" homosexual encounter. I then told him that I, too, was a sinner and that my struggles with *heterosexual* temptation were no less sinful than his struggles with homosexual temptation. I also assured him that his sin was forgiven through the blood of Jesus Christ.

Nick thanked me for my words of comfort. He went on to tell me how difficult it was for him to deal with homosexual desires. Then Nick said something that I would never forget. Nick said: "Why did God give me this burden to bear?" How could I answer his question?

We can't pretend to give answers to questions that God Himself has not revealed to us. Why did God allow Adam and Eve to be tempted in the first place? Why does God allow us to be conceived with a sinful nature and give us no choice in the matter? Why does God allow some people to be burdened with particular sin issues? God does not give us answers to these questions. But God **does** assure us that He loves us and that He has done something to rescue us from our sinful condition that is unbearable for us.

After Nick told me about his struggle with homosexuality being a "burden he had to bear" I soon came across the Scripture from Galatians where Paul writes: "Brothers, if someone is caught in a sin, you who are spiritual should restore him gently. But watch yourself, or you also may be tempted. Carry each other's burdens, and in this way you will fulfill the law of Christ." God was calling me to bear Nick's burden by being his friend and proclaiming to him the hope he had in the Gospel of Jesus Christ.

During my fourth year at Concordia in 1985 I wrote a paper for a class on the subject of homosexuality. I searched our college library for books on this issue, but I found very few that dealt with Scripture's teaching regarding homosexuality in any thorough way. However, I did find one impressively massive volume by a man named John Boswell. His book was entitled *Christianity, Social Tolerance, and Homosexuality.* I quickly checked out the book and began to read it – not realizing what I was about to encounter.

For some reason I assumed that the author would show me in great detail how and why Scripture condemns homosexual lust and behavior as sin. Instead, I found very thorough (and initially, very convincing) arguments that gave new interpretations to the usual texts used to teach that homosexuality is a sin. Boswell reinterpreted these texts in such a way as to show that Scripture in no way condemns adult, consensual homosexual behavior.[7] In fact, I later discovered that John Boswell himself was a practicing homosexual. I then realized that it was not enough for me to "bear the burden" of friends like Nick by helping them to see what Scripture teaches about homosexuality. I would also need to be prepared to use Scripture to give a faithful and intelligent response to those who would mislead people like Nick with their twisting of Scripture's teaching on this issue.

I graduated from Concordia College in the winter of 1986. I was still planning to go on to seminary in St. Louis in order to study for the pastoral ministry, but at that point in my life I decided to take some time off from study and work for a year or two so I could save some money for seminary expenses. I worked two different jobs – one as a security guard and the other as a care giver for special needs children and adults in various group homes and sheltered work shops. I worked at these jobs for 1 ½ years, and during that time I had a chance to meet many people – some of whom shared my Christian views, whereas others certainly did not!

My fellow employees who were non-Christians eventually came to learn that I was a Christian and planning to be a pastor. Many of them were eager to have discussions with me about various issues - such as

---

[7] I will be responding to some of Boswell's revisionist arguments later in this book.

the existence of God, the reliability of Holy Scripture, the theory of evolution versus Scripture's teaching about creation, the problem of evil and suffering, abortion and sexuality (including the issue of homosexuality). I now view these discussions, often confrontational, as a gift from God because they challenged me to think clearly and intelligently about what I believe so that I could learn how to "speak the Truth in love" (Ephesians 4:15) by using reason and Holy Scripture. During this time in my life I was able to increase my knowledge of what Holy Scripture teaches regarding homosexuality as well as develop my skill in responding to those who used the same Scriptures to affirm homosexual desire and behavior.

In September of 1987 I enrolled at Concordia Seminary in St. Louis, Missouri. A few weeks later I met a young woman named Andrea who was a Sunday school teacher at the congregation where I had been assigned to do field work. We began dating. We soon were engaged, and we were married on June 4th, 1988. My marriage to Andrea has been a blessing to me in so many ways! Andrea and I have many things in common. ***One of the things we have in common is that Andrea also has people in her life who struggle with same-sex desire and behavior.*** Andrea and I have had many conversations regarding Scripture's teaching on the issue of homosexuality and how we can serve those who want help with unwanted same-sex attraction. Andrea and I continue to pray to God for the wisdom to know how to best bear the burdens of such people in love and faithfulness to God's Word.

I graduated from Concordia Seminary in May, 1991, and I was ordained into the pastoral office on July 14th, 1991. As I write this introduction to my book I have been in the pastoral ministry for 19 years. I have served four different congregations as a full time pastor, and I am still serving as pastor at my fourth congregation. During these years as a pastor God has given me many opportunities to minister to individuals and families who bear the burden of homosexuality.

In fact, while I was serving a congregation in the St. Louis area I had the opportunity to become involved with a St. Louis area ministry which serves those who struggle with unwanted same-sex attractions. This ministry is known as FirstLight[8]. I served on their board of directors for almost two years and I also helped lead devotions and prayer during their evening counseling sessions with those who struggled with unwanted same-sex attractions. I had the chance to meet

---

[8] See their web page: www.firstlightstlouis.org

many people who thanked us for being willing to accept them in the midst of their struggles and loving them enough to speak the truth to them about their sin and the forgiveness and hope they have in Jesus.

During my years as a pastor I've had both negative and positive experiences with those who have same-sex attraction. The <u>negative</u> experiences I've had came from both men and women who refused to hear what God's Word says about homosexual sin. Because they refused to confess their sin they were also not able to receive the forgiveness that Christ longed to give them for that sin. I continue to pray for these individuals who are caught in the trap of homosexual sin. In contrast, the <u>positive</u> experiences I've had came from both men and women who came to me in repentance, acknowledging their sin of homosexual lust and behavior as well as longing for a message of forgiveness – and I was able to proclaim forgiveness and hope to them in Jesus' Name. I encouraged them to share their burden with other Christians. I also encouraged them to rejoice in God's gifts of Holy Baptism, Holy Absolution, the teaching and preaching of Holy Scripture, and Holy Communion – and thereby receive comfort and the strength to live a sexually pure life.

So, why does God work repentance and faith in some people whereas others resist the Holy Spirit and remain in unbelief? If God wants all people to be saved (and Scripture is clear about this!) and God is the One who works repentance and faith in our hearts (and Scripture is also clear about this!), then why do some resist the Holy Spirit and remain under God's wrath? God doesn't give us an answer that makes sense to our limited human reason. However, what God's Word <u>**does**</u> teach us is that no one loves us sinners more than God and no one longs for our salvation more than God. If we repent and trust in Christ for salvation, then we give all glory to God who saved us. But if we cling to our sin and refuse to trust in Christ, then we have no one to blame but ourselves. As Jesus Himself said with a heavy heart: "O Jerusalem, Jerusalem, you who kill the prophets and stone those sent to you, how often I have longed to gather your children together, as a hen gathers her chicks under her wings, but you were not willing." (Matthew 23:37)

However, even though we sinners are unfaithful, the good news is that God is always faithful! With that in mind, there's a hymn I love to sing. Its title is *Jesus Sinners Doth Receive.* If you are a person who struggles with same-sex attraction and/or behavior, you need to know Jesus is longing to receive you as His own! Homosexual lust and behavior are NOT unforgivable sins. The lust and sinful behavior of

heterosexuals are no less sinful. We are all guilty before God. One must remember that being a Christian does not mean that one is sanctified enough to be worthy of God's mercy. Instead, being a Christian means acknowledging that you deserve nothing but God's wrath and coming to him with your many sins knowing that you stand completely forgiven and holy in God's sight through Jesus Christ. *This is the message we must proclaim if we are to bear the burden of those who struggle with homosexuality!*

With God's help, I plan to continue to speak His Truth in love to both believers and unbelievers who are burdened by homosexuality. This book is part of that effort. I pray that this book will help fellow Christians as they strive to "bear the burden" of people they know who are caught in the sin of homosexuality so that these people may experience the freedom of forgiveness they can have in Jesus who took our burden of sin upon Himself and carried it to the cross where He sacrificed Himself for us.

Galatians 6:1-2

╬ *CHAPTER ONE* ╬

***If you have not yet read the "Introduction" section of this book, you are encouraged to do so before reading on in this chapter!*

"Why Single Out Homosexuality?"

This chapter will give a response to those who wonder why Christians put so much focus on the issue of homosexuality. This chapter will also respond to those who believe Christians are guilty of prejudice, hatred and homophobia when they teach that homosexual behavior is a sin. Finally, this chapter will show that <u>love</u> is the motivation for many Christians who speak God's truth regarding homosexuality. However, before I address these issues I want to make something perfectly clear.

Many Christians are sometimes guilty of unloving words and deeds toward those who bear the burden of same-sex attraction. The Church has failed to address the issue of homosexuality adequately, and when it has, the message has often been one of judgment and condemnation with little or no mercy and love.

Some Christians, in the name of Jesus, have attended gay pride parades, holding signs that read "God Hates Fags!" and "Turn or Burn!" and "AIDS is God's Judgment on Queers!"[9]

Of course, Scripture <u>does</u> teach that those who refuse to repent of their sins are rejecting God's forgiveness and thereby sending themselves to hell. *But God does not want this for any sinner!* Yes, we must preach God's judgment against sin. **But even more, we must proclaim God's love in Christ and stress that there is complete and total forgiveness for all sin through Christ's sacrifice for us!**

Christians need to reach out to those who bear the burden of same-sex attraction, and do so in a spirit of humility, kindness and love. We

---

[9] For example, see the web page: www.godhatesfags.com

have often failed to do this, however, and I'm just as guilty as anyone. Christians must repent of any unloving words or actions toward those who bear the burden of same-sex attraction. We can rejoice in the fact that our sins, too, are forgiven through faith in Jesus.

At this point I would like to quote from an LCMS document titled *Theological Implications of the 2009 ELCA Decisions.*[10] The following paragraph from this document sums up very well what it means for Christians to speak the truth in love to those who bear the burden of homosexual desire and behavior:

> **In discussions regarding homosexuality in church and society, legitimate concern is raised over the ways homosexual individuals have often been excluded and even vilified by Christians. Our Lord's intentional outreach to those who were marginalized and excluded during His earthly ministry is a reminder that the Scriptural judgments against homosexual behavior must not become the cause for hatred, violence, or an unwillingness to extend the Gospel's promises of forgiveness and reconciliation to the homosexual or any person caught in sin's traps. Homosexual sins, like heterosexual sins of adultery or promiscuity – or any sins in any area of life – are all atoned by Christ, who "came to seek and to save the lost" (Luke 19:10 ESV). Loving, compassionate recognition of the deep pain and personal struggles that same-sex inclinations produce in many individuals, families and congregations may not be neglected in the name of moral purity. To do so is indeed hypocritical, for all have sinned (Rom. 3:23).**[11]

Simply put, we must repent of any time we have been guilty of prejudice, hatred, homophobia or any other evil thoughts, words or deeds directed toward those who bear the burden of homosexuality. *At the same time, as we will see in rest of this chapter, Christians who*

---

[10] You can find this document in the following section of the LCMS web page: http://www.lcms.org/pages/internal.asp?NavID=16740

[11] *Theological Implications of the 2009 ELCA Decisions* , 3.

speak God's truth in love concerning the issue of homosexuality are NOT thereby guilty of these sins!

The Squeaky Wheel Gets the Grease!

It was the summer of 1992. I had served as a parish pastor for one year. I was attending the national LCMS youth gathering in New Orleans with some of the youth who were members of the two congregations I served. One afternoon we were asked to attend various sessions of our own choosing – sessions that dealt with issues and topics related to the Christian faith. I decided to attend a lecture on homosexuality.

After the speaker gave his presentation, he asked those in attendance if they had any questions or comments. At that point a young woman stood up. She was visibly upset. As I recall, her words went something like this: *"Why all this fuss about homosexuality? It's not the only sin out there, you know! Like, I know alcoholics who cause a lot more hurt and pain in people's lives than any homosexuals I know. Why don't I hear sermons about the sin of alcoholism? Why isn't there a session about alcoholism at this youth gathering? Why are we so focused on the issue of homosexuality? Like, do we think it's the worst of all sins or something? I just don't understand. I don't think it's fair!"* How should we answer her?

Many people feel the same way as the young woman in the above paragraph. Many wonder why society and especially Christians are putting so much attention on the issue of homosexuality. Are there not many other important issues? On top of that, many get the impression that some Christians are saying that homosexuality is the worst of all sins or even the unforgivable sin. Some who struggle with homosexual desire and behavior hear Christians focusing on the sin of homosexuality and conclude that they are not wanted whereas people who struggle with *heterosexual* sin or other sins, such as alcoholism, are welcome in the Church. Is this a fair assessment?

Most people have heard the old saying: "The squeaky wheel gets the grease!" What this means is that people or situations that demand our attention usually end up receiving more attention from us. We can use this fact of life to answer the young woman's question: "Why is the Church spending so much time focusing on homosexuality when alcoholism is just as bad?"

First of all, we must understand that homosexual lust or behavior is not the worst of all sins much less the unforgivable sin. For example, in Romans 1:18-32 (a section of Scripture I will examine in detail later in this book) the apostle Paul condemns even consensual homosexual behavior. However, Paul also mentions many other sins (such as greed, murder, gossip, disobeying parents), and then makes this comment: "Although they know God's righteous decree that those who do such things deserve death, they not only continue to do these very things but also approve of those who practice them." (Romans 1:32)

Even though we humans categorize sins and create various penalties for those sins based on how much harm they cause society, we must understand that God sees all sin as equally evil. *In other words, as far as God is concerned, getting drunk is just as sinful as homosexual behavior!* All sins of desire, thought, word and deed are equally condemned before God because they flow from the following sinful attitude: "I know God says this is sin. But I don't care what God says. I'm going to do it anyway!"

Of course, there is no sin – including homosexual lust or behavior – for which Christ did not shed His blood. Scripture teaches that those who acknowledge their sin, whatever it may be, and trust in Christ are completely forgiven and holy in God's sight! As the apostle Paul said of himself: "Even though I was once a blasphemer and a persecutor and a violent man, I was shown mercy … Here is a trustworthy saying that deserves full acceptance: Christ Jesus came into the world to save sinners – of whom I am the worst." (1st Timothy 1:12-15) *Therefore, the Church is NOT giving so much attention to homosexuality because it is the worst of all sins or the unforgivable sin!*

However, if homosexual lust or behavior is no worse than alcoholism, then why do we seem to focus on homosexuality so much more? My first response, first of all, is that I HAVE addressed the issue of alcoholism in my teaching and preaching. Even though the Scriptures allow for and even affirm the **moderate** use of alcoholic beverages, the same Scriptures also clearly teach that the **abuse** of alcoholic beverages – *what many call "drunkenness"* – is condemned by God as sin.[12] With that said, I must admit that in the past few years I have given more focus to the sin of homosexual lust and behavior than I have to drunkenness. Why is that?

---

[12] See Romans 13:13, Galatians 5:21, Ephesians 5:18.

The reason I (and many others) have focused more attention on homosexuality versus drunkenness is that I have never read books or heard sermons by Christians affirming drunkenness as a legitimate lifestyle. I have never heard of Walt Disney World holding "Drunkenness Days" at any of their theme parks. I have never heard of a "Drunkenness Pride Parade" being sponsored by any U.S. city. I do not believe there has ever been a TV series entitled: "Drunk Eye for the Sober Guy."

Simply put, even though drunkenness is no less sinful than homosexual lust or behavior, I don't have to fight against an aggressive pro-drunkenness movement in society and the Church. Of course, there are many people – even some Christians! – who do get drunk, but when they are confronted about their behavior many are usually willing to admit that getting drunk is not a good thing and maybe even a sin. In contrast, there are more and more people – even some who claim the name "Christian" – who refuse to acknowledge that homosexual lust or behavior is a sin condemned by God; there are more and more people who not only insist that we tolerate their homosexual behavior but some even insist that we affirm it.[13] *If I am going to be a faithful pastor who loves his people as well as those who do net yet trust in Jesus, I must be willing to speak God's truth in love especially concerning those issues in society and the Church where God's Word is being compromised.*

It would be so easy for me to preach and teach on issues that "don't rock the boat" and result in me being a popular guy. But the apostle Paul teaches that we must be willing to proclaim God's Word "out of season" (1st Timothy 4:2), that is, even when God's truth about a particular sin is not popular with some who hear it. The apostle Paul also says that "the time will come when men will not put up with sound doctrine. Instead, to suit their own desires, they will gather around them a great number of teachers to say what their itching ears want to hear. They will turn their ears away from the truth and turn aside to myths." (1st Timothy 4:3-4)

---

[13] See *The Gay Gospel?* by Joe Dallas, 37-100. In this section of his book Dallas addresses the history and confrontational nature of the pro-gay movement in America. Also see *The Homosexual Agenda* by Alan Sears and Craig Osten.

Some attribute the following words to Martin Luther[14]: *"If I profess with the loudest voice and clearest exposition every portion of the truth of God except precisely that little point which the world and the devil are at the moment attacking, then I am not confessing Christ, however boldly I may be professing Christ. Where the battle rages, there the loyalty of the soldier is tested."*[15]

God's Word (Holy Scripture) is not a smorgasbord from which we can pick and choose what we like and ignore or reject what we don't like. We must be willing to accept ALL of God's Word.[16] Anything less is rebellion and sin. As the apostle James writes: "For whoever keeps the whole law and yet stumbles as just one point is guilty of breaking all of it." (James 2:10)

Those who wonder why many Christians seem to be putting so much focus on homosexuality versus other sins need to understand how we are merely responding to forces in society and even in the Church that are compromising God's Word on the issue of homosexuality and thereby misleading many people.

Prejudice! Hatred! Homophobia!

Some accuse Christians of being guilty of prejudice, hatred and homophobia when they speak God's truth in love regarding the issue of homosexuality. But nothing could be farther from the truth!

First, I am NOT guilty of **prejudice** when I teach that homosexual lust and behavior are sinful As we will see later in this book, Scripture is clear that even consensual homosexual behavior is condemned by God. However, Scripture is also clear that various heterosexual behaviors – sex before marriage; adultery; incest; sexual thoughts for

---

[14] Some scholars question whether Luther ever wrote these words. For example, see *"If I Profess": A Spurious, if Consistent, Luther Quote?* by Bob Caldwell, 356-359 (Fall 2009 Concordia Journal – Volume 35/Number 4). **Whoever wrote these words, they are good words and worthy of our attention!**

[15] Theses words also apply to such modern day issues as abortion and the creation versus evolution debate.

[16] This does not mean that every passage of Scripture applies directly to ALL people of ALL times and places. For example, later on in this book I will distinguish between the civil and ceremonial laws given to Israel *only* and for a temporary period of time *only* versus the universal moral laws that apply to ALL people of ALL times and places.

someone other than your spouse – are also condemned by God, and I preach and teach accordingly! Does this mean I am prejudiced against people with *heterosexual* desires? As we learned earlier, Scripture also condemns drunkenness, and I preach and teach accordingly. Does this mean I am prejudiced against alcoholics? Scripture teaches that theft is sin, and I preach and teach accordingly. Does this mean that I am prejudiced against thieves?

Some think that those who believe homosexual behavior is sinful are no better than racists. But as we will see later in the book, believing that it is sinful to have a certain skin color is an evil notion that cannot even be compared to believing that certain sexual behaviors are sinful. Having black skin is NOT a sin whereas a man and a woman having sex outside of marriage IS a sin. I am not prejudiced against those who engage in homosexual behavior anymore than I am prejudiced against those who engage in various heterosexual sins when I preach and teach against such behavior.

Second, I am NOT guilty of **hatred** when I preach and teach that homosexual lust and behavior are sinful. For example, God is love! No one loves us more than God! Yet God clearly and firmly exposes and rebukes our sin. He does this so that we will acknowledge our sin, repent of it, and trust in Christ for mercy and the strength to live according to God's loving plan for our lives.

Of course, one can be guilty of speaking, preaching and teaching in a *hateful manner* without care or compassion for the people who are hearing you. But the mere act of pointing out someone's sin is not hatred. In fact, pointing out someone's sin with the goal of helping that person can be one of the most loving things one can do. As the apostle James writes: "My brothers, if one of you should wander from the truth and someone should bring him back, remember this: Whoever turns a sinner from the error of his way will save him from death and cover over a multitude of sins." (James 5:19-20)

Finally, I am NOT guilty of **homophobia** when I teach that homosexual lust and behavior are sinful. Just because someone believes a particular behavior is a sin does not mean that they have an unnatural fear of people who engage in such behavior – an unnatural fear that needs to be treated and cured! However, that is what many believe when they apply the label "homophobia" to people who believe that homosexual lust and behavior are sinful. Many think that people who hold the same views I do about homosexuality are suffering from a psychological condition – a phobia – that needs to be treated and cured. Many people who hold the same views I do about homosexuality have been forced to attend special classes or sensitivity training to help them overcome their "negative perception" of people who engage in homosexual behavior. *But the fact is that I (and many others who hold my views on homosexuality) do NOT have an unnatural fear of those who engage in homosexual behavior anymore than I have unnatural fear of those who engage in various heterosexual sins.*

The fact is that I have many friends who bear the burden of same-sex attraction. Some of them agree with me that homosexual lust and behavior are sinful, and they trust in Christ for mercy and strive to live a sexually pure life; others do not view their homosexual behavior as a sin, and yet we have been able to maintain a degree of friendship in some cases. Just because I view a person's behavior as sinful does not mean I have an unnatural fear of that person.

For example, if I believe that a person who produces pornography is engaging in sinful behavior, does that mean I'm guilty of "pornographerphobia?" If I believe that an adult man who has sex with a 5 year old child is engaging in sinful behavior, does that make me guilty of "pedophilephobia?" If I believe that a man who cheats on his wife is engaging in sinful behavior, does that make me guilty of "adultererphobia?" If I believe that a man and woman who have sex before marriage are engaging in sinful behavior, does that make me guilty of "fornicatorphobia?" Nobody would ever suggest this!

Those who agree with God's Word that homosexual lust and behavior are sinful – and who speak, teach and preach accordingly – are not automatically guilty of prejudice, hatred or homophobia. *On the contrary, those who speak, teach and preach the truth about homosexual lust and behavior are usually motivated by sincere love for those who bear this burden.*

Love is the Reason!

Many in our society are confused about the word "love." We use that English word "love" for so many things. "I love my wife." "I love my lovebird." "I love classic Star Trek episodes." "I love cold Diet Pepsi." "I love my children." "I love the ocean." "I love pizza." What does that word "love" really mean? Obviously, the English word "love" can have many different meanings, depending on the context.

However, in the original Greek language of the New Testament Scriptures we find three different Greek words that are translated by the one English word "love." Those three Greek words are *eros* , *philía* and *agape* . The New Testament Greek word *eros* most often refers to romantic or sexual love. The New Testament Greek word *philia* often describes the loyal, committed love that exists between friends and family members. Finally, the New Testament Greek word *agape* usually means a kind of love that is sacrificial and unconditional – a love given for the sake of another; even one's enemy!

We find this *agape* love in its purest form when we consider the attitude of God toward us sinners who are by nature His enemies. For example, the apostle John writes the following: "This is how God showed his love among us: He sent his one and only Son into the world that we might live through him. This is love: not that we loved God, but that he loved us and sent his Son as an atoning sacrifice for our sins." (1st John 4:9-10) What do we learn from this text about God's love for us? We learn at least two things.

First, we see that God "loved" (*agape*) us even though we have not loved Him. God's love for us is not based on whether we are lovable. In fact, God loves us even though we are by nature His enemies! The Apostle Paul writes: "But God demonstrates his own love for us in this: While we were still sinners, Christ died for us. Since we have now been justified by his blood, how much more shall we be saved from God's wrath through him! For if, when we were God's enemies, we were reconciled to him through the death of his Son, how much more, having been reconciled, shall we be saved through his life!" (Romans 5:8-10)

Second, not only does God love us even though we are by nature His enemies. Even more, His love for us expressed itself in the Father willingly sacrificing His One and Only Son for us. You see, as sinners who have rebelled against God in desire, thought, word and deed, we deserve nothing but His present and eternal wrath. However, instead of giving us what we deserve, the Father gave us His Son, Jesus! In order to save us from His holy wrath that He must pour out on evil, God placed the sins of all people on His innocent Son and damned Him in our place so that we might be saved. *Can we even begin to comprehend such love?*

For example, imagine a criminal who is guilty of multiple crimes – including first degree, cold blooded murder of a helpless woman who was also a wife and a mother. This evil man was found guilty in a court of law, and sentenced to the death penalty by the judge – *the very judge whose wife was killed by this criminal he just sentenced to death!* Several months later this criminal's sentence is about to be carried out. They place this criminal in the electric chair and prepare to throw the switch. However, just before the execution takes place a loud voice is heard: "Stop! Don't kill him! Let him go free!" The loud voice speaking these words is none other than the judge who condemned this criminal to death - *the judge whose dear wife was killed by this very same criminal.* The people at the execution respond: "Judge! How can you ask us to set this criminal free? He killed your wife! He is guilty! He deserves to die. Justice must be served." The judge then answers: "I understand that. I know that justice must be served, and I have a solution for that problem."

At that moment a young boy walks up and stands beside the judge. This boy is the judge's son – his only son! The judge's son has never commited any crime. In fact, the judge's son is a kind boy who has done many loving things for many people. At this point the judge then says: "Let the criminal go free. My son will suffer the punishment for this criminal's many crimes – including the crime of murdering my wife. Justice will be served. Let the criminal go free."

Do I have that much love in my heart? Would I place my only son, Joshua, on an electric chair in order to free a guilty criminal who had murdered my wife, Andrea, and deserves to die? I'll answer that right now: "No way!" I don't have that much love in my heart. I would never be able to make that kind of sacrifice.

Here's the amazing thing. God made that kind of sacrifice for you and me. All the various sins we commit – the evil things we do (including our sexual sins) and the many good things we fail to do – are ultimately against <u>God</u>, because it is His commandments that we are disobeying. For example, after his acts of adultery and murder, King David confessed to God: "Against you, you only, have I sinned and done what is evil in your sight, so that you are proved right when you speak and justified when you judge." (Psalm 51:4) We all have sinned against God, and His justice requires that we face His wrath for our sins. But God loves us so much that He sent His only Son to the cross with our sins on His back and there the Father damned His own Son in our place. Because of Jesus' sacrifice on the cross, forgiveness and freedom has been accomplished for all us sinners.

However, (and this is very important!) the forgiveness and freedom Jesus won for us by His death in our place does us no good unless we receive that forgiveness and freedom through God's gifts of repentance and faith.[17] In other words, if we deny what God says about our sin and

---

[17] See Acts 5:31, 1st Corinthians 2:13-16, Ephesians 1:13-14 & 2:8-9,

see no need for the forgiveness and freedom that Jesus won for us, we thereby reject God's loving gift and place ourselves under His wrath.

Remember the criminal who killed the judge's wife? What if this criminal, after having been set free, would have said the following to the judge: "I'm offended that you would suggest that my act of murdering your wife was a crime deserving death! You certainly didn't need to sacrifice your son for my crime because I didn't do anything wrong in the first place. In fact, I plan to murder someone else's wife tomorrow, and I hope you have the sense to see that I have a right to act this way and that you are the one who should be ashamed for condemning my behavior." *Can you imagine how that judge would respond to such evil thanklessness?!*

In the Book of Hebrews we read: "If we deliberately keep on sinning after we have received the knowledge of the truth, no sacrifice for sins is left, but only a fearful expectation of judgment and of raging fire that will consume the enemies of God. Anyone who rejected the law of Moses died without mercy on the testimony of two or three witnesses. How much more severely do you think a man deserves to be punished who has trampled the Son of God under foot, who has treated as an unholy thing the blood of the covenant that sanctified him, and who has insulted the Spirit of grace? For we know him who said, 'It is mine to avenge; I will repay,' and again, 'The Lord will judge his people.' It is a dreadful thing to fall into the hands of the living God." (Hebrews 10:26-31)

Please understand! God has <u>no</u> joy when He must condemn unrepentant sinners. The prophet Ezekiel records these words of God: "For I take no pleasure in the death of anyone, declares the Sovereign Lord. Repent and live!" The apostle Peter echos this truth when he writes: "[God] is patient with you, not wanting anyone to perish, but everyone to come to repentance." (2nd Peter 3:9b) Pouring out His wrath on His unrepentant and unbelieving enemies is not something God WANTS to do; it is something God MUST do. Sinners <u>must</u> be punished. The good news is that God provided a way for us sinners to be saved from the punishment we deserve through the sacrifice of His Son in our place. As Paul writes: "God made [Christ] who had no sin to be sin for us, so that in him we might become the righteousness of God." (2nd Corinthians 5:21) But if we resist the Holy Spirit who works through Holy Baptism and the preaching of God's Word to give us repentance and faith in Jesus, we thereby reject the forgiveness Christ won for us and place ourselvers under God's eternal wrath.

Therefore, because He LOVES us, God does all He can to convict us of our sins so that we will joyfully receive the forgiveness of sins Jesus won for us by His loving sacrifice on the cross. As James writes: "But he gives us more grace. That is why Scripture says: 'God opposes the proud but gives grace to the humble.'" (James 4:6) God opposes the pride of our sinful nature which denies, excuses or justifies our sins against God. God opposes our pride so that in broken humility before Him we may receive His grace in Christ through repentance and faith. King David writes: "Create in me a pure heart, O God, and renew a steadfast spirit within me … a broken and contrite heart, O God, you will not despise." (Psalm 51:10, 17b)

In *Luther's Small Catechism* we read the following in the section on confession : "Before God we should plead guilty of all sins, even those we are not aware of, as we do in the Lord's Prayer."[18] ***We learn from this that it may be possible for a person to be a repentant Christian who believes in Jesus for salvation, and yet be unaware of or misled about what Scripture teaches concerning his or her homosexual desire and behavior.*** However, if you are a Christian, then God will move you to "search the Scriptures"[19] concerning the issue of homosexuality and submit to His truth in this matter. God uses His Word to expose our many sins – including our sexual sins – so that we will acknowlege them as being rebellion against God's loving will for us and long for the *forgiveness for* and *freedom from* those sins that God has provided for us through His Son, Jesus.

Now, why have I spent several paragraphs speaking about the love of God, the sacrifice of Christ, and God's gifts of repentance and faith? The reason I have done this is to help you understand why people like me use God's Word to expose the fact that homosexual lust and behavior are sin. We are NOT guilty of prejudice, hatred or homophobia when we use God's Word to teach that homosexuality is sin. Instead, our motive is LOVE when we confront you with your sin and your need for the forgiveness and freedom that only Jesus can give you.

We live in a culture where many – even some who claim the name "Christian" - condemn the Christian teaching that homosexuality is sin. Some say that I and others like me are being unloving when we teach that homosexual desire and behavior are sin. But these same people

---

[18] See *Luther's Small Catechism,* 26.

[19] See the example of the people of Berea as found in Acts 17:10-11.

need to hear these words of Jesus Himself: "Those whom I love I rebuke and discipline. So be earnest, and repent." (Revelation 3:19)

If you want to know my motive for writing this book, here it is: "Love is the reason!" First, God loves you! Second, God's love for me in Christ moves me to show love for you – and such love includes speaking God's truth concerning homosexuality. I write this book out of love for those who bear the burden of homosexual desire and behavior.

This book will help you to see what Scripture teaches about God's loving plan for our sexual lives. This book will also help you to see through the lies and deception that the devil has used to keep people from seeing what Scripture clearly teaches about the sin of homosexual lust and behavior. **But most of all, this book will point you to <u>Jesus</u> through whom you have complete *forgivenes for* and complete *freedom from* your sins against God – including your many sexual sins.**

Galatians 6:1-2

╬ *CHAPTER TWO* ╬

"Let the Lord Have His Say!"

When I was attending Concordia Seminary, St. Louis, in the late 1980s I took a class on Holy Baptism taught by Dr. Norman Nagel. I wasn't sure what to expect. I thought we would begin by discussing the various opinions that Christians had about Holy Baptism. However, when Dr. Nagel began our first class session he said: "We will not say anything about Holy Baptism until we first let the Lord have His say!" We then began to examine the Holy Scriptures in the original Greek – specifically the texts dealing with God's gift of Holy Baptism.

When we consider homosexuality we find that people have various opinions about this issue. However, our opinions really mean nothing! At this point I would like to paraphrase Dr. Nagel: "We will not say anything about *homosexuality* until we first let the Lord have His say!" With that in mind, this chapter of my book will look at the pertinent texts of Holy Scripture that will help us understand what God says about sexual activity in general and homosexual activity in particular.

Of course, if we are going to examine Holy Scripture so that the Lord can have His say about homosexuality, we must then approach Holy Scripture with the assumption that we are reading the very words of God. At this point I will confess what I believe about Holy Scripture. ***I believe that the sixty six books of Holy Scripture are the inspired and inerrant Word of God.***

In other words, I believe that the men who wrote Holy Scripture were inspired by the Holy Spirit so that what they recorded in human language is the exact information that God wanted to communicate to us. In addition, because the Holy Scriptures are inspired by the Holy Spirit, they are without error.

Why do I believe that the Holy Scriptures are inspired by the Holy Spirit and, therefore, without error in all they teach? Is this merely my opinion? No! God Himself has revealed this truth about His Holy Scriptures. At this point I would like to quote from *A Brief Statement of the Doctrinal Position of the Missouri Synod* which explains what Scripture itself teaches about its inspiration and inerrancy:

1. We teach that the Holy Scriptures differ from all other books in the world in that they are the Word of God. They are the Word of God because the holy men of God who wrote the Scriptures wrote only that which the Holy Ghost communicated to them by inspiration, 2 Tim. 3:16; 2 Pet. 1:21. We teach also that the verbal inspiration of the Scriptures is not a so-called "theological deduction," but that it is taught by direct statements of the Scriptures, 2 Tim. 3:16, John 10:35, Rom. 3:2; 1 Cor. 2:13. Since the Holy Scriptures are the Word of God, it goes without saying that they contain no errors or contradictions, but that they are in all their parts and words the infallible truth, also in those parts which treat of historical, geographical, and other secular matters, John 10:35.

2. We furthermore teach regarding the Holy Scriptures that they are given by God to the Christian Church for the foundation of faith, Eph. 2:20. Hence the Holy Scriptures are the sole source from which all doctrines proclaimed in the Christian Church must be taken and therefore, too, the sole rule and norm by which all teachers and doctrines must be examined and judged. -- With the Confessions of our Church we teach also that the "rule of faith" (analogia fidei) according to which the Holy Scriptures are to be understood are the clear passages of the Scriptures themselves which set forth the individual doctrines.

3. We reject the doctrine which under the name of science has gained wide popularity in the Church of our day that Holy Scripture is not in all its parts the Word of God, but in part the Word of God and in part the word of man and hence does, or at least, might contain error. We reject this erroneous doctrine as horrible and blasphemous, since it flatly contradicts Christ and His holy apostles, sets up men

as judges over the Word of God, and thus overthrows the foundation of the Christian Church and its faith.[20]

If we refuse to submit to God's teaching in Holy Scripture regarding homosexuality, we will then be left with the mere opinions of people regarding this issue. Far be it from me to insist that it is necessary for you to agree with my *mere opinion* about homosexuality. In the same way, why should I feel compelled to agree with your *mere opinion* about homosexuality? In a world governed by such relativism, all that remains for us is toleration of each other's opinions or, worse yet, imposing our opinions on one another by various means. *But if the One who created the world and, therefore, also created sex has communicated to us His loving will for our sexual lives, then we will all be blessed if we set aside our opinions and listen carefully as we allow the Lord to have His say about homosexuality!*

However, before we begin to examine what the Scriptures say about sex in general and homosexuality in particular, I need to address some misconceptions about the ***purpose*** of Holy Scripture. Simply put, the Holy Scriptures were never meant to be viewed as an inspired rule book filled with "thou shalts" and "thou shalt nots" from a Sovereign God who expects us to make ourselves worthy of His respect and love by our obedience. Nor are the Holy Scriptures to be understood as a divinely inspired "how to" book that helps us to achieve our best life now.

Even though it is necessary for us to view Scripture as the inspired and inerrant Word of God if we are going to submit to its authority regarding what we believe and how we are to live, we must understand that our believing in the inspiration and inerrancy of Scripture is not Scripture's ultimate ***purpose.***

You see, the PRIMARY ***purpose*** of God's inspired and inerrant Scriptures is to lead us sinners to Jesus, our Lord and Savior! As the apostle Paul once wrote to Timothy: "...continue in what you have learned and have become convinced of ... and how from infancy you

---

[20] From the section "Of the Holy Scriptures" in *A Brief Statement of the Doctrinal Position of the Missouri Synod* . This document can be found at the following web address: **http://www.lcms.org/pages/internal.asp?NavID=563**

Another excellent document that deals with the nature of Holy Scripture is *A Statement of Scriptural and Confessional Principals*, and can be found at the following web address: **http://www.lcms.org/graphics/assets/media/LCMS/astatement.pdf**

have known the holy Scriptures, which are able to make you wise for salvation through faith in Christ Jesus." (1st Timothy 3:14-15) Also, Luke records these words of Jesus Himself: "He said to them, 'This is what I told you while I was still with you: Everything must be fulfilled that is written about me in the Law of Moses, the Prophets and the Psalms.' Then he opened their minds so they could understand the Scriptures. He told them, 'This is what is written: The Christ will suffer and rise from the dead on the third day, and repentance and forgiveness of sins will be preached in his name to all nations, beginning at Jerusalem. You are witnesses of these things.'" (Luke 24:44-48)

It's ALL About Jesus!

WHO is Jesus? Scripture teaches that Jesus is the eternal Son of God, the Father.[21] The Son of God, without ceasing to be fully God, became fully human when He was conceived by the Holy Spirit in the womb of the Virgin Mary.[22] Here we see that the one God reveals Himself to us as Father, Son and Holy Spirit – one God united as three separate Persons. We see this truth about God already "In the beginning" when God said: "Let us make man in our image, in our likeness,…" (Genesis 1:26)

When God said "Let us" He was thereby helping us understand *one* of the things it means for us humans – male and female - to be made "in His own image" (see Genesis 1:27).[23] The Father, Son and Holy Spirit are united as one God. We humans were created for union with God and union with each other.[24] Therefore, Genesis chapters 1 and 2 teach us that we humans – the descendants of the first two humans,

---

[21] See John 1:1-18.

[22] See Matthew 1:18-23 and Luke 1:26-38. The eternal Son of God taking on human flesh is what is known as "The Incarnation." Scripture teaches that Jesus is fully God and fully human (a perfect human, without sin). See John 1:14, Philippians 2:5-11, Colossians 2:9, Hebrews 1:1-3 and 4:15.

[23] See The Expositor's Bible Commentary *Genesis* by John Sailhamer, 37-38.

[24] The ultimate expression of human unity is found in God's gift of marriage where one man and one woman become "one flesh" (see Genesis 2:23-24). I will discuss God's gift of marriage more thoroughly later in this book.

Adam and Eve[25] - were meant to live forever in an eternal love relationship with God, Who is Father, Son and Holy Spirit.[26]

However, as I explained in the introduction to this book, God's loving plan for our eternal relationship with Him was lost when the devil, a rebellious angel, tempted Adam and Eve to doubt God's Word and decide for themselves what is good and what is evil. This tragic historic event resulted in us humans losing the "image of God." Because of our unbelief and sinful rebellion, we are separated from God because we do not love Him and we do not trust Him.

In addition, our separation from God also results in broken human relationships. Because we no longer love God as we ought, we can not love each other as we ought. God told Adam and Eve that the result of their rebellion would be "death" – not just *physical* death (which would come to them hundreds of years later), but ultimately *spiritual* death, which is separation from God and His love because of our sin.

However, already "In the beginning" God put into motion a plan to save us from our sins and restore "the image of God" in our lives. Now we're ready to learn about the WORK of Jesus! In Genesis 3:15 we read these words of God spoken to the devil[27]: "...I will put enmity between you and the woman, and between your offspring and hers; he will crush your head, and you will strike his heel." What do we learn from this?

First, only "the woman" is mentioned – no human father. This was fulfilled when Jesus was born of the Virgin Mary. Second, only God has the power to crush the devil. Therefore, the male Child (Jesus) was God Himself in human flesh. But exactly how would God's Son crush the devil and thereby save us? God gives us a hint in Genesis 3:21,

---

[25] See Luke 3:23-38 and Acts 17:26-27.

[26] A thorough teaching about the Holy Trinity is beyond the scope of this book. Simply put, in Holy Scripture God clearly reveals Himself to us as Father, Son and Holy Spirit (see Matthew 3:16-17 and 28:19-20). Even the Old Testament suggests that the One God exits as more than one Person. For example, the study of the Old Testament character known as "The Angel of the Lord" yields some interesting results in this area. The Angel of the Lord is sent <u>from</u> the Lord and yet this same Angel of the Lord IS also God Himself! (See Genesis 22:1-12 and Exodus 3:1-6)

[27] Scholars debate whether "the serpent" was a literal animal used by the devil to tempt Adam and Eve or merely a figurative way of speaking about the devil himself. (For example, see 2nd Corinthians 11:3 and Revelation 20:2). In either case, when God addressed "the serpent" he was essentially speaking to the devil and prophesying his defeat by the male Child born of the woman (Luke 4:1-13, Romans 16:20 and Galatians 4:4-5).

which reads: "The Lord God made garments of skin for Adam and his wife and clothed them." God clothed them with animal skin! An animal died. Blood was shed. This was God's first sacrificial picture pointing ahead to Jesus who has crushed the devil's plan to separate us from God by His sacrificial death on the cross in our place of separation and damnation.[28] *This truth helps us understand what I mean when I say of the Scriptures: "It's ALL about Jesus!"*

When I say that the Scriptures are ALL about Jesus I do NOT mean to suggest that the Scriptures do not contain information about many other things – they certainly do! Instead, the Scriptures are "ALL about Jesus" in the sense that God's purpose for us can not be understood properly apart from interpreting the Scriptures in light of the person and work of God's Son, Jesus the Christ.[29]

For example, we sinners naturally have the wrong idea about God and His way with us. Many people think that God's love for us is based on how well we obey His laws. Therefore, when such people read the Ten Commandments (found in Exodus chapter 20 and Deuteronomy chapter 5) or God's universal sexual laws (found in Leviticus chapters 18 and 20) they wrongly conclude that if we do our best to keep these laws then God will be pleased with us and reward us accordingly. However, such people also wrongly conclude that if we fail to obey these laws we must then do something to appease God's anger or else suffer His wrath. *But Holy Scripture itself gives us the key to properly understand the purpose of God's commandments – including God's sexual laws for ALL people of ALL times and places.*

First of all, before Adam and Eve were tempted by the devil and turned away from God in unbelief, they lived in a perfect relationship with God. In this sinless relationship God's moral laws would have been a positive description of God's loving plan for our lives as human beings. As the apostle Paul says, "...the law is holy, and the commandment is holy, righteous and good."

---

[28] See Romans 13:14 and Galatians 3:26-27.

[29] On page 262 of his book *What Does This Mean?* James Voelz writes: "...the entire history of Israel is, in a very real sense, prophetic. Not only words point to the future. People, activities, institutions, etc., also point to the future, because they are, in actual fact, foretastes of the future. **What is distinctively Christian is the notion that the form and essence of that future is our Lord and Savior, Jesus Christ, who has appeared already in history bringing with him that very eschatological future."**

The moral laws of God were never meant to be His Word that condemns us. Instead, "In the beginning," God's moral laws were a **positive** description of our lives as human beings.

Sadly, after Adam and Eves' rebellion against God (a rebellion in which we ALL participate!), the moral laws of God as summed up in the Ten Commandments now expose the fact that we are God's enemies. In other words, even though the Ten Commandments are a guide for how we get to live our lives as human beings, the tragic fact is that we are no longer "human," that is, we are not the sinless, perfect humans God created "In the beginning." By our unbelief and sin we show ourselves to be *inhuman* enemies of God.

Therefore, God's laws – whether we're talking about the Ten Commandments in general or the specific sexual laws based on the sixth Commandment – were never meant to be a list of rules for us to keep and thereby make ourselves worthy of God's love. Instead, God's laws are loving gifts to us humans who were created by an act of God's grace. However, now that we have rejected God's grace, those same laws of God expose the fact that we are in rebellion against His loving will for our lives.

For example, regarding the relationship of God's laws to us sinners, the apostle Paul writes: "Now we know that whatever the law says, it says to those who are under the law, so that every mouth may be silenced and the whole world held accountable to God. Therefore no one will be declared righteous in his sight by observing the law; rather, through the law we become conscious of sin." (Romans 3:19-20) Simply put, God doesn't love us and forgive us because we do our best to obey His laws – for instance, turning from sexual sin and striving to live sexually pure lives. Instead, God loves us IN CHRIST – even though we sinners can't obey His laws perfectly!

So, if you bear the burden of homosexuality and conclude that God will love you and forgive you if you just stop your homosexual behavior, clean up your act, live a celibate life or marry a person of the opposite sex, *then you have been deceived by the devil and you are resisting God's loving plan to save you from your sin!*

How, then, can we sinners be saved from our sin if we can not keep God's laws perfectly and God won't accept our best attempts at obeying His laws as the basis for Him loving us and forgiving us?

After the apostle Paul explains that we can't be saved by trying to obey God's laws, he goes on to give us God's wonderful good news! Paul writes: "But now a righteousness from God, apart from law, has been made known, to which the Law and the Prophets testify.[30] This righteousness from God comes through faith in Jesus Christ to all who believe. There is no difference, for all have sinned and fall short of the glory of God, and are justified freely by his grace through the redemption that came by Christ Jesus. God presented him as a sacrifice of atonement, through faith in his blood. He did this to demonstrate his justice, because in his forbearance he had left the sins committed beforehand unpunished – he did it to demonstrate his justice at the present time, so as to be just and the one who justifies those who have faith in Jesus. Where, then, is boasting? It is excluded. On what principle? On that of obeying the law? No, but on that of faith. For we maintain that a man is justified by faith apart from observing the law." (Romans 3:21-28) **Allow me to sum up what God is teaching us through Paul.**

Simply put, God's holy laws expose the fact that we have sinned against God, and "the wages of sin is death." (Romans 6:23a) We can do nothing to take away the guilt of our sin. In fact, our attempts at trying to appease God's wrath by offering him our works of obedience only make matters WORSE! The prophet Isaiah records these words of God: "All of us have become like one who is unclean, and all our righteous acts are like filthy rags…" (Isaiah 64:6a)

Why do our attempts at righteous acts of obedience appear as "filthy rags" before God? Two reasons. First, even the good works we attempt to do flow from a sinful heart. Our motivations are evil. We often do good works for selfish reasons or to manipulate God so that He will forgive us and not give us the punishment we deserve. Second, when we try to appease God's wrath by offering Him our righteous acts we thereby show that we do not trust in **The Righteous Acts of God's Son** who lived, died and conquered death FOR US.

Therefore, when God uses His laws to expose our sins He is NOT thereby telling us to "clean up our act" and obey His laws well enough until we are worthy of His mercy and love. No! When God uses His laws to expose our sins – including our sexual sins! – God is thereby showing us that we are rebellious sinners who deserve His wrath.

But why does God use His laws to say this to us if He loves us? The answer, as I already explained earlier in this book, is that God exposes our sin and the damnation we deserve so that, in desperate humility, we

[30] By "the Law and Prophets" Paul means the entire Old Testament which points us to the person and work of Christ. (See Romans 1:1-4)

will joyfully receive the good news that we are forgiven and innocent in God's sight through Jesus.

Now, the reason we can receive complete holiness and forgiveness through faith in Christ – who kept God's laws perfectly in our place, died on the cross in our place of damnation, and conquered death for us by His resurrection – is that the Holy Spirit has worked through the Gospel to give us new hearts which see God's laws (including His sexual laws!) as loving gifts that lead us into God's plan for our lives as His dearly loved children. In other words, Christians are moved to turn from sin and obey God's laws BECAUSE we are already completely forgiven and holy before God in Christ.

Therefore, if you are a person who bears the burden of homosexuality, you need to understand that when God uses Holy Scripture to show that your homosexual desire and behavior is sin, He does this because He LOVES you! God exposes your sin so that you can trust in Jesus, your Lord and Savior, through whom you are completely forgiven and holy in God's sight – *even as you continue to struggle with homosexual desires and behavior!* In fact, once we are set free by the Gospel of Jesus Christ, we are then able to see God's sexual laws as gifts from a loving Father.

At this point I would like to quote once again from the document *Theological Implications of the 2009 ELCA Decisions*:

> **Our stance on homosexuality, therefore, is affirmative of human life as God's gift. The healing voice of Jesus – Sacred Scripture – seeks to lead us into the richness of the life God intends for us. Prohibitions against adultery, homosexuality, and promiscuity of any sort are kind words, warning us against behavior that would diminish or destroy human wholeness. After all: The heart, center, and ultimate message of the Bible is that God wishes to be gracious for Christ's sake. Unless one hears this voice of the Gospel, that is, the voice from heaven speaking absolution to terrified consciences..., the whole point and purpose of the Scriptures has been missed.**[31]

[31] *Theological Implications of the 2009 ELCA Decisions* , 3-4.

Now you can understand why I say of the Scriptures: "It's ALL about Jesus!" In the rest of this chapter I will examine what Holy Scripture teaches about sex in general and homosexuality in particular. However, especially as we are confronted with God's prohibitions against homosexuality, please remember that these are "kinds words" used by God to lead you to JESUS – through whom you have *forgiveness for* and *freedom from* the sins that separate you from God and keep you in bondage.

"In the beginning…"

Before I examine biblical texts that clearly prohibit and condemn various sexual acts (with the focus being on homosexual acts), I will first deal with the context of Genesis chapters 1 and 2 where we find a positive description of God's loving plan for His gift of sex.

"In the beginning God created the heavens and the earth." (Genesis 1:1) This first verse of Holy Scripture is foundational for understanding the rest of Scripture. Unlike various pagan myths that assert an eternal universe from which the various gods themselves came into being, Holy Scripture teaches that God alone is eternal whereas "creation" – the universe (matter and energy) and all life – has a beginning. As Scripture says: "By the Word of the Lord were the heavens made, their starry host by the breath of his mouth … For he spoke, and it came to be; he commanded, and it stood firm. (Psalm 33:6, 9) Also, the author of Hebrews writes: "By faith we understand that the universe was formed at God's command, so that what is seen was not made out of what is visible." (Hebrews 11:3)[32]

In Genesis chapter 1 we see that God reveals to us that He made everything within the span of six ordinary days. The rest of Scripture speaks of God's creative work as recorded in Genesis chapter 1 as being a real historical event and NOT, as some suggest, only one creation myth among many other ancient creation myths – none of which have any basis in factual history.[33]

---

[32] Also see John 1:1-3, Acts 17:24-25, Colossians 1:15-17 and Hebrews 1:2.

[33] Later in this book I will deal with the idea that the creation account in Genesis can not be taken seriously. Many who wish to affirm homosexual behavior will often dismiss the creation account in Genesis because it teaches that God made humans "male and female" and gave them to each other in marriage – the ONLY God-pleasing context for sexual behavior.

Contrary to what some teach, Genesis chapter 2 is not a second, much less a contradictory, creation account as compared to Genesis chapter 1. Instead, in Genesis chapter 2 we get a "close-up" look at the creation of Adam and Eve that took place on the sixth day of creation. In fact, in Matthew 19:4-5 Jesus Himself quotes from both Genesis chapters 1 and 2 in such a way as to suggest that they are to be read as part of a unified account.[34]

Sadly, many people who affirm homosexual behavior end up denying the historicity of the Genesis creation account and reduce it to nothing more than an outdated myth. Such people will usually point out contradictions between Genesis chapter 1 and Genesis chapter 2.

For example, in her book *Hate They Neighbor* Linda J. Patterson writes: "...the story of Adam and Eve is one of two distinct and inconsistent creation myths found in the Bible ... According to Genesis 1, God first created water, followed by land, vegetation, fish, birds, animals, etc., and then humankind – both men and women. According to Genesis 2, however, God is said to have created land, followed by water, Adam, and vegetation. The creation of vegetation was then followed by the creation of animals, birds, and a woman – Eve."[35] **Sadly, Patterson does her best to find contradictions where they do not exist.[36]**

First, Patterson claims that Genesis 1 teaches God that created water and then land whereas Genesis 2 teaches that God created land and then water. But she fails to understand that when Genesis 2:4b reads "When the Lord God made the earth and the heavens" this is a brief summary of the entire six days of creation found in Genesis chapter 1. The water referred to in Genesis 2:5-6 does NOT mean that no water existed until

---

[34] On pg. 65 of *The Word Becoming Flesh* Horace Hummel writes: "There is no compelling reason why Gen. 1 and 2 need be read as two disparate creation accounts, as the critical dogma goes. One of its major supporting arguments is that Gen. 1 *ends* and climaxes with man (male *and* female) while chap. 2 *begins* with man (male only). But the two dovetail perfectly if we understand Gen. 1 as a 'wide-angel' introduction to *all* of creation, while Gen. 2 zooms in for a 'close-up' of the Bible's primary interest." Also see *Commentary on the Old Testament: The Pentateuch* by Keil-Delitzsch, 67-91.

[35] See *Hate They Neighbor* by Linda J. Patterson, 62.

[36] For a good response to those who teach that there are two contradictory creation accounts in Genesis, see *Bible Difficulties and Seeming Contradictions* by William Arndt, Robert Hoerber and Walter Roehrs, 133-134 (available from Concordia Publishing House).

AFTER God had created the land. Instead, Genesis 2:5-6 simply mentions that there was no rain at that time because water came up from the earth and watered the plants that had not yet sprouted.

Second, Patterson claims that Genesis 1 teaches that God created "men and women" whereas Genesis 2 teaches that God created only 1 man and then, later, only 1 woman. But she fails to see that Genesis 1:27 does NOT teach that God created multiple men and women. Instead, when Genesis 1:27 refers to "them" it means the 1 man and 1 woman – not multiple men and women (and Jesus' own interpretation of this text in Matthew chapter 19 confirms this!).

In addition, Patterson claims that Genesis 2 teaches that plant life was created AFTER Adam whereas Genesis 1 teaches that it was created BEFORE Adam. What she fails to realize is that Genesis 2 is not speaking about the creation of ALL plant life. Instead, Genesis 2 is pointing to the fact that certain types of plants had not yet begun to grow in the particular area of the Garden. Obviously, many other types of plant life had already been created BEFORE Adam or God would not have been able to tell Adam to eat from them AFTER God had created him![37]

Patterson also wrongly claims that Genesis 2 teaches that animals were created AFTER Adam whereas Genesis 1 teaches that animals were created BEFORE Adam. What she does not understand is that the Hebrew text of Genesis 2 refers to the fact that God *had already* created the animals BEFORE he brought them to Adam.[38] Genesis 2:19 reads: "Now the Lord God ***had formed*** out of the ground all the beasts of the field and all the birds of the air. He brought them to the man…"

Finally, Patterson thinks there is a contradiction between Genesis 1:27 (where we're told that God created humans as male and female) and Genesis 2 where Adam is created first and then, later, Eve. But this is no contradiction at all if we note that Genesis 1:27 simply gives us the *general information* about God's creation of the first humans whereas Genesis 2 gives us the *particular details* of how God actually did that – by creating Adam first and then, later, Eve.

---

[37] On page 133 of *Bible Difficulties and Seeming Contradictions* we read: "In Genesis 2:5 Moses is not giving an account of the origin of plant life … he speaks of 'any plant of the field' and 'any herb of the field,' not plant life in general. He is describing the region where the Garden of Eden was to be located and states that it was at this juncture of time, that is, when man was created, still a barren desert."

[38] See *Commentary on the Old Testament: The Pentateuch* by Keil-Delitzsch, 87-88.

When we read Genesis chapters 1 and 2 within the context of the entire witness of Scripture (especially Jesus' quotations from Genesis chapters 1 and 2 in Matthew chapter 19) we see that there are not two conflicting creation accounts but ONE creation account – the *general* overview of all six days of creation given in Genesis 1, and the *specific* details of God's creation of Adam and Eve given in Genesis 2.

Concerning God's creation of the first two humans, Moses[39] writes the following in Genesis chapter 1: "Then God said, 'Let us make man in our image, in our likeness ... So God created man in his own image, in the image of God he created him; male and female he created them." (Genesis 1:26-27)

Moses also writes in Genesis chapter 2: "The Lord God said, 'It is not good for the man to be alone. I will make a helper suitable for him ... So the Lord God caused the man to fall into a deep sleep; and while he was sleeping, [God] took one of the man's ribs and closed up the place with flesh. Then the Lord God made a woman from the rib he had taken out of the man, and he brought her to the man. The man said, 'This is now bone of my bones and flesh of my flesh; she shall be called "woman," for she was taken out of man.' For this reason a man will leave his father and mother and be united to his wife, and they will become one flesh." (Genesis 2:18, 21-24)

In the two texts above God teaches us about the crowning work of His very good creation. God creates a woman for the man and gives her to him as his wife. Here we see that marriage between one man and one woman is not some human invention that was created by society at some point in man's evolutionary development. No! God created the first humans as male and female and gave them to each other in marriage. *Here we see that marriage is God's creation and institution.*

We also see that God's very good gift of sexual activity is intended for one man and one woman within marriage. The purpose of sex is not limited only to creation of new human life (see Genesis 1:28a). In addition, the purpose of sex is ***also*** intended to celebrate the unique "one flesh" relationship that exists only between one man and one woman in marriage (see Genesis 2:23-24).

---

[39] Scripture and Jesus Himself (see Luke 24:44 and John 5:46) teach that Moses was the author of the first five books of the Old Testament. In the case of the account of Moses' death at the end of the Book of Deuteronomy, this was probably written by Joshua or some other inspired author.

For example, the Old Testament book known as The Song of Songs celebrates sexual activity between a husband and wife in a monogamous marriage *without even mentioning if they ever have any children!*[40] This is important! Why? Some wrongly teach that the ONLY purpose of sex between a husband and wife is reproduction. They will then argue that homosexual behavior is wrong because homosexual couples can't have their own biological children.

However, those who affirm homosexual behavior will then point out that many married men and women engage in heterosexual activity even though reproduction is not their goal or even possible in some cases. Some conclude from this that homosexual behavior should be affirmed because sexual activity can obviously take place without the focus being reproduction. The problem with this argument is that Scripture clearly teaches that the purpose of sexual activity is <u>not</u> limited to reproduction. Instead, the purpose of sexual activity also includes the celebration of the unique "one flesh" relationship that exists only between one man and one woman in marriage.[41]

In view of this, Thomas Schmidt writes: "Every sexual act that the Bible calls sin is essentially a violation of marriage, whether existing or potential. So it is that Paul makes reference to same-sex relations as a supplement to, or a substitution for, adultery. And so it is that Paul never makes direct reference to procreation in reference to sexual morality, because he is less concerned about reproduction than about union..."[42]

Therefore, God's gift of marriage becomes the foundation for understanding the proper place for God's good gift of sex in human life. **Any sexual activity outside of the context of one man and one woman within marriage is a perverted and sinful use of what God intended sexual activity to be.** The foundational nature of marriage for understanding God's gift of sex becomes clear when we see how texts from Genesis chapters 1 and 2 are used in the <u>New</u> Testament.

---

[40] See the Concordia Commentary *The Song of Songs* by Christopher Mitchell, 155-240. The Old Testament book The Song of Songs also points to the even greater marriage between Christ and the Church. We see this already in Genesis chapters 1 & 2 as portrayed by the apostle Paul in Ephesians 5:25-32.

[41] See *Straight & Narrow?* by Thomas E. Schmidt, 39-63. Also see *Welcoming But Not Affirming* by Stanley Grenz, 101-129.

[42] See *Straight & Narrow?* by Thomas E. Schmidt, 53.

Matthew 19:1-9

In Matthew 19:1-9 Jesus quotes from Genesis chapters 1 and 2 to show that divorce is not God's will because it separates what He has joined together. We will examine Matthew 19:1-9 more carefully later in this chapter (under the section *Jesus and Homosexuality*). For now allow me to point out that in Matthew 19:1-9 Jesus teaches that the only option to sex between one man and one woman in marriage is celibacy! Jesus teaches that God's good gift of sex is meant to take place only in the context of marriage between one man and one woman.

1st Corinthians chapters 5 and 6

In 1st Corinthians chapters 5 and 6 the apostle Paul condemns various types of sexual immorality taking place among the Christians in the city of Corinth.[43] One man was guilty of incest with his father's wife. (1st Corinthians 5:1) Some, both men and women, were guilty of "fornication" (that is, single people having consensual sex before marriage) and adultery. (1st Corinthians 5:11 and 6:9) Paul also mentions men who engaged in homosexual behavior. (1st Corinthians 6:9) In addition to *consensual* sexual immorality, others were also *purchasing* sexual immorality via the ancient sin of prostitution. (1st Corinthians 6:15) *All of these types of sexual immorality (and others I won't mention at this point) are taking place in our modern society as well!* All of these forms of sexual activity are condemned by God because they fall outside the one context where sexual activity is very good – the sexual activity between one man and one woman within marriage.

The apostle Paul writes: "The body is not meant for sexual immorality, but for the Lord, and the Lord for the body. By his power God raised the Lord from the dead, and he will raise us also. Do you not know that your bodies are members of Christ himself? Shall I then take the members of Christ and unite them with a prostitute? Never! Do you not know that he who unites himself with a prostitute is one with her in body? For it is said, 'The two will become one flesh.' But he who unites himself with the Lord is one with him in spirit." (1st Corinthians 6:13b-17) *What is Paul teaching us here?*

---

[43] I will deal with 1st Corinthians chapters 5 and 6 even more thoroughly under the section *The Apostle Paul and Homosexuality* in this chapter.

First of all, Paul reminds us that our bodies belong to the Lord. (1st Corinthians 6:13b) Paul also says: "You are not your own; you were bought at a price. Therefore, honor God with your body." (1st Corinthians 6:19b-20) These words of Paul point us back to creation and the cross. God is the one who created us "In the beginning" – and the human reproduction that has taken place over the centuries, starting with Adam and Eve, is simply an extension of God's creative process. (See Psalm 139:13-16) In addition, our bodies have been saved from the curse of death caused by our rebellion against God. This took place when Christ "purchased" us with His own blood, shed on the cross. (See 1st Peter 1:18-19) Therefore, we are to use our bodies in a way that honor the Lord. Of course, if we use our bodies for sexual immorality we DISHONOR the Lord.

Second, Paul says that God will raise our bodies from the dead just as Christ is risen from the dead. (1st Corinthians 6:14) Paul later writes: "...Christ has indeed been raised from the dead, the firstfruits of those who have fallen asleep. For since death came through a man, the resurrection of the dead comes also through a man. For as in Adam all die, so in Christ all will be made alive." (1st Corinthians 15:20-22) When believers are raised from the dead on the Final Day, we will be with the Lord forever[44] – joyfully living in His will. How then can we Christians use our bodies NOW to live in rebellion against the Lord? We CAN'T! The reason we can't is that our bodies have been united to Jesus' resurrection through Holy Baptism. (See Romans 6:1-4 and 1st Peter 3:21-22)

Third, Paul stresses that the bodies of Christians are united with Christ's Body. (1st Corinthians 6:15a) Very likely, Paul is referring to the mystery of The Lord's Supper in which we eat and drink the very Body and Blood of Christ as we eat the bread and drink the wine consecrated by Christ's Words: "This is My Body. This is My Blood." (See 1st Corinthians 10:14-17 and 11:23-32) Paul then stresses that we Christians can not use our bodies, which are united with Christ, to "unite" with a prostitute via sinful sexual behavior. (1st Corinthians 6:15b)

Fourth, Paul then shows us how **Genesis chapter 2** is foundational for his understanding of God's will for sexual behavior. (1st Corinthians 6:16) Paul quotes from Genesis 2:24 and points out

---

[44] See 1st Thessalonians 4:13-18.

that when a person has sex with a prostitute he or she[45] is thereby mocking God's gift of sex by using it in a context that has nothing to do with the "one flesh" relationship of marriage. *The intimate "one flesh" sex act is a beautiful, God-pleasing behavior within marriage. But the intimate "one flesh" sex act becomes an ugly abomination in God's sight when it is used outside of the context of one man and one woman within marriage.*

This mockery of God's gift of sex takes place not only in the context of prostitution, but also in the context of ANY sexual behavior outside of marriage (for example, adultery, incest, homosexuality, fornication – see 1st Corinthians 5:1-6:9). In fact, in 1st Thessalonians 4:1-8 the apostle Paul clearly teaches that sexual immorality (which is ANY sexual behavior outside of the context of heterosexual marriage) results in sin against the person with whom you are having sex. Paul writes: "...in this matter no one should wrong his brother or take advantage of him."

Finally, Paul reminds us Christians that our "unity with Christ" (which takes place in Holy Baptism and The Lord's Supper) means that we are "one with him in spirit." (See 1st Corinthians 6:17)

We who have been saved are "married" to Christ. He is the Bridegroom and we are His Bride! *(See Ephesians 5:25-32, which I will deal with next.)* Therefore, we should not use our bodies for sexual immorality because that DISHONORS the Lord and mocks His gift of marriage.

In fact, in 1st Corinthians chapter 7 Paul will stress that the only proper way for the Corinthian Christians (and US!) to deal with sexual sin is to 1) repent, 2) trust in Christ for forgiveness, and 3) then EITHER choose a life of celibacy OR get married – and by "marriage" Paul means one man and one woman! (See 1st Corinthians 7:2-7)[46]

[45] Even when a woman engages in sexual activity – whether heterosexual or homosexual – outside the context of marriage, she is thereby mocking the "one flesh" nature of sexual activity which is meant to celebrate the unique relationship that exists between one man and one woman within marriage. Therefore, in Romans 1:26 the apostle Paul also condemns female homosexual behavior.

[46] The apostle Paul also alludes to Genesis chapters 1 & 2 in 1st Corinthians chapter 11 where he writes: "In the Lord, however, woman is not independent of man, nor is man independent of woman. For as woman came from man, so also man is born of woman. But everything comes from God."

Ephesians 5:22-32

In Ephesians chapter 5 Paul writes: "Wives, submit to your husbands as to the Lord. For the husband is the head of the wife as Christ is the head of the church, his body, of which he is the Savior. Now as the church submits to Christ, so also wives should submit to their husbands in everything. Husbands, love your wives as Christ loved the church and gave himself up for her to make her holy, cleansing her by the washing with water through the word, and to present her to himself as a radiant church, without stain or wrinkle or any other blemish, but holy and blameless. In this same way, husbands ought to love their wives as their own bodies. He who loves his wife loves himself. After all, no one ever hated his own body, but he feeds it and cares for it, just as Christ does the church – for we are members of his body. 'For this reason a man will leave his father and mother and be united to his wife, and the two will become one flesh.' This is a profound mystery – but I am talking about Christ and the church." (Ephesians 5:22-32)[47]

The above text from Ephesians chapter 5 is a favorite of modern liberals and Bible skeptics. Why? They will say: "See! Paul was a misogynistic male chauvinist. Paul's opinions about women are barbaric, and so why should we listen to anything he has to say about homosexuality?" How do we respond to this complaint?

Simply put, in addition to such an attitude about Paul showing utter contempt for the authority of Holy Scripture, this view also completely fails to understand what Paul is teaching us. Far from being a "misogynistic male chauvinist," Paul is actually exalting the place of women within marriage. In Paul's day many men were misogynistic male chauvinists – *and these same men would have been shocked to read what Paul said about wives and husbands in Ephesians 5:22-32!*

So, then, what is Paul teaching us about the relationship between wives and husbands in marriage?

First of all, we must understand that Paul assumes that both the wife and husband are Christians who desire to relate to each other based on God's will for marriage. Paul forbids Christians marrying non-Christians[48] - and one of the reasons (besides complete spiritual incompatibility) is that non-Christian men are either clueless about or

---

[47] Also see Revelation 21:1-4 where the same marriage imagery is used to speak of Christ and His saints in the New Creation.

[48] See 1st Corinthians 7:39 and 2nd Corinthians 6:14-16.

rebellious against God's will for the role of husbands based on Genesis chapters 1 and 2.

Second, we need to understand what Paul meant when he wrote: "Wives, submit to your husbands as to the Lord." When I take engaged couples through pre-marriage counseling we always study this text from Ephesians chapter 5. When we read the part where Paul says "Wives, submit to your husbands as to the Lord" I always ask the woman: "So, what do you think of Jesus? Do you view Jesus as a power hungry, self-centered, misogynistic male chauvinist? Or do you view Jesus as your loving Lord and Savior who gave His life for you and has your best interests in mind?" I have not yet had a Christian woman go with the former option. All Christian women I know have no problem joyfully submitting to the Lord Jesus because they know He loves them and wants the best for them. Well, that's what Paul means when he tells Christian wives to submit to their Christian husbands "as to the Lord." In other words, Paul wants women to view their Christian husbands as gifts from God through whom Jesus loves them and serves them.

Third, Paul goes on to say: "For the husband is the head of the wife as Christ is the head of the church, his body, of which he is the Savior." Now, when we read that the husband is the "head" of the wife we immediately think in terms of male domination, dictatorship and treating the wife as inferior. But that is the farthest thing from Paul's mind! When Paul says that the husband is the "head" of the wife he uses the Greek word *kephale* [49] .

We find Paul using the same Greek word (kephale) in 1st Corinthians 11:3 where he says "the head of Christ is God."[50] Certainly Paul is not saying that God the Father is guilty of domination, dictatorship and treating the Son as inferior! Instead, we see that by the word "head" (kephale) Paul is teaching that those who are in a position of authority are to LOVE AND SERVE those who are under them.

For example, Paul says that the husband is the head of the wife in the same way that Christ is the head of the church. In what sense in Christ our head? He is our loving Lord and Savior! Therefore, just as

---

[49] For a thorough study on the meaning of this word in Scripture, see "The Meaning of *Kephalē* ("Head"): A Response to Recent Studies" by Wayne Grudem, found in *Recovering Biblical Manhood & Womanhood*, 425-468. Also see the Concordia Commentary *1 Corinthians* by Gregory Lockwood, 359-379.

[50] Even though the Father and the Son are completely equal, there is an order of submission within the Trinity – the Father being the "head" of the Son.

the Church joyfully submits to Christ's loving headship, a wife is to submit to her Christian husband's loving headship.

Finally, Paul says: "Now as the church submits to Christ, so also wives should submit to their husbands in everything." Once again, it sounds like Paul is a male chauvinist. However, Paul does not mean that wives should joyfully submit to the evil things their husbands wish to do – even if that means their husbands are leading them into sin. No! In such cases Peter's teaching that we must obey God rather than men would apply. (See Acts 4:19) Even though God normally wants us to submit to the various authorities He has placed over us (see Romans 13:1-7, Ephesians 6:1 and 1st Peter 2:13-17), God does not expect us to submit to earthly authorities who are leading us to sin against God's will for us.

Therefore, when Paul says that wives should submit to their Christian husbands "in everything," he means that wives should respect, encourage and joyfully submit to the godly leadership of their Christian husbands. *If a Christian husband is striving to love and serve his wife as Christ loves and serves the church, a Christian wife will have no problem submitting to her husband's godly headship.*

In Ephesians 5:25-32 Paul goes on to address the duties of Christian husbands. Remember what Paul said? "Husbands, love your wives, just a Christ loved the church and gave himself up for her..." Here Paul clearly teaches that male headship is NOT misogynistic male chauvinism. Far from it! Instead, male headship reflects the loving headship of Christ over His Bride, the Church, for whom He suffered and died "to make her holy, cleansing her by the washing with water through the word..."[51]

Now, this is all very interesting! Paul says that Christian marriage between a woman and a man is like the marriage that exists between Christ and His Bride, the Church. PLEASE DON'T MISS THIS! Paul does not say that the relationship between Christ and His Church is like ***earthly marriage*** – as though Paul were simply using earthly marriage as a metaphor to explain Christ's relationship to the Church. If that were the case, what a poor metaphor earthly marriage would be! We sinners do not live up to our promises, and even Christian husbands and

[51] When Paul mentions "the washing with water through the word" he is speaking of Holy Baptism, which is one of the means God uses to apply to us the saving benefits of Christ's life, death and resurrection. Also see Acts 22:16 and Titus 3:5.

wives often sin against each other. I certainly hope Christ's relationship to His Church is not like earthly marriage!

Instead, Paul is teaching us that earthly marriage should be like the **marriage that exists between Christ and His Bride, the Church.** In other words, Christ's perfect faithfulness to us, His Bride, and our willing submission to Christ's loving headship – this is the pattern for how husbands and wives should relate to each other in earthly marriage! Therefore, changing earthly marriage to anything other than what God intends it to be ends up mocking the <u>pattern</u> for earthly marriage – the true marriage between Christ and His Bride.

After Paul stresses that earthly marriage should be like the marriage between Christ and His Bride, Paul quotes from Holy Scripture to support his teaching – and from where does Paul quote? **Paul quotes Genesis 2:24!** *Once again, here Paul shows us that our foundation for understanding sexual activity and marriage is the creation account in Genesis chapters 1 and 2.*

I once read an article on Ephesians 5:22-32 in which the author wrote that Paul was a misogynist (even though he said that husbands should love their wives!) and based his sinful view of male and female relationships on a passage from Genesis that occurred <u>after</u> the fall into sin. The author wasn't reading her Bible very carefully! Simply put, Paul doesn't quote from Genesis chapter <u>3</u>, after the fall into sin. Instead, Paul quotes from Genesis chapter <u>2</u>, which is *before* sin ever entered the world! In other words, by quoting Genesis 2:24 Paul is showing that his teaching about the relationship between husbands and wives in Ephesians 5:22-32 was God's ideal plan from the very beginning. Now that we are saved, God wants us to conform to His loving plan for marriage that existed before sin ever entered the world.

The apostle Paul uses the creation account in Genesis as the basis for his teaching about the relationship between Christian wives and Christian husbands as found in Ephesians 5:22-32. Once again we see how the creation account in Genesis chapters 1 and 2 is the foundation for understanding the proper place for God's very good gift of sexual activity – and that proper place is marriage between one man and one woman. **Any other sexual activity outside of marriage *(including homosexual behavior)* is rebellion against God's loving will for our sexual lives.**

Sodom and Sodomy

A mistake often made by Christians who wish to give witness to the fact that homosexual behavior is sinful is that they will begin with the historical event of homosexual gang rape that took place in a city known as Sodom as recorded in Genesis 19:1-29. The problem with this approach is that it fails to begin with God's foundational teaching about sex and marriage in Genesis chapters 1 and 2. In addition, the text of Genesis 19:1-29 – *read in isolation from the wider context of the rest of Scripture* – says nothing about consensual, publicly accountable, life-long, monogamous same sex behavior. Instead, the sin of the men of Sodom was homosexual gang rape – and most of those today who affirm consensual homosexual behavior will agree with us that homosexual gang rape is sinful.

Nevertheless, there is something we can learn about consensual homosexual behavior from the event that took place at Sodom as recorded in Genesis 19:1-29. But first we must consider the context – Genesis 18:16-33. In Genesis 18:1-15 we see that Abraham and Sarah receive three visitors at their home – two of these visitors were angels, but the third was God Himself in human form (see Genesis 18:1, 10a, 13 and 19:1, 22).[52] The Lord reminds us of the promise He made to Abraham (see Genesis 18:17-19; also Genesis 12:1-3). Then in Genesis 18:20-21 the Lord tells Abraham about the sin of the cities of Sodom and Gomorrah, and alludes to His plan to destroy them.[53]

Abraham then pleads with the Lord to spare Sodom and Gomorrah for the sake of any believers that may be there (and Abraham was probably thinking of his nephew Lot and his family). The Lord finally

---

[52] Many scholars believe that the Old Testament appearances of God in some tangible, visible manner (such as one of the human visitors to Abraham and also the "Angel of the Lord" appearances) are examples of the pre-incarnate Son of God who reveals the Father to His Old Testament people (see John 1:1-18 and 14:1-11).

[53] In Genesis 18:20-21 God appears to be unclear whether the sin of Sodom and Gomorrah is as bad as He has "heard" (2nd Peter 2:6-8). Does this mean God doesn't know what is going on in cities unless believers inform Him in prayer and He checks it out *in the flesh?* No! Scripture is clear that God knows all things! So, why did God come to earth *in the flesh?* In many cases, God appears in visible, physical form for the purpose of leading people to repentance and giving them salvation. God wants ALL to be saved! For example, God had mercy on Nineveh when they repented after hearing the preaching of God's judgment proclaimed by Jonah. Also, in Genesis 18:18 God reminds us of His promise (see Genesis 12:1-3) that all nations will be blessed through Abraham's "seed" – and Abraham's "seed" is pointing to Jesus (see Galatians 3:6-25), God's Son, who came down to earth *in the flesh* to save us from our sins.

agrees to spare the cities if at least ten believers can be found in their midst. Sadly, this does not end up being the case, and the cities of Sodom and Gomorrah are destroyed.

But what was the sin (or sins) of Sodom? In the New International Version (NIV) English translation of Genesis 19:5 we are told that the men of Sodom wanted to have sex with the two male visitors. The NIV uses the English words "have sex" to translate the Hebrew word *venedeah* – based on the Hebrew verb *yada* . Is this a legitimate translation? The Hebrew word *yada* can have various meanings, depending on its context. Most often it means "to know" in the sense of having personal experience with something – and in the case of human beings, to "get to know" or "become acquainted with" them. However, in a few cases *yada* is used to refer to sexual relations (see Genesis 4:1, where *yada* is used in this sense). Simply put, the <u>context</u> must determine how the Hebrew word *yada* will be translated.

Some scholars such as Derek Bailey[54] and John Boswell[55] have argued that *yada* in Genesis 19:5 does not refer to homosexual relations. Instead, they argue that the men of Sodom wanted to "get acquainted with" the two visitors in Lot's house because they were suspicious of strangers in their city. When Lot refused, the crowd became angry. *Therefore, they say, the sin of the men of Sodom was not homosexual gang rape but inhospitality!*

But not even the highly respected <u>pro</u>-gay scholar Martti Nissinen agrees with this interpretation. Nissinen writes: "Although Bailey's interpretation of the verb *yada* has met with some approval, the theory ultimately fails. Lot tries to appease the troublemakers by offering them his daughters (Gen. 19:8), saying that his daughters are virgins, or, as the Hebrew text puts it, 'they do not know of man' ... In this context the verb *yada* is used with an explicitly sexual meaning – only a couple lines after the previous similar use. Bailey's explanation, that the daughters were only a tempting bribe to calm down the mob, may be correct but this does not alter the sexual connotation of *yada* ."[56] Other respected scholars also challenge this view of Bailey and Boswell - such as Thomas Schmidt[57], Stanley Grenz[58] and especially Robert Gagnon.[59]

---

[54] *Homosexuality and the Western Christian Tradition* by Derek Bailey, 2-3

[55] *Christianity, Social Tolerance, and Homosexuality* by John Boswell, 92-99.

[56] *Homoeroticism in the Biblical World* by Martti Nissinen, 45-49.

[57] *Straight & Narrow* by Thomas Schmidt, 86-99.

In addition to all the scholarly evidence against this interpretation of Bailey and Boswell, we also have the witness of the New Testament Scriptures. In 2nd Peter 2:7 the sin of the men of Sodom is described by the Greek word *aselgeia* , which refers to sexual sin. Also, in Jude 7 the sin of the men of Sodom is described by the Greek word *ekporneusasai* , which also refers to sexual sin. Simply put, when the immediate context of Genesis 19:1-29 is considered along with the New Testament witness, it becomes very clear that the sin of the men of Sodom was homosexual gang rape.

Some who affirm homosexual behavior, and who realize that all the evidence shows that the men of Sodom were guilty of homosexual gang rape, suggest that God did not destroy Sodom because of their sexual sin. Instead, they insist that God destroyed Sodom because of their many non-sexual sins. In support of this idea they will usually quote Ezekiel 16:49, which reads: "Now this was the sin of your sister Sodom: She and her daughters were arrogant, overfed and unconcerned; they did not help the poor and needy."

"There you have it!" they say. "God destroyed Sodom because they were gluttons and didn't feed the poor – not because of the homosexual sin of the men!" So, how do we respond to this? At least two points can be made.

First of all, we must acknowledge the fact that the people of Sodom were guilty of many other sins besides homosexual behavior. – just as WE are guilty of many other sins besides homosexual behavior. Certainly, gluttony and failing to help the truly needy when we have the opportunity are horrible sins. But that's just the point. To my knowledge there are no people in any Christian denomination who are suggesting that gluttony and failing to help the poor are sins that we should tolerate much less affirm. I agree that Scripture clearly condemns gluttony and failing to help the poor – and we should repent of these sins, trust in Christ for mercy, and strive to do better.

Second, even though Sodom was guilty of gluttony and failing to help the poor (and many other non-sexual sins, I'm sure), and even though all sin deserves God's wrath, the New Testament texts sited above make it clear that God was *also* angry with Sodom's sexual sin! In other words, we can't use Ezekiel 16:49 to justify homosexual behavior by suggesting that gluttony and failing to help the poor are the

---

[58] *Welcoming But Not Affirming* by Stanley Grenz, 36-40.

[59] *The Bible and Homosexual Practice* by Robert Gagnon, 71-90.

"REALLY BAD" sins compared to sexual sin. Such self-righteous thinking places various sins into categories of "not so bad, worse, and unforgivable" – as though God will overlook our sexual sins as long as we're not like those gluttons who fail to help the poor.

One other thing we must consider is that those who quote Ezekiel 16:49 to support their idea that God did not judge Sodom for their sexual sin usually don't quote the very next verse - Ezekiel 16:50, which reads: "They were haughty and did detestable things before me. Therefore I did away with them as you have seen." The English word "detestable" translates the Hebrew word *toevah* – a Hebrew word that is used in Leviticus 18:22 and 20:13 to describe consensual homosexual behavior.

Now, some will argue that the Hebrew word *toevah* also refers to various other non-sexual sins in the Old Testament. This is true. However, since Ezekiel 16:49 already lists various non-sexual sins, and in light of the fact that the New Testament texts sited above refer to the SEXUAL sin of the men of Sodom, it is very likely that the Hebrew word *toevah* in Ezekiel 16:50 is referring to the sexual sin, that is, the attempted homosexual gang rape of the men of Sodom.

When those who affirm homosexual behavior realize that they can't refute all the evidence against them, they then point out the fact that the sin of the men of Sodom was homosexual gang rape and NOT the consensual homosexual behavior we find in our society today. What is our response to this argument?

First, I admit that the sin of the men of Sodom was homosexual gang rape and that nothing is said about consensual homosexual behavior. But as we will see in our study of Leviticus and other New Testament texts, Holy Scripture clearly condemns even *consensual* homosexual behavior.

Second, we can't be too sure that there was no *consensual* homosexual sex taking place within the city of Sodom. For example, in Genesis 18:16-33 we see that God was planning to destroy Sodom before the homosexual gang rape depicted in Genesis 19:1-29 had even occurred! If there were *consensual* homosexual behavior in the city of Sodom (and there very likely was), then God would have seen such behavior as *toevah* , that is, "detestable" – as *toevah* is translated in the NIV texts of Leviticus 18:22 and 20:13 where even *consensual* homosexual behavior is condemned.

This takes us to the next section of this chapter where we will examine the universal sexual laws found in Leviticus chapters 18 and

20 – with focus on the prohibitions against homosexual behavior in Leviticus 18:22 and 20:13.

Leviticus chapters 18 and 20: Sexual Prohibitions

The Book of Leviticus was written by Moses around 1445 BC during Israel's journey in the wilderness of Sinai after God had delivered them from slavery in Egypt. The purpose of the Book of Leviticus is to show how Israel can share in God's holiness through faith in the promised Christ who is pictured by the many rituals and ceremonial laws found in Leviticus (see especially Leviticus chapter 16). In addition, the Book of Leviticus also contains many universal moral laws that apply to all people of all times and places.[60]

The Book of Leviticus can be very difficult to comprehend if one fails to understand its message within the wider context of the rest of Holy Scripture – especially as it is fulfilled in the person and work of Christ. In his commentary *Leviticus* John Kleinig writes: "The book of Leviticus consists of God's ritual legislation for the performance of the divine service at the tabernacle and, by extension, later at the temple in Jerusalem. The advent of Jesus Christ radically and irrevocably altered the way in which the OT revelation continues to speak to God's people … through the Word and Meal of Christ, we are involved in the liturgy performed together with the angels in the heavenly sanctuary … both Christ and his apostles show that the ritual legislation in Leviticus is relevant for us … Leviticus was used widely in the early church and later to preach the Gospel and our participation in God's holiness by virtue of our union with Christ. In contrast, the modern church generally ignores Leviticus … Leviticus cannot be sidelined as easily as that, for much of the NT is rightly interpreted only in its light. We depend on Leviticus for the proper understanding of Christ's death for sinners and the doctrine of his vicarious atonement, which is the heart of the NT Gospels and epistles."[61]

Since many fail to understand how Leviticus has been fulfilled in Christ, they conclude that its message is completely unrelated to our lives today. Some will use this erroneous opinion to suggest that we should ignore the entire book of Leviticus – *especially the texts that*

---

[60] See Leviticus 19:3a, 4, 11-13a, 14-18, 29, 31 & 35. Also see the Concordia Commentary *Leviticus* by John Kleinig, 405-422.

[61] Concordia Commentary *Leviticus* by John Kleinig, 24-26.

prohibit homosexuality! But this leads to some problems since there are many texts in Leviticus that clearly DO apply to us today.

For example, there are texts condemning idolatry, adultery, bestiality, murder, theft, oppression of the poor and those with disabilities. In addition, there are texts which are positive commands – such as "You shall be holy, for I the Lord your God am holy," "Every one of you shall revere his mother and father" and "You shall love your neighbor as yourself."

As I will explain more thoroughly in the next chapter, we must carefully distinguish between the **civil and ceremonial laws** in Leviticus that were given only to the *people of Israel* and only for a *temporary* period of time versus the **universal moral laws** that apply to ALL people of ALL times and places.

In his commentary on the Book of Ezekiel Horace Hummel writes: "…the OT places moral and ceremonial laws beside each other without the sharp distinction between them later made by Christians. Christ fulfilled the entirety of the OT for our sakes. The ceremonial law has been rendered obsolete, and indeed since the destruction of the temple in A.D. 70 much of it is impossible to perform, but God's moral law remains normative for Christians and for all peoples. To the best of my knowledge, no Christians prohibit intimacy during menstruation.[62] However, even most secular societies regard mother-son incest as heinous, and this is also an excellent example of 'natural law' (cf. Oedipus)."[63] Simply put, we would be foolish to ignore the **universal moral laws** (including the various ***sexual*** laws) in Leviticus chapters 18 and 20 simply because there are also **civil and ceremonial laws** in the Book of Leviticus that no longer apply to us today.

We will now examine Leviticus 18:22 and 20:13 – two texts that clearly condemn even *consensual* adult homosexual behavior. The universal sexual laws found in Leviticus chapters 18 and 20 are based on the foundational teaching about sex and marriage found in Genesis chapters 1 and 2.

Leviticus 18:22 reads: "Do not lie with a man as one lies with a woman; that is detestable." Leviticus 20:13 reads: "If a man lies with a man as one lies with a woman, both of them have done what is

---

[62] Leviticus 18:19 and 20:18 prohibit a man from having sexual relations with his wife during her period. I will deal with the ceremonial aspects of this Levitical law at the end of this section.

[63] Concordia Commentary *Ezekiel 21-48* by Horace Hummel, 684-685.

detestable. They must be put to death; their blood will be on their own heads."

Pro-gay scholars have various arguments against using Leviticus 18:22 and 20:13 to show that God condemns even consensual homosexual behavior. Some try to show respect for the authority of Scripture by suggesting that Leviticus 18:22 and 20:13 condemn only certain forms of homosexual behavior and only for that place and time – and they will then stress that these prohibitions do not apply to consensual homosexual behavior today. *I will respond to these types of arguments in this section.* Other pro-gay scholars suggest we should not take Holy Scripture seriously at all. *I will respond to those types of arguments in the next chapter.* [64]

So, what can be said about the prohibitions against homosexual behavior in Leviticus 18:22 and 20:13? First, Leviticus 18:22 is clear that, at the very least, the active partner in homosexual behavior is guilty of detestable behavior before God. However, in Leviticus 20:13 we see that the passive partner is also guilty of detestable behavior – and so even ***consensual*** homosexual behavior is condemned, with both men receiving the death penalty. Even though the death penalty is eventually removed (for reasons I will explain later in this section), we will see in this chapter that Jesus and the Apostle Paul assume that Leviticus 18:22 and 20:13 continue to apply to us today. I will now go on to respond to a few arguments that attempt to show why Leviticus 18:22 and 20:13 do not apply to modern day consensual homosexual behavior.

---

[64] For examples of both types of these revisionist arguments see: *Homosexuality and the Western Christian Tradition* by Derek Bailey; *Christianity, Social Tolerance, and Homosexuality* by John Boswell; *Homoeroticism in the Biblical World* by Martti Nissinen; *Homosexuality and Christian Faith* edited by Walter Wink; *The Church and the Homosexual* by John J. McNeill; *Gay Theology Without Apology* by Gary David Comstock; *The Children Are Free* by Jeff Miner and John Tyler Connoley; *Dirt, Greed & Sex* by L. William Countryman; *Love Between Women* by Bernadette J. Brooten; *Homosexuality and Religion* edited by Richard Hasbany; *Biblical Ethics & Homosexuality* edited by Robert L. Brawley; *Gay/Lesbian Liberation: A Biblical Perspective* by George R. Edwards; *What the Bible Really Says About Homosexuality* by Daniel A. Helminiak; *The Sins of Scripture* by John Shelby Spong; *Gay by God* by Michael Piazza; *Jesus, the Bible, and Homosexuality* by Jack Rogers; *Hate Thy Neighbor* by Linda Patterson; *Those 7 References* by John Dwyer; *Take Back the Word* edited by Robert Goss and Mona West; *Bulletproof Faith* by Candace Chellew-Hodge; *The New Testament and Homosexuality* by Robin Scroggs.

Only homosexual rape is condemned

Some who affirm consensual homosexual behavior have argued that Leviticus only condemns violent homosexual rape (as we found in Genesis 19:1-29 with the men of Sodom). But this interpretation can not stand because, as noted above, Leviticus 20:13 clearly shows that BOTH partners were to be put to death. The Old Testament would never have imposed the death penalty on a man who was raped against his will.[65] Therefore, Leviticus 20:13 is clearly condemning the *consensual* homosexual behavior of both the active and passive partners.

Only homosexual behavior during idol worship is condemned

Others have argued that Leviticus 18:22 and 20:13 are only condemning consensual homosexual behavior within the context of idol worship.[66] In other words, they argue that the truly detestable act is "idolatry" (the worship of false gods with heterosexual or homosexual rituals) and not the homosexual behavior per se. But this argument completely fails when one considers the fact that idolatry is not even mentioned within the context of the sexual laws in Leviticus chapters 18 and 20 (with the exception of Leviticus 18:21 and 20:3 which prohibit offering one's child as a sacrifice to Molech). In addition, if the idolatry argument were true, then does this mean that all the other sins listed in Leviticus chapters 18 and 20 - *such as incest, adultery, child sacrifice and bestiality* - are permissible as long as they do not take place within the context of idolatry? This is ridiculous![67]

Homosexual prohibitions are only for ancient Israelites

Still others suggest that God prohibited consensual homosexual behavior and other sexual sins only to distinguish Israel from the pagan nations and not because the sexual behaviors were evil in themselves.

---

[65] On page 124 of *The Bible and Homosexual Practice* Robert Gagnon writes: "Deut. 22:23-27 penalized an engaged virgin for having intercourse with another man only if she did not cry for help; a cry for help indicated rape ***and the victim of rape was not penalized.***" [Emphasis mine]

[66] For an example of this revisionist argument, see *The Children Are Free* by Jeff Miner and John Tyler Connoley, 10-12.

[67] For some other excellent responses to this pro-gay argument see *The Bible and Homosexual Practice* by Robert Gagnon, 129-132. Also *The Same Sex Controversy* by James R. White & Jeffrey D. Niell, 97-105.

This argument is used to suggest that the sexual prohibitions in Leviticus chapters 18 and 20 only applied to the Jews of that time and not to the Gentile nations of that time or to any people in the modern world today. But this argument fails to see the obvious! The reason that God condemned the sexual immorality of the Gentile nations of Egypt and Canaan (see Leviticus 18:1-3) is that their sexual sins WERE evil in and of themselves! In addition, when writing to Gentile Christians around 1400 years later, the apostle Paul shows that the sexual laws found in Leviticus chapters 18 and 20 (along with other universal moral laws) are still in force! This is why Paul could condemn a man for his incestuous behavior![68]

Homosexual behavior was "ritually unclean" but not sinful

Another argument used to dismiss the prohibitions against consensual homosexual behavior in Leviticus 18:22 and 20:13 is that the people of Israel viewed homosexual behavior as making one ritually "unclean" or "dirty" (on the same level as touching a dead animal or person) – but they did not view homosexual behavior as an actual sin. The problem with this argument becomes clear when we see that most of the purity laws are found in other sections of Leviticus, and the penalty for breaking these purity laws was a brief period of separation from the camp and then some form of ritual washing or cleansing.

In contrast, the penalty for breaking the *sexual* laws – such as certain forms of incest, adultery, bestiality and homosexuality – was death! Clearly, the sexual prohibitions are in the category of universal moral laws that apply to ALL people of ALL times and places instead of the purity laws given to ancient Israel only. In response to John Boswell, one of several scholars who promote the idea that homosexuality was merely ritually "dirty" in ancient Israel, the pro-gay scholar Louis Crompton writes: "Unlike the legislation on ritual, this law was also taken to apply to non-Jews living under Jewish jurisdiction. John Boswell is mistaken in arguing that it was akin to enactments on ritual and not binding on gentiles. Leviticus 18:26 specifically extends the prohibition to 'any stranger that sojourneth among you.' Such a law was one of the so-called Noachid precepts, binding on all the descendants of Noah – that is, on all humanity."[69]

---

[68] See 1st Corinthians 5:1-5.

[69] *Homosexuality & Civilization* by Louis Crompton, 33.

This quote from Crompton shows that even a pro-gay scholar recognizes that the Levitical prohibitions against consensual homosexual behavior are based on universal moral laws that have their foundation in the Genesis creation account – *foundational moral laws passed on to Noah!*

The waste of Israelite semen was the real issue

Yet another attempt to keep the Levitical prohibitions against homosexual behavior from applying to us today is the idea that God was only concerned about the waste of semen that would take place in homosexual behavior. In other words, this argument goes, God's primary concern was not with the homosexual behavior itself but with the need to ensure future generations of Israelites – and so, apparently, this means that the prohibitions against consensual homosexual behavior do not apply to us today. But there are several obvious responses to this view.

First, there is no mention about the concern for wasted semen in Leviticus chapters 18 and 20. Second, there is no prohibition against male masturbation in the entire Book of Leviticus or in the rest of Holy Scripture.[70] Third, the laws regarding the discharge of male semen are found in another section of Leviticus (chapter 15) where we find ceremonial laws that apply only to ISRAEL whereas God condemned the GENTILE nations for the sexual sins listed in Leviticus chapters 18 and 20. In addition, in Leviticus chapter 15 we see that the discharge of male semen was dealt with by ceremonial washing and a brief period of being ritually unclean whereas the penalty for consensual homosexual behavior in Leviticus 20:13 is death! Fourth, if the waste of male semen is the only issue, then why does God also condemn *heterosexual* prostitution, rape, incest or adultery? Such acts could produce offspring. Of course, the point is that heterosexual prostitution, rape, incest and adultery, along with consensual

---

[70] Some suggest that God's execution of Onan (Genesis 38:8-10) for "spilling his seed" is a condemnation of masturbation. But the context shows that God was angry because Onan refused to fulfill the Levirate law (which required a man to produce offspring for his dead brother via his dead brother's wife). Of course, this does not mean that masturbation should always be affirmed. Masturbation is sinful when accompanied by lustful thoughts (Matthew 5:27-28). Also, masturbation can lead to self-centeredness. For a good Christian treatment of the issue of masturbation, see *Human Sexuality: A Christian Perspective* by Roger Sonnenberg, 90-94.

homosexual behavior, were sinful in and of themselves quite apart from the issue of wasted semen!

One last attempt to support this view points out that there is no condemnation of female homosexual behavior in Leviticus chapters 18 and 20. Therefore, they argue, the issue with male homosexuality is wasted semen. However, not only does this argument ignore the fact that even *heterosexual* prostitution, rape, incest and adultery were forbidden even though they could be procreative. In addition, this argument ignores the fact that God expects us to **assume** that even female homosexuality is sinful based on the example of male homosexuality.

For instance, in the sections of Leviticus chapters 18 and 20 that condemn various forms of incest there is one type of incest that is not even mentioned: *a father having sex with his daughter!* In contrast, a mother having sex with her son IS mentioned and condemned. Now, based on this information, what conclusion should we draw? Should we conclude that the condemnation of mother/son incest assumes that father/daughter incest is also condemned? Or do we conclude that the failure to mention father/daughter incest means that such sexual behavior is affirmed by God? The answer should be obvious.

Another example of one type of prohibition assuming another is Jesus' condemnation of a man's lustful thoughts for a woman who is not his wife (see Matthew 5:28). Does this mean that God affirms a woman lusting after a man who is not her husband since Jesus only condemned lustful thoughts by a man? Of course not! *The point is: "What's bad for the gander is bad for the goose!"*

Finally, in Romans 1:26 the apostle Paul clearly condemns even consensual FEMALE homosexual behavior – showing he understood that God wants us to assume that *female* homosexual behavior is sinful based on the condemnation of *male* homosexual behavior in Leviticus 18:22 and 20:13.

Only male homosexual genital/anal intercourse is forbidden

In his book *What the Bible Really Says about Homosexuality* Daniel Helminiak writes: "...that two men shared a sexual experience was really not a problem. The only problem was when one man penetrated another. Among the early Israelites, as Leviticus sees it, to engage specifically in male-male intercourse was to mix the roles of man and woman." Helminiak wants us to believe that only male genital/anal intercourse was prohibited and that all other forms of male-male "sexual experience" (for example, kissing[71] and fondling, mutual masturbation, and oral sex) would have been permissible. This strained interpretation completely fails for the following reasons.

First, in no place does Helminiak condemn modern day male homosexual genital/anal intercourse and fails to give a reasonable explanation as to why this particular activity, which he suggests is the only thing being condemned in Leviticus 18:22 and 20:13, is now permissible.

Second, Helminiak fails to note that Leviticus 18:22 and 20:13 do not specifically mention genital/anal intercourse but merely teach that a man should not lie with another man as "with a woman." In other words, ANY type of sexual activity that a man would have with a woman is forbidden for him to have with another man! Other sexual acts (such as kissing and fondling, mutual masturbation or oral sex) are still SEXUAL ACTS! Imagine a wife catching her husband with another woman, and the husband attempts to comfort his wife by saying "Why are you upset? We were only doing some kissing and fondling." or "Why are you upset? We were only doing some mutual masturbation." Or "Why are you upset? We were only performing oral sex on one another."

Third, Helminiak fails to understand, as noted in the above paragraph, that FEMALE homosexual behavior is also assumed to be prohibited by Leviticus chapters 18 and 20 as well as being clearly prohibited by the apostle Paul – ***and there is no genital/anal intercourse possible between two women, and yet Scripture clearly forbids such behavior!***

We no longer enforce the Levitical death penalties today

One last argument used by those who want to affirm homosexual behavior is this: "If we insist on taking the Levitical prohibitions against homosexual behavior seriously then we must also be prepared to give homosexuals the death penalty today!" But since most Christians today are NOT suggesting we should give homosexuals the

[71] Obviously, some types of kissing are non-sexual. In some cultures men kiss each other on the cheek as a form of friendly affection - with no sexual intent whatsoever. In addition, parents and children will often kiss each other - with no sexual intent whatsoever. *Honestly, it really does not take a genius to distinguish between a non-sexual kiss and a sexual kiss!*

death penalty, this argument insists we can also ignore the Levitical prohibitions against homosexual behavior as well. How do we answer this?

First, one must understand that ancient Israel functioned as a theocracy, that is, they were both Church and State. However, after Christ finished His work, the purpose of Old Testament Israel was fulfilled. Therefore, the Old Testament civil laws were abolished and Christians now submit to the various laws of the governments under which they live.

Second, even though the death penalty for homosexual behavior is no longer required, ***homosexual behavior itself is still condemned as sin.*** Would those who affirm homosexual behavior argue that we should also affirm idolatry, children disobeying parents, adultery, incest and bestiality since we no longer apply the Levitical death penalties for those sins? I hope not!

The fact that God required the death penalty for homosexuality, adultery, bestiality, murder, etc., shows that God was very serious about His hatred of such behavior. In fact, in Romans 1:28-32 and 6:23 the apostle Paul clearly states that ALL sin is worthy of death. Even though Jesus did not encourage the death penalty for such sins, He still clearly taught that we must repent of such sins and trust in Him for salvation **or face something far worse than <u>physical</u> death!** (See Luke 13:1-5; Matthew 5:27-30, 7:13-21, 10:26-39, 11:20-24, 18:6-7; also see 1st Thessalonians 4:1-10).

Of course, Jesus taught us to "love our neighbor." But Jesus' own example shows us that "loving our neighbor" includes telling them to repent of their sin so they can receive forgiveness through His sacrifice for sinners on the cross. Jesus reached out in love to the tax collectors and prostitutes – but Jesus did NOT affirm their theft and sexual sin! Jesus said to the woman caught in adultery: "Go and sin no more!" (See John 8:11)

I would now like to deal with three other issues concerning the sexual prohibitions in Leviticus chapters 18 and 20. Those issues are **1)** incest (Leviticus 18:6-18), **2)** sacrificing one's child to Molech (Leviticus 18:21) and **3)** a husband having sex with his menstruating wife (Leviticus 18:19).

Incest

Most people today who *affirm* homosexual behavior and therefore attempt to reinterpret the clear prohibitions against consensual homosexual behavior in Leviticus 18:22 and 20:13 will usually be *opposed* to various types of incest – even though incest is condemned in the same section of Leviticus where we find the prohibitions against homosexuality. Why believe that one type of sexual prohibition (incest) still applies and then insist that another sexual prohibition (homosexuality) in the very same context does not apply? As we have seen, they have no good explanation.

Of course, some will argue that incest usually includes children who can not give consent. But what about a situation where two consenting adults – a mother/son or father/daughter want to have sex? Would those who affirm consensual adult homosexual behavior also be willing to affirm consensual adult mother/son or father/daughter incest? Not usually![72] But they thereby show themselves to be totally inconsistent. Some will then point out that adult consensual incest could result in birth defects. True. But what if the incestuous adults used birth control or had operations that would prevent them from having children? Would such incest be permissible then? Again, most who affirm homosexual behavior would say "No." But again, they are not being consistent!

However, there is one difficulty that faces those who **do** take the Levitical prohibitions against homosexuality seriously – and that difficulty is this: ***If we believe that the creation account in Genesis is an accurate record of a real historical event, then would not some type of incest have been necessary in order to produce human descendants from Adam and Eve?***

I am among those who agree with the whole of Scripture which teaches that the creation account in Genesis chapters 1 and 2 was a real historical event. Along with Holy Scripture, I believe that all humans today are descendants of Adam and Eve.[73] However, if this is true (and Scripture is clear that it is!), then we can't avoid the fact some of the children of Adam and Eve (see Genesis 5:4) – brothers and sisters – got married and had children together. However, in Leviticus chapter 18

---

[72] I say "not usually" because there are some groups who, in addition to affirming all types of homosexual behavior, also affirm polyamory (groups of men and women having sex with each other), incest, adult/child sex and even bestiality!

[73] See Genesis 3:20, 1st Chronicles 1:1, Luke 3:23-37, Acts 17:26, Romans 5:12-21.

we find that brother/sister incest is clearly prohibited! How do we answer this?

The only real solution, if one wishes to be faithful to Holy Scripture, is to assume that God originally allowed brothers and sisters to marry and have children in order to populate the world. But at some point in history, not long after creation (we don't know when for sure, because Scripture doesn't say), God prohibited this behavior and declared it to be sinful. This explains why God could condemn the GENTILE nations in Leviticus 18:1-3 for the sin of brother/sister incest. At some point in early history God prohibited brother/sister incest, and then this prohibition was passed down from generation to generation but simply ignored or forgotten (along with prohibitions against other sexual behaviors).

In any case, by the time we get to the point in human history that is the setting for the Book of Leviticus we see that various forms of incest (including brother/sister incest) are condemned by God. Of course, this need not cause a problem for those who believe that the creation account in Genesis is a real historical event. God is sovereign! God can permit a set of behaviors at one point in history and then prohibit those same behaviors later in history – and He doesn't have to give us any explanations! Our place as human creatures is to trust God's Word and accept His will – even when He decides to prohibit a behavior (such as brother/sister incest) that He once permitted.

Sadly, some will use my explanation in the above paragraph to suggest that maybe *"God is doing a new thing!"* – and that means He **now** permits homosexual behavior even though He once prohibited it! The only problem with that notion is that Holy Scripture is clear that the prohibitions against consensual homosexual behavior in Leviticus 18:22 and 20:13 are still in force today – and several New Testament texts affirm this! God has NOT abolished these prohibitions! Therefore, it is sinful for us to suggest otherwise.

Sacrificing one's child to Molech

The prohibition in Leviticus 18:21 which forbids God's people from sacrificing their children to Molech (a pagan god of the underworld who could provide fertility to humans and the land)[74] does not seem to

[74] On page 433 of the Concordia Commentary *Leviticus* John Kleinig writes: "Molech was a deity who resided in the underworld. He required child sacrifice as the price for the fertility of a family and the prosperity of its land."

fit with the prohibitions against the various sexual sins in the same chapter. For example, the sacrifice of one's child would make one guilty of murder, which is not a sexual sin per se. In addition, the sacrifice of one's child in the context of a pagan fertility rite would also make one guilty of idolatry – again, not a sexual sin per se. So, even though it is obvious why God would condemn this activity, why does it appear in this context?

The most reasonable explanation is that both the sacrifice of the child and the pagan ritual resulted in a distortion of God's good gift of sex. First, some married couples may have had sex with the full intention of sacrificing the "fruit of their womb" – and this would be a clear distortion of God's gift of sex which could result, if it was God's will, in the creation of human life.[75] Second, the act of sacrificing one's child to Molech was done in the hope of being more fertile in the future – and thus having even more children. In other words, the Israelite couple said to each other: "Let's give one child to Molech and he'll be sure that we get six more in return!" This form of pagan idol worship also distorted God's gift of sex because people were trying to control their reproduction via doing business with a pagan god rather than trusting in the One True God to give them children where and when it pleased Him.

A husband having sex with his menstruating wife

When we are confronted with this particular prohibition in Leviticus 18:19 we must ask ourselves: "Why does this prohibition exist here?"

---

[75] We see the same evil today with the practice of abortion – the act of murdering a baby boy or girl in the womb as a form of "birth control." Men and women who have sex with the intention of getting an abortion if a child were to be conceived, as a way of ensuring their "standard of living," are guilty of the same detestable act performed by the men and women of Israel who had sex with the intention of murdering any child that might be conceived by offering it to Molech in return for a higher "standard of living." **Of course, the good news is that Christ also shed His Blood for the sin of abortion. No One loves the millions of aborted children more than God, and we commend them to His mercy. In addition, no One loves those who've had abortions, performed abortions, paid for abortions, encouraged someone to have an abortion or simply failed to speak out against abortion more than God. We can all come to God with the sin of abortion and know that we are forgiven and holy in His sight through Jesus. The same Jesus will set us free to cherish all human life – from the womb to the tomb – for which He shed His precious Blood.** ***God is "pro-life" and so are His people!***

Is God teaching us that there is something inherently evil with a woman's monthly period? No! Scripture is clear that the female reproductive process was part of God's "very good" creation before sin entered the world. Then why does God give this prohibition in Leviticus 18:19? Scholars have offered various explanations.

Some suggest that God was prohibiting a kind of rape, that is, God was condemning any man who would force himself on his wife during a time when she would be uncomfortable with such an act. Certainly, Scripture does forbid rape – and this would include a husband forcing himself on his wife when she is unwilling because she is having her period. But this does not fully explain why God also condemns this act when the woman is a consensual participant, because in Leviticus 20:18 we see that both the husband and wife are to be punished - *and this would make no sense if the woman were a victim of rape!*

Therefore, the best explanation seems to be that we are dealing with a ceremonial law that has been placed in this context because of the sexual nature of the act.[76] Unlike adultery, incest, male and female homosexual behavior or bestiality (which are sinful in and of themselves), the prohibition against contact with a woman's menstrual blood is not a universal moral law binding on all people of all times but, as described in Leviticus 15:19-31, merely makes an Israelite ritually unclean. In contrast, there is no place in Scripture where adultery, incest, male and female homosexual behavior or bestiality are described as merely making one ritually unclean.

Jews (and Gentiles who lived with them) were not allowed to eat blood because of its associations with life and especially because of blood's connection with the temple sacrifices for the atonement of sin (which were a picture of the Blood of Christ and His sacrifice for us).[77] Because blood was associated with life and atonement for sin at the temple, Israelites were made to be temporarily ritually impure as a result of their contact with blood.

---

[76] In Leviticus 15:1-31 we see that the discharge of male semen or female menstrual blood makes one ritually unclean. One had to perform various washings, offer certain animal sacrifices and be considered ritually unclean for a temporary period of time. In other words, a ritually impure man or woman could not come near the temple during their time of temporary impurity. For a thorough examination of this issue, see the Concordia Commentary *Leviticus* by John Kleinig, 311-324.

[77] See Leviticus 17:10-12 and 19:26a.

In addition, according to Leviticus chapter 15, when a husband and wife had ACCIDENTAL contact with menstrual blood during a sex act, they were merely temporarily unclean and had to offer certain sacrifices and perform various ritual washings. But in Leviticus 20:18 the result of such behavior is that both the man and the woman are to be "cut off from their people." Why this intense punishment for the behavior described in Leviticus 20:18 when the same behavior described in Leviticus chapter 15 results in only temporary ritual impurity after the required purification rituals are performed?

The best answer is that in Leviticus 20:18 we appear to have a man who ***knowingly*** and ***willingly*** has sex with his wife during her period in open rebellion against the known ceremonial law and its required purifications. In the same way, it appears that the woman in Leviticus 20:18 ***knowingly*** and ***willingly*** participates in this act in open rebellion against the known ceremonial law and its required purifications. In other words, their ***intentional rebellion*** (whatever their reasons) against God's ceremonial law and its purification requirements is met with a harsh punishment whereas ACCIDENTAL contact with menstrual blood resulted only in being temporarily ritually unclean as long as one took part in the purification requirements.

Therefore, the best way to understand the prohibition against contact with a woman's menstrual blood in Leviticus 18:19 and 20:18 is that this was a ceremonial law (given only to Israel and only for a temporary period in history) that was included in this section of universal sexual prohibitions because of the sexual nature of the act itself. (For the same reason, the prohibition against offering one's child to Molech was placed in this section of universal *sexual* prohibitions even though this act had to do with the universal laws of murder and idolatry.)

One other thing we must note is that unlike adultery, incest, and homosexuality (which are clearly condemned in the New Testament Scriptures), the prohibition against contact with a woman's menstrual blood is not found anywhere in the New Testament! Because of the ceremonial aspect of this law, most Christians have understood it to be fulfilled in Christ who shed His Blood for us (just as the animal blood sacrifices were abolished because they were fulfilled in Christ).

Now, this doesn't mean that it is a good thing for a husband to have sex with his wife during her period. Certainly, a husband should NEVER force himself on his wife during her menstrual cycle (or anytime, for that matter!) because such a selfish, unloving act would be in direct conflict with the sacrificial love that God intends to be communicated in the "one flesh" sexual activity between a husband and wife. In addition, there could also be other reasons (health or hygiene) that it would be best for a husband and wife to refrain from sexual activity during the menstrual cycle. The point is that such an act (unlike the universal sexual laws!) is NOT prohibited for us today because the temporary ceremonial laws given to Israel have been abolished by their being fulfilled in Christ.

In conclusion of this section I must stress again that the sexual prohibitions found in Leviticus chapters 18 and 20 – including *homosexual* behavior – **are based on the teachings about sex and marriage found in Genesis chapters 1 and 2.** Therefore, consensual male and female homosexual behavior (along with all other kinds of sexual activity outside of heterosexual marriage) is sinful and condemned by God.

David and Jonathan: Homosexual Lovers?

The suggestion that King David and Jonathan (son of King Saul) might have been homosexual lovers is so strained beyond credibility that it would not be worth a response if it were not for the many people who have been misled by this erroneous notion.

One of the more popular proponents of a homosexual relationship between David and Jonathan is Tom Horner. Referring to Old Testament characters, Horner says that the relationship between David and Jonathan is "the only example of an unabashed homosexual love of one well-known character for another."[78]

Many who share Horner's opinion about David and Jonathan will usually, in support of their argument, quote these words of King David at the death of Jonathan: "I grieve for you, Jonathan my brother; you were very dear to me. Your love for me was wonderful, more wonderful than that of women." (2nd Samuel 1:26) So, does this text of Scripture prove that David and Jonathan had a homosexual relationship?

---

[78] See *Sex in the Bible* by Tom Horner, 85. Also see *Jonathan Loved David: Homosexuality in Biblical Times* by Tom Horner. A few other pro-gay authors also attempt to find a lesbian relationship between Ruth and Naomi. For an excellent refutation of the idea that Ruth and Naomi were lesbian lovers, see *Homosexuality in History and the Scriptures* by Ronald M. Springett, 78-81.

Many have written fine refutations of the idea that David and Jonathan were homosexual lovers.[79] In fact, even pro-gay scholar Martti Nissinen says the following: "Nothing indicates that David and Jonathan slept together 'as one sleeps with a woman.' Neither of the men are described as having problems in their heterosexual sex life ... The story of David and Jonathan was being told at the time when the Holiness Code with its commands and prohibitions of sexual contact between males regulated the Israelites' sexual morality."[80] With that understood, I offer the following additional responses to the idea that David and Jonathan were homosexual lovers.

First, even if we grant the unlikely possibility that David and Jonathan were homosexual lovers, this would in no way change the fact that Scripture clearly condemns even consensual homosexual behavior. When reading Holy Scripture, one must distinguish between PRESCRIPTIVE texts (commands intended for ALL people of ALL times and places) and DESCRIPTIVE texts (portions of Scripture that relate events in history).[81]

Simply put, just because Holy Scripture describes an event in history does not mean that God thereby condones or affirms that event. For example, Scripture describes how the men of Sodom threatened homosexual gang rape against Lot's guests. But Scripture in no way condones this behavior! In the same way, even if David and Jonathan were homosexual lovers (and all the evidence shows that they were NOT!) this does not mean that God affirmed their behavior. In fact, as we learned from our study of the creation account in Genesis as well as the sexual prohibitions in Leviticus chapters 18 and 20, God would have condemned such homosexual behavior between David and Jonathan.

Second, as noted in the above quote from Martti Nissinen, "The story of David and Jonathan was being told at the time when the Holiness Code with its commands and prohibitions of sexual contact between males regulated the Israelites' sexual morality." In other words, David himself would have acknowledged that homosexual

---

[79] For example, see *The Bible and Homosexual Practice* by Robert Gagnon, 146-154. Also see *Homosexuality in History and the Scriptures* by Ronald M. Springett, 70-74.

[80] *Homoeroticism in the Biblical World* by Martti Nissinen, 55-56.

[81] I give more information on the difference between prescriptive and descriptive texts in chapter 3.

behavior was sinful! When King David was guilty of adultery (by having sex with the WIFE of another man), he confessed his sin after being rebuked by the prophet Nathan.[82] However, in no place do we find that the prophet Nathan ever rebukes David for his homosexual behavior. If David had been guilty of homosexual behavior, then surely the prophet Nathan, who rebuked David for his heterosexual adultery (based on Leviticus 18:20), would also have rebuked David for his homosexual behavior with Jonathan (based on Leviticus 18:22).

Third, when 2nd Samuel 1:26 tells us that Jonathan's love for David was "more wonderful than that of women" this in no way implies a homosexual relationship. In fact, the wider context of 1st and 2nd Samuel proves the opposite! David had several wives,[83] and yet his relationship with some of them was less than ideal. In contrast, the brotherly love between David and Jonathan was sacrificial and unconditional. Jonathan sacrificed so much to be loyal to David, whom he knew was God's chosen one to be king over Israel in place of his evil father, King Saul. Jonathan was willing to be loyal to David even though this resulted in a tense relationship between him and his father, Saul. The Hebrew word *ahad* is used to describe the "love" that David and Jonathan had for each other. The same Hebrew word is used to describe the love that all Israel had for David (see 1st Samuel 18:16). The Hebrew word *ahad* in these and similar contexts has the meaning of the Greek word *philía* which describes a dedicated brotherly or family love (unlike the Greek word *érōs* which describes romantic or sexual love).

Finally, one other place that some try to find a homosexual relationship between David and Jonathan is 1st Samuel 20:41b, which reads: "Then they kissed each other and wept together – but David wept the most." How do we respond to this text? First, the wider context of 1st Samuel 20:41b has nothing to do with a sexual situaiton! In addition, the fact that David and Jonathan "kissed each other" has nothing to do with homosexual behavior when one considers that in the culture of that time it was perfectly natural for heterosexual men to express affection for each other via non-sexual kissing. Even pro-gay scholar Martti Nissinen acknowledges this when he writes: "Modern readers probably see homoeroticism in the story of David and Jonathan more easily than did the ancients. In the contemporary Western world,

---

[82] See 2nd Samuel 12:1-13. Also see Psalm 51.

[83] I will deal with the issue of polygamy in the Old Testament in the next chapter.

men's mutual expressions of feelings are more restricted than they were in the biblical world. Men's homosociability apparently was not part of the sexual taboo in the biblical world any more than it is in today's Christian and Islamic cultures around the Mediterranean ... The relationship of David and Jonathan can be taken as an example of ancient oriental homosociability, which permits even intimate feelings to be expressed."[84]

Simply put, there is no evidence whatsoever to suggest that David and Jonathan were homosexual lovers. Those who want to suggest such a relationship are forcing their views on the text of Holy Scripture. The love that David and Jonathan had for each other was a non-sexual, sacrificial friendship between two men. In view of this, Robert Gagnon writes: "Some companions destroy each other 'but there is a lover/friend ... who sticks closer than a brother' (Prov. 18:24). David and Jonathan had the latter type of relationship and it was one which was completely asexual."[85]

Jesus and Homosexuality

I recall an occasion back in the year 2000 when I was speaking with a man who believed that his homosexual behavior was completely compatible with his being a Christian. Regarding the prohibitions against even consensual homosexual behavior in Leviticus, he offered some of the revisionist arguments I dealt with in the above section. When I gave responses to his revisionist arguments and showed him their obvious error, he didn't know what to say. He then attempted to counter my points by saying: "But Jesus Himself never said one word about homosexuality! If homosexual behavior were such a horrible sin, don't you think Jesus would have addressed it? Jesus' silence on the issue of homosexuality convinces me that my homosexual desire and behavior are affirmed by God!" This argument is found among many who affirm homosexual desire and behavior. How do we respond?

I will admit that Jesus said nothing about the issue of homosexual desire and behavior – at least nothing that has been recorded in Holy Scripture. However, in this section of my book I will show that Jesus' silence on homosexual behavior does not mean that we can affirm it in direct conflict with the rest of Holy Scripture! In fact, I will show that

---

[84] *Homoeroticism in the Biblical World* by Martti Nissinen, 56.

[85] *The Bible and Homosexual Practice* by Robert Gagnon, 154.

Jesus' silence on the issue of homosexuality actually ***speaks loudly*** regarding what the rest of Scripture teaches about homosexual desire and behavior being sin and in conflict with God's loving plan for our sexual lives.

Many have offered excellent responses to the notion that Jesus' silence on the issue of homosexuality means that we are allowed to affirm this behavior – such as Stanley Grenz,[86] Joe Dallas[87] and Robert Gagnon.[88] *I encourage you to read their work on this issue.* At this point I will offer the following arguments for why Jesus would have been opposed even to consensual homosexual behavior.

First, Jesus' silence on the issue of homosexual behavior does not mean that He was indifferent about the issue much less that He affirmed it. For example, the Gospels give us no record of Jesus ever mentioning bestiality (see Leviticus 20:15-16). Does this mean that Jesus affirmed such behavior? Also, Jesus never directly speaks to the issue of incest (see Leviticus 18:6-18). Does this mean He would have approved of sex between an adult mother and her adult son or an adult father and his adult daughter? In addition, in no place does Jesus explicitly condemn the abuse of people with disabilities (see Leviticus 19:14). Does this mean that Jesus would overlook or even affirm such behavior?

Those who suggest that Jesus would affirm homosexual behavior usually respond to the above points by saying: "But sins such as bestiality, incest and abuse of people with disabilities are clearly condemned in the Old Testament and go against the moral teachings of Jesus about sex and love of one's neighbor." Precisely! In the same way, the sin of **homosexual behavior** is clearly condemned in the Old Testament and, as we will see, goes against the moral teachings of Jesus about sex and love of one's neighbor.

Second, the Jewish culture of Jesus' day condemned even consensual homosexual behavior between adults.[89] Therefore, Jesus did not need to "beat a dead horse" and "preach to the choir" by

---

[86] *Welcoming But Not Affirming* by Stanley Grenz, 60-61.

[87] *The Gay Gospel?* by Joe Dallas, 189-200.

[88] *The Bible and Homosexual Practice* by Robert Gagnon, 185-228.

[89] For a thorough treatment of the Jewish view of homosexual behavior in Jesus' day, see *The Bible and Homosexual Practice* by Robert Gagnon, 159-192.

condemning a sexual behavior that was viewed as sin by most Jewish people in His day.

Regarding this, pro-gay scholar Martti Nissinen writes: "To the extent that Rabbinic and Hellenistic Jewish literature sheds light on the norms of Jewish society in Jesus' time, it can be assumed that public expressions of homosexuality were regarded as anomalous, idolatrous, and indecent."[90] In addition, the pro-gay scholar Louis Crompton writes: "Since few men are uninfluenced by their culture and times, it is likely Jesus shared the traditional prejudices of his fellow Jews."[91]

If Jesus had **affirmed** consensual homosexual behavior, we would have expected Him to **condemn** the views of His own people who believed that homosexual behavior was an abomination. Jesus never hesitated rebuking and correcting His own people regarding their erroneous views on other issues! *Therefore, Jesus' silence on the issue of homosexual behavior* ***speaks loudly*** *about His own views on this matter.* Simply put, Jesus' silence on the issue of homosexual behavior shows that He agreed with His fellow Jews that such behavior was sinful and condemned by God.

Third, Jesus' use of Genesis chapters 1 & 2 in Matthew 19:1-12 shows that He viewed the creation account as a commentary on God's will for human sexuality. In Matthew 19:1-12 Jesus clearly teaches that the only option to sex between one man and one woman in marriage is a life of celibacy! The apostle Paul (as we will see in the next section) also alludes to the creation account to show that marriage between one man and one woman is the ONLY godly context for sexual activity.

Of course, some will try to spin this text to suggest that Jesus was open to the idea of homosexual behavior. They will point to Jesus' comments about eunuchs in Matthew 19:11-12. *However, Jesus' comments about eunuchs actually go against the argument that He would have affirmed homosexual behavior.* In Matthew 19:11-12 Jesus is responding to His disciples who suggested that if God does not want men to divorce their wives then it would be better not to marry (thus showing that they did not understand the sacrificial nature of what it

---

[90] *Homoeroticism in the Biblical World* by Martti Nissinen, 118.

[91] *Homosexuality & Civilization* by Louis Crompton, 111-112.

means to be a husband – see Ephesians 5:25-32). Jesus then tells them that not all men have this gift, that is, the gift of CELIBACY![92]

Jesus goes on to give examples of men who DO have the gift of celibacy. He mentions that some are "eunuchs" because they were born that way. The Greek word translated as "eunuchs" is *eunouchoi* - a word that refers to a man whose reproductive organs do not function or have been cut off, and so he is not able to have sexual relations at all.[93]

In other words, Jesus' comment about eunuchs that were "born that way" does not refer to those who engage in homosexual behavior (as though Jesus were somehow affirming homosexual behavior) but to those who do not practice any type of sexual behavior – heterosexual or homosexual. Jesus also mentions those who have been made eunuchs by men (referring to those who have been castrated versus those who were born with non-functioning reproductive organs).

Finally, Jesus mentions those who "have renounced marriage because of the kingdom of heaven." In this case Jesus is speaking of men who choose to remain single (and therefore, celibate!) so as to give their attention to serving the Lord with undivided commitment.

Simply put, in no way does Jesus use the word "eunuchs" to somehow affirm those who engage in homosexual behavior. Jesus' point is that CELIBACY is the only option to sex between one man and one woman in marriage.

However, some who affirm homosexual behavior will point out that whereas <u>heterosexual</u> people have the option of being sexually active within marriage, those with <u>homosexual</u> desires do not have this option if we teach that all forms of homosexual behavior are condemned by God. Therefore, they argue, we should allow those with same-sex attraction the option of being sexually active within consensual, adult, life-long, monogamous relationships. I have two responses to this view.

First, those who have same-sex desires are allowed the option of sexual activity within HETEROSEXUAL marriage. In other words,

---

[92] The Apostle Paul makes the same point in 1st Corinthians 7:1-7 where he clearly teaches that celibacy is the only option to sex between one man and one woman within marriage.

[93] The Expositor's Bible Commentary *Matthew* by D. A. Carson, 418-419.

they still have the biological ability to function in a heterosexual manner even though this is not their ideal preference.

For example, on one occasion I spoke with a man who left his wife and children to pursue a homosexual relationship. He said to me: "God made me a homosexual! I can't function in any other way." I then responded: "But you were married to a woman for several years and fathered three children!" He was silent for a few moments, and then said: "Alright! I PREFER to function as a homosexual."

Just because a person may PREFER homosexual sex does not mean we should affirm such behavior! For example, a heterosexual man may prefer to have sex with other women besides his wife, but this does not mean that his preference should be affirmed!

Second, if people with same-sex desires refuse to enter heterosexual marriage, then God asks them to deny themselves and strive to live a sexually pure life – and for a single person (whether heterosexual or homosexual) this means celibacy!

In regard to the second point above, Marva J. Dawn (who struggles with very poor eyesight in addition to other physical problems) writes the following: "When I ask homosexuals for celibacy, I am not asking anything more of them than I asked of myself all the years that I was single. Celibacy was a good (but sometimes painfully difficult) choice for me in order to be faithful to the purposes of God ... To be denied sexual fulfillment (as I also was for many single years) does not seem to me to be such a great suffering. Though I am passionately in love with my husband, I would gladly give up sexual happiness to get my vision back. (You see, my dear reader, I am easily as guilty of making an idol of visual pleasure as others might be of the idolatry of sexual pleasure. We are all sinners in rebellion against our Creator!)"[94]

The fourth reason that Jesus would have been opposed even to consensual homosexual behavior is that in Mark 7:21 we see that He condemns "sexual immorality" in addition to the sin of adultery. The Greek word translated as "sexual immorality" is *porneiai* – and in the Jewish culture of Jesus' day this word was used to refer to ALL forms of sexual immorality condemned by the sexual prohibitions in Leviticus

---

[94] *Sexual Character: Beyond Technique to Intimacy* by Marva J. Dawn, 107-108.

chapters 18 and 20, **and this would include the prohibition against consensual homosexual behavior.**[95]

But why does Jesus even mention adultery and other forms of "sexual immorality" (including homosexual behavior) if the Jews of His day already agreed that such behaviors were sinful? Simply put, most Jews were focused merely on the outward behavior and not the sinful ***desire*** that could lead to such behavior. That is why Jesus said: "For from within, out of men's hearts, come evil thoughts, sexual immorality, theft, murder, adultery..." (Mark 7:21)

Jesus makes the same point in Matthew 5:27-28 where He stresses that lustful thoughts are equal to adultery before God. The fact that Jesus speaks of "sexual immorality" (*porneiai*) in addition to adultery shows that He agreed with the Jews of His day regarding the universal applicability of the sexual prohibitions in Leviticus chapters 18 and 20 – which also condemn even consensual homosexual behavior.

Fifth, if Jesus had affirmed consensual homosexual behavior, then we would expect that His Jewish enemies (for example, many of the Pharisees) would have used this against Him. Remember, the huge majority of Jews in Jesus' day agreed with Holy Scripture that homosexual behavior was an abomination before God. If Jesus had been willing to affirm consensual homosexual behavior, His Jewish enemies would have immediately pointed out this fact as a way to discredit Jesus and His ministry. However, we find no evidence whatsoever that the Jews of Jesus' day used this argument against Jesus. This shows that Jesus shared the common Jewish view that homosexual behavior was sinful.

Sixth, Jesus' love for sinners did not mean that He tolerated or much less affirmed their sin. Instead, Jesus preached that people should repent of their sins – including various sexual sins! – and receive forgiveness and new life through faith in Him. But if people refused to repent of their sin, they faced eternal condemnation. Jesus was very likely referring to Leviticus 19:17-18 when He spoke the following words: "If your brother sins, rebuke him, and if he repents, forgive him. If he sins against you seven times in a day, and seven times comes back to you and says, 'I repent,' forgive him." (Luke 17:3-4)

---

[95] For example, in 1st Corinthians 5:1 Paul uses the Greek word *porneia* (translated in the NIV as "sexual immorality") to refer to the incest taking place among two members of the Corinthian congregation. The sin of incest is found in the same immediate context of Leviticus chapters 18 and 20 where we also find the condemnation of consensual homosexual behavior.

All the evidence shows that Jesus would have condemned homosexual behavior along with the other sexual sins condemned in Leviticus chapters 18 and 20. At the same time, He would have offered complete and total forgiveness to those who confessed their sin and longed for God's mercy.

However, the forgiveness that Jesus freely gives us results in us turning away from the very sins He has forgiven.[96] That is why Jesus defines the Christian life as "taking up your cross," "denying yourself," and "losing your life" (see Mark 8:34-37; Matthew 10:38-39; Luke 14:27 and 17:33; John 12:25).

Therefore, there is no reason to believe that Jesus would make an exception for homosexual behavior when He clearly expected people to repent of all other sexual sins.

Finally, Jesus entrusted His teaching to His chosen apostles (see John 17:16-20 and Acts 26:15-18). This means that Jesus' apostles delivered His teaching to others – including God's teaching for our sexual lives.

As I noted earlier, Jesus did not need to mention homosexual behavior explicitly because the Jews to whom He ministered already agreed with Scripture that homosexual behavior was sinful.

However, as we will see in the next section *The Apostle Paul and Homosexuality*, when Paul shares Jesus' teaching with the Gentiles (whose culture had many who AFFIRMED homosexual behavior!) he clearly addresses the issue of homosexual behavior and condemns it as sinful. **Since the apostle Paul speaks for Jesus, we see that Jesus would have been opposed to homosexual behavior!**

In spite of all the evidence to the contrary, some who affirm homosexual behavior will go to great lengths to try to show that Jesus not only affirmed homosexual behavior but may have actually practiced homosexual behavior Himself!

I will now respond to two arguments that attempt to show that Jesus would have viewed homosexual behavior in a positive way.

[96] See Ephesians 4:17-5:20, Titus 2:11-14 and 2nd Peter 1:3-9.

Did Jesus condone a Roman centurion's gay relationship?

A few years ago a friend of mine visited a congregation one Sunday. The pastor offered a Sunday morning class on the issue of homosexuality. The pastor held the position that Scripture does not forbid homosexual behavior but actually affirms it. Of course, she admitted that many texts of Scripture appear to condemn homosexual behavior, but then she suggested that there is one example where Jesus seems to affirm a male homosexual relationship. She was referring to Matthew 8:5-13 and Luke 7:1-10 where we read about the Roman centurion who asked Jesus to heal his sick servant.[97]

Some have attempted to find evidence of Jesus affirming a male homosexual relationship by suggesting that the Roman centurion and his servant were homosexual lovers.[98] Why would they make this assumption? The reason is that there is historical evidence showing that some (but not all!) Roman men who were slave owners would sometimes have sex with their slaves – both male and female.[99] They then conclude that the Roman centurion mentioned in Matthew and Luke must have had a homosexual relationship with his servant – whom Luke says his master "valued highly" (Luke 7:2). Since Jesus does not condemn this supposed homosexual relationship (in fact, He doesn't even mention it!), they argue, Jesus was thereby affirming their homosexual behavior.

Is this a reasonable interpretation of this event as recorded in Matthew 8:5-13 and Luke 7:1-10? Hardly! Many have exposed the ridiculous nature of this strained interpretation.[100]

---

[97] In Matthew's account we are told that the centurion asks Jesus for help whereas in Luke's account some Jews ask for Jesus' help on behalf of the centurion. Is this a contradiction? No. Matthew simply fails to mention that the centurion sent his message to Jesus through the Jews. Both Matthew and Luke include the centurion's words: "I do not deserve to have you come under my roof." Matthew and Luke agree that the centurion did not feel worthy to meet Jesus in person. Therefore, Matthew's account assumes what Luke's account explicitly states – that the centurion sent his message to Jesus through the Jews.

[98] For example, see *The Children are Free* by Jeff Miner and John Tyler Connoley, 46-51. Also *What the Bible Really Says About Homosexuality* by Daniel Helminiak, 127-130.

[99] For a detailed treatment of ancient Roman sexual practices see *Roman Sexuality* by Craig A. Williams as well as *Bisexuality in the Ancient World* by Eva Cantarella.

[100] For an excellent refutation of this argument, see the article *Did Jesus Approve of a Homosexual Couple in the Story of the Centurion at Capernaum?* by Robert Gagnon

I will now give the following brief responses to this revisionist argument.

First, even though there is evidence that *some* Roman slave owners had sex with their male and female slaves, not ALL of them did. Therefore, it would be wrong to assume that the Roman centurion mentioned in Matthew and Luke had sex with his servant when there is no clear evidence that such a sexual relationship existed. In their book *The Children Are Free*, Miner and Connoley make a lot of the fact that the Roman centurion refers to his servant as his *pais* [101] – a Greek word that could, in some contexts, refer to a male slave who was a homosexual partner with his master.

But even Miner and Connoley admit that this is not the only meaning of the word *pais* , which can also mean "son" or just plain "servant" (without any sexual connotations). In fact, within the New Testament the Greek word *pais* is best understood as being synonymous with another Greek word *doulos* – which also means "slave" or "servant" (without any sexual connotations whatsoever). Finally, as we will see in the following responses, the context in Matthew chapter 8 and Luke chapter 7 makes it very clear that the word *pais* could NOT have any homosexual meaning whatsoever in that situation.

Second, the cultural context in which we find this Roman centurion actually makes it quite impossible that he had a homosexual relationship with his servant. For example, in Luke chapter 7 we read: "The centurion heard of Jesus and sent some elders of the Jews to him, asking him to come and heal his servant. When they came to Jesus, they pleaded earnestly with him, 'This man deserves to have you do this, because he loves our nation and has built our synagogue.'" (Luke 7:4-5) Here we see that the Jews adore and respect this Gentile centurion. They even say that he *deserves* to have Jesus heal his servant. Why would the Jews say this about a Roman centurion when they usually despised most Gentiles – especially the Romans who were often oppressing them and whose various sinful behaviors (such as idolatry and homosexuality) were an abomination to them? The answer is that this Roman centurion was very likely a "God-fearer" (the Greek word for "God-fearer" being *phoboumenos*).

(available on his web page: **www.robgagnon.net**). Also see *The Gay Gospel?* by Joe Dallas, 194-200.

[101] See their book *The Children Are Free, 47-48.*

In Acts chapter 10 we read about another Roman centurion whom Luke explicitly refers to as a God-fearer (*phoboumenos* – see Acts 10:2). When we consider how the Jews in Luke chapter 7 adored the Roman centurion in their community, and when we note that the Roman centurion loved the Jewish nation and built the synagogue in Capernaum, the obvious conclusion is that this Roman centurion was a God-fearer.

Now, what did it mean for a Gentile man to be a God-fearer? In his commentary on the book of Acts, F. F. Bruce writes the following about the Roman centurion in Acts chapter 10: "It is further important to observe that Cornelius was one of those Gentiles who are commonly classed as 'God-fearers' … Many Gentiles in those days, while not prepared to enter this Jewish community as full proselytes, were attracted by the simple monotheism of Jewish synagogue worship and by the ethical standard of the Jewish way of life. Some of them attended synagogue and were tolerably conversant with the prayers and Scripture lessons, which they heard read in the Greek version; some observed with more or less scrupulosity such distinctive Jewish practices as Sabbath observance and abstinence from certain kinds of food."[102]

What we know of these Gentile God-fearers is that they *at the very least* worshipped only the God of Israel and submitted to all their moral laws – **including their sexual laws!** As F. F. Bruce noted, not only did the God-fearers submit to the ethical standards of the Jews, but some of these God-fearers would even observe many of the Jewish ceremonial laws. Therefore, if the Roman centurion in Luke chapter 7 were a God-fearer (and the evidence suggests that he was!), then he would NOT have been involved in homosexual behavior because this was clearly condemned in the Old Testament Scriptures.[103]

In fact, if the Jews had known that this Roman centurion was involved in homosexual behavior with his slave, they would have been greatly offended. But Luke tells us that they thought highly of this centurion and believed he deserved Jesus' help.

---

[102] The New International Commentary on the New Testament *The Book of Acts* by F. F. Bruce, 215-216.

[103] Unlike the pagan Romans who often abused their slaves, this God-fearing Roman centurion was influenced by the Old Testament Scriptures which teach that slaves should be treated with compassion. In other words, the centurion's concern for his servant has nothing to do with him having a homosexual relationship with him.

In their book *The Children Are Free,* Miner and Connoley suggest that the Jewish crowd knew about the centurion's homosexual behavior and despised the fact that Jesus was willing to help such a man.[104] But this view is in direct conflict with what Scripture teaches us about the event!

The Jews respected this Roman centurion because he loved their nation (and therefore, also loved their moral laws – including their prohibition of homosexuality!) and they pleaded with Jesus to help him! Miner and Connoley did not read the Scriptures very carefully.

The third reason we should not accept the idea that Jesus affirmed a homosexual relationship between the Roman centurion and his servant is that, as we have already learned in this section, Jesus would have been opposed to even consensual homosexual behavior.

Therefore, if this Roman centurion had been involved in homosexual behavior, Jesus would have called him to repentance just as He did with the tax collectors, prostitutes and other sinners. The fact that Jesus said nothing about this centurion's homosexual behavior with his slave is strong evidence that such homosexual behavior did NOT exist!

In their book *The Children Are Free*, Miner and Connoley write: "We must let the word of God speak for itself, even if it leads us to an uncomfortable destination."[105] *I find this sentence to be ironic.* If Miner and Connoley were actually willing to let the Word of God "speak for itself" on the issue of homosexuality they would quickly realize that God clearly condemns even consensual homosexual behavior as being sinful.[106] This might be an "uncomfortable destination" for those who wish to impose their affirmation of homosexual behavior on the pages of Holy Scripture, but the Holy Spirit moves us to face the Truth of God's Word even when it exposes our cherished sins. **But even more, the Truth of God's Word points**

---

[104] See their book *The Children Are Free, 49-50.*

[105] See their book *The Children Are Free, 48.*

[106] Even pro-gay author Daniel Helminiak, who would love to find evidence for Jesus affirming homosexual behavior, admits that there is not much proof for the idea that the Roman centurion in Matthew chapter 8 and Luke chapter 7 had a homosexual relationship with his servant. On pages 128-129 of his book *What the Bible Really Says About Homosexuality* he writes: "...what was the relationship between the centurion and the servant? There is no way of knowing for certain. The historical evidence is scanty." **To say the least!**

us to Christ through whom we have complete forgiveness and new life with God!

Were Jesus and the apostle John homosexual lovers?

The ridiculously strained revisionist argument that Jesus condoned a centurion's homosexual behavior (refuted above) is not even close to being as twisted and unbelievable as the notion that Jesus and the apostle John were homosexual lovers. Where do people get this idea? Some point to the fact that John refers to himself as "the disciple whom Jesus loved" and that he leaned against Jesus' chest during the last supper (see John 21:20).

I will not spend much time refuting this argument because even most pro-gay biblical scholars admit that it is ridiculous. For example, Martti Nissinen writes: "Clearly the Gospel of John in particular presupposes a close teacher-student relationship between Jesus and his immediate circle, and in this company the favorite disciple clearly enjoys special status. He is the one whom Jesus quite especially 'loved' and who always stood closest to Jesus. Nevertheless, the homoerotic or pederastic dimension of their relationship could be argued only in a strained way … Only the scene at the last supper might suggest this direction – and it is questionable evidence at that. The custom of a student resting against his teacher's chest manifests cultural conventions rather than homoeroticism…"[107] With that said, I will now offer the following refutations.

First, as we have already learned from this section, Jesus and His apostles would have shared the common view of most Jews in their day who believed that even consensual homosexual behavior was condemned by the Old Testament. Therefore, Jesus and John would NOT have engaged in such sinful behavior.

Second, John uses the Greek verbs *agapao* and *phileo* to describe Jesus' love for him and his love for Jesus. Never once does John use the Greek verb *erao* (the Greek verb used for sexual behavior) to speak of his relationship with Jesus. Regarding this fact, Robert Gagnon writes the following: "The fact that the verb *phileo*, which refers to friendship love, and the related noun *philos*, 'friend,' are used

---

[107] *Homoeroticism in the Biblical World* by Martti Nissinen, 122.

interchangeably with *agapao* and cognates in John's Gospel confirms the non-erotic character of this love."[108]

Simply put, there is no evidence whatsoever to support the notion that Jesus and the apostle John may have had a homosexual relationship. In fact, all the evidence shows that Jesus (and His apostles) would have considered even consensual homosexual behavior to be a sinful abomination before God.

As I mentioned earlier in this section, Jesus' silence on the issue of homosexual behavior actually ***speaks very loudly*** to the fact that Jesus would have denounced homosexual behavior as being sinful. I also noted that Jesus entrusted His teaching to His apostles, who then passed on His teaching to others after His ascension. *We're now ready to examine what one of Jesus' apostles teaches us about homosexual behavior as we consider some of the letters of Paul.*

The Apostle Paul and Homosexuality

When Jesus taught His own Jewish people He did not even need to mention the fact that homosexual behavior was sinful because most Jews agreed with Scripture on this issue. However, when the apostle Paul (who had been entrusted with Jesus' teaching) proclaimed God's Word to the Gentiles (in whose culture many AFFIRMED even consensual homosexual behavior) he clearly deals with the issue of homosexuality and condemns it as being sinful and contrary to God's will for our sexual lives. We will now examine what Paul says about homosexual behavior in Romans 1:18-32, 1st Corinthians 6:9-11 and 1st Timothy 1:8-11.

Romans 1:18-32

Paul's letter to the Romans is a favorite of many Christians. Paul wrote Romans in 55 AD, and in this epistle he explains in detail how the person and work of Christ are connected to other doctrines of the Christian Faith.

Martin Luther was greatly influenced by the book of Romans, and in his preface to this epistle he writes: "We, therefore, find in this Epistle most copiously treated whatever a Christian ought to know; namely,

---

[108] See the article *Was Jesus in a Sexual Relationship with the Beloved Disciple?* by Robert Gagnon (found on his web page: www.robgagnon.net).

what are the law and the Gospel - sin, punishment, grace, faith, and righteousness, Christ and God, good works, charity, hope, and crosses; how we ought to act towards every one, whether he be a religious man or a sinner, strong or weak, friend or foe, and how we ought to act towards ourselves. And all this so admirably lain down with examples from Holy Writ, and so exemplified both by himself and from the Prophets, as to leave nothing to wish for. It would seem as if St. Paul in this Epistle wished to epitomize the whole faith and doctrine of the Gospel of Christ, and thus prepare us an introduction to the whole of the Old Testament."[109]

Paul begins Romans with these words: "Paul, a servant of Christ Jesus, called to be an apostle and set apart for the gospel of God – the gospel he promised beforehand through his prophets in the Holy Scriptures regarding his Son, who as to his human nature was a descendant of David, and who through the Spirit of holiness was declared with power to be the Son of God by his resurrection from the dead: Jesus Christ our Lord." (Romans 1:1-4)

There is enough information packed into those first four versus of Romans chapter 1 to fill an entire book. Therefore, at the risk of being simplistic, I will briefly sum up what Paul is teaching us here so that we may better understand Paul's teaching about homosexual behavior in light of the entire context of the message of the book of Romans.

First, Paul says that he was called to be an apostle – and this was by Christ Himself (see Acts 9:1-19 and Galatians 1:1). Second, Paul was "set apart for the gospel of God." In other words, the "gospel" (the "good news" about Jesus) is not something Paul made up, but it was given to him by God. Third, this gospel from God finds its source in the Old Testament Scriptures which point us to Jesus (see Romans 3:21 and 15:1-4). Fourth, this Jesus is fully human as a descendent of King David (the ancestor of the Virgin Mary – see Luke 3:23-38 and Galatians 4:4) and also fully God as revealed to us by the Holy Spirit who points us to Jesus' resurrection as proof that He is the Son of God.

The Son of God was given the name "Jesus" (which means "God saves" – see Matthew 1:21) and the title "Christ" (which is the Greek translation of the Hebrew title "Messiah" – meaning "The Anointed One," the Savior of all nations promised in the Old Testament).

---

[109] Luther's prefaces to the books of the Bible can be found in Volume 35 of the American Edition of Luther's Works: *Word & Sacrament I* (Fortress Press).

However, Jesus the Christ is also "The Lord." The English word "Lord" translates the Greek word *kurios* – a Greek word used by the Jews in place of the Old Testament Holy Name of God, *Yahweh* (which means "I Am that I Am").

Therefore, when Paul writes "Jesus Christ our Lord" he is teaching us that Jesus is not only the Messiah promised in the Old Testament Scriptures but also God Himself – *Yahweh,* the God of Abraham, Isaac and Jacob (see John 8:58-59 and Philippians 2:5-11).

Later on in chapter 1 of Romans Paul explains the essence of the gospel of Christ in these words: "I am not ashamed of the gospel, because it is the power of God for the salvation of everyone who believes … For in the gospel a righteousness from God is revealed, a righteousness that is by faith from first to last, just as it is written: 'The righteous will live by faith.'" (Romans 1:16-17) Here Paul teaches that the essence of the gospel of Christ is that we receive a righteous from God – *a righteousness we could never produce for ourselves.*

In other words, we do not stand holy and pure before God because of who we are and what we do for God – such as obeying His commandments. Instead, we unworthy sinners stand holy and pure before God because He gives us the holiness and purity of **Jesus** – a gift we receive through faith, which is itself a gift from God (John 6:44 and Ephesians 2:8-9).

At this point it would be helpful to quote the words of Martin Luther regarding **the righteousness of God** : "…I anxiously and busily worked to understand the word of Paul in Rom. 1:17: The righteousness of God is revealed in the Gospel. I questioned this passage … for the expression 'righteousness of God' barred my way. This phrase was customarily explained to mean that the righteousness of God is a virtue by which He is Himself righteous and condemns sinners … as often as I read this passage, I wished that God had never revealed the Gospel; for who could love a God who was angry, who judged and condemned people? This misunderstanding continued until, enlightened by the Holy Spirit, I finally examined more carefully the word of Habakkuk: 'The just shall live by faith' (2:4). From this passage I concluded that life must be derived from faith … Then the entire Holy Scripture became clear to me, and heaven itself was opened to me."[110]

---

[110] See the study note for Romans 1:17 in *The Lutheran Study Bible* , available from Concordia Publishing House.

What was the insight into the heart of God that the Holy Spirit gave to Luther through the words of the prophet Habakkuk? This: "The righteousness of God" describes God's desire to save the very sinners who deserve nothing but His wrath. Sinful human reason concludes that God will punish sinners unless we can do something to appease Him. But God has revealed to us that He longs to be merciful to sinners through Jesus Christ our Lord who lived a holy life FOR US, suffered God's wrath FOR US and conquered death FOR US – *and we believe and receive this good news personally through God's gift of faith!*

Tragically, there are two kinds of unbelief that keep us sinners from receiving the righteousness of God through Christ – and these two kinds of unbelief are ***licentiousness*** and ***legalism*** .

In Romans 1:18-32 (the section where Paul deals with homosexual desire and behavior) we see a description of licentiousness – meaning that people openly rebel against God's loving plan for their lives and embrace the sins exposed by God's Word. Such people understand God's grace, that is, the righteousness of God, as being a "license" to sin all they want[111] because they ignore the fact that they deserve God's wrath and think that they will escape His judgment - *thereby denying their need for Christ's atoning death on the cross!*

On the other hand, in Romans 2:1-3:20 Paul addresses the legalism of the Jews who trust in their obedience of God's Law as the basis for their righteousness before God. Because these Jews try to establish their own righteousness before God based on their good works (see Romans 9:30-33) they fail to recognize that they need a Savior from sin's curse – *thereby denying their need for Christ's atoning death on the cross!*

In other words, the solution to licentiousness is not legalism! If we trust in either our *vice* or our *virtue* we will remain under God's wrath! Therefore, the solution for the two kinds of unbelief – licentiousness and legalism – is repentance and faith in Christ's work FOR US.

At this point someone might ask: "So, where does obedience to God's Law fit in with all of this?" In Romans 1:5 the apostle Paul writes: "Through [Christ] and for his name's sake, we received grace and apostleship to call people from among all the Gentiles to the obedience that comes from faith." Also, in Romans 12:1-2 Paul writes:

---

[111]See Jude 3-4.

"Therefore, I urge you, brothers, in view of God's mercy, to offer your bodies as living sacrifices, holy and pleasing to God – this is your spiritual act of worship. Do not conform any longer to the pattern of this world, but be transformed by the renewing of your mind. Then you will be able to test and approve what God's will is – his good, pleasing and perfect will."

Simply put, the God who declares us righteousness in Christ also creates in us a new heart that grieves over sin and longs to submit to God's Law because we know His will for us is a loving gift. In other words, those who trust in Christ do not turn from sin and strive obey God's Law because they are trying appease God or earn His mercy. No! Those who trust in Christ are moved by the Spirit to turn from sin and obey God's loving will for our lives because we love and trust Him who has completely and totally saved us for Jesus' sake.

In Titus 2:11-14 Paul writes about this truth: "For the grace of God that brings salvation has appeared to all men. It teaches us to say 'No' to ungodliness and worldly passions, and to live self-controlled, upright and godly lives in this present age, while we wait for the blessed hope – the glorious appearing of our great God and Savior, Jesus Christ, who gave himself for us to redeem us from all wickedness and to purify for himself a people that are his very own, eager to do what is good."

However, even though the Spirit will move believers to do good works out of love for God, we will never be free from sin this side of heaven. Paul writes these words about himself as a Christian: "I know that nothing good lives in me, that is, in my sinful nature … When I want to do good, evil is right there with me." (Romans 7:16, 21)

Therefore, even though Christians are moved by the Spirit to turn from sin and obey God's Law, we should not be deceived into thinking that we are becoming less sinful and more holy over time – and therefore need Jesus' mercy just a little bit less every day. No! We never leave behind our need for Christ and the righteousness from God we receive through faith in Him. Just as the salvation and faith we receive from God are pure gifts (see Ephesians 2:8-9), our life of good works is also a pure gift from God (see Ephesians 2:10; also Philippians 1:6 and 2:13).

What a comfort this is! Thank God He doesn't save us and then say: "Now, do your best to obey My Law and maybe I'll keep on loving you!" No! God loved us in Christ even when we were His unbelieving enemies (see Romans 5:10), and He will continue to love us in Christ even as we continue to struggle with the desires and deeds of our sinful nature. This is why the life of the Christian is defined by daily repentance and faith in Jesus!

Now that we understand the essential message of Paul's letter to the Romans, we're ready to consider what he teaches us about homosexual desire and behavior in Romans 1:18-32, which reads:

> **"The wrath of God is being revealed from heaven against all the godlessness and wickedness of men who suppress the truth by their wickedness, since what may be known about God is plain to them. For since the creation of the world God's invisible qualities – his eternal power and divine nature – have been clearly seen, being understood from what has been made, so that men are without excuse. For although they knew God, they neither glorified him as God nor gave thanks to him, but their thinking became futile and their foolish hearts were darkened. Although they claimed to be wise, they became fools and exchanged the glory of the immortal God for images made to look like mortal man and birds and animals and reptiles. Therefore God gave them over in the sinful desires of their hearts to sexual impurity for the degrading of their bodies with one another. They exchanged the truth of God for a lie, and worshiped and served created things rather than the Creator – who is forever praised. Amen. Because of this, God gave them over to shameful lusts.** ***Even their women exchanged natural relations for unnatural ones. In the same way the men also abandoned natural relations with women and were inflamed with lust for one another. Men committed indecent acts with other men, and received in themselves the due penalty for their perversion.***[112] **Furthermore, since they did not think it worthwhile to retain the knowledge of God, he gave them over to a depraved mind, to do what ought not be done. They have become filled with every kind of wickedness, evil, greed and depravity. They are full of envy, murder, strife, deceit and malice. They are gossips, slanderers, God-haters, insolent, arrogant and boastful; they invent ways of doing evil; they disobey their**

[112] The italic emphasis is mine.

parents; they are senseless, faithless, heartless, ruthless. Although they know God's righteous decree that those who do such things deserve death, they not only continue to do these very things but also approve of those who practice them."

This passage from Romans chapter 1 is probably the most well known section of Scripture regarding the issue of homosexuality. Paul clearly condemns both male and female homosexual desire and behavior. *Of course, there are many who affirm homosexual desire and behavior who offer various reasons why Romans 1:18-32 does NOT speak to consensual homosexual behavior today, and I will deal with those arguments later in this section.* However, before I do that, I will first summarize what Paul is teaching us in Romans 1:18-32.

Paul begins by telling us about the "wrath of God." Why? Didn't I just explain that the essential message of Romans is that God desires to be merciful to sinners for Christ's sake? Yes, I did. We need to understand God's wrath in light of the Gospel. You see, God does not want to pour out His wrath on any sinner. However, God pours out His wrath anyway - for **two** reasons.

The **first** reason God pours out His wrath is that He MUST - God MUST pour out His wrath even though He doesn't WANT to do this. Why? The reason is that God is Holy and He can not tolerate or, much less, affirm sinners. The apostle Paul says: "God will not be mocked!" (Galatians 6:7) Why will God not be mocked? Not because He has a temper problem and needs to protect His sensitive ego. Such a *false god* is merely a projection of our own sinful nature. The reason God will not be mocked is that those who mock Him can not abide in His love! Those who mock God also lead others away from God's love as well. God must destroy sinners who refuse to repent in order to protect His creation and any others who would be misled by their unbelief. *But God doesn't want this to happen to any sinner.* That's why He sent Jesus to be our Savior!

Now we're ready to hear about the **second** reason God pours out His wrath. God pours out His wrath "this side of the Final Day" so that sinners will fear God's judgment and long for His mercy before it's too late. On the Final Day when Christ returns God will pour out His wrath in such a way that there will be no escape for those who refused to repent and trust in Christ (see 1st Corinthians 11:32b, 1st Thessalonians 1:10, 2nd Thessalonians 1:5-10, Revelation 6:16-17). Therefore, while we live "this side of the Final Day" God pours out His wrath in the hope that sinners will repent and trust in Christ Who suffered God's wrath in our place so that we might be saved (see Isaiah 59:20, Ezekiel 18:30-32, Matthew 4:17, Luke 13:5, Acts 3:19, 2nd Peter 3:9-10, Revelation 2:21-22 and 3:19). *In other words, God pours out His wrath in service to His GOSPEL!*

Therefore, in Romans 1:18 we do not have a God who takes pleasure in pouring out His wrath on sinners. Instead, we have a God who longs to save sinners and will do whatever it takes to bring them to repentance so they may receive forgiveness through faith in Christ.

Paul goes on to teach that those who are in bondage to licentious unbelief "suppress the truth by their wickedness." Even though they know there is a God because creation is evidence of this fact, and even though they know what God's will is for their lives (including their sexual lives) because God has given them a conscience ("written His Law on their hearts" – see Romans 2:12a, 14-15), they willingly suppress the truth of God and embrace what they know is evil (see 1st John 1:8, 10). They create their own false gods who will do their bidding. *You see, at the heart of all idolatry is the desire to have a god whom we can appease and bribe so that he/she/it will give us what we want. But even our own false gods let us down eventually when the reality of sin and death crushes us and our false gods can do nothing to save us.*

So, what does God do in response to this licentious unbelief? He gave them over in the sinful desires of their hearts to "sexual impurity." The Greek word translated "sexual impurity" is *akatharsian* - a Greek word Paul uses in other sexual vice lists (see 2nd Corinthians 12:21, Galatians 5:19, Ephesians 5:3, 1st Thessalonians 4:7). Apparently, one of the things these licentious unbelievers wanted from their false gods was the freedom to indulge any and every sexual desire. God finally gives them over to this desire. Why? God hopes that when they have their way and are alone with their sin they will eventually be crushed by guilt and the suffering that inevitably comes from all our wicked choices. **Simply put, God's goal in "giving us over to sin" is to lead us to repentance!**

In contrast, the devil lies to us and thereby convinces us that indulging the sinful desires of our hearts will be good for us. But the devil's goal is to use our sin to kill and destroy us (see John 8:44 and 10:10a). Sadly, some people convince themselves that their sin – in spite of the pain it eventually brings – is better for them than God's loving plan for their lives. By their own choice they remain under

God's wrath. **Paul then goes on in Romans 1:26-27 to mention a specific type of sexual impurity - *homosexual desire and behavior.***

Paul begins by mentioning that women "exchanged natural relations for unnatural ones." Here Paul clearly condemns consensual female homosexual lust and behavior. In the above section on Leviticus chapters 18 and 20 we answered the argument: "Leviticus does not mention female homosexuality and, therefore, God must not condemn it!"

We learned that just as father/daughter incest is not mentioned in Leviticus chapters 18 and 20 and yet is condemned because of the example of mother/son incest, and just as female heterosexual lust is not mentioned by Jesus in Matthew chapter 5 and yet is condemned because of the example of male heterosexual lust, in the same way female homosexual lust and behavior is condemned by the example of male homosexual lust and behavior in Leviticus chapters 18 and 20. This is confirmed by the fact that in Romans 1:26 Paul explicitly condemns female homosexual behavior - showing that we must **assume** the prohibition against Lesbianism in Leviticus chapters 18 and 20 based on the prohibition of male homosexual behavior.

After Paul condemns female homosexual behavior, he goes on to say that "the men also abandoned natural relations with women and were inflamed with lust for one another." Here Paul clearly condemns consensual male homosexual lust and behavior. Paul adds that these men committed "indecent acts" with each other. What were these "indecent acts?" Paul is referring to any type of sexual behavior[113] between men. In the same way, any type of sexual behavior between women would also be an "indecent act."

However, what does Paul mean when he says that the men received in themselves the "due penalty" for their perversion? Scholars debate about what this "due penalty" might be. Some suggest it could be a hard heart that is incapable of repentance.[114] Others suggest some type of physical and emotional problems associated with male homosexual behavior.[115] Whatever the "due penalty" may be, Paul is pointing out

---

[113] Such "sexual behavior" between men could be kissing, other types of foreplay or genital "intercourse" (oral or anal).

[114] See Exodus 8:15-10:1, 2nd Chronicles 36:13, Daniel 5:20, Hebrews 3:13 & 6:6.

[115] For examples of physical and emotional problems associated especially with the male homosexual lifestyle, see: *Understanding Homosexuality* by David N. Glesne, 25-33; *Homosexuality and the Politics of Truth* by Jeffrey Satinover, 49-70; *The Bible and Homosexual Practice* by Robert Gagnon, 471-484.

that all sin – including the sin of homosexuality – has negative spiritual, physical, emotional and mental consequences.

Finally, in Romans 1:28-32 Paul goes on to stress that God gave these licentious unbelievers over to many other sins besides homosexuality. We see here a list of sins against every one of the Ten Commandments – sins of desire, thought, word and deed! Paul then writes: "Although they know God's righteous decree that those who do such things deserve death, they not only continue to do these very things but also approve of those who practice them." (Romans 1:32)

Paul clearly teaches that ALL sin is worthy of death! That may surprise us, because some of the sins Paul lists seem trivial from a human point of view. In the same way, some think that God over-reacted when Adam and Eve merely ate a piece of fruit from the forbidden tree. But what we must understand is that at the heart of each and every sin is the rebellious attitude: "I know God says this is evil. But I don't care what God says. I'm going to do it anyway!" No wonder Paul says: "The wages of sin is death!" (Romans 6:23a)

What do we learn from Romans 1:28-32? First, we learn that homosexual lust and behavior are NOT the worst of all sins. No sin is more evil than another before God, and no sin is too evil that it can't be forgiven by Christ's shed blood. Second, we dare not stand in judgment over those who practice homosexual behavior as though our sins are less evil. Paul is very clear that ALL sin is worthy of death and deserves God's wrath.

But then why does Paul single out female and male homosexual lust and behavior and list it separately from the other sins mentioned in Romans 1:28-32? The context helps us understand what Paul is trying to do. Paul teaches that licentious unbelievers ignore the Creator and worship created things.

In other words, unbelievers create false gods whom they can appease and bribe so they can live as they please – and the result of denying God's laws (written on their hearts) is that they turn God's plan for human life *upside down!*

Now, what is a very obvious example of turning God's plan for human life *upside down?* Even though various sins could serve as examples, **homosexual** behavior clearly and obviously distorts the created order by reversing the natural function of sex between male and female – the "one flesh" union of male and female described in the Genesis account!

Romans 1:18-27 brings to mind the creation account in Genesis chapters 1 and 2 where we read that God created the first two humans as "male and female" and gave them to each other in marriage. In fact, the Greek words that Paul uses for "men and women" (*arsenes* and *theleias* , respectively) in Romans 1:27 are based on the same Greek words for "male and female" (*arsen* and *thelu* , respectively) used in the **Septuagint** – the Greek translation of the Hebrew Old Testament, which was the common Bible among Jews in Paul's day. Paul obviously wants us to think about God's creation of the first man and woman in Genesis!

The created anatomy of male and female are obviously structured to be compatible with each other. This fact is so obvious that some people today even refer to certain electrical components as having "male" or "female" parts. However, the obvious sexual compatibility of male and female is mocked and turned *upside down* by **homosexual** behavior.

Therefore, Paul uses homosexual behavior as a clear example of what happens when licentious unbelievers suppress the truth of God in creation and choose to rebel against it. Because their suppression of the truth is so obvious (as with the example of homosexual lust and behavior), God says they are "without excuse" because "they know God's righteous decree that those who do such things deserve death" and yet "they not only continue to do these very things but also approve of those who practice them."

After Paul shows us the end result of unrepentant licentiousness, he then goes on in Romans 2:1-3:20 to confront those who separate themselves from God's love by their unrepentant self-righteous legalism. Once Paul makes his point about Jewish legalism being just as evil as Gentile licentiousness, he then gives us the solution to our sin problem in Romans 3:21-28.

The solution to our sin problem is JESUS and the salvation that only He can give us! God uses His law to expose the evil and hopelessness of our licentiousness and legalism (see Romans 3:19-20) so that we will despair before God's judgment and joyfully receive the salvation He longs to give us in Christ. The apostle Paul writes: "But now a righteousness from God … has been revealed … This righteousness from God comes through faith in Jesus Christ to all who believe. There is no difference, for all have sinned and fall short of the glory of God, and are justified freely by his grace through the redemption that came by Christ Jesus." (Romans 3:21-24)

Now that I've explained the meaning of Paul's teaching on homosexual behavior in Romans 1:26-27 within the wider context of the message of the book of Romans, I will continue by responding to various arguments that attempt to show why Romans 1:18-32 does NOT apply to consensual homosexual behavior today. In this section I will deal with arguments that attempt to retain some respect for the authority of Holy Scripture whereas in the next chapter I will respond to arguments that openly assert we should not always take Holy Scripture seriously.

Paul is condemning heterosexuals who behave as homosexuals!

In his influential book *Christianity, Social Tolerance, and Homosexuality,* John Boswell argues that when Paul says that men gave up "natural relations" for other men just as the women gave up "natural relations" with other women – by "natural" Paul meant that heterosexuals were going against their natural orientation and engaging in homosexual behavior. In other words, according to Boswell, Paul is not condemning homosexual behavior per se, but only homosexual behavior that is contrary to "nature," that is, contrary to one's heterosexual orientation. Therefore, argues Boswell, if a person who has a *homosexual* orientation engages in *homosexual* behavior, this is NOT sin because it is not contrary to his or her "nature."[116] How do we respond?

First, one must note that Boswell admits that Paul is condemning even consensual homosexual behavior – quite apart from whether it is associated with idol worship. Boswell writes: "…it is clear that the sexual behavior itself is objectionable to Paul … and possibly more important, Paul is not describing cold-blooded, dispassionate acts performed in the interest of ritual or ceremony: he states very clearly that the parties involved 'burned in their lust toward one another' …" So how does Boswell get around Paul's condemnation of homosexual behavior? Boswell's solution is to argue that Paul is only condemning homosexual behavior by those who have a heterosexual orientation and who are thereby by acting contrary to their "nature."

However, the problem with Boswell's argument is obvious. When Paul talks about "nature" he is not referring to one's "sexual orientation" (a modern category which Boswell imposes on the text of

[116] See *Christianity, Social Tolerance, and Homosexuality* by John Boswell, 108-117 & 303-332.

Romans). Instead, when Paul speaks of "nature" (the Greek word is *phusiken*) in the context of Romans chapter 1 he means God's created order! In other words, based on the creation account, it is "natural" for a man to have sex with a woman and it is "natural" for a woman to have sex with a man. However, it is CONTRARY to "nature" when men have sex with men or when women have sex with women.

Even pro-gay scholars, who would be happy to agree with Boswell, admit that his argument fails when one considers the context of Romans 1:26-27. For example, even though Martti Nissinen shows some appreciation for Boswell's argument, he goes on to acknowledge that Boswell's argument does nothing to change the fact that Paul was condemning any type of homosexual behavior - whether performed by a person with a heterosexual or homosexual orientation.

Nissinen writes: "The distinction between sexual orientations is clearly an anachronism that does not help to understand Paul's line of argumentation. Paul does not mention *tribades* or *kinaidoi*, that is, female and male persons who were habitually involved in homoerotic relationships; but if he knew about them (and there is every reason to believe that he did), it is difficult to think that, because of their apparent 'orientation,' he would *not* have included them in Romans 1:26-27."[117]

In addition, Nissinen also writes the following: "It is essential to notice that Paul speaks of homoeroticism precisely as a practice … for him, there is no individual inversion or inclination that would make this conduct less culpable … nothing would have made Paul approve homoerotic behavior. Clearly, Paul, to whom marriage was the only acceptable venue for sexual life, could not have approved of any same-sex interaction that even resembled sex between a man and a woman."[118]

Another pro-gay scholar who disagrees with Boswell is the lesbian New Testament scholar Bernadette Brooten. In her book *Love Between Women* she writes: "Paul could have believed that *tribades, kinaidoi,*[119] and other sexually unorthodox persons were born that way and yet still condemn them as unnatural and shameful, this all the more so since he

---

[117] *Homoeroticism in the Biblical World* by Martti Nissinen, 109.

[118] *Homoeroticism in the Biblical World* by Martti Nissinen, 111-112.

[119] As noted also in the quote from Nissinen, the *tribades* and *kinaidoi* were people in Paul's day who had same-sex desires and acted on them. So the argument that Paul knew nothing about "homosexual orientation" simply can not stand.

is speaking of groups of people rather than of individuals ... I believe that Paul used the word 'exchanged' to indicate that people knew the natural sexual order of the universe and left it behind ... Paul is condemning all forms of homoeroticism as the unnatural acts of people who had turned away from God."[120]

Pro-gay scholar Louis Crompton, in his book *Homosexuality & Civilization,* responds to Boswell's argument with these words: "Some interpreters, seeking to mitigate Paul's harshness, have read the passage as condemning not homosexuals generally but only heterosexual men and women who experimented with homosexuality ... But such a reading, however well-intentioned, seems strained and unhistorical. Nowhere does Paul or any other Jewish writer of this period imply the least acceptance of same-sex relations under any circumstances. The idea that homosexuals might be redeemed by mutual devotion would have been wholly foreign to Paul or any other Jew or early Christian."[121]

The above quotes from <u>pro</u>-gay biblical scholars are enough to put Boswell's argument to rest. However, many others have refuted Boswell's argument as well.[122] Simply put, like many other pro-gay revisionist arguments below, Boswell's interpretation of Romans 1:26-27 twists and distorts the clear teaching of Holy Scripture.

Paul is condemning pederasty, not consensual homosexuality!

In his book *The New Testament and Homosexuality*, Robin Scroggs argues that Paul was only condemning <u>abusive</u> forms of homosexual behavior – such as pederasty.[123] However, as with Boswell, even many <u>pro</u>-gay scholars disagree with Scroggs.

For example, Bernadette Brooten writes: "Robin Scroggs has argued that in Rom 1:27 Paul was opposing the principal form of homosexuality known in the Roman world, namely pederasty ... If

---

[120] *Love Between Women* by Bernadette Brooten, 244.

[121] *Homosexuality & Civilization* by Louis Crompton, 114.

[122] *The Same Sex Controversy* by James White and Jeffrey Niell, 125-127; *Welcoming But Not Affirming* by Stanley Grenz, 49-50; *Straight & Narrow?* by Thomas Schmidt, 77-83; *The Bible and Homosexual Practice* by Robert Gagnon, 254-269; *Understanding Homosexuality* by David Glesne, 115-124; *The Gay Gospel?* by Joe Dallas, 202-206.

[123] Pederasty refers to an adult man who has sex with a male teenager or boy – often against his will.

Paul directed Rom 1:27 mainly against pederasty out of humanitarian concern for the passive boy partner, several interpretive problems emerge. Why does Paul apply the phrase 'deserve to die' (Rom 1:32) to all of the foregoing acts, not distinguishing between victims and perpetrators? ... Rom 1:27, like Lev 18:22 and 20:13, condemns all males in male-male relationships regardless of age, making it unlikely that lack of mutuality or concern for the passive boy were Paul's central concerns."[124]

Simply put, Paul nowhere mentions that abusive homosexual behavior is his concern. Instead, when Paul says that men "were inflamed with lust for one another" he thereby stresses that the consensual homosexual act itself is sinful and condemned by God.

Another bit of evidence that refutes Scroggs' argument is the fact that Paul also condemns consensual FEMAL homosexual behavior – and there is no evidence of FEMALE pederasty in the culture of Paul's day. In other words, if abusive forms of male homosexual behavior were Paul's only concern, then why condemn consensual female homosexuality?

In view of this, Bernadette Brooten writes: "If however, the dehumanizing aspects of pederasty motivated Paul to condemn sexual relations between males, then why did he condemn relations between females in the same sentence? ... Scroggs ... maintains his thesis concerning pederasty even though the sources on women do not support it."[125] Brooten also adds: "The ancient sources, which rarely speak of sexual relations between women and girls, undermine Robin Scroggs's theory that Paul opposed homosexuality as pederasty."[126]

In addition, concerning Scroggs' pederasty argument, Martti Nissinen writes that Paul's "mention of women shows that his arguments are not limited to pederasty."[127]

---

[124] *Love Between Women* by Bernadette Brooten, 256-257.

[125] *Love Between Women* by Bernadette Brooten, 253, footnote #106.

[126] *Love Between Women* by Bernadette Brooten, 361.

[127] *Homoeroticism in the Biblical World* by Martti Nissinen, 112-113.

Paul condemns lustful but not loving homosexual behavior!

Some try to suggest that Paul is merely condemning lustful homosexual behavior outside of a loving, committed relationship. However, based on what we have learned about homosexual behavior from Scripture so far, this argument is easy to refute.

First of all, the creation account clearly teaches that the only proper place for sexual activity is between one man and one woman within marriage. Therefore, the Levitical prohibitions against homosexual behavior as well as Paul's condemnation of homosexual behavior (which are based on the creation account in Genesis) would not condone homosexual behavior simply because the two involved are in a committed, loving relationship.

Simply put, homosexual behavior itself is sinful and is not made right simply because two people love each other! Once again, allow me to quote pro-gay scholar Louis Crompton: "The idea that homosexuals might be redeemed by mutual devotion would have been wholly foreign to Paul or any other Jew or early Christian."[128]

In addition, should we then affirm other sexual sins as long as they take place within a committed, loving relationship? Is adult mother/son or father/daughter incest acceptable if it occurs within a committed, loving relationship? Certainly not! Paul condemned such an incestuous relationship even though the two involved were consensual and very likely loved each other.[129]

Or maybe we should affirm adultery as long as a husband and wife give each other permission and as long as they love the people with whom they are committing adultery. This is crazy! Adultery is condemned by God quite apart from whether a husband and wife give each other permission and love the people with whom they are committing adultery.

Not only does Paul condemn homosexual behavior itself – whether or not it occurs within a committed, loving relationship. But one could argue that the **ongoing** nature of homosexual behavior within a committed, loving relationship (in contrast with a "one night stand") is *all the more* sinful because it prolongs a sinful behavior condemned by God's Word.

---

[128] *Homosexuality & Civilization* by Louis Crompton, 114.

[129] See 1st Corinthians 5:1-5.

For example, a person who agrees with God's Word that homosexual behavior is sinful but who has a lustful homosexual "one night stand" during a time of weakness can repent of his or her sin and be forgiven. In contrast, people who practice homosexual behavior within a committed, loving relationship are refusing to repent of their sin and thereby deny the forgiveness of Christ.

Paul is condemning only homosexuals who worship idols!

Some suggest that in Romans 1:18-27 Paul is not condemning homosexual behavior per se but only homosexual behavior by those who reject the Triune God and worship idols. In other words, as long as you worship the Triune God and trust in Jesus as your Lord and Savior, your homosexual behavior is NOT condemned by God.

In their book *The Children Are Free*, Jeff Miner and John Tyler Connoley write: "The model of homosexual behavior Paul was addressing here is explicitly associated with idol worship … But this is not the experience of the vast majority of gay, lesbian, and bisexual people … These are lovers of God who, nevertheless, have been attracted to people of the same sex from early in life … Paul simply does not address our model of stable, loving homosexual relationships among people of faith."[130]

As with the previous two revisionist arguments, even many pro-gay scholars take issue with this view. As noted in the quotes above from pro-gay authors, Paul would have condemned any type of homosexual behavior – whatever the context!

In addition, Paul's point is not that homosexual behavior is wrong only when it is performed in the context of idol worship. Instead, his point is that homosexual behavior is just one sin *among many other sins* that show how people have turned away from the One, True God.

For example, idolatry is one obvious way that people reject the One, True God. However, homosexual behavior (along with many other sins Paul lists) are also examples of how people have turned away from the One, True God. If someone claims to worship the Triune God and yet rejects what He clearly teaches about sins such as adultery, incest, bestiality, homosexuality, greed, theft, gossip, murder, etc. – then such a person has rejected God and is living in a state of unrepentant unbelief.

---

[130] *The Children Are Free* by Jeff Miner and John Tyler Connonley, 14-16.

Another thing to consider is that Paul mentions many other sins *in addition to* homosexuality in the **very same context** where he mentions the sin of idolatry. Paul says that just as God "gave over" some people to their homosexual behavior He also "gave over" some people to various other sins – which Paul lists in Romans 1:28-32.

Therefore, those who insist that homosexual behavior is only wrong when performed in the context of idol worship would also have to argue that *other* sins – such as adultery, greed, murder, deceit, gossip, disobeying parents – are just fine and dandy as long as they are not performed within the context of idol worship. But who would argue for that ridiculous notion? Not very many people! In fact, in Colossians 3:5 the apostle Paul says that various sins are equal to idolatry. In other words, all sin – including homosexual behavior – results in the rejection of God and the worship of one's own sinful desires and actions.

Paul teaches that homosexuality is "dirty" but not sinful!

In his book *Dirt Greed & Sex,* L. William Countryman argues that Romans 1:26-27 is NOT teaching that homosexual behavior is sin. Instead, he suggests that the apostle Paul was teaching that homosexual behavior was merely "dirty," that is, something that would be considered crude by Paul's culture but not sinful.[131] For example, if I drop a hotdog on a dirty sidewalk and then pick it up and eat it, you would consider such an act crude or dirty but NOT sinful. So, is homosexual behavior no different than eating a hotdog after it has fallen on a dirty sidewalk? *There are so many problems with this argument I'm not sure where to begin!*[132]

First, Paul's Jewish culture clearly understood that Scripture condemned homosexual behavior as being sinful and not merely crude or dirty. Second, in the very same context Paul mentions homosexual behavior along with many other sins (see Romans 1:28-32). Why should we believe that Paul would single out only homosexual behavior as being merely dirty when all the other desires and acts he mentions are clearly sinful?

---

[131] *Dirt Greed & Sex* by L. William Countryman, 104-123.

[132] For a thorough response to Countryman's argument, see *Straight & Narrow?* by Thomas Schmidt, 64-85. Also *The Bible and Homosexual Practice* by Robert Gagnon, 273-277.

In response to Countryman, White and Niell write: "This revisionist argument is surely one of the weakest offered, for it requires us to believe all of the following propositions: first, that in the midst of demonstrating the awful sinfulness of idolatry and its punishment, Paul would insert a sentence where he switches subjects to something that, while possibly 'unusual' in a social sense, is not actually sinful; second, that the context is to be broken up with no connection seen (despite the summary statement of 1:32); and finally, that when Paul spoke of 'degrading passions,' 'indecent acts,' and how those committing them would receive the 'due penalty of their error,' these are not indications of sinfulness."[133]

In addition, Robert Gagnon writes: "...the context surrounding 1:26-27 makes clear that same-sex intercourse is sin for Paul. First, all the other conduct described in 1:18-32 is evaluated as sinful, so surely same-sex intercourse is as well. Second, the heading for 1:18-32 as a whole refers to God's wrath 'upon *every* ungodliness and unrighteousness of human beings who suppress the truth in unrighteousness' (1:18). Third, same-sex intercourse parallels the sin of idolatry since both suppress the truth of God and God's creation. Fourth, the description of gentile behavior in 1:18-32 is presented as partial proof of the 'charge' that 'all are under sin' (3:9; cf. 3:23: 'all have sinned')."[134]

Finally, <u>pro</u>-gay scholar Bernadette Brooten responds to Countryman with these words: "...Countryman ... argues that Paul explicitly defines homosexual acts as impurity, rather than as sin ... Countryman's sharp distinction between sin and impurity, however, does not hold up. He argues that homosexual acts were a purity issue for Leviticus (which ... define sexual relations between males as an 'abomination,' rather than an 'impurity'), but 'impurity' (or 'abomination') and 'sin' are not mutually exclusive categories. Further, in Rom 3:9, 23 Paul applies the category 'sin' to both Jews and gentiles, which I understand to refer back to the preceding chapters; Countryman does not discuss Rom 3:9, 23. Finally, the structure Countryman proposes (Rom 1:18-23: about sin; Rom 1:24-27: about impurity, not sin; and Rom 1:28-32: about sin) would be more convincing if the text contained stronger markers for indicating that the middle section concerns itself with mere impurity, rather than serious

---

[133] *The Same Sex Controversy* by James White and Jeffrey Niell, 133-134.

[134] *The Bible and Homosexual Practice* by Robert Gagnon, 276.

sin. In contrast, I see the three units as substantially interconnected..."[135]

Paul only condemns Jewish legalism, not homosexuality!

Various pro-gay authors try to argue that Paul's apparent condemnation of consensual homosexual behavior in Romans 1:26-27 is not truly a condemnation of homosexual behavior but only serves his true purpose. What is Paul's "true purpose," according to these pro-gay scholars? Simply put, Paul's true purpose was to condemn Jewish legalism. In other words, the only real sin is judging others for their sin as though you are more righteous than they are. Paul only mentions the evil of homosexuality to set a trap for those who would say: "That's right, Paul! Give it to those homosexuals! They are horrible sinners, unlike us law-abiding Jews."

In his book *The Bible and Homosexuality,* Victor Furnish writes: "In Rom. 1:24-32 Paul is not enumerating specific 'sins' but listing some representative consequences of sin ... Far from singling out any particular group or practice for special criticism, the apostle is insisting that when people condemn others they are also condemning themselves (Rom. 2:1). This 'bad news' about the human condition is followed in Rom 3:21-8:39 with the 'good news' ... that ... saving grace is bestowed as a sheer gift (e.g., 3:24), with absolutely no conditions (e.g., 5:6, 8). Clearly, he has not written the earlier paragraphs in order to 'condemn sinners,' to frighten them into repenting, or to specify what one should and should not do."[136] **The danger of this argument is that it mixes some truth with serious error!**

First, I agree that we should not condemn others for their sin as though we ourselves are not sinful. In Romans 3:19-20, 23 Paul clearly teaches that ALL people are equally sinful before God. ***However, this truth should not result in the error that we should never rebuke anyone for their sins.***

Galatians 6:1-2, which is the basis for the title of this book, reads: "Brothers, if someone is caught in a sin, you who are spiritual should restore him gently. But watch yourself, or you also may be tempted. Carry each other's burdens, and in this way you will fulfill the law of

---

[135] *Love Between Women* by Bernadette Brooten, 235-236, footnote #57.

[136] See *The Bible and Homosexuality* by Victor Furnish, 29 (quoted on page 278 of *The Bible and Homosexual Practice* by Robert Gagnon).

Christ." In addition, Jesus Himself says the following: "If your brother sins, rebuke him, and if he repents, forgive him." (Luke 17:3) Even though we are all equally sinners, God calls us to confront others in love regarding their sin so that they may repent and receive forgiveness in Christ.

Second, I agree with Furnish that "saving grace is bestowed as sheer gift … with absolutely no conditions." But this does not mean that people can deny or justify sin and at the same time receive God's mercy for that sin. In the book of Jude we read about "godless men, who change the grace of God into a license for immorality and deny Jesus Christ our only Sovereign and Lord." (Jude 4)

In other words, people can talk about "loving and trusting Jesus" all they want, but if they deny what God's Word says about their sin they are thereby denying Jesus as their Lord and Savior.

Third, I also agree that repentance is NOT a condition for salvation in the sense that we must do something to make ourselves worthy of God's mercy – as though repentance means "cleaning up your act" and "avoiding sinful behavior" until you are holy enough to deserve God's forgiveness.

On the other hand, Scripture clearly teaches that repentance IS a condition for **RECEIVING** salvation in that it is **God's** work in the heart of a sinner – a work of God that forces the sinner to confess his or her various sins and acknowledge that they deserve God's wrath. *God's work of repentance in the heart of a sinner prepares him or her to receive God's gift of faith (produced by the proclamation of the Gospel) and thereby believe and receive God's mercy in Christ.* However, if someone refuses to repent he or she thereby resists the Holy Spirit. Such a person has rejected God's mercy because of unbelief (see 1st John 1:7-2:2).

Therefore, God uses His people to proclaim His Word of judgment through which He convicts us of sin and convinces us that we deserve God's eternal wrath. Even more, God uses His people to proclaim His Word of forgiveness in Christ which comforts the despairing sinner and creates faith in his or her heart.

Acts 5:31 reads: "God exalted [Jesus] to his own right hand as Prince and Savior that he might give repentance and forgiveness of sins to Israel." 2nd Corinthians 7:10 reads: "Godly sorrow brings repentance that leads to salvation…" Finally, regarding how a pastor should respond to those who reject God's Word, Paul writes: "Those who oppose him he must gently instruct, in the hope that God will grant them repentance leading them to a knowledge of the truth…" (2nd Timothy 2:25)

Finally, if Furnish wants us to believe that Paul's condemnation of homosexual behavior in Romans 1:26-27 is not to be used by us to show others that homosexual behavior is sinful, then would he also argue that Paul's condemnation of various *other* sins in Romans 1:28-32 should not be used by us to show others that *those* desires and behaviors are sinful?

In other words, should we tolerate or even affirm people who want to engage in such sins as idolatry, murder, theft, greed, disobedience of parents, adultery, lust, or gossip? Would it be sinful for us to "speak the Truth in love" to people who are caught in such sins? According to Furnish's logic, he would have to say "Yes."

But Scripture clearly teaches that we should confront one another about any sin – including *homosexual* behavior – with the goal of leading one another to repentance so that the forgiveness of Christ for that sin can be proclaimed. The result of receiving such forgiveness is that the Holy Spirit moves us to grieve over the sin condemned by God's Word and to strive to conform our behavior (including our *sexual* behavior!) to God's loving plan for our lives.

1st Corinthians 6:9-11

The apostle Paul wrote 1st Corinthians around 55 AD. He wrote this letter, in part, as a response to some information he received concerning false teaching and sinful behavior taking place within the Christian congregation of Corinth.[137] One type of sinful behavior in the Corinthian congregation was sexual immorality of a various kinds.

For example, in 1st Corinthians 5:1-5 Paul addresses the sin of incest – a man was having sexual relations with his father's wife. Paul writes: "It is actually reported that there is sexual immortality among you, and of a kind that does not occur even among pagans: a man has his father's wife." (1st Corinthians 5:1)

The Greek word translated as "sexual immorality" is *porneia* – **and this is evidence against those who want to claim that the Greek word *porneia* only referred to prostitution and not any other sexual**

[137] For an excellent commentary on the book of 1st Corinthians, see the Concordia Commentary *1 Corinthians* by Gregory Lockwood.

sin. The fact is that among the Jewish culture of Paul's day the Greek word *porneia* was used to refer to all forms of sexual immorality condemned in Leviticus chapters 18 and 20 – including the sin of homosexual behavior.

This is why Jude 7 used a verbal form of *porneia* to refer to the homosexual behavior of Sodom. In the same way, Jesus' use of the Greek word *porneiai* in Mark 7:21 **in addition to** the Greek word for adultery (*moicheiai*) shows that Jesus was condemning all forms of sexual immorality listed in Leviticus chapters 18 and 20 – including consensual homosexual behavior.

In 1st Corinthians 5:4-5 Paul commands the Corinthian congregation to hand the incestuous man "over to Satan." In other words, by the authority of Jesus, they are to withhold forgiveness of sins from this man and publicly excommunicate him from Christ's Church. (Also see Matthew 18:15-20) This means that he is to be considered an unbeliever. In other words, he is MISSION material! Even though he is allowed to hear God's Word proclaimed, he is NOT allowed to receive the Lord's Supper as long as he refuses to repent and remains in unbelief.

Why would Paul ask them to do this to the incestuous man? The answer is: **LOVE!** Paul writes: "...hand this man over to Satan, so that the sinful nature may be destroyed and his spirit saved on the day of the Lord." (1st Corinthians 5:5) In other words, the goal of excommunication is always the salvation of one who is burdened by unrepentant sin.

The good news is that the excommunication of the incestuous man achieved the desired goal! This man repented of his sin, and then Paul insisted that the Corinthian congregation forgive him in Jesus' Name and receive him back into their fellowship (see 2nd Corinthians 2:5-11).

In 1st Corinthians 5:9-11 Paul mentions that he had previously instructed them not to associate with sexually immoral people as well as people who practiced other types of sins. However, they misunderstood what Paul meant. Some thought they should avoid ALL people – *unbelievers and maybe even repentant Christians* – who were involved in sexual immorality or other sins. Therefore, Paul clarifies that he only wanted them to avoid associating with people who claimed to be Christians and yet expected others to affirm their sexual immorality or other sins.

But what exactly did Paul mean when he told them to "avoid associating" with people who claimed to be Christians and yet refused to repent of their sexual immorality or other sins? In 1st Corinthians 5:11 Paul writes: "…I am writing you that you must not associate with anyone who calls himself a brother but is sexually immoral or greedy, an idolater or a slanderer, a drunkard or a swindler. With such a man do not even eat."

What does Paul mean when he says "with such a man do not even eat?" Paul does NOT mean that we can't eat at Burger King or have Thanksgiving Dinner with such people. Instead, Paul is speaking of a very particular kind of "eating." What kind of "eating" does Paul mean? 1st Corinthians 5:6-8 gives us a clue. Paul refers to the Passover when he says that "Christ, our Passover Lamb, has been sacrificed." The Passover was the Old Testament *picture* of the REALITY we receive in the Lord's Supper – **the Body and Blood of Christ!** (See 1st Corinthians 10:14-17 and 11:23-32)

In 1st Corinthians 5:8 Paul writes: "Therefore let us keep the Festival, not with the old yeast, the yeast of malice and wickedness, but with bread without yeast, the bread of sincerity and truth." Simply put, when Paul tells them not to eat with people who claim to be Christians and yet refuse to repent of their sins, Paul thereby means that they should not receive **the Lord's Supper** with unbelievers! What is the purpose of this practice? The goal is to humble those who are burdened by unrepentant sin so that they will confess their guilt and be in a position to receive the forgiveness of Christ for their sins.

In 1st Corinthians 6:1-8 Paul goes on to rebuke the Corinthian Christians for taking each other to court. *Paul is NOT thereby condemning the legitimate use of our legal system.* Instead, Paul is condemning the greed and vengeance that was moving Christians in the very same congregation to take advantage of their fellow Christians in a legal manner. Paul's response to this sinful behavior is: "Why not rather be wronged? Why not rather be cheated? Instead, you yourselves cheat and do wrong, and you do this to your brothers." They had forgotten Christ's teaching that it would be better for us to "turn the other cheek" than to be overcome by greed and vengeance (see Matthew 5:39 and Romans 12:14-21).

But why does Paul mention the issue of sinful lawsuits just after he deals with sexual immorality? This is very likely Paul's way of showing us that sexual immorality is not the worst of all sins. ALL sin is equally evil before God. A person who is burdened by the sin of greed or vengeance (or any other sin Paul mentions) has no right to stand in self-righteous judgment over another who is burdened by sexual immorality.

This is why Paul says what he does in Galatians 6:1-2. After telling us to bear the burdens of those caught in sin by restoring them through the preaching of repentance and forgiveness, Paul then says: "But watch yourself, or you also may be tempted." In other words, we must remove the "log" in our own eye before we attempt to remove the "speck" from our brother's eye (see Matthew 7:3-5).

This does NOT mean that we must be sinless before we can help someone who is caught in sin. *In that case, I'd never be able to help a fellow sinner who is caught in sin's trap.* What this DOES mean is that we must acknowledge the sin in our lives and trust in Jesus for mercy before we attempt to help others who are caught in various sins.

Now we're ready to consider Paul's words in 1st Corinthians 6:9-11. Paul writes: "Do you not know that the wicked will not inherit the kingdom of God? Do not be deceived: Neither the sexually immoral nor idolaters nor adulterers nor male prostitutes nor homosexual offenders nor thieves nor the greedy no drunkards no slanderers no swindlers will inherit the kingdom of God. And that is what some of you were. But you were washed, you were sanctified, you were justified in the name of the Lord Jesus Christ and by the Spirit of our God." **In order to understand what Paul is teaching us here, we must first take a look at the Greek words behind the English translation.**

The Greek word translated as "sexually immoral" is *pornoi* – and in this case *pornoi* refers either to prostitution (which Paul addresses in 1st Corinthians 6:16) or to fornication (sex between people who are not married) or to incest (which Paul addresses in 1st Corinthians 5:1-5) – or to all three forms of sexual sin! The reason that the meaning of *pornoi* in this context is more limited is that Paul goes on to mention other particular sexual sins.

The Greek word translated as "adulterers" is *moichoi* – which is related to the Greek word Jesus uses for "adultery" in Mark 7:21. The Greek word *moichoi* refers to people who have sex with another person's spouse.

The Greek word translated as "male prostitutes" is *malakoi* . The basic meaning of this Greek word is "soft" and was used to describe a man who had an effeminate demeanor and who was ALSO involved in homosexual behavior.[138]

---

[138] For an excellent examination of the meaning of *malakoi* in 1st Corinthians 6:9, see *The Bible and Homosexual Practice* by Robert Gagnon, 306-312.

I want to stress the point that *malakoi* refers to effeminate men who were **also involved in homosexual behavior** because there are some men who are less masculine and more effeminate than other men – but this characteristic in and of itself is not sinful! There are many men who have effeminate characteristics and yet are purely heterosexual in orientation. Therefore, *malakoi* refers to effeminate men who willingly (and without remorse or repentance) engage in homosexual behavior.

Scholars debate about whether *malakoi* merely refers to effeminate men who took the passive role in homosexual behavior or whether *malakoi* also entails the act of prostitution. In view of the fact that the very next word Paul uses in his list of sins – the Greek word *arsenokoitai* - can refer to both the active and passive partners in homosexual behavior (see the next few paragraphs for my evidence of this), I am more inclined to conclude that *malakoi* refers to effeminate males who sell their sexual favors as the passive homosexual partner. In other words, by putting *malakoi* and *arsenokoitai* immediately next to each other in his list of sins, Paul is thereby condemning not only homosexual prostitution but ***also*** consensual homosexual behavior without the element of prostitution.

The Greek word translated as "homosexual offenders" is *arsenokoitai* - which literally means "men who go to bed with men" (from the Greek word *arsen* = "male" and the Greek word *koite* = "bed"). I disagree with the New International Version translation of *arsenokoitai* as "homosexual offenders" because the word "offenders" can lead to the erroneous idea that Paul was only condemning pederasty, that is, a man forcing himself on another man or young boy who was not willing to have sex.

As we learned in our examination of Leviticus 20:13 and Romans 1:26-27, Scripture also condemns CONSENSUAL homosexual behavior. In fact, a closer examination of the Greek word *arsenokoitai* will help us to see that Paul is using this word to condemn even consensual forms of homosexual behavior and not merely homosexual rape.[139]

Some scholars have suggested that we can't know for sure what Paul meant by the Greek word *arsenokoitai* because it is not found in

---

[139] For thorough examinations of the meaning of *arsenokoitai* in 1st Corinthians 6:9, see *The Bible and Homosexual Practice* by Robert Gagnon, 312-332; *The Same Sex Controversy* by James White and Jeffrey Niell, 146-150; *Homosexuality* by James B. De Young, 175-214.

any other Greek literature before or during Paul's time.[140] However, if we recall that Paul used the universal sexual prohibitions found in Leviticus chapters 18 and 20 as the basis for his teaching about sexual sins, we can then find a strong clue as to what Paul meant by the word *arsenokoitai* .

The Greek translation of the Hebrew Old Testament is known as the Septuagint.[141] The Septuagint was a common translation of the Old Testament for both Jewish and Gentile Christians in Paul's day. If one reads the Septuagint translation of Leviticus 18:22 and 20:13 we discover the likely source for Paul's unique word *arsenokoitai* .

The Septuagint (Greek) translation of Leviticus 18:22 is *kai meta* ***arsenos*** *ou koimethese* ***koiten*** *gunaikos Bdelugma gar estin* . Notice the two words in bold print: ***arsenos*** and ***koiten*** .

The Septuagint translation of Leviticus 20:13 is *kai hos an koimethe meta* ***arsenos koiten*** *gunaikos, Bdelugma epoieisan amphoteroi Thanatousthosan, enochoi eisin* . Notice the two words in bold print: ***arsenos*** and ***koiten*** .

Many scholars believe that Paul coined his own Greek word based on the Greek translation of Leviticus 18:22 and 20:13. Paul made a compound Greek word out of *arsenos* and *koiten* in order to stress to his readers (who would have been familiar with the Septuagint!) that even consensual homosexual behavior is sinful – **which is the clear teaching of Leviticus 20:13!**

In view of the meaning of *arsenokoitai* in 1st Corinthians 6:9 and its connection to the Septuagint translation of Leviticus 18:22 and 20:13, Robert Gagnon writes: "…the likely derivation of the word from the Levitical prohibitions … strengthens the case for an inclusive meaning. What kind of same-sex intercourse would have hurdled the obstacle of Lev 18:22 and 20:13 in Paul's mind? Surely none since these prohibitions speak generically of all men who have sexual intercourse with any and every kind of male."[142]

---

[140] For example, see *Arsenokoites and Malakos: Meanings and Consequences* by Dale Martin (in *Biblical Ethics & Homosexuality,* edited by Robert L. Brawley, 117-136). For a detailed response to Martin, see *The Bible and Homosexual Practice* by Robert Gagnon, 316-332.

[141] The word "Septuagint" is based on the Greek word for seventy. Jewish tradition says that seventy Jewish scribes translated the Hebrew Old Testament into Greek to accommodate the many Jews for whom Greek was their first language.

[142] *The Bible and Homosexual Practice* by Robert Gagnon, 326.

In addition to Paul's clear allusion to Leviticus 20:13, we must also note that in Romans 1:27, where Paul deals with male homosexual behavior, he mentions "men with men" – and the Greek is *arsenes en arsesin* . Paul uses a Greek word for "men" that is also used in the Septuagint translation of Genesis 1:27 and Leviticus 18:22. When we compare Paul's use of *arsenokoitai* in 1st Corinthians 6:9 with his use of *arsenes en arsesin* in Romans 1:27 it becomes clear that Paul is using *arsenokoitai* to refer even to consensual forms of homosexual behavior.

Therefore, when Paul uses *arsenokoitai* after *malakoi* in 1st Corinthians 6:9 he is stressing that both the **active** and **passive** partners in a **consensual** homosexual relationship are guilty of sin before God. Just like Romans 1:26-27, Paul's teaching about homosexual behavior in 1st Corinthians 6:9 also applies to consensual homosexual behavior today!

However, we have not yet considered the most important part of Paul's teaching in 1st Corinthians 6:9-11! Paul lists many other sins besides homosexual behavior. Once again, this reminds us that homosexual behavior is NOT the worst of all sins. Homosexual behavior is one sin among many. Paul stresses that all these sins (and many others he didn't bother to list!) will prevent us from inheriting the kingdom of God if we refuse to repent of these sins and trust in Jesus for salvation.

Therefore, we must understand that when Paul says that those who practice homosexual behavior "will not inherit the kingdom of God" he is speaking about UNBELIEVERS – those who refuse to acknowledge their sin and thereby reject the forgiveness that Jesus longs to give them for that sin.

In contrast, there are many men and women today who bear the burden of homosexual desire and behavior but who acknowledge this as sin and trust in Jesus for mercy and the strength to live a new life.

We must realize that Paul is NOT saying that if you have ever committed any of the sins he lists in 1st Corinthians 6:9-10 that you are automatically denied access into God's Kingdom. Those who remain outside God's Kingdom are those who refuse to acknowledge their sin and will not trust in Jesus for mercy. **However, when the Spirit convicts you of sin and moves you to trust in Jesus as your Savior, you are then completely forgiven and holy in God's sight – *even as you continue to bear the burden of homosexual desire and behavior!***

Paul reminds the Corinthian Christians (and US!) that we were once unrepentant unbelievers apart from Christ. But we who have been washed, sanctified and justified in the name of the Lord Jesus Christ and by the Spirit of our God can know that we are NOW part of God's Kingdom of mercy and love.

When Paul tells repentant believers who bear the burden of homosexuality that they once were unrepentant unbelievers, this does not mean that such people have ceased to have homosexual desires. As I noted earlier in this book, being a Christian does not mean that you no longer struggle with sin.

There are some Christians who will struggle with homosexual desire and behavior until the day they die. But these same people acknowledge their sin and trust in Jesus as their Savior – and so they are NOW in God's Kingdom.

When Paul says that Christians were "washed" (the Greek word is *apelousasthe*) he is very likely referring to God's gift of Holy Baptism wherein God washes away the guilt of our sin by the power of Jesus' shed Blood![143]

When Paul says that Christians were "sanctified" (the Greek word is *eigiastheite*) he is teaching that we have been "set apart" as holy to the Lord. We belong to Him and nothing – not any sin (not even homosexuality) – can separate us from His love.

When Paul says that Christians were "justified" (the Greek word is *edikaiotheite*) he is reminding us that God has pronounced us to be righteous in His sight; God has declared us "not guilty" before His throne. This verdict is true and certain in spite of the fact that we continue to struggle with various sinful desires and behaviors.

Paul says that we Christians were washed, sanctified and justified "in the name of the Lord Jesus Christ and by the Spirit of our God." With these words Paul points us to the mystery of the One God who is Father, Son and Holy Spirit. We Christians were baptized into His Name – the Name of the Father and of the Son and of the Holy Spirit.

Our Baptism defines our identity, not our sin! **So, if you bear the burden of homosexual desire and behavior, know that this sin does**

---

[143] The Greek verb translated "washed" (*apelousasthe)* in 1st Corinthians 6:11 is used only one other time in the New Testament – and that is in Acts 22:16 where we see that Paul was told to be baptized and thereby **wash** away his sins. In addition, the Greek words *loutro* and *loutrou* are used in Ephesians 5:26 and Titus 3:5 respectively – and in both cases these texts are speaking about the "washing" God gives us in Holy Baptism!

not define who you are! If you have been baptized, then your identity is in Christ – and He defines who you are!

In Romans 6:4 the apostle Paul writes: "We were therefore buried with [Christ] through baptism into death in order that, just as Christ was raised from the dead through the glory of the Father, we too may live a new life."

1st Timothy 1:8-11

Many scholars believe 1st Timothy was written by the apostle Paul around 65 AD.[144] Paul writes to a young pastor named Timothy. Paul calls Timothy his "true son in the faith" (see 1st Timothy 1:2) – which is very likely a reference to Paul being used by God to convert Timothy to faith in Christ. Paul was also instrumental in Timothy's decision to serve the Lord as a pastor in Christ's Church (see 2nd Timothy 1:6).

Paul begins his letter by urging Timothy "to command certain men not to teach false doctrines any longer nor to devote themselves to myths and endless genealogies" (see 1st Timothy 1:3-4). Who were these men who taught false doctrines? What false doctrines did they teach? We don't have specific details, but based on the wider context of 1st Timothy (as well as 2nd Timothy and Titus) we can come to some conclusions.

Based on Titus 1:14 (where Paul condemns "Jewish myths") and 1st Timothy 4:1-5 (where Paul condemns those who denounce things in God's creation – such as certain foods and even marriage), these false teachers were likely men who combined aspects of Judaism with an early form of Gnosticism.

The word "Gnosticism" is based on the Greek word *gnosis* which means "knowledge." This early form of a later philosophy known as

---

[144] Since the early 1800s some biblical scholars have questioned whether 1st Timothy was written by Paul. One reason for this is that the vocabulary found in 1st Timothy differs from the other letters of Paul. But this can easily be explained by the different subject matter in 1st Timothy. Other reasons for denying that Paul wrote 1st Timothy are based on the assumption that issues he addresses (for example, Church structure and various false teachings) occurred at a point in history after Paul had died. But there is no proof for this. The fact is that the early Church accepted 1st Timothy as an authentic letter of Paul. For responses to those who question the Pauline authorship of 1st Timothy, see: *A Commentary on the Pastoral Epistles* by J. N. D. Kelly, 1-36; *The Word of the Lord Grows* by Martin H. Franzmann, 165-167; *The Interpretation of St. Paul's Epistles to the Colossians, to the Thessalonians, to Timothy, to Titus and to Philemon* by R. C. H. Lenski, 473-484.

Gnosticism stressed the following: **1)** The physical creation is itself evil and not part of the good will of God;[145] **2)** Salvation entails not the forgiveness of sins but one's immaterial soul escaping from this physical world; **3)** Salvation from imprisonment in this physical world is achieved through special knowledge of this process – knowledge conveyed by enlightened teachers upon those whom they deem worthy of such knowledge. *These quasi-Gnostic teachings were combined with aspects of Jewish teaching and this resulted in the "false doctrines" that Paul wanted Timothy to silence.*

In addition to requiring as much separation as possible from aspects of life in this physical world (see 1st Timothy 4:1-5), these false teachers also focused on "myths and endless genealogies" not taught in Holy Scripture. The myths referred to stories of a spiritual or philosophical significance to the false teachers – myths that had no basis in the historical events recorded in Holy Scripture. The genealogies likely referred to these false teachers' focus on ancestry being a key to whether you were worthy of the special knowledge necessary for salvation from this physical world.[146]

The apostle Paul says the following about these Jewish Gnostics: "They want to be teachers of the law, but they do not know what they are talking about or what they so confidently affirm." (1st Timothy 1:7) Apparently, one aspect of their false teaching was that they did not understand the purpose of God's Law (the Ten Commandments) in this fallen world. Paul then goes on in 1st Timothy 1:8-11 to talk about the proper use of God's Law in this fallen world.

In 1st Timothy 1:8-11 Paul writes: "We know that the law is good I one uses it properly. We also know that law is made not for the righteous but for lawbreakers and rebels, the ungodly and sinful, the unholy and irreligious; for those who kill their fathers and mothers, for murderers, for adulterers and perverts, for slave traders and liars and

---

[145] In contrast, Scripture teaches that God's physical creation is "very good." The problem with our physical world is not that it is evil in itself. The problem is that God's good creation – including our physical bodies! – has been cursed by our sin against God. But through Christ we have the certain hope that this physical world – and our physical bodies! – will be redeemed from this curse and we will live in the perfect physical creation God gave us "In the beginning" (see Romans 8:18-25 and 2nd Peter 3:1-13).

[146] In Philippians 3:5 Paul confesses how his ancestry was part of his self-righteousness as an unbelieving Pharisee. It is possible that this focus on ancestry among Jews was used by the Jewish Gnostics as part of their religious system to determine if one was worthy of the special knowledge required for salvation from this physical world.

perjurers – and for whatever else is contrary to the sound doctrine that conforms to the glorious gospel of the blessed God, which he entrusted to me." What is Paul teaching us here?

First of all, Paul stresses that God's Law is GOOD! But God's Law can be *misused* for evil purposes. One way the Law is misused is when it becomes a list of rules that one must obey to become worthy of salvation. It is possible that the Jewish Gnostics were using the prohibitions against various sins in God's Law as the basis for making oneself worthy of "salvation" (that is, "salvation" as they understood it in their religious system). They believed that by avoiding certain sins condemned by God's Law one could make himself/herself worthy of the special knowledge needed for salvation.

However, Paul then stresses that the Law in this fallen world was never intended for those who wish to make themselves righteous before God by their obedience. Instead, the purpose of the Law in this fallen world is **1)** to curb sinful behavior and **2)** to expose the sins in one's life and the fact that we are guilty before God and deserve nothing but His wrath (see Romans 1:18, 3:19-20, 7:7; also Galatians 3:10-14). Paul then goes on to list various sins condemned by the Ten Commandments. (We find a similar list of sins in Romans 1:26-32!)

We also must understand that Paul is NOT denying what is sometimes called "The third use of the Law," which means that God's Law is a guide for Christians so we can know God's will for our lives – *the **sinful behavior** we are to avoid and the **good behavior** we are to embrace.* Instead, Paul is condemning the Jewish Gnostics' misuse of God's Law by turning it into a list of rules for us to obey and thereby merit salvation. God's Law is used properly when it exposes our sins of thought, word and deed so that we will recognize that we deserve God's wrath and long for a Savior!

Once we have been saved by Christ, the Spirit gives us a new heart that longs to obey God's will out of love in response to the salvation He has freely given us in Christ. The list of sins in 1st Timothy 1:9-10a is "contrary to the sound doctrine that conforms to the glorious gospel of the blessed God…" (see 1st Timothy 1:10b-11).

In other words, we don't avoid the sins condemned by God's Law so that we can thereby make ourselves worthy of His salvation. *Instead, we avoid the sins condemned by God's Law because Christ has saved us.* As Paul said in his letter to the Corinthians: "And that is what some of you were. But you were washed, you were sanctified, you were justified in the name of the Lord Jesus Christ and by the Spirit of our God." (1st Corinthians 6:11)

The list of sins in 1st Timothy 1:9-10a includes two references to sexual sins: **1)** adulterers (the Greek word is *pornois*) and **2)** perverts (the Greek word is *arsenokoitais*) .

The New International Version translation of *pornois* as "adulterers" is unfortunate. Paul had access to a more technical term for "adulterers" in Greek (*moichos*) . Therefore, the Greek word *pornois* is best translated as "the sexually immoral" – referring to various types of sexual immorality in general.

In the same way, the New International Version translation of *arsenokoitais* as "perverts" is also unfortunate – for two reasons. First, the English word "pervert" does not adequately define the specific type of sexual sin described by *arsenokoitais* . Second, in 1st Corinthians 6:9 the New International Version translates *arsenokoitai* as "homosexual offenders." Why translate *arsenokoitai* in 1st Corinthians 6:9 as "homosexual offenders" and then translate *arsenokoitais* in 1st Timothy 1:10 as "perverts?" There is no good reason.

As we learned in the previous section dealing with 1st Corinthians 6:9-11, the Greek word *arsenokoitai* refers to men who have consensual sex with other men. Therefore, whether we're dealing with *arsenokoitai* in 1st Corinthians 6:9 or *arsenokoitais* in 1st Timothy 1:10 – the better translation in both cases would be "men who practice homosexual behavior."[147]

The reason I prefer the words "practice homosexual behavior" is that they stress the fact that Paul is referring to **unrepentant unbelievers.** We need to make this clarification because the modern word "homosexual" can refer to a repentant Christian man or woman who struggles with same-sex attraction and behavior.

By translating *arsenokoitai* and *arsenokoitais* merely as "homosexuals" could lead one to the erroneous conclusion that one can't be a Christian and struggle with same-sex attraction at the same

[147] Some pro-gay scholars suggest that *arsenokoitais* in 1st Timothy 1:10 refers to pederasty or some other form of exploitive homosexual sex and not to consensual homosexual behavior. But as we have already learned in the section on 1st Corinthians 6:9-11, the likely source of *arsenokoitais* being the Greek translation of Leviticus 18:22 and 20:13 shows that Paul means to condemn even consensual homosexual behavior. For a response to those who deny that *arsenokoitais* in 1st Timothy 1:10 also refers to consensual homosexual behavior, see *The Bible and Homosexual* Practice by Robert Gagnon, 332-336.

time. However, Scripture is clear that Christians continue to struggle with the desires of their sinful nature in this life. Therefore, Paul is speaking of those who affirm of their homosexual desires and behavior and refuse to repent.

Some may wonder why Paul would single out a specific type of sexual sin (homosexual behavior) after using a Greek word (*pornois*) to refer to various types of sexual sin in general. We can't know for sure what Paul's reasons were. But based on Paul's use of homosexual behavior in Romans 1:26-27 as an obvious example of how we sinners turn God's created order "upside down," Paul may be focusing on homosexual behavior in 1st Timothy 1:10 as an obvious example of how we sin against the 6th Commandment.

In any case, we must understand that Paul is NOT teaching that homosexual behavior is the worst of all sins. In *other* sections of Paul's letters he condemns various sexual sins without mentioning homosexual behavior. Also, in Mark 7:21 Jesus singles out adultery and includes homosexual behavior under the more general category of "sexual immorality." We find the same thing in Hebrews 13:4. Does this mean that adultery is the worst of all sins? No!

In 1st Timothy 1:12-13 Paul points us back to his life as a non-Christian Pharisee and confesses that he was guilty of being a blasphemer, a persecutor and a violent man. He then writes: "Here is a trustworthy saying that deserves full acceptance: Christ Jesus came into the world to save sinners – of whom I am the worst." (1st Timothy 1:15)

Paul does NOT think that he is less sinful than those who practice homosexual behavior. Paul calls himself the "worst of sinners." Nevertheless, Paul confronts people about their sins – including their homosexual behavior – because he loves them and wants them to repent and trust in Jesus.

We learn from 1st Timothy 1:12-17 that Christ came into the world to save sinners! If we acknowledge the sins in our lives exposed by God's Law and trust in the Savior we have been given Who is revealed to us by God's Gospel, then we can say with Paul: "…I was shown mercy so that in me, the worst of sinners, Christ Jesus might display his unlimited patience as an example for those who would believe on him and receive eternal life." (1st Timothy 1:16)

╬ CHAPTER THREE ╬

"Can We Trust The Bible?"

In the previous chapter I responded to reinterpretations of various Biblical texts which clearly teach that even consensual homosexual behavior is sinful. The reinterpretations of these texts all attempt to maintain a certain level of respect for the authority of Holy Scripture. In other words, these various reinterpretations suggest that we can take the Bible seriously and submit to its authority – it's just that we've *misinterpreted* the texts dealing with homosexuality. Of course, in the previous chapter I've given solid evidence that the proper interpretation of the texts addressing homosexuality is that God condemns even consensual homosexual behavior.

However, in this chapter I will deal with other arguments put forth by those who affirm homosexual behavior – but these arguments are of a kind that question whether we can take the Bible seriously in some or all matters. In fact, some who put forth these arguments will admit that the Bible clearly condemns even consensual homosexual behavior – *and then they will conclude that the Bible is simply WRONG!*

In other words, the arguments I'm responding to in this chapter all stem from the idea that Scripture is not the inspired and inerrant Word of God. Instead, those who put forth the arguments in this chapter will assert that the Bible contains errors and therefore we can ignore some or all of what it teaches us. The people who put forth the arguments in this chapter differ from each other regarding what portions of Scripture they deem acceptable. However, what they all have in common is the idea that the Bible need not be taken seriously on various issues – *especially when the Bible clearly condemns even consensual homosexual behavior.*

An Anonymous Letter

At this point I would like share with you an experience I had about three years ago. At that time in my life I was publishing a monthly article in our local newspaper. I was writing a series of articles on the Ten Commandments. In my article on the Sixth Commandment I addressed various sexual sins condemned in Holy Scripture – such as sex before marriage, adultery, incest, bestiality, pornography, lust and homosexual behavior. **I also clearly stated that we can come to God will ALL our sins – sexual and non-sexual – and know that we have complete forgiveness and a new beginning through faith in Christ who died for our sins and conquered death for us.**

A few days later I received a letter in the mail. There was no return address and nothing inside the envelope to indicate who may have sent the letter to me.[148] The only thing in the envelope was a copy of an article titled: "Biblical Verses Are Used As Crutches to Prop Up Biases."

There was no information about the author of the article or the place where it had been published – only the words of the article itself. On the back of the copy of this article was a hand-written note which condemned me for using Scripture to suggest that homosexual behavior was sinful. (I thought it was interesting that this person did NOT condemn me for using Scripture to teach that sex before marriage, adultery, incest, bestiality, pornography or lust are sinful!)

Of course, I read the article sent to me by this anonymous person. *The content of this article is a perfect example of the confused thinking that leads some people to reject parts of Scripture they DON'T like while embracing other parts of Scripture they DO like.* **Therefore, I decided to reprint this article in this book as an example of the faulty ideas we must be prepared to refute with sound reason and faithful teaching of Holy Scripture.**

Since the copy of this article that was sent to me did not contain any information about the author or place that it was published, I can not offer that information here. With that understood, here is the article sent to me by an anonymous person:

---

[148] I must confess that I have a hard time respecting anyone who would send such an anonymous letter. If a person is not willing to identity himself/herself for the purpose of respectful and intelligent dialog, this does not say much about the certainty of such a person's convictions.

BIBLICAL VERSES ARE USED AS CRUTCHES TO PROP UP BIASES

An engineering professor is treating her husband, a loan officer, to dinner for finally giving in to her plea to shave off the scraggly beard he grew on vacation.

His favorite restaurant is a casual place where they both feel comfortable in slacks and cotton/polyester-blend golf shirts. But, as always, she wears the gold and pearl pendant he gave her the day her divorce decree was final.

Quiz: How many biblical prohibitions are they violating? Well, wives must be "submissive" to their husbands (1 Peter 3:1). And all women are forbidden to teach men (1 Timothy 2:12), wear gold or pearls (1 Timothy 2:9) or dress in clothing that "pertains to a man" (Deuteronomy 22:5).

Shellfish and pork are definitely out (Leviticus 11:7, 10), as are usury (Deuteronomy 23:19), shaving (Leviticus 19:27) and clothes of more than one fabric (Leviticus 19:19). And since the bible rarely recognizes divorce, they're committing adultery, which carries the rather harsh penalty of death by stoning (Deuteronomy 22:22).

So why are they having such a good time? Probably because they wouldn't think of worrying about rules that seem absurd, anachronistic or – at best – unrealistic.

Yet this same modern-day couple could easily be among the millions of Americans who never hesitate to lean on the Bible to justify their own anti-gay attitudes.

Bible verses have long been used selectively to support many kinds of discrimination. Somewhere along the way, Jesus' second-greatest commandment gets lost: "You shall love your neighbor as yourself."

Once a given form of prejudice falls out of favor with society, so do the verses that had seemed to condone it. It's unimaginable today, for example, that anyone would use the Bible to try to justify slavery.

Yet when the abolitionist movement began to gain momentum in the early nineteenth century, many

Southern ministers defended the owning of human beings as a divinely approved system: "Slaves, obey in everything those who are your earthly masters..." (Colossians 3:22)

In an influential anti-abolitionist essay, South Carolina Baptist leader Richard Furman declared in 1822 that "the right of holding slaves is clearly established in the holy Scriptures."

Meanwhile, anti-slavery crusaders were taking an interpretative approach to the Bible, since a literal reading "gave little or no support to an abolitionist position," author Carl Degler says in *Place over Time: The Continuity of Southern Distinctiveness.*

Nearly one hundred years after the Emancipations Proclamation, a Virginia court defended racial segregation by saying, "The Almighty God created the races white, black, yellow, malay and red and he placed them on separate continents ... He did not intend for the races to mix." The U.S. Supreme Court rejected that ridiculous reasoning in 1967 when it struck down laws in sixteen states forbidding interracial marriage.

Like advocates of racial equality, suffragists found the literal reading of the Bible was their biggest stumbling block. Many ministers even condemned using anesthesia during labor because pain in childbirth was punishment for Eve's bite of forbidden fruit. (Genesis 3:16)

Susan B. Anthony eventually declared in frustration, "I distrust those people who know so well what God wants them to do, because I notice it always coincides with their own desires."

Studying the Bible is often akin to looking at Rorschach ink blots, says biblical scholar Joe Barnhart, author of *The Southern Baptist Holy War*. "What we get out of it is sometimes what we put into it," he explains.

The punishment the Bible metes out to all men for Adam's downfall is toiling "in sweat of your face (Genesis 3:19). Yet, Barnhart notes with a laugh, there's one bit of progress never denounced by preachers hot under the clerical collar: air conditioning.

So, what do you think of this article that was sent to me by an anonymous person? Does this brief article refute all the points I have made so far in this book? HARDLY! In fact, this kind of article (and I have read others that are similar) is a perfect example of the biblical ignorance and lack of reasonable thinking that are far too common even among some pastors in our society today. There are so many errors, bad analogies and faulty interpretations of Scripture in this one brief article that I don't know where to begin.

However, since I have to begin somewhere, I will start out by discussing the importance of taking Scripture seriously and submitting to its authority. I will also make a distinction between a "literal" (proper) versus a "literalistic" (improper) interpretation of Holy Scripture. After this, I will respond to various arguments which suggest that since we don't take the Bible seriously on **some issues** we need not take seriously what the Bible says about **homosexual behavior**, either. *Finally, regarding the article (printed above) sent to me by the anonymous person, I will respond to various points it makes and show how misleading, ridiculous and confused is the reasoning of the person who wrote this article.*

Holy Scripture: Revelation from God <u>or</u> Subjective Human Opinion?

In 1st Timothy 3:15-17 the apostle Paul writes: "...the holy Scriptures are able to make you wise for salvation through faith in Christ Jesus. All Scripture is God-breathed and is useful for teaching, rebuking, correcting and training in righteousness, so that the man of God may be thoroughly equipped for every good work." When Paul mentions "the Holy Scriptures" he is referring to the books of the Old Testament. Paul says that this Scripture is "God-breathed."

In other words, the books of the Old Testament (Genesis – Malachi) were inspired by the Holy Spirit. Therefore, they are God's revelation to us. The apostle Peter writes about this: "...no prophecy of Scripture came about by the prophet's own interpretation. For prophecy never had its origin in the will of man, but men spoke from God as they were carried along by the Holy Spirit." (2nd Peter 1:20-21) Also, in Matthew 22:43-44 Jesus quotes from Psalm 110 and says that these words are the result of king David "speaking by the Spirit."

During the 19th century some scholars began to question whether the Jews even had an established canon of Scripture in Jesus' day. Such scholars will usually suggest that the Jews didn't have a set canon of

Scripture until some rabbis established the books of Old Testament at a meeting in Jamnia around 90 A.D.

However, there is no evidence that the purpose of the meeting at Jamnia was to establish an Old Testament canon. On the contrary, the facts show that the Old Testament canon must have already existed by this time! There is evidence that *some* (not all!) rabbis at Jamnia questioned whether the Song of Songs and Ecclesiastes belonged in the Old Testament canon – which would make no sense unless these books were already part of an established canon! Also, many references in the Gospels assume an accepted canon of the Old Testament in Jesus' day. For example, when Jesus mentioned "The Law of Moses, the Prophets and the Psalms" (see Luke 24:44) he was likely referring to the three-fold division of the Old Testament canon as we have it today.[149]

In the same way, the books of the New Testament are also God's revelation to us. Jesus says of His apostles: "…when he, the Spirit of truth, comes, he will guide you into all truth … He will bring glory to me by taking from what is mine and making it known to you … Sanctify them by the truth; your word is truth … My prayer is not for them alone. I pray also for those who will believe in me through their message." (John 16:13-14 & 17:17, 20)

In addition, Luke records these words of Ananias regarding the apostle Paul: "The God of our fathers has chosen you to know his will and to see the Righteous One and to hear words from his mouth. You will be his witness to all men of what you have seen and heard." (Acts 22:14-15)

The apostles of Jesus spread His Word through preaching, teaching and writing – and we have the apostles' teaching (which is JESUS' teaching) in the books of the New Testament. The apostle Paul writes: "…stand firm and hold to the teachings we passed on to you, whether by word of mouth or by letter." (2nd Thessalonians 2:15) Paul also writes: "…when you received the word of God, which you heard from us, you accepted it not as the word of men, but as it actually is, the word of God, which is at work in you who believe."

The apostle Peter writes: "Dear friends, this is now my second letter to you. I have written both of them as reminders to stimulate you to

---

[149] For a thorough treatment of the Old Testament canon see *The Biblical Canon* by David G. Dunbar (found in *Hermeneutics, Authority, and Canon* edited by D. A. Carson and John D. Woodbridge, 299-315).

wholesome thinking. I want you to recall the words spoken in the past by the holy prophets and the command given by our Lord and Savior through your apostles." (2nd Peter 3:1-2)

Peter then goes on to write the following about the letters of Paul: "...Paul also wrote you with the wisdom that God gave him. He writes the same way in all his letters, speaking in them of these matters. His letters contain some things that are hard to understand, which ignorant and unstable people distort, as they do the other Scriptures, to their own destruction."

In these two quotes from 2nd Peter we see that the writings of Peter and Paul (and the other apostles) are to be viewed as Scripture along with the Old Testament!

Why am I taking time to stress that Holy Scripture (both the Old and New Testaments) is God's revelation to us? The reason is that some want to reduce Holy Scripture to nothing more than the subjective religious opinions of ancient people.

In other words, some assume that Holy Scripture is NOT the inspired and inerrant revelation of God. Instead, they assume that Scripture is nothing more than human opinion about God and His will – and since OUR opinion about God and His will is just as valid, we are free to dismiss the teaching of Holy Scripture and trust our own opinions instead.

But where does this leave us? If our knowledge about God and His will has not been revealed to us by God Himself, then we are left in utter chaos! No wonder there are so many different religions in the world. If people are free to speculate about God and His will by using their own reason and senses as the basis for that knowledge, then we are doomed to worship gods that have been created by us! Not only will we never have objective knowledge of the True God.[150] We will never have objective foundation for morality.[151] Instead, we will suffer

---

[150] In Romans 1:18-20 Paul teaches that creation is proof that there is a Creator. This is what some call the natural knowledge of God. However, this knowledge of God is very limited and can never save us. For example, the examination of creation via our reason and senses would never lead us to the truth that we sinners are righteous before God through the death and resurrection of His Son, Jesus the Christ!

[151] In Romans 2:14-15 Paul teaches that God's laws are written on the human heart. In other words, we have a conscience. But the problem is that we sinners do not always recognize that our conscience comes from God. In fact, we often rebel against our conscience. In some cases the human conscience can become so corrupt that it is no longer possible to discern good from evil (see 1st Timothy 4:2 and Titus 1:15).

the fate of people during the time of the Judges: "In those days Israel had no king; everyone did as he saw fit." (Judges 21:25)[152]

We are left with one of two choices. Either we take Scripture seriously as the inspired and inerrant Word of God and submit to its authority regarding what we are to believe (especially how we sinners are saved through the Person and Work of Christ) and how we are to live. Or we deny what Scripture says about itself and conclude that it is nothing more than a collection of subjective human opinions about God and His will – subjective opinions that we can replace with our own subjective opinions.

But the Holy Spirit is working through the Word of God to rescue us from that evil <u>second</u> choice so that we might believe God's Truth that sets us free from our sinful opinions about God and His will for us (see John 8:31-59 and 1st Corinthians 2:1-16).

The same Holy Scriptures that condemn homosexual behavior as being contrary to God's loving plan for our lives also point us to Jesus through Whom we have complete *forgiveness for* and *freedom from* the sin that separates us from God and destroys us in the end.

In other words, submitting to the authority of Holy Scripture is not about obeying a bunch of rules in order to appease an angry God. Instead, submitting to the authority of Holy Scripture means that we trust the Word of the God who loved us so much that He sacrificed His only Son in our place of damnation so that we can live now and forever as His dearly loved children! (See 1st John 1:7-2:2, 3:1-10, 4:9-10, 19)

A "Literal" versus a "Literalistic" Interpretation of Holy Scripture

During the mid-1980s I was trying to save money for seminary by working as a security guard. One of the men at the place where I worked found out that I was a Christian and planning to become a Lutheran pastor. One day this man came up to me and asked me point blank: "Do you believe the Bible is the literal Word of God?" How did I answer him?

Initially, I simply said, "Yes!" He then immediately responded in this manner: "So, you believe in a geocentric universe!" (See Psalm 93:1) "You must also believe that rivers have hands and that mountains can sing!" (See Psalm 98:8) "I suppose you also believe

[152] Ironically, Israel DID have a King. Their King was God. But they rejected His Word (see Judges 2:6-19).

that God created the world in six days and that Mary was a virgin when she gave birth to Jesus!" (See Exodus 20:11 and Matthew 1:18-23) Such statements imply that it is foolish to believe that the Bible is the literal Word of God. How do we answer statements like these?

First, just because I believe that the Bible is the literal Word of God does NOT mean that I must read every passage of Scripture in a *literalistic* manner. Scholars who study Scripture in the original languages of Hebrew and Greek are well aware of the fact that there are different types of literature in the Bible – such as historical narrative, poetry, prophecy, legal material, genealogies, parables, apocalyptic and more.

Second, those who believe that the Bible is the literal Word of God insist that passages of Scripture must be understood within their immediate context as well as in the wider context of all of Scripture.

Regarding the statement about Psalm 93:1, we must first understand that the Bible does NOT teach either a heliocentric (that the earth revolves around a stationary sun) or a geocentric[153] (that the sun revolves around a stationary earth) solar system. Such an interpretation of Psalm 93:1 - along with Psalms 96:10 and 104:5 - is missing the point of the text!

The Hebrew word translated as "moved" in Psalms 93:1, 96:10 and 104:5 is *mot* – and in the contexts of these Psalms the Hebrew word *mot* merely teaches that humans can not move the earth from its "place" – only GOD can do that! *In other words, God has a plan for the earth and no power (human or otherwise) can change that plan!*

We find the same thing in Psalm 16:8 where David writes: "I will not be shaken." The Hebrew word translated "shaken" is also *mot* – and certainly David was not suggesting that he would stay on the same

---

[153] Some also point to Joshua 10:13 (where God commands the sun to "stand still") as another bit of evidence that Scripture teaches a geocentric solar system. I have two responses. First, when Scripture talks about the sun "standing still" it is simply using normal observational language. We do the same in our modern world when we talk about a "sunrise" or a "sunset." We would not accuse a scientist of believing in a geocentric solar system simply because he says: "What a beautiful sunrise we have this morning!" Second, even though Joshua 10:13 is not teaching a geocentric solar system, we must acknowledge the fact that the sun stopped moving! This means, based on the heliocentric theory of the solar system, that the earth stopped rotating for a period of time. How do we explain this? Simply put, this is just one of many miracles performed by God – mysterious events that are beyond our reason and experience. God created the world out of nothing. God created the laws of nature. God can cause the sun to "stand still" if He so chooses and maintain order on earth during this time.

spot of ground for his entire life! Instead, David's point is that no evil force could "shake" or "move" (Hebrew = *mot*) him from the plan God has for his life. We find the same teaching (using the Hebrew word *mot*) in Psalms 15:5, 21:7 and 62:2.

In the same way, according to Psalm 10:6 the wicked man says: "Nothing will shake me!" Again, the Hebrew word translated "shake" is *mot*. The wicked man's point is NOT that He will remain in the same spot his whole life! His point is that nothing can "move" or "shake" his wicked plans. Of course, he is a fool, because God WILL "move" him (see Psalm 10:12-18).

Therefore, when Psalm 93:1 says that the world can not be "moved" it does NOT mean that the earth remains motionless in space! Instead, it means that God has established this world and no power (human or otherwise) can change His plans for it.

In fact, God DOES "move" (Hebrew = *mot*) this world when He deems fit! In Psalm 62:2 David says that God has "shaken the land…" David does NOT mean that God moved the land from one place to another! Instead, David is using the Hebrew word *mot* as a figure of speech to describe the desperate times God has given to His people (see Psalm 62:3).

We see the same thing in Isaiah 24:19 where it says that the earth is "shaken" (Hebrew = *mot*) by God. The context of Isaiah chapter 24 shows that the prophet is talking about God's judgment upon the wicked of this earth – pointing ahead to the ultimate judgment on the Final Day when Christ returns.

However, the good news is that those who trust in Jesus do not have to fear being "moved" by God's judgment! In Isaiah 54:10 God says that His covenant of peace will not be "removed" (Hebrew = *mot*). In other words, God will be faithful to His promise to save those who trust in His Son!

The reason for the previous paragraphs explaining the use of the Hebrew word *mot* is to show that Psalm 93:1 is NOT teaching us about a geocentric solar system! Those who read it that way are forcing a modern astronomical theory on the text of Scripture and failing to read it within the wider context of the Psalms!

In fact, one could argue that Psalm 93:1 is at least open to supporting a <u>helio</u>centric theory of the solar system in that we humans can do nothing to change God's plan for the orbit of the earth around the sun! The earth continues to revolve around the sun without any help (or in spite of any possible hindrance) from us!

What about Psalm 98:8? Are those who believe that the Bible is literal Word of God required to read Psalm 98:8 in a *literalistic* manner? Of course not! When Psalm 98:8 talks about rivers "clapping their hands" and mountains "singing" it is obviously using figurative language. The context and style of literature of a particular text makes it clear whether one is to understand it literally or figuratively.

However, regarding God creating the world in six days and Mary being a virgin when Jesus was born, I must confess that I DO believe that these were literal historical events. I believe this because the context and language of Scripture is clear that these truths are to be understood literally. Even though such events are outside our experience, we believe that such events are possible because nothing is IMPOSSIBLE with God.

Some would argue that we can't believe in such things as the world being created in six days or a virgin conceiving and giving birth because modern science suggests that such things are not possible. However, we must remember that empirical science is an extension of our reason and senses by which we try to understand the nature of our universe.

Science is a blessing from God that allows us a partial understanding of our universe – and this has resulted in many blessings for humans (for example, medical science). However, science has also made many errors and there are many things about the universe that science simply does not understand.

Ministerial versus Magisterial Use of Reason

When one believes that the Bible is the literal Word of God, then one must also distinguish between a MINISTERIAL use of reason and a MAGISTERIAL use of reason.

The MINISTERIAL use of reason allows us to understand language and context so that we can study the Scriptures and determine what God is teaching. In this sense our reason is a "minister" (a servant) of the Scriptures. We use our reason to determine what God is teaching us in Holy Scripture, and then we trust that God's Word is truth. Therefore, the ministerial use of reason would lead one to say: "I'm not able to understand or comprehend this particular truth that God is teaching me in His Scriptures, but I believe that His Word is truth."

However, the MAGISTERIAL use of reason ceases to be a servant of the Scriptures and strives to become its master! The magisterial use of reason stands in judgment over God's teaching in Scripture and says: "What God is saying to me in this text of Scripture makes no sense to my reason or experience, and so I refuse to take this portion of Scripture seriously!"

Let's distinguish between the MINISTERIAL and MAGISTERIAL uses of reason by showing how they would respond to the following teaching of Holy Scripture: The Virgin Birth.

The **ministerial** use of reason would read Matthew 1:18-23 and conclude: "The language of Matthew as well as the immediate and wider context of Scripture clearly show that Mary was a virgin when she gave birth to Jesus. This goes against what modern science says about biological reproduction, and I don't understand how such a thing is possible. But with God all things are possible, and I trust His Word. Therefore, I believe that Mary was a virgin when she gave birth to Jesus."

In contrast, the **magisterial** use of reason would read Matthew 1:18-23 and conclude: "I don't believe what the Bible says about itself – that it's God's inspired and inerrant Word. Instead, I believe that the Bible is merely a collection of human opinions about God. Therefore, even though this text of Matthew clearly teaches that Mary was a virgin when she gave birth to Jesus, I know better. Modern science insists that such a thing is impossible. The idea of a virgin giving birth to a child makes no sense to me, and so it can't be true."

A good example of this kind of sad thinking is found in the book *Bulletproof Faith* written by openly lesbian United Church of Christ pastor Candace Chellew-Hodge. In her book Hodge writes: "For liberals … such things as reason and experience can trump both Bible and tradition … I contend that even if the Bible does condemn homosexuality, we are free to disregard its prohibitions based on our modern knowledge and experience."[154]

When it comes to the interpretation of Holy Scripture, many people are guilty of the MAGISTERIAL use of reason. Many in our culture today come to the Scriptures with their presuppositions about WHO God is and HOW He must act – and then they pick and choose from Scripture accordingly. People will believe the parts of Scripture that make sense to them, and reject the other parts that don't.

---

[154] *Bulletproof Faith* by Candace Chellew-Hodge, 44-46.

However, as I pointed out earlier in this book, we can't treat Holy Scripture like a smorgasbord – taking what we like and ignoring what we don't like. God's Word is a unity. If we reject some of God's Word, we reject God Himself!

Therefore, when the devil tempts us to ignore what Scripture clearly says about **homosexual behavior** we are guilty of rejecting God Himself. It doesn't matter if we're willing to accept some or most of what Scripture teaches on other issues. If we willingly reject what Scripture teaches about homosexual behavior (or any other sin or teaching of God's Word) we are guilty of UNBELIEF!

Some will insist that Scripture is simply too complex for anyone to understand clearly. Therefore, we can ignore what it says about various issues – including homosexual behavior.

In response to this way of thinking we must remember these words from the apostle Peter regarding the letters of the apostle Paul: "His letters contain some things that are hard to understand, which ignorant and unstable people distort, as they do the other Scriptures, to their own destruction." (2nd Peter 3:16)

Please note that Peter does NOT say that Paul's letters are IMPOSSIBLE to understand. Instead, Peter says that Paul's letters are HARD to understand. However, Peter assumes that we can understand what Paul is teaching via the <u>ministerial</u> use reason and that those who believe will submit in faith to what Paul is teaching. In contrast, those who interpret Paul's letters via the <u>magisterial</u> use of reason are unstable people who distort Paul's letters, as they do the other Scriptures, to their own destruction!

We Must Let Scripture Interpret Scripture!

When one believes that the Bible is the literal Word of God, then one must be willing to let Scripture interpret Scripture. In other words, those who believe that the Bible is the literal Word of God are more than willing to admit that some individual Bible passages are difficult to understand in isolation from the rest of Scripture. Therefore, we do not reject the whole of Scripture simply because we can't understand a particular passage nor do we base an entire doctrine of the Christian Faith on one isolated passage that is difficult to understand.

For example, some people are confused when Jesus' says that you can't be His disciple unless you hate your father and mother. (See

Luke 14:26) Is Jesus' actually teaching that I must hate my mother and father? No! Why not?

First, the immediate context of Luke chapter 14 teaches that we should be willing to turn away from anything that would keep us from trusting Jesus. Some people had family (a mother and/or father) who refused to trust in Jesus, and they would expect you to do the same. Jesus says we must "hate them" in the sense that we can't let an unbelieving father and mother keep us from trusting Jesus. (Jesus makes the same point in Luke 12:49-53)

Second, there are many examples in Luke's Gospel that we should love our mother and father. For instance, Jesus showed love and respect for His own parents (see Luke 2:51). Also, Jesus quotes the fourth commandment to teach the importance of honoring one's father and mother (see Luke 18:20).

Third, Jesus teaches that we should show love even for our enemies (see Luke 6:27). Therefore, if we are to love even our enemies, then how much more our mothers and fathers!

Finally, in Matthew 10:37 Jesus teaches that we should not love our mother and father *more* than Him. This text from Matthew helps us understand that when Luke uses the word "hate" he does not mean that you should literally hate your mother and father but that you should not love them *more* than Jesus.

Another reason we must allow Scripture to interpret Scripture is that we can then find solutions to what appear to be contradictions in Holy Scripture.

For example, if you compare the end of Matthew's Gospel (which teaches that Jesus' disciples were to meet Him in Galilee – see Matthew 28:7) with the end of Luke's Gospel (which teaches that Jesus first appeared to His disciples in Jerusalem and then later ascended to heaven – see Luke 24:33-53), one might conclude that Scripture is contradicting itself. But this can't be possible if Scripture is God's inspired and inerrant Word! However, if we allow Scripture to interpret Scripture, this apparent contradiction is resolved.

First, if you read John chapters 20 and 21 you will find that Jesus first appears to His disciples in Jerusalem (in harmony with Luke's Gospel) and then appears to His disciples in Galilee (in harmony with Matthew's Gospel). Matthew never says that Jesus did NOT meet with His disciples first in Jerusalem. Matthew merely mentions the fact that

Jesus wanted to meet with His disciples in Galilee – which He DID after He first met them in Jerusalem!

Second, if you read Acts chapter 1 (also written by Luke!) you will discover that Jesus remained on earth for forty days after His resurrection and before He ascended to His Father. This gave Jesus plenty of time to go to Galilee, and other places, and then return for His ascension. Also, if you read Luke chapter 24 you will note that Luke never says that Jesus did NOT go to Galilee. The end of Luke's Gospel simply skips over the events that took place during the forty days between Jesus' appearance to His disciples in Jerusalem and His ascension near Bethany 40 days later.

The Scripture interprets Scripture principle also applies to how we understand what Scripture teaches about **homosexuality.** For example, as noted in the previous chapter, some use the fact that the Gospels do not record Jesus ever saying anything explicitly about homosexual behavior as evidence that He affirmed it. But when we examine the rest of Scripture along with Jesus' use of the creation account in Matthew chapter 19, it becomes clear that Jesus clearly condemned homosexual behavior as being sinful.

Distinguishing Prescriptive vs. Descriptive Texts

Earlier in this book I briefly noted the importance of distinguishing between prescriptive and descriptive texts in Holy Scripture. When one believes that the Bible is the literal Word of God, such a distinction between texts of Scripture becomes obvious!

For example, when the ELCA voted to approve the ordination of practicing homosexuals at their national convention in August of 2009 there were several letters to the editor in my town's local paper regarding this issue. Two of the letters mocked those who believe that the Bible condemns homosexual behavior by pointing to texts that Christians no longer observe today. Their argument was that since we no longer observe the commands in the texts they quoted, we need not observe Scripture's prohibitions against homosexual behavior.

For example, in one letter a woman referred to Leviticus chapters 21 and 22 where we find ceremonial laws regarding the Levitical priests in Old Testament Israel. She pointed to Leviticus 21:16 as evidence that these laws were meant to be observed "forever" – and she argued that since we no longer observe these laws, we can also ignore what

Scripture says about homosexual behavior and pastors. *The problems with this interpretation are obvious!*

First, even though the ceremonial laws in Leviticus chapters 21 and 22 were PRESCRIPTIVE – we must note that they were prescriptive ONLY for the Levitical priests and NOT for pastors in the New Testament Church. (See 1st Timothy 3:1-7 and Titus 1:5-9)

Second, Leviticus 21:16 does not teach that these laws for the Levitical priests must be in force "forever" in the sense that they must never be abolished. Instead, the Hebrew text refers to "generations" of Levitical priests – and their "generations" as priests ENDED when Christ, our great High Priest (from the tribe of Judah!) abolished the Levitical priesthood by His sacrifice of Himself once for all! (See Hebrews 7:11-10:39)

One other letter to the editor was from a man who pointed to Genesis chapter 22 where God commands Abraham to sacrifice his son, Isaac. The man who wrote the letter argued that no father today would ever sacrifice his son. Therefore, since we ignore what God teaches in Genesis chapter 22 we can ignore what God teaches about homosexual behavior. *I wonder if this man would be willing to use the same logic to ignore what Scripture teaches about theft or bestiality. The problems with this interpretation are even more obvious than the other letter.*

First, even though God's command in Genesis chapter 22 was PRESCRIPTIVE for Abraham – it was prescriptive ONLY for Abraham. The context clearly shows that this command was given ONLY to Abraham and not meant to be followed by all other fathers throughout time!

Second, Genesis chapter 22 clearly teaches that God did NOT allow Abraham to sacrifice his son. In fact, Abraham trusted that God would provide a lamb in place of Isaac (see Genesis 22:8). Even if God had allowed Abraham to sacrifice Isaac, Abraham trusted that God would not go back on His promise that the Savior of the world would be a descendant of Isaac – and so Abraham believed that God would then have to raise Isaac from the dead (see Hebrews 11:17-19). But why did God ask Abraham to sacrifice Isaac if God did not allow Abraham to go through with it?

First, God was using this event to strengthen Abraham's faith in God's Word. You could say that God was teaching Abraham about the MINISTERIAL use of reason!

Second, God uses this event as a picture of the sacrifice that God Himself would offer to save us sinners from damnation. What God did NOT allow Abraham to do God Himself DID when He offered His One and Only Son on the cross for us! (See John 3:16 and 1st John 4:9-10)

Those two letters to the editor in my town's local paper are perfect examples of how some people do not understand that certain prescriptive texts are ONLY for certain groups or individuals – NOT for all people of all times and places.

In addition, we must understand that there are also many texts of Scripture that are DESCRIPTIVE. In other words, these texts describe events in history as teaching tools for us but not as laws for us obey. In fact, some descriptive texts actually describe evil behavior that we are NOT to obey but avoid with all our might!

For example, when Genesis chapter 19 describes the attempted homosexual gang rape by the men of Sodom – this is a description of an evil we must avoid! Also, when Romans 1:26-27 describes women and men engaging in homosexual behavior – this is a description of an evil we must avoid! Just because God describes an event or behavior in history does not mean that He approves of that event or behavior. In some cases God describes evil events and behaviors as examples for us so that we can avoid those same events and behaviors!

I could say so much more about what it means for us to believe that the Bible is the literal Word of God – but a detailed examination of this subject is far beyond the scope of this book. I simply wanted to point out that a person can believe that the Bible is the literal Word of God while avoiding a *literalistic* approach to Scripture that ignores the variety of language and interpretation within context.

In addition, I've shown that one who believes that Bible is the literal Word of God must **1)** distinguish between the ministerial vs. the magisterial use of reason, **2)** let Scripture interpret Scripture, and **3)** distinguish between prescriptive and descriptive texts.

I will now go on to respond to various pro-gay arguments which suggest that we need not take Scripture seriously when it condemns homosexual behavior as being sinful. Such arguments come from people who admit that Scripture condemns even consensual homosexual behavior – but they go on to assert that we need not take Scripture seriously at this point![155]

The Genesis creation account is a myth!

In chapter two of this book I explained that when we want to know what Scripture teaches about homosexual behavior we must begin with the creation account in Genesis. As we learned in chapter two, the Genesis creation account clearly teaches that God made the first two humans male and female (Genesis 1:27) and gave them to each other as husband and wife in marriage (Genesis 2:21-24). God's gift of sex was to be used by a husband and wife for 1) the creation of new human life (Genesis 1:28) and 2) the celebration of their "union" in marriage (Genesis 2:24).

We learned how the Song of Songs teaches that sex between a husband and wife in monogamous marriage is a celebration of the special love unique to their relationship.

In Matthew 19:1-12 we learned how Jesus used the creation account as the foundation for God's teaching that His gift of sex is to be celebrated ONLY within the context of one man and one woman in marriage – and how outside of such a marriage the only option is celibacy!

Finally, we learned how the apostle Paul directly quotes from the creation account in 1st Corinthians chapter 6 and Ephesians chapter 5 to show that God condones sex only between one man and one woman

---

[155] For example, on page 39 of his book *Gay Theology Without Apology* Gary David Comstock writes: "…in the interest of convincing ourselves and the church that the Bible does not condemn us, we have brought our own bias to our reading of it. We have tended to overlook the danger and hostility that lurk in the very passages with which we have tried to become friends … I would suggest that our approach to the Bible become less apologetic and more critical – that we approach it not as an authority from which we want approval, but as a document whose shortcomings must be cited." In addition, on page 11 of his book *The Sins of Scripture* John Shelby Spong writes: "At first I convinced myself that the problem was not in the Bible itself, but in the way the Bible was used. That, however, was a defensive and ultimately dishonest response. I had to come to the place where I recognized that the Bible itself was often the enemy. Time after time, the Bible, I discovered, condemned itself with its own words." Finally, after giving extensive evidence that Paul condemns all forms of homosexual behavior in Romans 1:26-27, Bernadette Brooten writes the following on page 302 in her book *Love Between Women*: "I hope churches today, being apprised of the history that I have presented, will no longer teach Rom 1:26f as authoritative."

within marriage. Paul also alludes to the creation account when he condemns homosexual behavior in Romans chapter 1.

Because Scripture as a whole clearly teaches that the creation account in Genesis is the foundation for understanding that God limits sex to one man and one woman in marriage, some have insisted that the creation account is only one of several ancient creation myths that need not be taken seriously by modern humans. *In other words, if God did not actually create the first humans and give them to each other in marriage, then we are free to redefine sex and marriage according to our desires and designs.*

However, Scripture itself clearly teaches that the creation account in Genesis chapters 1 and 2 is literal history! In fact, as I noted earlier in this book, the creation account in Genesis chapters 1 and 2 is foundational for understanding the message of Scripture from Genesis 3:1 to the end of the book of Revelation. If we deny or redefine the creation account in Genesis we must also deny or redefine the central teachings of the Christian Faith.

Therefore, those who want to dismiss the creation account in Genesis in order to affirm homosexual behavior need to understand what they are giving up!

I once met a man who denied the historicity of the creation account in Genesis because he believed that science had proven beyond a doubt that we humans evolved from lower life forms. Nevertheless, he considered himself to be a faithful Christian because he believed in original sin, the deity of Christ, the atonement, as well as the hope of the resurrection and eternal life in the New Creation.[156]

Even though I was glad that he believed in those doctrines that are so clearly taught in the Scriptures, I then attempted to help him understand that his denial of the historicity of the creation account logically leads to the denial of ALL the other doctrines he claimed to believe as a Christian.

Some who deny that the creation account in Genesis is literal history end up also denying the existence of God altogether – or at least they deny that we can *know* if such a God exists (contrary to Romans 1:18-20).

---

[156] I thought it was interesting that this man WAS willing to trust what Scripture teaches about God creating a new heaven and earth on the Final Day but he was NOT willing to trust what Scripture teaches about God creating the universe and all life in six days as taught in Genesis chapter 1.

On the other hand, there are others, like the man mentioned in the above paragraphs, who deny the historicity of the creation account and yet still hold to other doctrines of the Christian Faith. Such people will usually teach that God created the world through the process of "macro-evolution" - the theory that all life forms descended from a common ancestor via the process of natural selection working with biological mutations over the course of millions of years. *(I will be treating the issue of creation versus evolution more thoroughly in Appendix II of this book.)* **However, there are huge problems with the notion that God created all life via the process of macro-evolution!**

First, Scripture teaches that the creation account is literal history and so there is no way to harmonize the idea that God used macro-evolution with the text of Genesis.

Second, if we believe that God used macro-evolution then we are claiming that God used a process that requires suffering, mutation and death in order to create new life forms.

Third, if death is a natural part of God's creative process, then we must reject what Genesis chapter 3 teaches about death being the result of Adam's sin.

Fourth, if we reject the historicity of Adam's rebellion against God we also must reject original sin itself (see Romans 5:12-14).

Finally, if we deny the reality of original sin we are only a step away from denying the need for the atoning work of Christ who suffered and died to rescue us from the sin we inherited from Adam (see Romans 5:15-21 and 1st Corinthians 15:45-49).

Some may accuse me of overreacting when I suggest that a denial of the historicity of the creation account in Genesis logically leads to a denial of the entire Christian Faith. However, please read carefully the following quotes from *The Sins of Scripture* by John Shelby Spong regarding the creation account and its relationship to other doctrines of the Christian Faith:

> "Can anyone seriously argue today that these words[157] are the 'Word of God'? ... Since this story has been so influential in defining the sexes to this day, it is worth retelling, especially if

[157] When Spong writes "these words" he is referring to Genesis 2:18-23.

it can be … understood not as literal history but as an ancient Hebrew myth."[158]

"The primary way in which the Jesus story has been traditionally and historically told portrays the holy God involved in a cruel act of divine child abuse that was said to have occurred on a hill called Calvary. We are told that there, instead of punishing *us* for our sins, God required the suffering and death of the divine Son. God's righteousness was restored when the Son of God was punished as a substitute for us. Does that sound strange? … That is the traditional way in which Christianity has prescribed the cure for human sin … Let me state this boldly and succinctly: Jesus did not die for your sins or my sins. That proclamation is theological nonsense."[159]

"This interpretation of Jesus as the sacrificed victim is a human creation, not a divine revelation. It was shaped in a first-century world by the disciples of Jesus, who drew on their Jewish liturgical symbols as a way the crucifixion of Jesus might be understood. They borrowed this understanding directly from the Jewish Day of Atonement, Yom Kippur, in which an innocent lamb was slaughtered to pay the price for the sins of the people … Jesus was interpreted by his earlier disciples inside these Jewish liturgical images. They are all based, however, on an understanding of human life that is quite simply wrong. ***We are not fallen, sinful people who deserve to be punished. We are frightened, insecure people who have achieved the enormous breakthrough into self-consciousness that marks no other creature that has yet emerged from the evolutionary cycle. We must not denigrate the human being who ate of the tree of knowledge in the Genesis story. We must learn rather to celebrate the creative leap into a higher humanity. Our sense of separation and aloneness is not a mark of our sin. It is a symbol of our glory. Our struggle to survive, which manifests itself in radical self-centeredness, is not the result of original sin. It is a sign of emerging consciousness. It should not be a source of guilt. It is a***

[158] *The Sins of Scripture*, 75.

[159] *The Sins of Scripture*, 171-173.

source of blessing[160] ... Jesus did not die for our sins ... That is a god-image that must be broken; but when it is, the traditional way we have told the Jesus story will surely die with it. I believe it *must*. When it does, I think it will be good riddance..."[161]

"If the biblical explanation of the source of evil is no longer operative ... then from where does evil come? What is its origin? How is it to be explained? ... If the task of the Christian faith is not about rescuing and restoring the fallen sinner to wholeness ... then what is the task of this religious system? ... we need to raise the question as to whether Christianity as we know it can survive without its doctrines of atonement and incarnation, both of which hang on the sin and rescue themes we have discussed ... To all these inquiries I would answer not only that we *can*, but also that we *must* ... ***The deconstruction begins with the dismissal of the story with which the Bible opens. It has already moved from being thought of as literal history to being viewed as interpretive myth. The next step is to dismiss it as not even an accurate interpreter of life. It is a bad myth, a false myth, a misleading myth. There never was a time, either literally or metaphorically, when there was a perfect and finished creation. That biblical idea is simply wrong ... Whatever else we know about creation, we are now certain that it is an ongoing, evolving and still-incomplete process ... Since there was no perfect beginning, no Garden of Eden and no first man and woman who walked with God in perfect communion, there can also be no fall into sin and thus no act of disobedience that destroyed the perfection of God's world*** [162] ... Since these understandings are basic to the whole superstructure of Christian creeds, doctrine, dogma and theology, this realization means that they will all eventually come crashing down."[163]

---

[160] Bold and italic emphasis is mine.

[161] *The Sins of Scripture*, 173-174.

[162] Bold and italic emphasis is mine.

[163] *The Sins of Scripture*, 175-177.

"...we have evolved into a status that we judge to be only a little higher than the ape's ... Our humanity is not flawed by some real or mythical act of disobedience that resulted in our expulsion from some fanciful Garden of Eden ... We do not need some divine rescue accomplished by an invasive deity to lift us from a fall that never happened and to restore us to a status we have never possessed. The idea that Jesus had to pay the price of our sinfulness is an idea that is bankrupt ... It is like an unstoppable waterfall. Baptism ... becomes inoperative. The Eucharist ... becomes empty of meaning ... Even the afterlife symbols of heaven and hell ... now lose their credibility ... in acknowledging our evolutionary origins ... means that we rid ourselves of the idea that the world was created for the benefit of human beings, or even that the planet earth is somehow different or special in the universe ... we humans are simply the self-conscious form of life that has emerged out of the evolutionary soup ... We might be a dead end in the evolutionary process, a creature like the dinosaur, destined for extinction ... From where does evil come? ... It rises ... from the incompleteness of the evolutionary process."[164]

"Jesus can only be a product of humanity, created out of its gene pool ... the doctrines of the incarnation, the atonement and the Trinity were necessitated in traditional Christianity by the premise of the fall. God alone could overcome the fall, and since Jesus was perceived as the rescuer, then Jesus had to be a divine visitor accomplishing this divine task. When the fall is dismissed, traditional Christology cannot help but go with it and a new Christology must emerge..."[165]

I have provided these extensive quotes from Spong to shown the logical result of denying the historicity of the Genesis creation account. ***Please understand!* I'm NOT saying that all who deny the historicity of the Genesis creation account reject all the basic Christian doctrines that Spong does!** However, I AM saying that

[164] *The Sins of Scripture*, 177-179.

[165] *The Sins of Scripture*, 180.

Spong[166] is taking his denial of the creation account in Genesis to its logical conclusion.[167]

Therefore, those who attempt to affirm homosexual behavior by saying "The Genesis creation account is a myth!" need to understand what is at stake!

Some who have rejected the Genesis creation account in order to affirm homosexual behavior ARE comfortable rejecting the entire Christian Faith. However, there are other Christians who reject the Genesis creation account in order to affirm homosexual behavior – *and yet they want to hang on to all the other Christian doctrines that are based on the very Genesis creation account they have rejected!*

Not only is this inconsistent. But denying the historicity of the Genesis creation account is nothing less than unbelief and denial of God's Word when the rest of Scripture is clear that Genesis chapters 1-3 are literal history.[168] **Therefore, denying the historicity of the Genesis creation account is a high price to pay in order to affirm homosexual behavior.**

On the other hand, if you accept that the creation account in Genesis is literal history – as the rest of Scripture clearly teaches! – then you must also accept what the creation account (and the rest of Scripture,

---

[166] What amazes me about Spong is that on page 10 of *The Sins of Scripture* he says he is "a Christian, a deeply committed, believing Christian." *Does the word "Christian" have any meaning at this point?* Imagine someone saying: "I believe the Torah is a worthless document! I think Moses was an idiot! I think the Ten Commandments are hopelessly barbaric and outdated! I think Yahweh is an imaginary war god invented by ancient people to justify their oppression of other nations! By the way, I want you know that I a deeply committed, believing Jew!" Or imagine someone saying: "I deny the existence of Allah. I think Mohammed was a joke! I reject the five pillars of Islam. I think the Koran is full of ridiculous errors. By the way, I want you to know that I am a deeply committed, believing Muslim!"

[167] Another example of the denial of the creation account leading to a denial of original sin and the atonement can be found in the book *Doing Without Adam and Eve* by Patricia A. Williams. On pages 182 and 201 of her book she writes: "Adam and Eve's mythological disobedience cannot be atoned by Jesus' historical actions, nor can Adam and Eve's mythological sin be responsible for our sinful nature or our death … Christianity can embrace this … only if it consents to doing without Adam and Eve."

[168] The following are some excellent books on the creation versus evolution issue: *The New Answers Book – Volumes 1 & 2*, edited by Ken Ham (www.answersingenesis.org); *In Search of the Genesis World*, by Erich Von Fange (www.cph.org); *Refuting Compromise* by Dr. Jonathan Sarfati.

based on this creation account) teaches about God's gift of sex being limited to one man and one woman within marriage.

However, even more important, if you believe in the historicity of the Genesis creation account then you can also believe in the historicity of Jesus, the Son of God, and His atoning sacrifice on the cross for you! You can come to Jesus with your sexual sin – and all your other sins! – and know that you are forgiven and holy in God's sight through faith in Him. The Holy Spirit will help you to resist the desires of your sinful nature, and you can look forward to spending eternity with God in the New Creation He will provide for His people on the Day when Christ returns!

Red Lobster fans can't take Leviticus seriously!

I have a confession to make. I love, REALLY LOVE, shrimp! I'll take shrimp any way I can get it! I recall the immortal words of Bubba from the movie *Forest Gump*: "Anyway, like I was sayin', shrimp is the fruit of the sea. You can barbecue it, boil it, broil it, bake it, sauté it. Dey's uh, shrimp-kabobs, shrimp creole, shrimp gumbo. Pan fried, deep fried, stir-fried. There's pineapple shrimp, lemon shrimp, coconut shrimp, pepper shrimp, shrimp soup, shrimp stew, shrimp salad, shrimp and potatoes, shrimp burger, shrimp sandwich. That - that's about it."

I remember one occasion when I was having a dialog with a man about Scripture's teaching regarding homosexual behavior. This man believed Christians should affirm homosexual behavior. Of course, I made it clear that Scripture condemns all forms of homosexual behavior as sin – and I quoted Leviticus 18:22 and 20:13 as examples. He then responded: "And the next time you eat shrimp at Red Lobster you are also guilty of great sin!" What was this man's point?

Simply put, this man's point was that if I believed Leviticus 18:22 and 20:13 still applied to us today then I would also have to believe that Leviticus 11:10 still applied to us today, and Leviticus 11:10 reads: "But all creatures in the seas or streams that do not have fins or scales – whether among all the swarming things or among all the other living creatures in the water – you are to detest."

This man's point was that since no person today (including me, the shrimp lover!) takes Leviticus 11:10 seriously, we need not take the condemnations of homosexual behavior in Leviticus chapters 18 and

20 seriously, either! In other words, *Red Lobster fans can't take Leviticus seriously!* How do we answer this?

Honestly, of all the arguments that attempt show that we need not take Scripture's prohibitions against homosexual behavior seriously, this one is by far the weakest! People who use this argument are either completely ignorant of a proper understanding of the book of Leviticus or they are trying to be deliberately deceptive.

For example, if someone uses Leviticus 11:10 to suggest that we can reject the entire book of Leviticus (especially the prohibitions against homosexual behavior in Leviticus chapters 18 and 20), simply ask them: "Do you think mother/son incest is wrong? Do you think adultery is wrong? Do you think bestiality is wrong? Do you think children should respect their mother and father? Do you think feeding the poor is good? Do you think stealing is wrong? Do you think telling a lie is wrong? Do you think slandering an innocent person is wrong? Do you think refusing to pay an employee is wrong? Do you think mocking deaf and blind people is wrong? Do you think courts of law should be fair and impartial? Do you think murder is wrong? Do you think prostitution is wrong? Do you think consulting demons is wrong? Do you think dishonest business practices are wrong? Do you think that showing love for others is a good thing?"

Unless a person is morally bankrupt, they will answer all those questions by saying: "Yes!" Then simply point out to such a person that all those things that he or she agrees are sinful or good are laws that are found in the book of Leviticus!

In other words, if you reject the entire book of Leviticus because you believe that Leviticus 11:10 no longer applies to us, then you are also rejecting many good laws that most would agree still apply to us today!

Simply put, when a person reads the book of Leviticus he or she must distinguish between ***ceremonial laws*** that were given ONLY to the people of Israel and ONLY for a temporary period in history[169]

---

[169] In addition to the temporary ceremonial food laws given only to Israel as found in Leviticus chapter 11, there are also other temporary ceremonial laws given only to Israel that are found in the midst of universal moral laws intended for ALL people of ALL times and places. For example, Leviticus chapter 19 is filled with universal moral laws that even those who affirm homosexual behavior would agree still apply to us – for instance, the command: "...love your neighbor as yourself." (Leviticus 19:18b) However, in the midst of all the universal moral laws found in Leviticus chapter 19 we find a few temporary ceremonial laws intended only for Israel. Leviticus 19:19 reads:

versus the ***universal moral laws*** that continue to apply to ALL people of ALL times and places.

For example, the various food laws found in Leviticus chapter 11 are clearly given ONLY to the Jews. God never says that He condemns the Gentile nations for eating unclean animals. In contrast, in Leviticus chapters 18 and 20 God clearly condemns the GENTILE nations for their sexual immorality – *including their homosexual behavior.*

In addition, the New Testament clearly teaches that the Levitical ceremonial food laws have been abolished because they have been fulfilled by Christ (see Mark 7:19, Acts 10:9-23, Romans 14:14, 1st Timothy 4:3-4). In contrast, the New Testament is clear that the Levitical universal sexual prohibitions are still in force for ALL people – whether Jew or Gentile (see Mark 7:21, John 8:11, Romans 13:9-10, 1st Corinthians 5:1-5 & 6:9-20, Galatians 5:19-21, Ephesians 5:3, Colossians 3:5-6, 1st Thessalonians 4:1-8, Hebrews 13:4, 2nd Peter 2:14-22, Jude 7, Revelation 22:14-15).

At this point someone might ask: "What was the purpose of the temporary Levitical food laws given to the Jews?"[170] Simply put, as with many of the other ceremonial laws given to the Jews, the laws against unclean foods were a sign that Israel was to be a unique nation among the peoples of the earth. Why? The reason is that God wanted them to separate themselves from the sinful beliefs and behaviors of the unbelieving nations. But even more, God wanted Israel to stand out in the world because the Savior of ALL nations would come into the world through Israel (see Genesis 12:1-3).

However, once Jesus (the eternal Son of God who was descended from Abraham!) came into the world and finished His work of salvation, the purpose of Israel as a unique nation had served its

---

"Do not mate different kinds of animals. Do not plant your field with two kinds of seed. Do not wear clothing woven of two kinds of material." Obviously, no one would reject the command to "love your neighbor as yourself" as irrelevant simply because Leviticus 19:19 does not apply to us today. This shows the importance of distinguishing between the temporary ceremonial laws given only to Israel and the universal moral laws intended for all people of all times. For a good explanation of the purpose of the ceremonial laws in Leviticus 19:19, see the Concordia Commentary *Leviticus* by John Kleinig, 413-414.

[170] For an excellent treatment of the meaning of the food laws for ancient Israel and how they have been fulfilled by Christ, see the Concordia Commentary *Leviticus* by John Kleinig, 241-262.

purpose. All the ceremonial laws (for example, the food laws, circumcision, the animal sacrifices in the Jerusalem Temple, the Sabbath Day ritual, and many others) were fulfilled in Christ! As Paul writes: "…do not let anyone judge you by what you eat or drink, or with regard to a religious festival, a New Moon celebration or a Sabbath day. These are a shadow of the things that were to come; the reality, however, is found in Christ." (Colossians 2:16-17)[171]

In the beginning, before Adam and Eve rebelled against God, there was no eating of meat but only plant life (see Genesis 1:29-30). However, after the Flood, God gave permission for humans to eat meat (see Genesis 9:1-3). For this reason the apostle Paul wrote the following: "For everything God created is good, and nothing is to be rejected if it is received with thanksgiving…"

In other words, the Levitical food laws about unclean animals were not implying that some animals (for example, pigs or shrimp) were evil in and of themselves. Instead, certain animals were designated as unclean for Israel to distinguish them from the other nations. However, once Christ completed His work He thereby fulfilled all these Levitical ceremonial laws. The result is that there are now no animals that God considers "unclean" - *and that means we are free to eat shrimp!* **THANKS BE TO GOD! HALLELUJAH!**

However, just because Leviticus 11:10 no longer applies to us today does NOT mean that the universal sexual prohibitions in Leviticus chapters 18 and 20 no longer apply to us today. According to the rest of the Old Testament as well as the witness of the New Testament, the Levitical sexual laws are STILL in force for us today – *including the sexual prohibitions against even consensual homosexual behavior!*

There are no universal sex laws in Scripture!

Some who believe we should affirm homosexual behavior suggest that we can not take Scripture seriously as a standard for sexual morality because, supposedly, there are no universal sex laws in Scripture that apply to all people of all times and places. *I am going to devote some extra space to this section because this particular notion of Scripture having no universal sex laws has deceived so many people!*

---

[171] Also see Hebrews chapters 8-10.

One of the most well known proponents of this view is Walter Wink. In the book *Homosexuality and Christian Faith* (edited by Wink) he contributes a chapter titled *Homosexuality in the Bible*. In this chapter Wink questions whether 1st Corinthians 6:9 and 1st Timothy 1:10 even apply to consensual homosexual relations today – but he completely ignores all the evidence to the contrary! However, he is willing to admit that Leviticus 18:22, Leviticus 20:13 and Romans 1:26-27 clearly prohibit even consensual homosexual behavior (although Wink is in error about the purpose of these prohibitions against homosexual behavior). Regarding these three texts, Wink writes: "...all ... unequivocally condemn homosexual behavior."[172]

So, how does Wink get around the fact that these three texts (not to mention the clear prohibitions against even consensual homosexual behavior in 1st Corinthians 6:9 and 1st Timothy 1:10) clearly condemn even consensual homosexual behavior? His argument is that we need not take them seriously because we humans are always changing our standards for sexual morality.

In his chapter *Homosexuality and the Bible* Wink gives several examples of biblical commands and prohibitions (some sexual in nature; others not), and then concludes that most Christians follow only four of them today – those four being prohibitions against incest, rape, adultery and bestiality.

Wink then goes on to write: "But we disagree with the Bible on most other sexual mores. The Bible condemned or discouraged the following behaviors which we generally allow..." Wink then gives us this list: **intercourse during menstruation, celibacy** (some texts), **exogamy** (marriage with non-Israelites), **naming sexual organs, nudity** (under certain circumstances), **masturbation and birth control**. Wink then adds this comment: "And the Bible regarded semen and menstrual blood as unclean, which most of us do not."[173]

After giving the list above of prohibited behaviors we now allow, Wink then writes: "Likewise, the Bible permitted behaviors that we today condemn or have discontinued." Wink then gives this list: **prostitution, polygamy, levirate marriage, sex with slaves,**

---

[172] *Homosexuality and Christian Faith* edited by Walter Wink, 34.

[173] *Homosexuality and Christian Faith* edited by Walter Wink, 43.

concubinage, treatment of women as property, very early marriage (for girl, age 11-13).[174]

After giving all these lists, Wink then adds this comment: "And while the Old Testament accepted divorce, Jesus forbade it. In short, of the sexual mores mentioned here, we agree with the Bible only on four of them, and disagree with it on sixteen! … So why do we appeal to proof texts in Scripture in the case of homosexuality alone, when we feel perfectly free to disagree with Scripture regarding most other sexual practices? Obviously many of our choices in these matters are arbitrary."[175]

Sadly, many people have been convinced by Wink's argument that Scripture can not be used as a standard for sexual morality. But if we can not use Scripture as our standard for sexual morality, what standard SHOULD we use?

Wink writes: "The crux of the matter … is simply that the Bible has no sexual ethic … The Bible knows only a love ethic, which is constantly being brought to bear on whatever sexual mores are dominant in any given country, or culture, or period … Just within one lifetime we have witnessed the shift from the ideal of preserving one's virginity until marriage to couples living together for several years before getting married … So we must critique the sexual mores of any given time and clime by the love ethic exemplified by Jesus. Such a love ethic is nonexploitative (hence no sexual exploitation of children, no using of another to his or her loss); it does not dominate (hence no patriarchal treatment of women as chattel); it is responsible, mutual, caring, and loving. Augustine already dealt with this in his inspired phrase, 'Love God, and do as you please.'"[176]

How do we respond to Wink? First, I will briefly examine Wink's examples from Scripture of prohibitions we now allow or commands we no longer obey and show how they do NOT apply to Scripture's prohibitions against consensual homosexual behavior. Second, I will show how the four biblical sexual prohibitions Wink lists as being

---

[174] *Homosexuality and Christian Faith* edited by Walter Wink, 43.

[175] *Homosexuality and Christian Faith* edited by Walter Wink, 43.

[176] *Homosexuality and Christian Faith* edited by Walter Wink, 44-45.

accepted by most Christians today (incest, rape, adultery and bestiality) are perfect examples of why consensual homosexual behavior must also be condemned. Third, I will show how Wink's "love ethic" conflicts with the teaching of Jesus and allows for many other sexual sins. Finally, I will show how Wink's quote from the early Church father, Augustine, actually REFUTES Wink's argument.[177]

One of Wink's examples of a biblical sex prohibition we no longer follow is **the law against a man having sexual intercourse with a menstruating woman.**[178] Wink suggests that since we no longer follow this law we are free to ignore the biblical prohibitions against homosexual behavior. I have already responded to this flawed argument on pages 67-70 of this book. Simply put, the prohibition against intercourse with a menstruating woman was a ceremonial law (one of the many ceremonial laws fulfilled by Christ) given only to the people of Israel and only for a temporary period in history. The New Testament doesn't even mention it much less prohibit the behavior. Therefore, this law can NOT be compared to the universal sex laws (including the prohibition against homosexual behavior) intended for all people of all times and places. As Wink himself admits, the Levitical prohibitions against consensual homosexual behavior are maintained by the apostle Paul in Romans 1:26-27.

Robert Gagnon offers a great response to Wink's attempt to use the Levitical prohibitions against intercourse with a menstruating woman as a reason for us to ignore the biblical prohibitions against homosexual behavior. Gagnon writes: "In other parts of the Old Testament - outside the book of Ezekiel which has strong affinities to the Holiness Code - we hear not a word about the problem of sex with a menstruating woman. Consequently, it is not surprising that explicit mention of it does not appear in the New Testament. The best explanation for this omission is simply that New Testament authors lumped the proscription of sex during menstruation with other Old Testament legislation regarding ritual purity that had been abrogated by the new covenant in Christ. Yet adultery, incest, same-sex

---

[177] I don't have space in this book to give a thorough response to Wink's argument. However, if you wish to read such a thorough response, see the article *Are There Universally Valid Sex Precepts? A Critique of Walter Wink's Views on the Bible and Homosexuality* by Robert Gagnon (available on his web page: www.robgagnon.net).

[178] *Homosexuality and Christian Faith* edited by Walter Wink, 37.

intercourse, bestiality, prostitution, and premarital sex were not lumped together with defunct purity regulations; rather they were retained under the rubric of *porneia* , 'sexual immorality' … sex with a menstruating woman does not carry with it quite the 'unnatural' quality of having sex with one's parent, or another of the same sex, or an animal. It happens inadvertently, in the course of normal sexual activity. The notion of 'inadvertent' incest, same-sex intercourse, or bestiality makes little sense."[179]

Another one of Wink's examples of a biblical teaching we no longer follow is **the Levitical command that those who are guilty of adultery must be stoned to death.**[180] Wink suggests that since we no longer give the death penalty to adulterers (or to practicing homosexuals, for that matter), then we are free to ignore the biblical prohibitions against homosexual behavior. However, I have already responded to this flawed argument on pages 63-64 of this book. Simply put, Old Testament Israel functioned as a theocracy – both Church and State. However, after Christ fulfilled His work the purpose of Old Testament Israel ceased to exist. Therefore, the Christian Church no longer functions as a theocracy but submits to the laws (and to the punishments for breaking those laws) of the nations in which it exists. However, just because we no longer give the death penalty for sins like adultery, incest, bestiality and homosexuality does NOT mean that these behaviors are no longer condemned as being sinful. That's why Jesus could rescue an adulteress woman from stoning and still say to her: "Go and sin no more!"

Regarding Wink's flawed death penalty argument, Robert Gagnon writes: "Further evidence of Wink's flawed use of hermeneutical arguments is the following contention in his article: 'anyone who wishes to base his or her beliefs on the witness of the Old Testament must be completely consistent and demand the death penalty for everyone who performs homosexual acts.' Most Christians recognize that the movement from old covenant to new covenant represented a movement from a theocratic state in this age to the proclamation of a transcendent kingdom of God in the age to come. In such a movement, the assumption of a ready transfer of all civil penalties into the new covenant is out of place. At the same time it is irresponsible to argue, as Wink apparently does, that the Old Testament provides us with no

---

[179] *Are There Universally Valid Sex Precepts? A Critique of Walter Wink's Views on the Bible and Homosexuality* by Robert Gagnon, 102.

[180] *Homosexuality and Christian Faith* edited by Walter Wink, 37-38.

insight into God's views on any matter to which a now disused civil penalty was attached. Adultery is a good example. The Old Testament regards adultery as a capital offense; our civil jurisprudence does not. By Wink's reasoning, then, we cannot base any part of our theological views about adultery on anything that the Old Testament says. Who would argue this? Jesus certainly based his strong views on adultery at least in part on the Hebrew Bible. Yet, if we are to give any credence to the story of the woman caught in adultery in John 7:53-8:11, Jesus did not demand the death penalty for adultery. Why did Jesus skirt the death penalty? Was it because he did not regard adultery to be a severe infraction of God's will? No. In fact, Jesus expanded and deepened the injunction against adultery and warned people of the risk of being sent to hell for serial unrepentant acts of sexual immorality (Matt 5:27-32, with independent parallels in Mark 9:43-48; Mark 10:2-12; Luke 16:18) ... By analogy one can take the same stance toward same-sex intercourse: even though we do not apply the death penalty, the strong Old Testament censure of male-male intercourse is a good indication of God's abhorrence of such behavior."[181]

Still another one of Wink's examples of a biblical practice we no longer follow is **the fact that some Israelite men practiced polygamy.**[182] Most Christians today condemn this practice, and so Wink thinks this means we are free to ignore what Scripture teaches about homosexual behavior. But once again, this argument is seriously flawed!

First, in no place does Scripture ever *command* or even *commend* polygamy whereas all homosexual behavior is clearly *condemned.* Second, even though some Israelite men practiced polygamy, this does NOT mean that God approved of this behavior. The Genesis creation account clearly teaches monogamy (one woman for one man in marriage), and this is confirmed by Jesus (Matthew 19:1-12) and the apostle Paul (1st Corinthians 6:12-7:40; Ephesians 5:22-33; 1st Timothy 3:2). In addition, Old Testament texts such as Proverbs 18:22,

---

[181] *Are There Universally Valid Sex Precepts? A Critique of Walter Wink's Views on the Bible and Homosexuality* by Robert Gagnon, 91-92.

[182] *Homosexuality and Christian Faith* edited by Walter Wink, 38. **In addition, Wink's other examples of "concubinage," "prostitution" and "sex with slaves" (see pages 40-42 of his book) fall into the same category as polygamy and would also be condemned even if engaged in by a single man (see my response below regarding Wink's claim that the Old Testament did not prohibit pre-marital sex). The New Testament also clearly condemns all three behaviors!**

Ecclesiastes 9:9 and Malachi 2:15 show God wanted Israel to view monogamy as His will. God allowed polygamy for Israelite men in some cases because it was better than promiscuous sexual behavior – prostitution or pre-marital sex (which could result in pregnancy and leave a woman alone to raise a child by herself).

Therefore, God allowing polygamy among Israelite men was not unlike the reason for His decision to allow Israelite men to divorce their wives – the reason God allowed this was that their hearts were hard (see Matthew 19:7-9) and He knew they were going to do it anyway, and so He created a system (the certificate of divorce) to give women some protection. Nevertheless, Jesus and His apostles clearly teach that God now expects Christians to avoid polygamy completely. Therefore, Wink's use of Old Testament male polygamy as a reason to affirm homosexual behavior has no merit.

Two other ridiculous examples that Wink puts forward of biblical practices we no longer follow are **1) shame regarding public nudity (Wink gives the example of Ham being cursed when he saw his father, Noah, naked)** *and* **2) euphemistic terms for sexual organs (such as "foot" or "thigh").**[183] Why does Wink think these examples should affect how we understand what Scripture clearly teaches about homosexual behavior? Wink's examples do not make sense!

First of all, many people still today (both Christian and non-Christian alike) DO share similar views as the ancient Israelites on these issues. With the exception of a minority of people involved in the pornography business or nudist organizations, most people in most cultures do not approve of public nudity. Most people today also avoid referring to sexual organs unless it is necessary. Second, the New Testament clearly teaches that Christians should be modest and not cause others to sin sexually.

Regarding these two ridiculous examples, Robert Gagnon writes: "Modesty in sexual expression remains a contemporary Christian virtue and the graphic sexual character of many biblical texts still has the power to make us blush … Ham in Gen 9:20-27 is not cursed merely for 'seeing' his father's nakedness any more than the prohibition in Lev 20:17 against a man 'seeing' his sister's nakedness refers merely to

[183] *Homosexuality and Christian Faith* edited by Walter Wink, 38-39.

sight (cf. the parallel phrase 'uncover the nakedness of' in Lev 18:9 and 'lie with' in 20:11-20). Ham is cursed for having sex with his father."[184]

Yet another of Wink's examples of a biblical practice we no longer follow is **levirate marriage.**[185] Again, Wink argues that since we no longer obey this Old Testament law we are free to ignore what the whole of Scripture teaches regarding the sin of homosexual behavior. *What is levirate marriage?* Simply put, if an Israelite man died before he could have any children with his wife, then the dead man's brother was required to marry his dead brother's wife and produce children for his dead brother through his dead brother's wife in order to maintain his dead brother's family line.

The problem with this example is that levirate marriage was a temporary civil law given only to the nation of Israel. Why? God had promised Abraham that the Savior of all nations would be one of his descendants (see Genesis 12:1-3). Therefore, maintaining one's family line in Israel was very important not only because of legal inheritance issues but also because of the promise of the Messiah being a descendant of Israel.

However, once Christ completed His work of salvation the purpose for levirate marriage ceased to exist. In contrast, unlike levirate marriage, the prohibitions against homosexual behavior were also intended for Gentiles and continued to be in force for New Testament Christians.

Regarding Wink's example of levirate marriage, Gagnon writes: "Because this regulation is primarily designed to protect patrimony within the theocratic state of Israel, and indeed the property rights of the husband, it is not surprising that no New Testament author calls for its enforcement. There is no reference to a violation of this rule in New Testament vice lists, or even (to my knowledge) in vice lists in early Jewish and rabbinic texts; nor is there reference to violation of this rule as a prime indicator of human depravity. The New Testament vision of inheriting the kingdom of God is not about maintaining property rights in this world-age. This is precisely the kind of Old Testament sex precept that one would expect to pass away with the change of covenantal dispensations. So the silence of the New Testament is not

---

[184] *Are There Universally Valid Sex Precepts? A Critique of Walter Wink's Views on the Bible and Homosexuality* by Robert Gagnon, 95.

[185] *Homosexuality and Christian Faith* edited by Walter Wink, 38-39.

likely to point to a universally presumed adherence to this command … Finally, the principle of levirate marriage, unlike the proscription of same-sex intercourse, is not grounded in creation structures. And there is nothing 'unnatural' about not impregnating a dead brother's childless wife."[186]

One of the more erroneous examples that Wink offers is his idea that **the Old Testament nowhere prohibits sex between unmarried consenting heterosexual adults.**[187] Wink then points out that some Christians today believe that people should remain virgins until marriage, in conflict, according to Wink, with the teaching of the Old Testament. Wink then uses this as an example of inconsistency and a reason why we can ignore what Scripture teaches about homosexual behavior. How do we answer this?

Simply put, Wink is just plain wrong concerning the Old Testament's teaching about pre-marital sex. Even though we don't find a specific prohibition against pre-marital sex as we do with homosexual behavior, the sin of pre-marital sex is simply assumed. The Genesis creation account assumes that sex is to be reserved for marriage only - *and the New Testament clearly confirms this!* Also, whenever pre-marital sex did take place in the Old Testament it was frowned upon, compared to prostitution, and in some cases there were penalties![188] In addition, contrary to Wink, The Song of Songs clearly teaches that one is to remain a virgin until marriage.[189]

Regarding the issue of pre-marital sex in The Song of Songs, Robert Gagnon writes: "At one point the male lover likens his beloved to a garden that no one has yet entered (4:12). The young woman is described as facially veiled (4:1, 3), suggesting modesty on her part and imagination on the part of the male lover in describing her erotic attractiveness. The Song also contains a thrice-repeated adjuration to

---

[186] *Are There Universally Valid Sex Precepts? A Critique of Walter Wink's Views on the Bible and Homosexuality* by Robert Gagnon, 99-100.

[187] *Homosexuality and Christian Faith* edited by Walter Wink, 39.

[188] In Exodus 22:16-17 we see that if a man "seduces" (meaning the woman is a willing participant!) a virgin woman who is not betrothed to any man, they are required to marry!

[189] For detailed evidence of this, see the Concordia Commentary *The Song of Songs* by Christopher Mitchell.

the daughters of Jerusalem that could be read as a warning not to kindle erotic passion until the day of one's wedding (2:7; 3:5; 8:4)."[190]

Wink also offers as an example of Old Testament teaching we no longer follow **the Levitical purity regulations regarding semen and menstrual blood.**[191] Wink then suggests that since we no longer follow these laws we are free to ignore what Scripture teaches about homosexuality. *I have already dealt with this issue on pp. 61-62 of this book.* Simply put, the purity regulations regarding semen and menstrual blood are found in Leviticus chapter 15 where we clearly see that we are dealing with ceremonial laws given only to Israel for a temporary period of time. Unlike homosexual behavior, these purity regulations did not apply to the Gentiles. In addition, these purity laws were fulfilled in Christ whereas the prohibitions against homosexual behavior are still in force.

Wink then points to evidence which suggests that **women were viewed as property in Old Testament Israel**[192] – and then, like the other examples, Wink argues that since we no longer treat women like property this supposedly means we are free to ignore what Scripture teaches about homosexual behavior. The problem with this example is that the Old Testament never commands or condones the mistreatment of women. Instead, the Old Testament prohibits abuse and regulates the way men treat women. When we get to the New Testament we see that Jesus and the apostles appeal to the Genesis creation account (before the fall into sin) as the basis for men respecting women as well as loving and serving their wives. So, the few examples of women being mistreated in the Old Testament are not *condoned* by God! In contrast, the Scriptures clearly *condemn* homosexual behavior along with other sexual sins.

In response to Wink's example of Old Testament women being treated as property, Gagnon writes: "Wink's listing of ... the **'treatment of women as property'** is also a bad analogy to the Bible's proscription of same-sex intercourse, for many reasons. (a) This is not a proscription of a type of sexual intercourse. (b) There is no biblical proscription against the obverse. (c) 'Property' has to be seriously

---

[190] *Are There Universally Valid Sex Precepts? A Critique of Walter Wink's Views on the Bible and Homosexuality* by Robert Gagnon, 109.

[191] *Homosexuality and Christian Faith* edited by Walter Wink, 39-40.

[192] *Homosexuality and Christian Faith* edited by Walter Wink, 40.

qualified in the same way that treatment of children as property in the Old Testament has to be qualified (i.e., there are numerous ways in which their treatment differs from the treatment of inanimate property or animals). (d) There are many examples of a more liberating dynamic to women within the Bible itself, particularly the New Testament but also in the Old ... (e) The biblical view of women looks good in comparison to the broader cultural environments out of which this view emerged. Finally, (f) in Christian circles today we do not do away entirely with a sense of belongingness and obligation in marriage; rather we equalize it mutually between husband and wife in a manner already foreshadowed in 1 Cor 7:2-5 and other texts."[193]

Another example of Old Testament teaching we no longer follow, according to Wink, **is the idea that life-long celibacy was abnormal.**[194] Since the New Testament and some modern Christians have no problem with people who choose not to marry and remain celibate, Wink suggests that since we choose to ignore the Old Testament view about life-long celibacy being abnormal we are also free to ignore what Scripture teaches about homosexual behavior.

The problem with this example is that even though Old Testament Israel encouraged marriage it never condemned those who chose to remain single and celibate. Therefore, even though Old Testament Israel viewed singleness/celibacy as "abnormal" or "not the norm," it NEVER condemned it as sin. In contrast, the Old Testament clearly condemns homosexual behavior as sin. In addition, even though the New Testament seems to be more open to singleness/celibacy, the reasons for this are 1) the fulfillment of Christ's work does away with the emphasis on most Israelites marrying and having children (because the Messiah was to come from their nation), and 2) singleness/celibacy is only encouraged for those who wish to do so for the sake of having more time to serve Christ's Church. Nevertheless, marriage is still expected to be the norm even in the New Testament – not just for laypeople but also for <u>pastors</u> (see 1st Corinthians 9:5, 1st Timothy 3:2, Titus 1:6). Therefore, modern day Christians are not being inconsistent

---

[193] *Are There Universally Valid Sex Precepts? A Critique of Walter Wink's Views on the Bible and Homosexuality* by Robert Gagnon, 96-97.

[194] *Homosexuality and Christian Faith* edited by Walter Wink, 41.

if they affirm a minority of people who choose to remain single and celibate.

In response to Wink's celibacy example, Gagnon writes: "while there is generally a strong expectation of marriage in the Old Testament (with exceptions), there is neither an explicit proscription against nor penalty, imposed for celibacy … There is no radical overhauling of a pointed Old Testament proscription and what shift there is, manifested already in the New Testament, exists partially as a result of the change of covenantal dispensations: the shift to Gentile mission and conversion makes physical procreation less vital for the preservation of God's people."[195]

In addition, Wink also points to the fact that **ancient Israel allowed girls to marry at a very young age (sometimes as young as 11).** [196] Since most modern nations do not allow this, Wink uses this as an example of why we need not obey what Scripture teaches about homosexual behavior. But once again, this is a very flawed example!

Even though Old Testament Israel allowed some girls to marry at a very young age, they almost always waited until the girl/woman had reached puberty and child-bearing age. Many of our elderly married couples today were married as young teenagers! Even though we should rightly condemn abuse of children, in no place does the Bible give a specific age for when it is proper for a girl/woman to marry. The assumption is that a girl/woman is ready to marry when she has reached puberty and child-bearing age. Just because women today often choose to wait until they are much older before getting married does not mean that we are disobeying a command of Scripture because in no place does Scripture ever command that a girl/woman should get married at a particular age! In contrast, the Scripture is very clear that homosexual behavior is to be condemned as sinful.

Regarding Wink's example of Israelite girls getting married at a young age, Gagnon responds: "Wink lists … **very early marriage**, especially among girls, as another analogue. It is questionable how widespread this practice may have been in ancient Israel, let alone early Christian circles. Regardless, in ancient cultures a significantly shorter

---

[195] *Are There Universally Valid Sex Precepts? A Critique of Walter Wink's Views on the Bible and Homosexuality* by Robert Gagnon, 96.

[196] *Homosexuality and Christian Faith* edited by Walter Wink, 43.

lifespan and a significantly higher infant mortality rate perhaps necessitated some compromises in minimum age requirements for marriage in order to increase the chances for childbearing. Most importantly, since the Bible nowhere mandates marriage at an early age, we do not override any strong biblical proscription when we prohibit marriage to those under the ages of 16, 17, or 18. Even in our own culture we would have to admit that these are not magic numbers: within any given culture some people above the minimum age limit may exhibit less maturity than some a few years below that age limit. Different social mechanisms across cultures, ancient and modern, can also affect maturity levels. For example, the minimum marriage age in our culture is partly conditioned by a relatively lengthy period of schooling. Furthermore, there is no evidence that sexual relationships with prepubescent girls were ever allowed in ancient Israel or early Christianity - one more element that Wink could add to a list of biblical sexual mores that we would agree in rejecting."[197]

Wink also mentions **the practice of exogamy (Israelite men marrying only Israelite women and not Gentiles) as the normal practice in Old Testament Israel**[198] (although Wink admits there were exceptions). Wink points to a similar practice in the American south when white people were not allowed to marry black people. Then Wink notes that most people in our modern world do not put such limitations on whom people can choose to marry. He then argues that since we no longer imitate this Old Testament practice we are now free to ignore what Scripture teaches about homosexual behavior. Sadly, Wink is again guilty of faulty reasoning.

First, Wink's comparison of racial segregation in the American South with the Old Testament practice of exogamy is in error. The reason for Old Testament Israel's exogamy had nothing to do with racial segregation. Instead, the practice of exogamy was to keep believers (Israelites who trusted the One, True God) from being led astray by unbelievers (pagan Gentiles who worshipped false gods) – and this could especially happen when a believer married an unbeliever! We see the same teaching in the New Testament where Paul stresses that Christians should marry only other Christians. What is interesting is that the Bible in no place condemns intermarriage

---

[197] *Are There Universally Valid Sex Precepts? A Critique of Walter Wink's Views on the Bible and Homosexuality* by Robert Gagnon, 97-98.

[198] *Homosexuality and Christian Faith* edited by Walter Wink, 40.

between people of different races because the Bible assumes that there is only ONE race – the HUMAN race, descended from Adam and Eve (see Acts 17:26).

Second, Wink fails to show how Israel's practice of exogamy for SPIRITUAL reasons relates to the issue of homosexual behavior. In fact, one of the reasons God commanded that Israel not intermarry with unbelievers is that Israel might thereby be tempted to engage in many of the sinful behaviors practiced by unbelievers at that time – *one of those sinful behaviors being homosexuality!* Therefore, Israel's example of exogamy for SPIRITUAL reasons actually supports the argument for upholding Scripture's condemnation of homosexual behavior.

In response to Wink's exogamy argument, Gagnon writes: "...(marriage to non-Israelites) in the Old Testament, especially in the post-exilic period, also shifts in the new covenant dispensation with the new program of God for active mission to Gentiles. Again, this shift is firmly ensconced already in the New Testament. In addition, the concern for exogamy is in the first instance a concern about exclusive religious allegiance to the God of Israel. A strong reservation about marriage to unbelievers continues in the New Testament (1 Cor 7:12-16, 39; cf. 2 Cor 6:14-18). There are also plenty of positive instances of marriages to Gentile women in the Old Testament, of which the story of Ruth is the prime example."[199]

Yet another example Wink offers of an Old Testament prohibition we no longer follow **is masturbation.**[200] Wink suggests that since even many Christians today do not completely condemn masturbation in all cases, this then means we can ignore what Scripture teaches about homosexual behavior. However, Wink is totally off base on this example.

First, contrary to Wink's assertion, there is NO Old Testament prohibition (or New Testament, for that matter) against masturbation. *(I have already shown in footnote #65 that the example of Onan in Genesis 38:8-10 has nothing to do with masturbation!)* Second, even though there is no biblical prohibition against masturbation there are many Christians today who recognize that masturbation can be

---

[199] *Are There Universally Valid Sex Precepts? A Critique of Walter Wink's Views on the Bible and Homosexuality* by Robert Gagnon, 96.

[200] *Homosexuality and Christian Faith* edited by Walter Wink, 42-43.

associated with sinful behavior in many cases (for example, if masturbation is accompanied by lustful thoughts or leads to self-indulgent behavior apart from sexual activity with one's spouse). In contrast, Scripture has clear prohibitions against homosexual behavior.

Gagnon responds to Wink's masturbation example with these words: "**Masturbation** is another weak analogy. (a) There is nothing about masturbation in the Old Testament (the story about Onan 'spilling his semen' in Gen 38:8-10 is not about masturbation) so its degree of significance is questionable. (b) The one who broadens the law's sphere to include 'adultery of the heart' is none other than Jesus (Matt 5:27-28), certainly relevant to the issue of masturbation ... Contemporary ecclesiastical approval of masturbation, then, would be inappropriate. (c) Consistent with this understanding is the fact there is no 'masturbation lobby' in the church today advocating that we should celebrate masturbation as part of a broad diversity of sexual expression that God allegedly gives us in Christ. (d) The church's response to masturbation is of one piece with its response to adultery (or fornication) of the heart: the church recognizes it as an ongoing problem - like any attempt to deal with sin in one's thought life. The church does not encourage it or endorse it. However, the fact that it is normally done in private without any direct involvement of, knowledge by, or impact on another does not make it a suitable issue for church discipline. (e) Most - including Wink, I suppose - rightly recognize that, so far as church action is concerned, there is a significant difference between the public effects of someone committing concrete acts of adultery with other persons and the public effects of someone stimulating him- or herself through mental fantasies."[201]

Wink also mentions the issue of **birth control**[202] as a reason we can ignore what the Scriptures say about homosexual behavior – but why Wink uses this example is not at all clear. First, in no place does the Bible condemn the use of birth control (although Scripture's teaching against abortion would lead us to conclude that

---

[201] *Are There Universally Valid Sex Precepts? A Critique of Walter Wink's Views on the Bible and Homosexuality* by Robert Gagnon, 97.

[202] *Homosexuality and Christian Faith* edited by Walter Wink, 42-43.

methods of "birth control" that end a human life that has *already been conceived* would be condemned). Second, even though Genesis encourages Adam and Eve to be "fruitful and multiply," it gives no commands as to how many children they must have. In contrast, Scripture has clear condemnations against all forms of homosexual behavior.

Regarding Wink's birth control example, Gagnon writes: "**Birth control** is not comparable to same-sex intercourse. There are no pointed prohibitions of birth control in the Bible, let alone any of a severe, pervasive, and absolute nature. Some would construe the creation command to be fruitful and multiply as necessarily precluding all birth control but this is not a necessary inference. Scripture does not forbid sex with infertile spouses and in various places celebrates sexual pleasure in marriage in its own right. There is considerably more ambiguity concerning the Bible's posture on this issue than on same-sex intercourse. The degree of abhorrence expressed for same-sex inter-course is a world away."[203]

Finally, one last example Wink uses is **divorce.**[204] Wink points out that even though Jesus condemned divorce, the modern Christian church allows it. This supposedly means we should also affirm homosexual behavior. *But this is NOT a very good analogy at all!*

First, just because some modern day Christians ignore what Scripture teaches about divorce does NOT mean that we are now free to ignore what Scripture teaches about homosexuality. *Wink's argument suggests that two wrongs make a right!* Instead, we should call modern Christians to repentance regarding the sin of divorce. In the same way, we should call modern Christians to repentance regarding their refusal to submit to Scripture's teaching on homosexual behavior.

Second, even though both the Old and New Testaments clearly teach that God despises divorce because He wants marriages to stay together (Malachi 2:15-16, Matthew 19:1-6, 1st Corinthians 7:10-11), the Bible also recognizes that there are situations where a divorce may

---

[203] *Are There Universally Valid Sex Precepts? A Critique of Walter Wink's Views on the Bible and Homosexuality* by Robert Gagnon, 98.

[204] *Homosexuality and Christian Faith* edited by Walter Wink, 41.

be necessary (Deuteronomy 24:1-4, Matthew 19:8-9, 1st Corinthians 7:12-16) – such as in cases of unrepentant adultery, desertion or other kinds of "evil abuse" (which would be a kind of "desertion" from one's marriage vows).

Lastly, most Christian churches I know of today do NOT affirm divorce in direct conflict with Scripture's teaching - *as many are doing with homosexual behavior!* Wink makes it sound like most churches today are celebrating divorce as an "alternate lifestyle." This is simply not the case! When married couples do get divorced they are first encouraged to remain single and to try to reconcile. If this is simply not possible, then they are told to 1) confess their sins that led to the divorce, 2) trust in the forgiveness that Christ gives to repentant sinners, and 3) be willing to follow God's will for marriage if He ever gives them another opportunity to marry. **In other words, people who get divorced are told to repent and not do it again!** This is a far cry from those (like Wink) who want us to ignore what Scripture teaches about homosexual behavior and affirm it as a God-pleasing lifestyle.

If one actually wants to use divorce as an analogy to affirm homosexual behavior, then one would have to make the following argument: "Not only do I think we should ignore what Scripture teaches about the evil of divorce. I think we should celebrate divorce as a godly lifestyle! I think people should be encouraged to get divorced and remarried as often as possible because we now consider divorce to be a behavior we ought to affirm!" But what Christians today are making this kind of argument about divorce? NONE!

Therefore, if we are to make any comparison between Scripture's teaching on divorce and Scripture's teaching on homosexual behavior it should be this: "God condemns all homosexual behavior. However, if you struggle with homosexual desires and behaviors, you can come to Jesus with those sins and know that you are forgiven by His sacrifice for you. This same Jesus will help you to live a pure life as He nurtures your faith in Him through His gifts you receive in His Church and through the support of your fellow brothers and sisters in Christ." In other words, we say to people who struggle with homosexuality the same thing that we say to people who are guilty of the sin of divorce: "Repent of your sin. Trust in the forgiveness you have in Christ. Turn away from this behavior and conform your life to God's loving will."

In response to Wink's divorce analogy, Gagnon writes these words: "[Jesus] saw that 'Moses' had made a concession to human - primarily male – 'hardness of heart' in the domain of sexual fidelity and monogamy, and removed the concession. Then he went even further than the OT restrictions on women by declaring that both the person who divorces and remarries and the person who remarries a divorced person commit adultery. So Jesus' stance on limiting the number of lifetime sex partners to one appears to be clear. Most pro-homosex advocates then contend that the deviation of current church doctrine and practice from Jesus' teaching on divorce provides a precedent for deviating from the strong New Testament view against same-sex intercourse ... Wink goes so far as to suggest ... that Jesus was more staunchly opposed to divorce than to homoerotic intercourse, if indeed he was opposed to the latter at all. Wink has not adequately thought through the matter. Shall we claim that Jesus felt less strongly about bestiality and incest on the grounds that he said not a word about these subjects? Jesus said nothing directly about such extreme forms of sexual immorality simply because the position of the Hebrew Bible on such matters was so unequivocal and visceral, and the stance of early Judaism (Palestinian and Diaspora) so undivided, with the incidence of concrete violations so rare, that nothing needed to be said - unless, of course, he had a different view, which he clearly did not have. There was no reason for him to spend time addressing issues that were not points of contention in his own cultural context and on which he had no dissenting view. Jesus could turn his attention to a sexual issue that was a problem in his society: the threat posed by divorce to the indissolubility of the one valid form of sexual union - the matrimony of one man and one woman. Jesus did not loosen the restrictions on sexual freedom; he tightened them, albeit in the context of an aggressive outreach to the lost. When Jesus cited back-to-back Gen 1:27 ("male and female he made them") and Gen 2:24 ("For this reason a man . . . will be joined to his woman [wife], and the two will become one flesh") he obviously understood - with all other Jews of his day - that an absolutely essential prerequisite to any valid marital union was that the two participants be male and female, man and woman. That Jesus used these two Scripture texts to focus on the 'God made' and the 'will be joined' - thereby emphasizing the divinely intended indissolubility of the union of male and female, husband and wife - in no way suggests that he regarded the gender of the participants as nonessential. Indeed, the precise opposite conclusion is the only logical and historically reasonable option. Both the Scriptures that Jesus cited with approval and the audience that Jesus addressed presumed the complementary male and female genders of the two participants as an essential prerequisite. It is also evident, by comparison with bestiality and incest, that Jesus did not regard the monogamous permanence of a given sexual union to be more important than the intrahuman, nonincestuous, and heterosexual prerequisites. If the longevity and fidelity of a sexual union had been the most important components for Jesus, then Jesus could not have been absolutely opposed to any form of sexual union, so long as it showed evidence of endurance. But as it is, longevity and fidelity would not have constituted for Jesus sufficient reason to validate incest and bestiality. The same would have held for same-sex intercourse. Bestiality, same-sex intercourse, and incest - in that order- were more severe infractions of God's will for human sexuality than short-term relationships. Only after these prerequisites were met- and others, such as the non-paying, non-coercive, and adult dimensions - would issues such as longevity and fidelity have come into play."[205]

Now that we have examined all of Wink's examples of Old Testament sexual or non-sexual behaviors or practices that we no longer follow we can clearly see how NONE of them can be used to suggest that we should ignore what Scripture clearly teaches about homosexual behavior being sinful.

After giving us his list of sexual and non-sexual behaviors from Scripture that we no longer follow, Wink then mentions four examples of sexual prohibitions from Scripture that most Christians DO follow today, and those are: **incest, rape, adultery and bestiality.**

However, what Wink completely fails to understand is that most Christians agree with Scripture on these issues because Scripture itself clearly teaches that these four sexual prohibitions are still in force. In contrast, Wink would argue that even these four sexual prohibitions (incest, rape, adultery and bestiality) are not examples of universal sex laws from Scripture that are still in force today. Instead, Wink would argue that we do not condone incest, rape, adultery and bestiality today because they do not meet the criteria of Jesus' "love ethic" – *a "love ethic" that Wink uses to AFFIRM homosexual behavior!*

However, what Wink fails to see (or refuses to see) is that incest, rape, adultery and bestiality are condemned in Scripture for the very same reason that all forms of homosexual behavior are condemned in Scripture – because they are ALL opposed to God's will for our sexual behavior, *and God's will for our sexual behavior is not changed by Wink's idea of Jesus' "love ethic."*

---

[205] *Are There Universally Valid Sex Precepts? A Critique of Walter Wink's Views on the Bible and Homosexuality* by Robert Gagnon, 113-115.

Once again, let's hear about Wink's idea of Jesus' "love ethic" with his own words: "The crux of the matter … is simply that the Bible has no sexual ethic … The Bible knows only a love ethic, which is constantly being brought to bear on whatever sexual mores are dominant in any given country, or culture, or period … Just within one lifetime we have witnessed the shift from the ideal of preserving one's virginity until marriage to couples living together for several years before getting married … So we must critique the sexual mores of any given time and clime by the love ethic exemplified by Jesus. Such a love ethic is nonexploitative (hence no sexual exploitation of children, no using of another to his or her loss); it does not dominate (hence no patriarchal treatment of women as chattel); it is responsible, mutual, caring, and loving. Augustine already dealt with this in his inspired phrase, 'Love God, and do as you please.'"

Do you see the problem with Wink's "love ethic" argument? This "love ethic" that Wink uses to affirm homosexual behavior within ***non-exploitative, non-dominating, responsible, mutual, caring, loving*** relationships can also be used to affirm at least adultery, incest and even bestiality!

For example, there are some people today who have what are called "open marriages" (spouses allowing each other to have sex with other people). Scripture clearly condemns this as adultery, but we could use Wink's "love ethic" to affirm such "open marriages." As long as such "open marriages" were ***non-exploitative, non-dominating, responsible, mutual, caring, and loving*** (as some who practice "open marriage" argue that they are!) we would have no reason NOT to affirm them! In fact, you would be considered a bigot if you didn't! (Just as some accuse Christians like me of being bigots because we believe homosexual behavior is sinful.)

What about incest between a brother/sister or mother/son or father/daughter (or brother/brother, mother/daughter, father/son – to include *homosexual* incestuous examples)? We could also use Wink's "love ethic" to affirm such incestuous relationships as long as they were ***non-exploitative, non-dominating, responsible, mutual, caring, and loving*** - as some today who practice incest actually insist is the case!

Of course, some would argue: "It would be exploitation if children were involved!" But what if the "children" involved – the son or daughter – are consenting adults? Not a problem then! But some would then argue: "What if they have children? There would be risk of birth defects." Answer: "What if they used birth control or had operations to make themselves incapable of having children? Problem solved!" At this point one would have to affirm such incestuous relationships if one used Wink's "love ethic" instead of Scripture as a standard for proper sexual behavior.

What about bestiality? "That's gross!" you say. But there are people today who want to have their "bestiality lifestyle" at least tolerated or, ideally, affirmed! Such people would argue that it's possible to have a sexual relationship with an animal that is ***non-exploitative, non-dominating, responsible, mutual, caring, and loving.*** They have a point! Just as there are animals that appear to enjoy <u>homosexual</u> behavior, there may also be animals that would find pleasure from a sexual relationship with a <u>human being</u>. Once again, how can we dare argue against this if we use Wink's "love ethic" instead of Scripture as a standard for proper sexual behavior?

At this point we can also see how we could use Wink's "love ethic" to affirm polygamy, polyamory (group marriage between several men and women together) and *even adult sex with pre-pubescent minor children!* That's right! What if a pre-pubescent minor child insists that he/she enjoys sex with an adult, gives his/her consent, and this sexual relationship is ***non-exploitative, non-dominating, responsible, mutual, caring, and loving?*** We can't argue against such things if we use Wink's "love ethic" as the standard for proper sexual behavior.

When Wink insists that he is opposed to adultery, incest and bestiality while at the same he uses his "love ethic" to affirm ***non-exploitative, non-dominating, responsible, mutual, caring, and loving*** <u>homosexual</u> behavior he is simply being inconsistent and completely arbitrary!

In contrast, when Christians use the clear teaching of Holy Scripture to condemn consensual homosexual behavior along with adultery, incest, rape and bestiality we are thereby being completely consistent and NOT arbitrary in any way!

When Jesus taught us to "love our neighbor" He did NOT mean that "anything goes" as long as the behavior is ***non-exploitative, non-dominating, responsible, mutual, caring, and loving.*** Instead, Jesus taught that one of the greatest ways we can love others is to proclaim repentance and forgiveness of sins – *and this includes telling people to repent of their homosexual behavior and receive forgiveness from Christ for that sin.*

Finally, in an attempt to give credibility to his twisted "love ethic," Wink *misquotes* the fourth century Church father, Augustine.

Regarding his "love ethic," Wink quotes Augustine as follows: "Augustine already dealt with this in his inspired phrase, 'Love God, and do as you please.'" Wink is using this quote from Augustine to suggest that as long as we "love God" (whatever that means) we are free to live as we please as long as our behavior is ***non-exploitative, non-dominating, responsible, mutual, caring, and loving.***

However, since I don't want to accuse Wink of being deliberately deceptive, I must conclude that he simply did not read Augustine's quote within its context – *because Augustine's quote read in context actually REFUTES Wink's "love ethic" argument!*

Robert Gagnon has done an excellent job exposing Wink's error regarding his quote from Augustine. Therefore, read these words from Gagnon: "This is another example of Wink taking a text out of context and grossly distorting its meaning. Indeed, one has to wonder whether he ever examined the original context for the quote that he loves so much. The saying is taken from Augustine's Ten Homilies on the First Epistle of John 7.8. It reads in Latin: Dilige, et quod vis fac ('Love, and what you want do'). In context, the implied object of the love may be 'one another' or 'your neighbor' rather than 'God.' Regardless, Wink's interpretation stands in serious tension with Augustine's application of his own words. Wink applies the words to support his contention that the Bible has no sex ethic and no universally valid sex precept but only a communal love ethic. Wink makes this application within a broader context that calls for tolerance and finds Scripture's restriction of sex to marriage between a man and a woman to be cruel. Augustine, for his part, gives no hint that he understands his own words as a denial of universally valid moral precepts. Rather, Augustine formulates the saying to show that love cannot be watered down to mean gentleness, permissiveness, and tolerance. A father disciplines rigorously his child, while a 'boy-stealer' caresses a boy. Which expresses love? The one who disciplines (7.8). So if you act out of love you can do what you want - **meaning that you can implement strong disciplinary measures for the purpose of turning someone away from sinful behavior. Conversely, if one does not act in love, actions that to the eye seem loving would in fact be cruel.**" [206]

[Gagnon now gives us the context for Wink's Augustine quote]

If any of you perhaps wish to maintain love, brethren, above all things do not imagine it to be an abject and sluggish thing; nor that love is to

[206] **Bold** and *italic* emphasis is mine.

> be preserved by a sort of gentleness, nay not gentleness, but tameness and listlessness. Not so is it preserved. Do not imagine that . . . you then love your son when you do not give him discipline, or that you then love your neighbor when you do not rebuke him. This is not love, but mere feebleness. Let love be fervent to correct, to amend. . . . Love not in the person his error, but the person; for the person God made, the error the person himself made.

[The Gagnon response continues below]

"There is a certain irony here. Wink argues in his review that restricting sex to heterosexual marriage is necessarily a 'cruel abuse of religious power.' Yet a proper application of Augustine's saying would suggest the opposite conclusion; namely, that this restriction, however hard it may seem to some, is an act of love. How so? Because it has in view things better than the mere satisfaction of sinful erotic impulses: conformity to God's life-giving will, transformation into the image of Christ by taking up one's cross, and, ultimately, inheritance of the kingdom of God. This is at least the perspective on discipleship taken by Jesus and Scripture generally, which Augustine certainly shared. For Augustine 'incorruption of chastity' fell under the rubric of love (8.1). To be sure, any restriction or discipline can be cruel if it is not motivated by love and correction. Thus: 'Even if you are severe at any time, let it be because of love, for correction' (7.11). Yet, by the same token, tolerance of behavior that Scripture pervasively deems egregious sin is also unloving. God 'loved the unrighteous, but he did away with the unrighteousness. . . [and] did not gather them together into (or: for) unrighteousness' (7.7). In another context Augustine states: 'The one who loves God loves his precepts' (10.3). ***So to 'love and do what you want' means, in Augustine's view, that it is entirely within the purview of love to apply strong measures to persons when the intent is correction and the goal is salvation. Undoubtedly, Augustine would have been appalled by Wink's reverse application of the saying in order to excuse behavior that Scripture abhors.***[207] Reading on in the same work we can see an additional irony. As noted above, Wink finds the notion of a God who might exclude any from his kingdom, on any grounds, to be 'reprehensible.' What would Augustine have said about this? We have an answer in Augustine's comments on 1 John 4:17: 'Love has been perfected among us in this: that we may have boldness on the Day of Judgment.' Augustine refers to people 'who do not believe in a Day of Judgment; these cannot have boldness in a Day

---

[207] **Bold** and *italic* emphasis is mine.

which they do not believe will come.' However, persons who correct themselves by putting to death sinful desires and deeds, including sexual 'uncleanness' (Col 3:5), learn to desire what they once feared: the Day of Judgment (9.2). This is a message from Augustine that Wink should consider adding to his repertoire."[208]

The Bible condones slavery!

About three years ago a pastor in the United Church of Christ wrote a letter to the editor of the newspaper in my community. Simply put, he argued that we should be willing to affirm homosexuality even though the Bible appears to condemn it. Why? The reason he gave was that Scripture approves of slavery. Therefore, he argued, since we no longer approve of slavery today we a free to ignore what Scripture teaches about homosexual behavior - *implying that Scripture can't be taken seriously on moral issues because is supposedly condones slavery.*

However, people who suggest that we can ignore what the Bible teaches about homosexual behavior because the same Bible also supposedly condones slavery are not consistent! These same people usually approve when the same Bible condemns adultery (Leviticus 18:20), bestiality (Leviticus 18:23), injustice (Leviticus 19:15) and theft (Leviticus 19:11) as well as commanding that we love one another (Leviticus 19:17-18). In addition, as we will see, the Bible does NOT condone *all forms* of slavery! Therefore, it is wrong to use the issue of slavery as a reason to reject the authority of Holy Scripture on the issue of homosexual behavior.

At this point I must stress that some are guilty of the opposite error. Some people teach that the Bible condemns *all forms* of slavery. But the fact is that in both the Old and New Testaments we see that certain forms of slavery were tolerated and regulated -- ***even though the institution of slavery itself was not commanded or condoned.*** Simply put, Christians need to be able to give an intelligent answer to those who ask honest questions about the Bible's teaching on slavery.

---

[208] *Are There Universally Valid Sex Precepts? A Critique of Walter Wink's Views on the Bible and Homosexuality* by Robert Gagnon, 87-89.

So, what DOES the Bible teach about slavery?[209] First, we must be willing to define the word "slavery." There were various types of slavery in the ancient world – all of them found in the Bible: **1)** One type of slavery was for those who were guilty of criminal behavior – a kind of prison sentence. **2)** Another type of slavery was for prisoners of war. **3)** There were also some people who WILLINGLY entered into a contract of slavery to ensure they would not be homeless or starve to death. **4)** There were some people who were forced to be slaves against their will – even though they were not criminals or prisoners of war.

Even though the Bible *tolerates* and *regulates* the first three forms of slavery, it never *condones* such slavery nor does it *command* it! As for the fourth type of slavery, the Bible is clear that such slavery should not exist. Sadly, some hardened their hearts and practiced such slavery anyway.

In fact, one major difference between the slavery found in the Bible and the slavery that was practiced in the American South has to do with the issue of racism. We find NO support for **race-based slavery** in Scripture![210] (In fact, race-based slavery was very rare even among *unbelievers* of the ancient world.) *Therefore, those who used Scripture to justify race-based slavery in the American South were guilty of reading their own opinions into the pages of Holy Scripture!*

The Bible clearly teaches that all humans are descended from one man, Adam! (See Luke 3:23-38 & Acts 17:26). According to Scripture, there is really only one race – the HUMAN race!

---

[209] The subject of slavery in Scripture is far beyond the scope of this paper. For a thorough treatment of the issue of slavery in Holy Scripture, see the Concordia Commentary *Philemon* by John Nordling.

[210] On page 75 of his commentary *Philemon* John Nordling writes: "'Race relations' were quite different in antiquity from what many today merely assume them to have been. Truth-seeking Christians of all races and ethnicities should not read modernist perspectives into the ancient texts – and especially not into the NT." Nordling then provides this quote from *Before Color Prejudice* by Snowden: "In antiquity slavery was independent of race or class, and by far the vast majority of the thousands of slaves was white, not black. The identification of blackness with slavery did not develop. No single ethnic group was associated with slave status or with the descendents of slaves. The Negro as slave or freedman was in a no more disadvantageous position than anyone else unfortunate enough to be captured as a prisoner of war or to be enslaved for some other reason." After this quote from Snowden, Nordling writes: "The inhumane idea that brutal slavery should exploit black Africans and other people of color developed, apparently, in early modern times."

But why doesn't Scripture simply forbid all forms of slavery and insist that Christians free their slaves? First, some Christians DID free their slaves! Second, many slaves did NOT wish to be freed because this would have meant homelessness and starvation in their ancient culture.

However, in complete contrast with the pagan culture of his day, the apostle Paul writes the following to Christians who have slaves: **"Masters, provide for your slaves what is right and fair, because you know that you also have a Master in heaven." (Colossians 4:1)** Paul also writes: **"...masters ... do not threaten [your slaves], since you know that he who is both their Master and yours is in heaven, and there is no favoritism with him." (Ephesians 6:9)**

Therefore, contrary to what some wrongly teach, the Bible does NOT condone much less command slavery – *especially not the kind of race-based slavery we had in the American South.* Instead, the Bible tolerated and regulated an institution that was part of ancient culture – even forbidding certain practices that could not be reconciled with Christ's teaching.

The Old Testament book of Exodus shows how God delivered His people from slavery in Egypt! The New Testament book of Philemon shows how the Gospel of Christ was beginning to transform the institution of slavery already in Paul's day!

Therefore, those who want to blame the institution of slavery on the teaching of Holy Scripture are simply in error. In fact, it is the teaching of Holy Scripture – *especially the Gospel message!* - that is responsible for the abolition of slavery in many places around the world!

With that understood, we must note how the Bible teaches that the greatest evil is not physical slavery but our SPIRITUAL slavery to **SIN** that is based on our rejection of God's Word! (See John 8:31-47, Romans 6:6 & 2nd Peter 2:17-22)

Therefore, those who point to slavery in the Bible as a reason to ignore the Bible's clear condemnation of all forms of homosexual behavior are dooming those whom they mislead to a SPIRITUAL "slavery" that is far worse than any physical slavery experienced by any slave – past or present. *As we've already learned, in no place does the Bible command or condone slavery. In contrast, the Bible very clearly condemns all forms of homosexual behavior for all times and places!*

Of course, the Good News is that our Master, Jesus, willingly sacrificed Himself to atone for our sins so that we might be forgiven and set free FROM our slavery to sin and set free FOR a life lived in conformity to God's loving plan for us! (See John 10:14-18, Romans 6:1-23, Galatians 5:13-26, Colossians 1:21-23, Hebrews 9:14-15 and 1st Peter 2:16-25)

The Bible condones the oppression of women!

Many who want to ignore what Scripture clearly teaches about homosexual behavior being sinful will attempt to discredit Scripture as a whole by suggesting that the Bible condones the oppression of women. Their argument goes like this: "In our modern world we treat women with respect and as equals with men. But the Bible is filled with examples of women being treated as second class citizens and even being abused. Since we no longer follow what the Bible teaches about women we are then obviously justified in rejecting what the Bible teaches about homosexual behavior." How do we answer this argument?

First of all, we must understand that Scripture does NOT condone the oppression of women! In Genesis chapters 1 & 2 we see that Eve was created in God's image along with Adam. Even though they had different roles and functions as male and female, they were both of equal worth before God!

But what about what God Himself says to Eve after she rebelled against Him? Genesis 3:16 reads: "I will greatly increase your pains in childbearing; with pain you will give birth to children. Your desire will be for your husband, and he will rule over you." What are we to make of this?

Regarding **women's pain during childbirth,** this is one of the ways that God reminds women that they live in a fallen world. All of the various types of suffering that we endure as sinners are God's way of reminding us that we live in a world that is in bondage to decay because of our rebellion against Him. But this suffering is intended to humble us so that we joyfully receive the Good News that we have forgiveness and the hope of a New Creation in Jesus. (See Romans 8:18-39) In addition, we need to remember that God also cursed Adam with suffering as well as with death – not just for himself but for ALL humanity (see Genesis 3:17-19 and Romans 5:12-14).

Now, this doesn't mean that it is sinful for people to try to alleviate the suffering that we experience in this fallen world. Even though God has cursed us with suffering to remind us that this is a fallen world, God also mercifully gives us much relief from suffering and even many experiences of pleasure. Therefore, women can certainly make use of any gifts God provides that would help them ease their pain during childbirth – for example, many of the pain relief drugs or treatments available from modern medicine.

However, even though God's gift of modern medicine alleviates much of the suffering and pain we would otherwise experience, the fact is that we STILL suffer. Even with the pain relief available from modern medicine, childbirth can still be a painful experience for women – a reminder that we do not live in the perfect creation that God created in the beginning.

Regarding what God says about **the husband ruling over his wife**, we must understand that this was NOT part of God's plan for the husband and wife relationship in His "very good" creation before the fall into sin. In other words, Genesis 3:16b is not a PRESCRIPTIVE text for how men ought to treat women. Instead, Genesis 3:16b is a DESCRIPTIVE text that shows the consequences of sin on the relationship between husbands and wives.

In the beginning God created the man to be the "head" of his wife, that is, her loving servant (see pp. 44-47 of this book where I deal with Ephesians 5:22-33). However, the result of sin is that many men throughout history have used their God-given strength to dominate and mistreat women.

The good news is that when God's mercy and forgiveness capture the heart of a man who has been humbled by God's curse, this man is then moved by God's Spirit to love and serve his wife as God intended before sin entered the world.

For example, in the day of the apostle Peter it was normal for most men to look down on women and use their strength as males to manipulate and oppress women. In contrast, note what Peter says to Christian husbands: "Husbands … be considerate as you live with your wives, and treat them with respect as the weaker partner and as heirs with you of the gracious gift of life, so that nothing will hinder your prayers." (1st Peter 3:7) What does this mean?

First of all, Peter tells Christian husbands to be considerate toward their wives and to respect them as the "weaker partner." Now, in today's modern world of politically correct language it seems as though those words "weaker partner" are a put down of women. But this is NOT Peter's intention! Peter is simply describing a fact of nature. In most every case the average male is going to have more physical strength than the average female. The question is: "How does God want men to use their natural strength in regard to their relationship with women?" Peter's answer is that men should use their natural strength to SERVE women. We men should use our strength to provide for and protect our wives just as Christ uses His strength to provide for and protect His Bride, the Church!

Second, Peter clearly teaches that women are equal heirs with men "of the gracious gift of life." In other words, even though God created male and female with differences, we are both equal in worth before God. God does not love men more because they are men. In the same way, God does not love women more because they are women. Both men and women are equally precious to God – and the proof is that Christ shed His blood to reconcile all humans to the Father!

Finally, Peter says that men should use their strength to serve women "so that nothing will hinder your prayers." What does Peter mean when he suggests that men's prayers could be hindered? Simply put, Peter is warning Christian men that if they reject God's will for them as males and follow the sinful examples of unbelieving men who oppress their wives and other women, then God will not hear their prayers. In other words, God is saying: "If you treat your wives or other women like garbage, you are thereby cutting off your relationship with me!"

That's a very serious warning to men from God! We find an example of the same warning in Malachi chapter 2. At that point in history some of the men of Israel were divorcing their believing wives so they could marry unbelieving women who were more appealing to them. Simply put, these men were treating their wives like garbage! These same men then wondered why God would not accept their worship at the Temple (see Malachi 2:13-14), and God answered them: "It is because the Lord is acting as the witness between you and the wife of your youth, because you have broken faith with her, though she is your partner, the wife of your marriage covenant."

Here we see that God expects Christian men to be faithful to their marriage vows and treat their wives (and other women!) with love and respect. God was saying this during a time in history when almost all the unbelieving men of the world used their strength to manipulate and oppress women.

Therefore, the Bible's teaching about women is counter-cultural! In contrast with the unbelieving world, the Bible did NOT condone the oppression of women. Instead, the Bible exalts women and expects believing men to treat them with love and respect.

But what about all those examples in the Bible of men who mistreat their wives and other women? Once again, we need to distinguish between PRESCRIPTIVE texts of Scripture and DESCRIPTIVE texts of Scripture. I agree that there are many DESCRIPTIVE passages where men sinfully mistreat women. But God does NOT condone this! These are examples of how sin affects relationships between men and women. In contrast, there are many PRESCRIPTIVE passages where God commands men to love, respect and serve women – and even die for them, if necessary.

In addition, we also have many examples in both the Old and New Testaments of women who were respected and honored for their wisdom, skills and godliness. We think of Old Testament women such as Miriam, Deborah, Huldah, Esther and the "honorable wife" in Proverbs chapter 31. We also think of New Testament women such as the Virgin Mary, Elizabeth, Anna, Mary Magdalene, Joanna, Susanna, Mary and Martha (sisters of Lazarus), Priscilla, Lydia, Euodia and Syntyche.

Of course, some will point out the fact that Jesus chose only men to be His apostles (see Matthew 10:1-4) and pastors (see 1st Timothy 2:11-3:7) as examples of God viewing women as inferior. However, the fact that God does not allow women to serve as pastors has nothing to do with God viewing them as inferior or incapable. ***In chapter 4 of this book I will deal more thoroughly with this issue of why God wants only men to be pastors.*** For now, allow me briefly to point out that God allows and encourages women to serve His Church in various ways and to be witnesses for Christ – with the exception of serving in the pastoral office.

Simply put, the Bible does NOT condone the oppression of women! **In fact, properly interpreted, the Bible CONDEMNS the oppression of women and exalts their God-given femininity!** Nevertheless, the Bible also clearly teaches that God created humans as male and female. Men and women have different gifts and roles in God's creation, and yet we are of equal value and worth before God.

Sadly, in an attempt to right the wrongs of male oppression of women and the sinful stereotypes many men have of women, modern feminism has led us to the other evil extreme with the result that the biblical uniqueness of male and female has been denied. In the pursuit of power and social equality many women have lost sight of the beautiful plan God has for the relationship between men and women – especially within the marriage relationship. Many men no longer know what it means to be a man; many women no longer know what it means to be a woman – *at least not the way* <u>*God*</u> *defines male and female.*

At this point I would like to quote at length from an article written by Elizabeth Elliot: "We must and we do deplore the stereotypes that caricature the divine distinctions. We deplore the abuses perpetrated by men against women – and, let us not forget, by women against men, for all have sinned – but have we forgotten the archetypes? ... An archetype is the original pattern or model, embodying the essence of things and reflecting in some way the internal structure of the world. I am not here to defend stereotypes, but to try to focus on the Original Pattern. The first woman was made specifically for the first man, a helper, to meet, respond to, surrender to, and complement him. God made her *from* the man, out of his very bone, and then He brought her *to* the man. When Adam named Eve, he accepted responsibility to 'husband' her – to provide for her, to cherish her, to protect her. These two people together represent the image of God – one of them in a special way the initiator, the other the responder. Neither the one nor the other was adequate alone to bear the divine image. God put these two in a perfect place and – you know the rest of the story. They rejected their humanity and used their God-bestowed freedom to defy Him, decided they'd rather not be a mere man and woman, but gods, arrogating to themselves the knowledge of good and evil, a burden too heavy for human beings to bear. Eve, in her refusal to accept the will of God, refused her femininity. Adam, in his capitulation to her suggestion, abdicated his masculine responsibility for her. It was the first instance of what we would recognize now as 'role reversal.' This defiant disobedience ruined the original pattern and things have been in an awful mess ever since. But God did not abandon His self-willed creatures. In His inexorable love He demonstrated exactly what He had had in mind by calling Himself a Bridegroom – the Initiator, Protector, Provider, Lover – and Israel His bride, His beloved. He rescued her, called her by name, wooed and won her, grieved when she went whoring after other gods. In the New Testament we find the mystery of marriage again expressing the inexpressible relationship between the Lord and His people, the husband standing for Christ in his headship, the wife standing for the church in her submission. This Spirit-inspired imagery is not to be shuffled about and rearranged according to our whims and preferences. Mystery must be handled not only with care but also with reverence and awe ... I would be the last to deny that women are given gifts that they are meant to exercise. But we must not be greedy in insisting on having all of them, in usurping the place of men. We are women, and my plea is *Let me be a woman*, holy through and through, asking for nothing but what God wants to give me, receiving with both hands and with all my heart whatever that is ... The world looks for happiness through self-assertion. The Christian knows that joy is found in self-abandonment ... A Christian woman's true freedom lies on the other side of a very small gate – humble obedience – but that gate leads out into a largeness of life undreamed of by the liberators of the world, to a place where the God-given differentiation between the sexes is not obfuscated but celebrated ... as essential to the image of God, for it is in male *and* female, in male as male and female as female, not as two identical and interchangeable halves, that the image is manifested. To gloss over these profundities is to deprive women of the central answer to the cry of their hearts, 'Who am I?' No one but the Author of the Story can answer that cry."[211]

Those who accuse the Bible of condoning the oppression of women in order to justify ignoring what the Bible says about homosexual behavior are simply in error. The Bible does NOT condone the oppression of women! However, the Bible DOES reveal to us God's plan for humans as male and female – a plan that many, tragically, have rejected. The result of rejecting God's plan for male and female has resulted in the modern confusion about the sexes – and this has also led to the additional error of affirming homosexual behavior.

Gay is the new Black!

Some who affirm homosexual behavior suggest that the Bible condones racism and that it was used in American history to justify the oppression of Black people. Since we no longer use the Bible as justification to deny basic civil rights to Black people, they argue that we are free to ignore what the Bible says about homosexual behavior. In other words, just as we no longer use the Bible to condemn people for being Black. In the same way, we should no longer use the Bible to condemn people for being homosexual. Simply put, "Gay is the new Black!"

---

[211] See *The Essence of Femininity: A Personal Perspective* by Elisabeth Elliot, found in *Recovering Biblical Manhood & Womanhood* edited by John Piper and Wayne Grudem, 394-399.

However, the "Gay is the new Black!" argument is in error for at least two reasons. First, this argument wrongly assumes that the Bible condones racism and the oppression of Black people. Nothing could be further from the truth! Second, this argument wrongly assumes that being Black is the same as being homosexual. But as we will see, this is false comparison.

At the beginning of the United States Constitution we find these words: **"We hold these truths to be self-evident, that all men are created equal, that they are endowed by their Creator with certain unalienable rights, that among these are life, liberty and the pursuit of happiness."** Sadly, it took several decades before the truth behind these words would be fully realized for some people – first for women and then later for Black people. *Tragically, ever since 1973, these words from the Constitution still do not apply to humans – both male and female – who live in the womb of their mothers.*

However, many who wish to affirm homosexual behavior will argue that being homosexual is the same as being Black. Therefore, those who use Scripture to teach that homosexual behavior is sinful are often lumped together with those who wrongly use the Bible to justify racism and prejudice against Black people. In addition, most who affirm homosexual behavior will insist that gays are being denied their basic civil rights if they are not allowed to be legally married just like heterosexual couples. How do we answer this?

First, please understand that I am NOT going to argue that those who practice homosexuality should be deprived of basic civil rights. Most Christians who agree with Scripture's teaching regarding homosexual behavior want to reach out to homosexuals in love and treat them with respect. We do NOT want homosexuals to be deprived of "life, liberty and the pursuit of happiness." *(Later in this section I will address the limitations for ALL people regarding what we CAN and CAN NOT do as we strive for "life, liberty and the pursuit of happiness.")*

Second, please understand that most Christians are concerned about the physical and especially the SPIRITUAL well being of those who practice homosexuality. We want them to know what God teaches about their homosexual behavior so they can recognize their sin. **Even more, we want them to know what God teaches about their Savior, Jesus Christ, so they can rejoice in the forgiveness, love and new beginning that He gives to all repentant sinners.**

However, some would oppose me by saying: "Gay is the New Black!" In other words, just as it was wrong for some Christians to misinterpret Scripture in order to justify treating black people as sub-human. In the same way, it is wrong for some Christians today to misinterpret Scripture in order to justify teaching that homosexual behavior is sinful. How do we respond?

First, Scripture clearly teaches that being black is NOT a sin. In fact, Scripture also clearly teaches that ALL humans are descended from Adam. Therefore, Scripture, properly interpreted, is opposed to racism because there is really only ONE race – the HUMAN race! One must twist and distort the clear teaching of Scripture in order to justify affirming racism.

In contrast, Scripture stresses that homosexual behavior (along with other sexual sins) is against God's will for our sexual behavior – *a behavior which is meant to be expressed only between one man and one women within marriage!* One must twist and distort the clear teaching of Scripture in order to justify affirming homosexual behavior. All the evidence shows that Scripture clearly teaches that all forms of homosexual behavior ARE sinful – *and even many pro-gay scholars admit this, and then find ways to reject the authority of Scripture in order to justify their affirmation of homosexual behavior.*

Now, regarding the issue of whether being gay is the same as being Black, I would now like to quote from parts of a letter to the editor written by a black woman by the name of Crystal Dixon. She wrote this letter to the editor in 2008 for the Toledo Free Press. She wrote in response to a previous letter to the editor which argued, among other things, that being gay is the same as being Black. In response, Crystal Dixon, a Black woman and a Christian, wrote the following:

> **"First, human beings, regardless of their choices in life, are of ultimate value to God and should be viewed the same by others. At the same time, one's personal choices lead to outcomes either positive or negative. As a Black woman who happens to be an alumnus of the University of Toledo's Graduate School, an employee and business owner, I take great umbrage at the notion that those choosing the homosexual lifestyle are 'civil rights victims.' Here's why. I cannot wake up tomorrow and not be a Black woman. I am genetically and biologically a Black woman and very pleased to be so as my Creator intended. Daily, thousands of**

homosexuals make a life decision to leave the gay lifestyle evidenced by the growing population of PFOX (Parents and Friends of Ex Gays) and Exodus International just to name a few. Frequently, the individuals report that the impetus to their change of heart and lifestyle was a transformative experience with God; a realization that their choice of same-sex practices wreaked havoc in their psychological and physical lives. Charlene E. Cothran, publisher of Venus Magazine, was an aggressive, strategic supporter of gay rights and a practicing lesbian for 29 years, before she renounced her sexuality and gave Jesus Christ stewardship of her life. The gay community vilified her angrily and withdrew financial support from her magazine, upon her announcement that she was leaving the lesbian lifestyle. Rev. Carla Thomas Royster, a highly respected New Jersey educator and founder and pastor of Blessed Redeemer Church in Burlington, NJ, married to husband Mark with two sons, bravely exposed her previous life as a lesbian in a tell-all book. When asked why she wrote the book, she responded 'to set people free... I finally obeyed God.' ... My final and most important point. There is a divine order. God created human kind male and female (Genesis 1:27). God created humans with an inalienable right to choose. There are consequences for each of our choices, including those who violate God's divine order. It is base human nature to revolt and become indignant when the world or even God Himself, disagrees with our choice that violates His divine order. Jesus Christ loves the sinner but hates the sin (John 8:1-11.) Daily, Jesus Christ is radically transforming the lives of both straight and gay folks and bringing them into a life of wholeness: spiritually, psychologically, physically and even economically. That is the ultimate right."

A few days after writing her letter to the editor, Crystal Dixon was fired from her job simply because she publicly expressed her beliefs about the homosexual lifestyle.[212]

---

[212] Imagine the outcry if a practicing homosexual man or woman was fired from his or her job for writing a letter to the editor in which he or she expressed his or her positive views about homosexual behavior!

Crystal Dixon made a very important distinction. Being gay is NOT the same as being Black. Of course, some would argue: "But I have a homosexual orientation. I have had desires for the opposite sex ever since I can remember!"[213] This may be true. Many people do not choose to have same-sex attraction. However, some people with same-sex attraction DO choose to **act** on their desires! Some people with same-sex attraction DO choose to **practice** the homosexual lifestyle!

Just because a person has a certain desire does not mean that he or she MUST or SHOULD act on that desire. A man or woman may have sexual desires for people other than his or her spouse. Does this mean they MUST or SHOULD act on those desires? Many single men and women have heterosexual desires. But does this mean they MUST or SHOULD act on those desires outside of the context of marriage? Some adults have sexual desires for pre-pubescent children. Does this mean they MUST or SHOULD act on those desires? Some people have the desire to steal items from a store. Does this mean they MUST or SHOULD act on that desire? Many alcoholics have the desire to drink. Does this mean they MUST or SHOULD act on that desire? No! In fact, we tell alcoholics: "Your desire to abuse alcohol is not good! You must acknowledge your problem and get the help that is available. There are many people who are able to refrain from alcohol and remain sober, even though they have the desire to drink." Many other examples could be given. The point is that just because a person has sexual desires for people of the same sex does not mean that he or she MUST or SHOULD act on those desires.

However, in spite of the common sense of the above argument, some will still insist that homosexuals are being deprived of their basic "civil rights" – and by "civil rights" they mean that those who practice homosexuality should be able to get legally married. They argue this right based on the fact that the United States Constitution teaches that all people should have access to "life, liberty and the pursuit of happiness." *But are there no limitations on behavior in pursuit of these rights?*

What about the right to life? For example, the Constitution (and Scripture!) teaches the sanctity of human life. Obviously, if humans don't have the right to life then they can not have liberty or the pursuit of happiness. *Ironically, many (not all!) who insist that homosexuals should have the right to marry also support the legalized murder of*

---

[213] I will deal with the issue of whether there is a genetic link to homosexual desire or behavior in the next section.

humans while they are in the womb. None of these aborted boys and girls will ever have the opportunity for liberty and the pursuit of happiness this side of Heaven.

But there are some cases where the right to life can be taken away in a proper manner! Scripture teaches that governments may (not must!) use the death penalty to punish those who are guilty of murder (see Genesis 9:5-6, Luke 23:41 and Romans 13:1-7). In addition, law enforcement officials have the right to take the life of a criminal in defense of the innocent. In the same way, soldiers have the right to take human life in a just war in order to protect other people.

In contrast, not even governments, law enforcement officials or soldiers have the right to deliberately murder innocent humans! This is why legalized abortion is not only against Scripture but also against the United States Constitution! I can respect those (even though I disagree with them) who believe that opposing abortion means that we must also oppose capital punishment. On the other hand, I have no respect for those who oppose capital punishment and at the same time support the murder of innocent children in the womb. Such confused thinking is a perfect example of the inability of many people to make reasonable distinctions.

Simply put, the point is that even though the Constitution argues for the "right to life," in some cases people can lose their "right to life" if they commit crimes or deeds that would warrant capital punishment, deadly force by police or the act of just war.

What about the right to liberty? Does the right to liberty mean that I am free to do ANYTHING? No! When our founding fathers wrote about the right to liberty they did NOT mean that all citizens should be free to do whatever they please – even if their behaviors were harmful to themselves and other people. Instead, by "freedom" our founding fathers meant that we humans are truly free when we live our lives according to laws that are based on God's will for us. In other words, they wanted to create a society where humans would be free to be the BEST they could be, not the WORST they could be!

The fact is that we citizens of the United States are not free to do things that hurt ourselves (illegal drugs, suicide, etc.) or other people (murder, rape, theft, slander, etc.). Therefore, the right to liberty must be qualified and can not be used to legalize all behavior!

Finally, **what about the right to pursue happiness!** Once again, my pursuit of happiness ends when my happiness results in me engaging in behavior that is hurtful to me or others and when it is in conflict with what it means to be a human being. Part of what it means to be human is that we are male and female. Throughout history and across various cultures marriage has almost always been understood (especially by those who take Scripture seriously) as the unique relationship between one man and one woman.[214]

In fact, we often talk about married "couples" – and that word "couple" implies the number TWO. Even those who want to legalize gay marriage talk in terms of gay "couples." But why this focus on the number TWO? The answer should be obvious. The reason we think in terms of married "couples" – TWO people – is that humans are divided into TWO sexes: male and female.

Therefore, those who wish to **deny** that humans being male and female should have anything to do with legalized marriage need to explain why they are still focused on the number TWO? In other words, if we deny God's order of creation (humans are male and female) as the basis for what marriage is, then why insist on only TWO people in marriage?

If we decide to legalize gay marriage we should also be consistent and legalize polygamous marriage, polyamorous marriage as well as incestuous marriage. **Of course, I do NOT believe we should do this – *but I have a reasonable argument against these types of marriages as well as against gay marriage.*** On the other hand, those who promote gay marriage are not being consistent if they are also not willing to support polygamous, polyamorous or incestuous marriages.

Simply put, people who have same-sex desires have every legal right to marry just like every other United States citizen. People with same-sex desires are free to marry a person of the opposite sex! No one is refusing them this right! But we must not redefine marriage to be between two men or two women because this redefines what it means for us to be **human.** Also, if we open the door to legalized marriage for homosexuals, what justification do we then have for not allowing other types of "marriages" as well?

Sadly, in past United States history marriage between White people and Black people was not legal. This was wrong! This racist practice was based on a sinful misinterpretation of Scripture in order to justify prejudice.

---

[214] For an excellent treatment of the issue of same-sex marriage, see the chapter titled *Same-Sex Marriage* by Bill Maier in *The Complete Christian Guide to Understanding Homosexuality* by Joe Dallas and Nancy Heche.

In contrast, one can NOT attempt to justify the legalization of gay marriage by uttering the slogan: "Gay is the new Black!" Being gay is NOT the same as being Black. Being Black is not sinful. Black is not a sinful behavior. In contrast, Scripture clearly teaches that homosexual desire and behavior is NOT God's will for us as humans.

Therefore, according to Scripture, those who have same-sex desires should acknowledge that these desires are not God's will for us as humans (just as all the *other* sinful desires we have are not God's will for us). They should resist such desires and do their best to avoid acting on those desires – just as many heterosexual people should resist their sinful sexual desires and do their best to avoid acting on those desires (such as premarital sex, adultery, pornography, prostitution, incest, etc.).

Finally, one can NOT attempt to dismiss what Scripture teaches about homosexual behavior by claiming that the Bible also condones racism. The Bible does NOT condone racism! In fact, the Bible is our best defense AGAINST racism! *Those who attempt to affirm homosexual behavior by uttering the slogan "Gay is the new Black!" need to understand how they are offending black people and are also guilty of confused thinking as well as failing to make proper distinctions.*

The authors of Scripture knew nothing about the modern view of homosexual orientation being genetic!

Some who affirm homosexual behavior will argue that the authors of the Scriptures knew nothing about the modern view of homosexual orientation being genetic. They suggest that if the authors of Scripture had known about a genetic cause for homosexual desire they would not have condemned homosexual behavior as being sinful. Therefore, according to this argument, we can ignore what the Bible says about homosexual behavior.

However, this argument is erroneous for several reasons. First, this argument assumes that the authors of Scripture knew nothing about a "homosexual orientation." As I will show, this is not the case! Second, this argument assumes that science has proven with certainty that there is a genetic cause for homosexual behavior. I will also provide evidence to show that this assertion is in error. Finally, even if we CAN prove that there is a genetic cause for homosexual orientation this does NOT mean that we must affirm homosexual behavior. I will provide evidence for a genetic link to alcoholism to show that this is true.

Were Scripture's authors clueless about homosexual orientation?

So, did the authors of Scripture have no knowledge about a homosexual orientation? Obviously, they had no scientific knowledge of genetics as we do today. Nevertheless, there were several theories available during biblical times which suggested some sort of natural cause for homosexual desire and behavior. Robert Gagnon has provided extensive evidence for this.[215]

However, though it can be shown that the apostle Paul and other biblical authors were aware of theories about inborn homosexual desires, even if they had known about modern scientific arguments suggesting a genetic cause for homosexual orientation this would NOT have influenced their teaching that homosexual behavior is sinful. *They condemned all forms of homosexual behavior regardless of the motivation or cause for such behavior!*

Robert Gagnon comments on this fact: "Romans 1-8 indicates … that Paul considered the sinful passions that buffet humanity to be innate and controlling … Paul paints a picture of humanity subjugated and ruled by its own passions; a humanity not in control but controlled … Based on a reading of Rom 5:12-21 and 7:7-23, it is clear that Paul conceived of sin as 'innate' (a category available in antiquity which is close enough for our purposes to the concept of genetic). Paul viewed sin as a power operating in the 'flesh' and in human 'members,' … Adam transmitted sin, conceived as an impulse, a power, or congenital defect or disease, through the reproduction of human flesh. For Paul, all sin was in a certain sense innate in that human beings do not *ask* to feel sexual desire, or anger, or fear, or selfishness – they just *do*, despite whether they want to experience such impulses or not. If Paul could be transported into our time and told that homosexual impulses were at least partly present at birth, he would probably say, 'I could have told you that' … The experience of homosexual urges is part of a larger phenomenon of various sinful impulses that all humans experience,

---

[215] See *The Bible and Homosexual Practice* by Robert Gagnon, 380-432.

though in different proportions for different kinds of sin. According to Rom 8:1-7, the power of sin, that internal 'law' of the mind … can now be mastered by a … internal 'law,' the Spirit, which indwells those who believe in Christ. Sinful impulses remain, even among those who have been saved, but for believers it is now possible to live Spirit-led lives, at least in the main."[216]

By "Spirit-led lives" Gagnon does NOT mean that Christians never act on their sinful desires. Instead, the Spirit helps us to resist those sinful desires and, if we DO act on them in times of weakness, the Spirit convicts us of sin and leads us to trust in Jesus for the assurance that we are forgiven and for the strength to live a new life.

In addition, regarding Scripture's understanding of the relationship between a homosexual orientation and homosexual behavior, Joe Dallas, who struggled with a homosexual orientation himself and who once engaged in homosexual behavior, writes the following: "…there's no contingency in the Bible about homosexuality. It doesn't say, 'Thou shalt not lie with man as with woman, unless that's your orientation.' The biblical authors probably weren't concerned about what caused certain behaviors – they were concerned with the behaviors themselves. By the way, it's quite an insult to God and His Word to ignore what the Bible says about homosexuality just because its authors never heard of 'sexual orientation.' They may never have heard about alcoholism either, but don't you think they knew what they were talking about when they prohibited drunkenness? Orientation, in itself, doesn't justify behavior."[217]

Simply put, even though the biblical authors may not have had a modern understanding of the possible genetic cause for a homosexual orientation, this does not mean that GOD did not understand this! God knows all things!

Therefore, if there is a direct genetic cause for homosexual orientation (and this is questionable, as we will see below), then the Holy Spirit knew this when He inspired the biblical authors to write words that clearly condemn all forms of homosexual behavior. Using limited modern science as a reason to dismiss the authority of Scripture is arrogant and sinful!

---

[216] *The Bible and Homosexual Practice* by Robert Gagnon, 430-431.

[217] *The Complete Christian Guide To Understanding Homosexuality* edited by Joe Dallas and Nancy Heche, 149.

Has science proven a genetic cause for homosexual orientation?

Regarding whether there is scientific evidence for a direct genetic cause for homosexual orientation, recent studies answer this in the negative or at least cautiously suggest that genetic influence may only play a partial role in forming a homosexual orientation.[218]

In fact, in 2010 the American Psychological Association (APA), an organization known for its strong pro-gay stance, admitted that the scientific evidence for a genetic cause of homosexual orientation is not conclusive.

For example, in 1998 the APA published a brochure titled *Answers to Your Questions about Sexual Orientation and Homosexuality* – and in this document they wrote: "There is considerable recent evidence to suggest that biology, including genetic or inborn hormonal factors, play a significant role in a person's sexuality."

However, in the APA's recently published brochure titled *Answers to Your Questions for a Better Understanding of Sexual Orientation & Homosexuality* they write the following: "There is no consensus among scientists about the exact reasons that an individual develops a heterosexual, bisexual, gay or lesbian orientation. Although much research has examined the possible genetic, hormonal, developmental, social, and cultural influences on sexual orientation, no findings have emerged that permit scientists to conclude that sexual orientation is determined by any particular factor or factors. Many think that nature and nurture both play complex roles..."

Even though informed pro-gay advocates admit that the scientific evidence for a genetic cause of homosexual orientation is inconclusive, there are still many uninformed individuals who reference outdated studies as though those studies have proven conclusively that homosexual orientation is genetic.

For example, in 1991 Dr. Simon LeVay used the brains from 41 cadavers of which 19 were homosexual men, 16 were heterosexual men and six were heterosexual women. LeVay examined the portion of these brains known as the anterior hypothalamus. He discovered that this region of the brain was larger in the heterosexual men than it was in the homosexual men or heterosexual women. He thereby concluded

---

[218] For example, see *Homosexuality and the Politics of Truth* by Jeffrey Satinover; *Homosexuality: The Use of Scientific Research in the Church's Moral Debate* by Stanton Jones and Mark Yarhouse; *The Complete Guide to Understanding Homosexuality* edited by Joe Dallas and Nancy Heche.

that this evidence proved a genetic link for homosexual behavior based on the smaller size of the hypothalamus in the homosexual men whose brains he examined. Many people continue to reference this study as conclusive proof that homosexual behavior is genetic.

However, many flaws are associated with LeVay's study. First, the results of this study were not uniform because three of the *hetero*sexual men had a smaller hypothalamus than the average *homo*sexual man in the study. Second, it was discovered that LeVay did not measure the hypothalamus properly. Third, many pointed out that it is unclear whether brain structure affects behavior or whether behavior affects brain structure. In other words, there is a real possibility that homosexual behavior may affect the size of the hypothalamus! Fourth, LeVay himself admitted that he was not certain which of his subjects were homosexual and which were heterosexual. Finally, some questioned whether LeVay could examine the data objectively because he himself was openly homosexual.[219]

Another problematic study that is often referenced as conclusive proof of a genetic cause for homosexual orientation is the Pillard and Bailey twin study. In 1991 Psychologist Michael Bailey and psychiatrist Richard Pillard compared sets of identical twins with fraternal twins – and in each set at least one twin was known to be homosexual. The results of the study show 52% of the identical twins were both homosexual whereas only 22% of the fraternal twins were both homosexual. They used these results as proof that there must be a genetic cause for homosexual orientation.

However, at the very least, this twin study actually proves that a gene can NOT be the sole cause of homosexual orientation because 48% of the identical twins did NOT share a homosexual orientation. If a gene were the sole cause of homosexual orientation, we would expect 100% of identical twins to share the same sexual orientation. In addition, the 52% of identical twins who shared a homosexual orientation were both raised in the same home – and this means that *environment* could also have played a part in their homosexual orientation. If Pillard and Bailey could have found identical twins who shared a homosexual orientation but were raised in different environments, this would have been stronger evidence for a sole genetic link. Finally, as with LeVay, people also questioned whether Pillard and Bailey could examine their data objectively because Pillard

---

[219] *The Complete Christian Guide to Understanding Homosexuality* edited by Joe Dallas and Nancy Heche, 181-183.

was openly homosexual and Bailey was a well known gay rights advocate.[220]

Other more credible studies of a possible genetic link for homosexual orientation have been done since 1991, but even these studies are not conclusive.[221]

Would a genetic cause for homosexual behavior mean that it is NOT sinful or harmful and should be affirmed?

In his book Homosexuality and the Politics of Truth Jeffrey Satinover writes the following:

"What would you think if a relative, friend, or colleague had a condition that is routinely, even if not always, associated with the following problems:

- **A significantly decreased likelihood of establishing or preserving a successful marriage**
- **A five-to ten-year decrease in life expectancy**
- **Chronic, potentially fatal, liver disease – hepatitis**
- **Inevitably fatal esophageal cancer**
- **Pneumonia**
- **Internal bleeding**
- **Serious mental disabilities, many of which are irreversible**
- **A much higher than usual incidence of suicide**

---

[220] *The Complete Christian Guide to Understanding Homosexuality* edited by Joe Dallas and Nancy Heche, 183.

[221] *The Complete Christian Guide to Understanding Homosexuality* edited by Joe Dallas and Nancy Heche, 184-187.

- **A very low likelihood that its adverse effects can be eliminated unless the condition itself is eliminated**
- **An only 30 percent likelihood of being eliminated through lengthy, often costly, and very time-consuming treatment in an otherwise unselected population of sufferers (although a very high success rate among highly motivated, carefully selected sufferers)**

"We can add four qualifications to this unnamed condition. First, even though its origins are influenced by genetics, the condition is, strictly speaking, rooted in behavior. Second, individuals who have this condition continue the behavior in spite of the destructive consequences of doing so. Third, although some people with this condition perceive it as a problem and wish they could rid themselves of it, many others deny they have any problem at all and violently resist all attempts to 'help' them. And fourth, these people who resist help tend to socialize with one another, sometimes exclusively, and form a kind of 'subculture.' No doubt you would care deeply for someone close to you who had such a condition. And whether or not society considered it undesirable or even an illness, you would want to help. Undoubtedly, you would also consider it worth 'treating,' that is, you would seek to help your relative, friend, or colleague by eliminating the condition entirely. The condition we are speaking of is alcoholism." [222]

Scientific studies show that there is actually more evidence for a genetic link to alcoholic behavior than there is for homosexual behavior. However, even though the evidence for a genetic cause for alcoholism is strong, this does not stop Christians from agreeing with Scripture that the abuse of alcohol is sinful.

In addition, because Christians love people who are burdened by alcoholism, we want to help set them free from this behavior that is not

---

[222] *Homosexuality and the Politics of Truth* by Jeffrey Satinover, 49-50.

only spiritually harmful but also has many hurtful emotional and physical consequences.

In fact, even those who do NOT take Scripture seriously will at least admit that there are many negative things associated with alcoholic behavior. As a result, even though there appears to be a genetic cause for alcoholism, this does not stop such people from insisting that this alcoholic behavior is wrong, that people ought to get help for this condition, and that people can stop their alcoholic behavior if they are motivated to do so.

In his book *Homosexuality and the Politics of Truth* Jeffrey Satinover also writes the following:

"And now imagine another friend or colleague who had a condition associated with a similar list of problems:

- **A significantly decreased likelihood of establishing or preserving a successful marriage**
- **A *twenty-five to thirty-year* decrease in life expectancy**
- **Chronic, potentially fatal, liver disease – infectious hepatitis, which increases the risk of liver cancer**
- **Inevitably fatal immune disease including associated cancers**
- **Frequently fatal rectal cancer**
- **Multiple bowel and other infectious diseases**
- **A much higher than usual incidence of suicide**
- **A very low likelihood that its adverse effects can be eliminated unless the condition itself is**
- **An at least 50 percent likelihood of being eliminated through lengthy, often costly, and very time-consuming treatment in an otherwise unselected group of sufferers (although a very high success rate, in some instances nearing 100 percent, for groups of highly motivated, carefully selected individuals)**

> **"As with alcoholism: First, even though its origins may be influenced by genetics, the condition is, strictly speaking, a pattern of behavior; second, individuals who have this condition continue in the behavior in spite of the destructive consequences of doing so; third, although some people with this condition perceive it as a problem and wish they could rid themselves of it, many others deny they have any problem at all and violently resist all attempts to 'help' them; and fourth, some of the people with this condition – especially those who deny it is a problem – tend to socialize almost exclusively with one another and form a 'subculture.' This condition is homosexuality. Yet despite the parallels between the two conditions, what is striking today are the sharply different responses to them."** [223]

Just as scientific evidence for a likely genetic cause for alcoholism does not keep Christians from agreeing with Scripture that alcoholic behavior is sinful, in the same way, if science ever proves that there is a genetic cause for *homosexual orientation* this will not keep Christians from agreeing with Scripture that such behavior is sinful.

In addition, because Christians love people who are burdened by homosexual orientation and behavior, we want to help set them free from this behavior that is not only spiritually harmful but also has many hurtful emotional and physical consequences.

However, in contrast with their views of people burdened with alcoholism, those who do NOT take Scripture seriously will often affirm those with a *homosexual orientation* who choose to engage in homosexual behavior – even though evidence shows that there are many negative and hurtful things associated with homosexual behavior. Is this not being inconsistent?

Those who agree with Scripture that homosexual behavior is sinful understand that people do NOT choose to have a homosexual orientation – just as people do NOT choose to be burdened with alcoholism or any other number of sinful desires and orientations. But just because a person has a particular desire does NOT mean that this desire should be affirmed much less acted out.

---

[223] *Homosexuality and the Politics of Truth* by Jeffrey Satinover, 50-51.

Therefore, even if science one day proves that there is a genetic cause for homosexual orientation, this will in no way change the fact that Christians will continue to use Holy Scripture to teach that homosexual behavior is sinful and should be avoided.

In the book *The Complete Christian Guide To Understanding Homosexuality* Joe Dallas writes the following:

1. **Homosexual orientation, like a number of other tendencies, *may* be influenced by faulty parenting, or sinful choices, or trauma, or a combination of all three. It could also be influenced, or even created by, inborn characteristics, since the Fall of man has affected all of us physically, psychologically, and spiritually. "Behold, I was brought forth in iniquity, and in sin did my mother conceive me" (Psalm 51:5).**
2. **Attempts to prove homosexuality is inborn may *at times* be engineered to legitimize the behavior, but it's inaccurate and unfair to presume *all* such research is so tainted it can't be considered. "He who answers a matter before he hears it, it is folly and shame to him" (Proverbs 18:13).**
3. **Repenting of a sinful behavior by no means guarantees losing all temptations toward that behavior, as many who've repented of homosexuality will attest. Inborn or not, it tends to be deeply ingrained, so the desire for it may remain long after repentance. And the need for it to be resisted may last for many years – or for a lifetime. That's a reality of life in this fallen world. "The flesh lusts against the Spirit, and the Spirit against the flesh; and these are contrary to one another, so that you do not do the things that you wish" (Galatians 5:17).**
4. **No concession is made to a pro-gay viewpoint by acknowledging that homosexuality *could be* inborn. Acknowledging possible inborn tendencies toward a sin is a far cry from legitimizing the sin itself. "Do not let**

sin reign in your mortal body, that you should obey it in its lusts" (Romans 6:12). [224]

Sadly, some Christians have wrongly taught that if a person who has homosexual desires trusts in Jesus those desires will then go away. But Scripture does NOT teach this! On the contrary, Scripture clearly teaches that repentant believers in Christ will continue to struggle with the desires of their sinful nature until the day they die.

Some who are involved in homosexual behavior say: "I tried to change! I did my best to have sexual feelings for the opposite sex and eliminate my desires for the same sex. But no matter how hard I worked, I was never able to stop having sexual feelings for the same sex. Therefore, I decided that God wants me to affirm my homosexual desires and act on them." How do we respond to such a person?

Imagine an alcoholic saying: "I tried to change! I did my best to live a sober life and eliminate by desires for alcoholic beverages. But no matter how hard I worked, I was never able to stop having desires for alcoholic beverages. Therefore, I decided that God wants me to affirm my alcoholic desires and act on them." How do we respond to such a person?

I don't know many people who would say to an alcoholic: "You obviously tried to stop being an alcoholic. But you should never have done that in the first place! God made you the way you are and you should celebrate your alcoholism!"

On the contrary, most people would say to an alcoholic: "I don't care how many times you've tried to stop drinking, you must try again! You need to admit that you have a problem and that you need help. Many people with your problem have received help and are successful at remaining sober – even though they continue to have desires for alcohol from time to time. We love you and we want to help you!"

Many who are burdened with a homosexual orientation have been misled into thinking that "getting close to Jesus" means that our sinful desires – including our sinful sexual desires – will diminish and one day disappear. But God never says that our struggle with sinful desires will disappear when we are converted to faith in Christ. In fact, Scripture suggests that our struggle with sinful desires will actually

---

[224] *The Complete Christian Guide To Understanding Homosexuality* edited by Joe Dallas and Nancy Heche, 187-188.

INCREASE when we come to faith in Christ because now the devil must work overtime to tempt us in order to lead us away from Christ.

A well know practicing homosexual, Mel White, has written about his past experience as a Christian with homosexual desires. On one occasion he gave in to his desires and got involved in a homosexual affair while he was still married to his wife. He had tried to resist his homosexual desires for years and hoped to eliminate them through faith in Jesus. But his desires remained. He eventually concluded that it was God's will for him to act out his homosexual desires.

In his book *Stranger at the Gate* Mel White writes: "Mark and I undressed and climbed into bed … He got out of bed and returned a short time later with a jar of heated massage oil. As he rubbed the warm oil into my body, for some strange reason I remembered the woman anointing Jesus' body in the open tomb … But even while I lay there worrying that this sinful act would be the end of me, something in my brain kept reminding me that after death came the resurrection … For the next few weeks, I was hounded by guilt and fear … I survived the next year in large part because of Mark's generous, loving spirit. What my friendship with Mark provided was far more than 'recreational sex,' a practice that doesn't fit into the ethical pattern of Old Testament Judaism or New Testament Christianity. I had postponed appropriate male intimacy so long that I was desperate … I believe without any doubt that [Mark] was another of God's gifts … My friends on the religious right will read this story and accuse me of giving way to lust. 'He only needs to confess his sins,' they'll say, 'and be reborn.' Or, 'He just needs a good dose of God's Holy Spirit to take away this sinful bent.' In fact, I gave my life to Jesus at their altars in my childhood and I spent my lifetime in their churches, listening to their sermons and praying with my whole heart for God's loving Spirit to heal me. On several occasions I even went to Christian healers secretly asking to be exorcised of my homosexuality. Catholic and Protestant exorcists alike knelt around me with their hands on my head and shoulders asking God to cast out the 'demon' who had 'haunted me from my childhood.' In fact, it was their homophobic ghost who was haunting me. Like all the rest, their simplistic solution to my God-given sexual orientation only made matters worse."[225]

My heart goes out to people like Mel White. In the first 100+ pages of his book *Stranger at the Gate* Mel White recounts for us many years

---

[225] *Stranger at the Gate* by Mel White, 132-133.

of his struggle with a homosexual orientation. Not only does Mel continue to bear the burden of homosexual orientation and behavior, but now he has been deceived into thinking that God wants him to celebrate his homosexual behavior. One thing that may have led Mel to this tragic state is the error that if he had just truly "committed his life to Jesus" then his homosexual desires would have disappeared. Of course, this never happened for Mel. Therefore, he wrongly concluded that his homosexual desires were from God and that Jesus affirmed his homosexual behavior.

One thing I have learned in my 47 years of being a Christian is that the closer I get to Jesus the more sinful I realize I am. I never cease to thank God that my Lutheran tradition has correctly taught me what Scripture teaches about the Christian life. We are by nature enemies of God – and even after the Holy Spirit gives us repentance and faith in Jesus we continue to struggle with the desires of our sinful nature. In the midst of this daily struggle our hope is that we are completely forgiven and holy in God's sight because of Jesus' death and resurrection for us. This Good News not only comforts me! This Good News also gives me the desire and strength to say "No" to my sinful desires and "Yes" to God's loving plan for my life. (See Romans 6:1-14 and 12:1-2)

So, do I, a Christian and a pastor, continue to struggle with sinful desires (even sinful *hetero*sexual desires!) every day? Yes! I honestly can not relate to people like Mel White who bear the burden of homosexual desire. I have NEVER had sexual desires for men. However, I certainly DO understand what it means to struggle with ungodly *hetero*sexual desires.

I recall one occasion when I was asked to be the guest teacher at a men's Christian retreat. They asked me to speak on the topic of homosexuality. The first thing I wanted to stress to them is that *hetero*sexual sin is just as sinful as *homo*sexual sin.

So, assuming that most of the men there had a heterosexual orientation, I said to them: "Raise your hand if you have never had sexual desires for a woman who was not your wife." Not one man raised his hand – including me! I then said to them: "Raise your hand if you think you can go for one day without struggling with lust for a woman who is not your wife." Once again, not one man raised his hand – including me!

Why do I tell you this story? In Mel White's book *Stranger at the Gate* he describes in detail the pain and conflict he faced as he struggled with his homosexual orientation over the years. Mel wants us to have sympathy for him, and he succeeds! However, even though we should have compassion for the pain that people like Mel endure, we must realize that in his book Mel is a playing the victim and leading us astray by trying to convince us that his struggle with homosexual desire and behavior is God's sign that we should affirm and celebrate his lifestyle. Instead of acknowledging his sin and trusting in Christ for forgiveness, Mel affirms his sin and condemns those whose "homophobic attitudes" lead them to condemn his homosexual behavior.

I can NOT relate to Mel's struggle with *homo*sexual desire. But I (and many other men) certainly DO understand what it means to struggle with ungodly *hetero*sexual desires. Does that mean I should play the victim and lead you astray by trying to convince you that God wants you to affirm my heterosexual lust and celebrate with me if I choose to act on those desires and engage in sinful heterosexual behavior? By no means!

My prayer is that Mel White and many others like him will realize that they have deceived themselves (see 1st John 1:8 & 10). My prayer is that the Holy Spirit will work through God's Word to convict them of the sin of their homosexual lust and behavior. Even more, my prayer is that the Holy Spirit will work through God's Word to assure them that they are completely forgiven and holy in God's sight through Jesus. The Spirit will then lead them to resist their sinful desires and strive to live according to God's loving plan for their lives. If they do give in to temptation during a moment of weakness, they can come before God in repentance and know that they are already forgiven because of Jesus and His work for us. God will then give them a new beginning – and He will do this every day; every moment of their lives.

Therefore, even if science one day proves that there is a genetic cause for homosexual orientation, this will change nothing for those of us who trust God's Word in Holy Scripture. None of us choose the sinful desires we have, and Scripture suggests that ALL sinful desire is innate and part of our fallen "flesh."

But in Christ we are New Creations! (See 2nd Corinthians 5:17-21) In Christ we can stand before God, sinners though we are, and know that we are SAINTS! We must remember that our identity is not defined by our genes! Our identity is not defined by our sexual orientation – whether heterosexual or homosexual.

Our identity is defined by our BAPTISM! God has placed His Name on us! (See Matthew 28:19-20) God has given us New Birth! (See John 3:5 and Titus 3:5) God has given us forgiveness of sin and the Holy Spirit! (See Acts 2:38-39) We share in Christ's death and resurrection! (See Romans 6:3-4) We have been clothed with Christ! (See Galatians 3:26-27) Christ has saved us! (See 1st Peter 3:21) The apostle Paul writes: "I have been crucified with Christ and I no longer live, but Christ lives in me. The life I live in the body, I live by faith in the Son of God, who loved me and gave himself for me." (Galatians 2:20)

Only a few Bible verses address homosexuality!

In their book *The Children Are Free* Jeff Miner and John Tyler Connoley write the following regarding the number of Bible passages that explicitly address homosexual behavior: "...Given how often some Christians preach against homosexuality, you would think there must be hundreds of Scriptures on the subject. In fact, there are only six traditional clobber passages and, as we will show, none of them speaks to the situation of twenty-first century gay people who desire to live in loving relationships with the blessing of God. By contrast, there are literally hundreds of passages that regulate every aspect of heterosexuality."[226] How do we respond to this?

First, Miner and Connoley assert that none of six Bible passages addressing homosexual behavior have anything to do with "the situation of twenty-first century gay people who desire to live in loving relationships with the blessing of God."

However, in the previous and present chapter of this book I have provided tons of evidence showing that this assertion from Miner and Connoley is simply false!

Second, Miner and Connoley want us to think that since there are only six Bible passages (in their opinion) that deal explicitly with homosexual behavior this must mean that God doesn't think homosexual behavior is a very big deal. Some find this argument convincing!

But what would you think if I were to write the following: "Given how often some Christians preach against *bestiality*, you would think there must be hundreds of Scriptures on the subject. In fact, there are

[226] *The Children Are Free* by Jeff Miner and John Tyler Connoley, 1.

only *two* traditional clobber passages (both in the Old Testament book of Leviticus!) and, as I will show, none of them speaks to the situation of twenty-first century people and *animals* who desire to live in loving *sexual* relationships with the blessing of God. By contrast, there are literally hundreds of passages that regulate every aspect of heterosexuality."

Or, what would you think if I were to write the following: "Given how often some Christians preach against *incest*, you would think there must be hundreds of Scriptures on the subject. In fact, there are only *four* traditional clobber passages (two in the Old Testament book of Leviticus; two in the New Testament) and, as I will show, none of them speaks to the situation of twenty-first century mothers/sons, fathers/daughters, or brothers/sisters who desire to live in loving *sexual* relationships with the blessing of God. By contrast, there are literally hundreds of passages that regulate *other* aspects of *normal* heterosexuality."

How would you respond to my two arguments in favor of bestiality and incest? Most people (even some who affirm homosexual behavior!) would say: "Wait just a minute! Just because the Bible has very little to say about bestiality and incest does not mean that these behaviors should be affirmed! First, the Bible passages that address them are very clear that these behaviors are sinful. Second, there are no other Bible passages that affirm these behaviors. Third, how many Bible passages condemning a behavior as sinful do we need before we are willing to agree with Scripture that such behavior is sinful?" **What is interesting is that the very same points can be made about *homosexual behavior*!**

Simply put, I do not need to devote much space in this section to addressing the argument "Only a few Bible passages addresses homosexuality!" because the problems with this argument are so obvious!

In fact, one reason that the Bible has "only" six (actually, there are others) passages that address homosexual behavior is that homosexual behavior (like bestiality) is so obviously against God's will that not much needs to be said about it.

In addition, the reason Scripture has so much more to say about sinful *hetero*sexual behavior (adultery, premarital sex, lust) is that heterosexual behavior among humans is the norm and so the sins associated with heterosexual behavior are far more common.

In his book *The Bible and Homosexual Practice* Robert Gagnon writes: "On the descriptive level, throughout the Bible there is not a single hero of the faith that engages in homosexual conduct: no patriarch, no matriarch, no prophet, no priest, no king (certainly not David), no apostle, no disciple. The Song of Solomon is devoted to singing the praises of committed heterosexual love. On a prescriptive level, every regulation that affirms the sexual bond affirms it between a man and a woman – without exception. In addition, every proverb or wisdom saying refers to heterosexual – not homosexual – relationships as fitting for the lives of the faithful. There is an abundance of Old Testament laws and proverbs regulating and establishing proper boundaries for sexual intercourse between male and female (e.g., regarding virginity, mate selection, engagement, marital fidelity). By way of contrast, there are no laws distinguishing proper homosexual conduct from improper homosexual conduct, because in every law code homosexual conduct is presumed to be forbidden *in toto*. This includes the Ten Commandments ... "you shall honor your father and mother." ... "you shall not commit adultery." ... you shall not covet...your neighbor's wife." These only make sense where heterosexual couplings alone are sanctioned. Likewise, every discussion in the New Testament about marriage or sexual unions always and only seeks to regulate heterosexual unions because there is no conception of a proper homosexual union. There was no need to talk about fidelity and loving concern in same-sex unions because it was universally understood that homosexual unions were abominable. The relationship between Yahweh and Israel and between Christ and the church is imaged as a marriage between a husband and a wife. It would have been absolutely unthinkable for any prophet or New Testament author to conceive of this relationship in homosexual terms. In short, the universal silence in the Bible regarding an acceptable same-sex union, when combined with the explicit prohibitions, speaks volumes for a consensus disapproval of homosexual conduct. To say that there are only a few texts in the Bible that do not condone homosexual conduct is a monumental understatement of the facts. The reverse is a more accurate statement: there is not a single shred of evidence anywhere in the Bible that would even remotely suggest that same-sex unions are any more acceptable than extramarital or premarital intercourse, incest, or bestiality."[227]

---

[227] *The Bible and Homosexual Practice* by Robert Gagnon, 438-439.

You must respect my bound conscience!

In preparation for their August 2009 National Convention, the Evangelical Lutheran Church in America (ELCA) wrote for its congregations a document entitled *Human Sexuality: Gift and Trust*. On pp. 19-20 of this document we find these words:

This Church recognizes that, with conviction and integrity:

- **On the basis of conscience-bound belief, some are convinced that same-gender sexual behavior is sinful, contrary to biblical teaching and their understanding of natural law. They believe same-gender sexual behavior carries the grave danger of unrepentant sin. They therefore conclude that the neighbor and the community are best served by calling people in same-gender sexual relationships to repentance for that behavior and to a celibate lifestyle. Such decisions are intended to be accompanied by pastoral response and community support.**
- **On the basis of conscience-bound belief, some are convinced that homosexuality and even lifelong, monogamous, homosexual relationships reflect a broken world in which some relationships do not pattern themselves after the creation God intended. While they acknowledge that such relationships may be lived out with mutuality and care, they do not believe that the neighbor or community are best served by publicly recognizing such relationships as traditional marriage.**
- **On the basis of conscience-bound belief, some are convinced that the scriptural witness does not address the context of sexual orientation and lifelong loving and committed relationships that we experience today. They believe that the neighbor and community are best served when same-gender relationships are honored and held to high standards and public accountability, but they do not equate these relationships with marriage. They do, however, affirm the need for community support**

and the role of pastoral care and may wish to surround lifelong, monogamous relationships or covenant unions with prayer.

- **On the basis of conscience-bound belief, some are convinced that the scriptural witness does not address the context of sexual orientation and committed relationships that we experience today. They believe that the neighbor and community are best served when same-gender relationships are lived out with lifelong and monogamous commitments that are held to the same rigorous standards, sexual ethics, and status as heterosexual marriage. They surround such couples and their lifelong commitments with prayer to live in ways that glorify God, find strength for the challenges that will be faced, and serve others. They believe same-gender couples should avail themselves of social and legal support for themselves, their children, and other dependants and seek the highest legal accountability available for their relationships.**

Although at this time this church lacks consensus on this matter, it encourages all people *to live out their faith in the local and global community of the baptized with profound respect for the conscience-bound belief of the neighbor.*[228]

According to this ELCA document, we ought to respect the "conscience-bound belief" of those who conclude that God wants us to affirm homosexual behavior within a publicly accountable, lifelong, monogamous relationship. What are we to make of this?

There is serious error associated with the idea that your conscience-bound interpretation of Scripture must be respected and validated by others – even if others believe, based on the clear teaching of Scripture, that your conscience-bound interpretation is wrong.

What does this idea about conscience-bound interpretation mean for the clarity of Scripture? Is Scripture nothing more than a vague document that can be interpreted in any number of ways by any

[228] *Italic* emphasis is mine.

number of people – with the result that all the various interpretations of conscience-bound people must be respected and recognized as valid? How then would the Church ever be able to arrive at any certain position regarding Scripture's teaching on sexuality not to mention any other Christian doctrines? How would Christians be able to exercise any type of Church discipline without violating the principles of conscience bound interpretation?

For instance, in the quote from the ELCA document above we were given four examples of conscience-bound interpretations of Scripture that people within the ELCA have regarding the issue of homosexual behavior. What if we simply replaced the issue of homosexuality with adultery or incest or bestiality? Would this ELCA document still be asking its members to respect the conscience-bound interpretation of those who believe that Scripture allows us to affirm adultery, incest or bestiality? If we must respect everyone's conscience-bound interpretation of Scripture as valid, then at what point can we ever proclaim "Thus says the Lord!" in any objective way?

Allow me to suggest the following scenario. In 1st Corinthians 5:1-5 the apostle Paul condemns the incest taking place between two people – one of them being a man who was a member of the Corinthian congregation. Paul also commands the rest of the members to place the guilty man under Church discipline.

Now, imagine that some of the members of the Corinthian congregation had responded to Paul's condemnation and command with the following letter: "Why are you condemning this incestuous couple, Paul? Why are you asking us to put the man involved, one of our own brother's in Christ, under Church discipline? We have the Holy Spirit, too! We have studied the Scriptures with this man and our conscience-bound interpretation has led us to believe that God actually affirms this incestuous relationship – and that is why we are proud of this man's behavior. Paul, we understand that you also have your own conscience-bound interpretation of Scripture regarding the issue of incest, and we respect that. All we ask is that you also respect our conscience-bound interpretation and continue in fellowship with us. As you know, Jesus wants us to be one. We pray that you will respond favorably to our request and not insist on dividing the body of Christ."

How do you think Paul would have responded to such a letter? Do you think he would have written back and said: "I'm so convicted! How arrogant of me to think that my interpretation of what Scripture teaches about incest could be the only possible truth. Just so you know, I'm not saying I've changed my mind about incest. I still think

God condemns it as sinful behavior. But I respect the fact that you have a completely different interpretation of God's Word on this issue, and I must respect your conscience-bound interpretation for the sake of the unity that Christ wants for His Church. Please forgive me!"

The fact is that there may have been members of the Corinthian congregation who would have insisted that their reading of Scripture led them to believe that God wanted them to affirm incestuous behavior. *If there had been such a group at Corinth we can be sure that Paul would NOT have respected their conscience-bound affirmation of the incestuous relationship taking place in their midst!*

In fact, Paul would have most certainly said: "This is what we speak, not in words taught us by human wisdom but in words taught by the Spirit, expressing spiritual truths in spiritual words. I care very little if I am judged by you or by any human court; indeed, I do not even judge myself. My conscience is clear, but that does not make me innocent. It is the Lord who judges me.[229] 'Do not go beyond what is written.' Who makes you different from anyone else? What do you have that you did not receive? For I do not want you to be ignorant of the fact, brothers, that our forefathers were all under the cloud and that they all passed through the sea. Nevertheless, God was not pleased with most of them; their bodies were scattered over the desert. We should not commit sexual immorality, as some of them did – and in one day twenty-three thousand of them died. I hear that when you come together as a church there are divisions among you. No doubt

---

[229]After Paul writes "It is the Lord who judges me" (1st Corinthians 4:4b) he goes on to write something else that many misinterpret. 1st Corinthians 4:5 reads: "Therefore judge nothing before the appointed time; wait till the Lord comes. He will bring to light what is hidden in darkness and will expose the motives of men's hearts. At that time each will receive his praise from God." Some interpret Paul's words to mean that we should not condemn anyone's teaching or behavior as being sinful. Instead, we should respect all teaching and behavior as valid because God is the only Judge. ***But this is NOT what Paul means at all!*** All one has to do is read 1st Corinthians in its entirety to see that Paul does not hesitate to judge and condemn various sinful teachings and behaviors. Then what DO Paul's words in 1st Corinthians 5:5 mean? Paul is telling us that we should not waste our time attempting to judge things that we can not know – such as the motives of men's hearts. For example, some were questioning Paul's motives for his ministry at Corinth. Paul responds by saying that he doesn't even judge his own motives – but he leaves that to God! So, as far as the motives of men's hearts are concerned, we must let God deal with that on the Final Day. Nevertheless, Paul insists that we MUST judge the teaching and behavior of others – and we use God's Word, Holy Scripture, as the sole basis for that judgment! This is what Paul means when he says: "Do not go beyond what is written." (1st Corinthians 4:6)

there have to be divisions among you to show which of you have God's approval. Did the word of God originate with you? Or are you the only people it has reached? If anybody thinks he is a prophet or spiritually gifted, let him acknowledge that what I am writing to you is the Lord's command. If he ignores this, he himself will be ignored."

The apostle Paul would never have respected a conscience-bound interpretation of Scripture that would have led a person, couple or group to affirm incestuous behavior – or any other sin clearly condemned by Holy Scripture.

In fact, even though some members of the Corinthian congregation apparently had a "clear conscience" about their sinful sexual behaviors, this did not keep Paul from writing the following to them: "Do you not know that the wicked will not inherit the kingdom of God? … The body is not meant for sexual immorality, but for the Lord, and the Lord for the body … Flee from sexual immorality! … You are not your own; you were bought at a price. Therefore honor God with your body." (1st Corinthians 6:9, 13b, 18, 19b-20)

The ELCA's promotion of a conscious-bound interpretation of Scripture ultimately leads to a purely subjective interpretation of Scripture that completely denies the clarity of Scripture which is a necessary assumption of biblical interpretation if we are ever going to establish any kind objective doctrinal teaching that applies to all people of all times and places.

However, some will respond to me by saying: "But if the teaching of Holy Scripture is clear, then why do we have so many different interpretations of its meaning? Why does one person read it and conclude that homosexual behavior is sinful? Why does another person read the same Bible and conclude that homosexual behavior ought to be affirmed?"

The answer to the above questions is simply that we must learn to interpret the Bible properly. Any person can make the Bible mean anything by interpreting a passage out of context. As we learned at the beginning of this chapter, 1) we must distinguish between a literal versus a literalistic interpretation of Scripture; 2) we must distinguish between the ministerial versus the magisterial use of reason when interpreting Scripture; 3) we must allow Scripture to interpret Scripture – reading a particular text within the immediate and wider context in which it appears as well as using the majority of clear Scripture passages to help us deal with individual passages that are obscure if read in isolation from the rest of Scripture; 4) we must distinguish between descriptive texts and prescriptive texts; 5) we must especially recognize that the purpose of Holy Scripture is to point us to Jesus and the salvation that we have only in His person and work. *Allow me to give some examples of how this all plays out in a practical way.*

Imagine that a man says to me: "Jesus never says one single word about bestiality! Therefore, I have a clear conscience when I have sex with animals. I realize that you have a different interpretation of Scripture on this issue. But my interpretation is just as valid as yours!" How should we respond?

Here's what I would say: "I'm sorry, but Scripture's teaching on bestiality is very clear. Therefore, both of our interpretations can't be valid. One of us is in error. Simply put, there are two passages in the book of Leviticus that clearly condemn bestiality. These two passages appear in a wider context where we find condemnations of other sexual sins that apply to all people of all times and places. In addition, the creation account in Genesis clearly teaches that God's gift of sex was intended for one man and one woman in marriage – and Jesus Himself confirms this in Matthew chapter 19. The reason neither Jesus nor His apostles ever mentioned bestiality is that the Jews to whom they witnessed agreed with the Old Testament that bestiality is sinful. In the same way, even most of the Gentiles – most of whom were unfamiliar with Holy Scripture's teaching about sex – assumed that bestiality was wrong by their understanding of nature. So Jesus and His apostles did not even need to mention bestiality because the people they were witnessing to already agreed that it was sinful. My friend, you are in error! God's Word is clear on the issue of bestiality. You need to repent and trust in Jesus for forgiveness and the strength to live a new life."

Or imagine that a woman says to me: "I'm offended that you would rebuke me for having sex with my father! I'm a consenting adult and we love each other very much! Besides, the Bible says that after God destroyed Sodom Lot's daughters both had sex with him. Therefore, I have a clear conscience when I have sex with my father!" How should we respond?

Here's what I would say: "I'm sorry, but you're misinterpreting what Scripture clearly says about father/daughter incest. I agree with you that Lot had sex with his daughters. But this is an example of a <u>descriptive</u> text. In other words, God is describing an event in history for us. But this does NOT mean that He condones this behavior! In the book of Leviticus we see that God condemns sex between a mother and her son as well as sex between a grandfather and his granddaughter. True, God doesn't mention sex between a father and his daughter. But the reason for this is that such an act is assumed to be sinful because of the other similar examples. We find the same thing when God clearly condemns male homosexual behavior in Leviticus chapters 18 and 20. God doesn't mention female homosexual behavior. Does this mean God approves of lesbianism? No! Female homosexual behavior is assumed to be sinful based on the example of male homosexual behavior – and the proof is that Paul condemns female homosexual behavior in Romans chapter 1. Another thing you need to know is that the apostle Paul condemned an incestuous relationship between a man and his father's wife. Obviously, if Paul condemned this type of incest he also would have condemned father/daughter incest. No where does Scripture ever condone sex between a father and his daughter – even if they are both consenting adults who love each other. Your interpretation is wrong! You need to repent and trust in Jesus for forgiveness and the strength to live a new life."

Finally, imagine a single man saying to me: "Who are you to judge me for having sex with prostitutes?! I'm not even breaking the law, because I only visit prostitutes in areas of Nevada where it's legal. Besides, Samson was a great hero of the Bible – and he visited prostitutes! Therefore, I have a clear conscience when I have sex with prostitutes – and YOU are the one who needs to repent by suggesting that I'm guilty of sinful behavior. Remember! Jesus said that we should not judge people!" How should we respond?

Here's what I would say: "I'm a sinner just like you are! When I rebuke you for your sin of having sex with prostitutes I am merely pointing out that it is the Word of God that is judging and condemning your behavior. I realize that you visit prostitutes in areas of Nevada where it's legal. But just because a behavior is legal does not mean that God approves of it. As for you using Samson's example as a reason to justify your behavior, you fail to see that this is a descriptive text. God is merely describing what Samson did. This does NOT mean that God condoned Samson's behavior. The creation account in Genesis clearly teaches that sex is intended only for one man and one woman in marriage. Both the Old and New Testaments clearly condemn having sex with prostitutes. Not only are you putting yourself at risk of getting an STD. Even worse, you are openly rebelling against God's clear will for your life and that means you are living as an unbeliever! But God loves you. That's why the Holy Spirit is using me to show you what Scripture teaches about your sin.

The Holy Spirit will also use me to show you that you have forgiveness in Jesus, and He will give you the strength to live a new life."

I could give countless more examples of how reasonable and careful examination of Holy Scripture leads us to see what God clearly teaches about numerous issues. Those who believe that we should respect and validate those whose conscience-bound interpretation of Scripture leads them to affirm homosexual behavior are replacing the authority of Holy Scripture with the authority of the subjective opinions of individuals. *Not only does such a view mock Holy Scripture. In addition, such a view keeps us from bearing the burden of those who are caught in sin's trap by preventing us from calling them to repentance and faith in Jesus.*[230]

The ELCA's view of "bound conscience" embraces relativism over Holy Scripture and prevents us from proclaiming repentance and forgiveness of sins to erring sinners. This is why many other Lutherans are offended and concerned when on page 19 of *Human Sexuality: Gift and Trust* we read these words: "...this church draws on the foundational Lutheran understanding that the baptized are called to discern God's love in service to the neighbor. In our Christian freedom, we therefore seek responsible actions that serve others and do so with humility and deep respect for the conscience-bound beliefs of others. We understand that, in this discernment about ethics and church practice, faithful people can and will come to different conclusions about the meaning of Scripture and about what constitutes responsible

---

[230] We find a similar error in the book *Love Is an Orientation* by Andrew Marin. He wrongly interprets 1st Corinthians 6:9-11 by suggesting that we should NOT proclaim repentance to those involved in homosexual behavior. Instead, we should just love them and wait for God to change their minds. On pages 133-134 of his book Marin writes: "When do gays and lesbians have the right to be their own person in Christ, regardless of whether a Christian agrees with their conclusion – whether that conclusion is to be a gay Christian or nonbeliever? Love and grace still must persist even when ... two believers ... don't see eye to eye ... To release responsibility for a person to God is to remain unconditionally there for them and always provide the unrestricted path to God in both faith and deeds, all the while trusting in God's ultimate power to continue to shape their journey of faith – just as Paul did with the Corinthian Church." What Marin fails to note is that for Paul "love and grace" also included telling the members of the Corinthian congregation to rebuke the man in the incestuous relationship and then excommunicate him if he refused to repent. Marin is wrong to interpret Paul's words to mean that we should never proclaim repentance to someone caught in the sin of homosexual behavior. Certainly, we should build a trusting relationship with such a person and lovingly show him or her what Holy Scripture teaches about his or her behavior. But there finally comes a point when we must proclaim repentance for the sake of the person's salvation (see 1st Corinthians 5:4-5).

action. We further believe that this church, on the basis of 'the bound conscience,' will include these different understandings and practices within its life as it seeks to live out its mission and ministry in the world."

When the ELCA defines "the foundational Lutheran understanding that the baptized are called to discern God's love in service to the neighbor" as being fulfilled in its view of the "bound conscience," this is a horrible misunderstanding of what Lutheran's teach about what it means to love one's neighbor. Loving one's neighbor means many things – but it especially means "speaking the truth in love" to those who are "blown here and there by every wind of teaching and by the cunning and craftiness of men in their deceitful scheming." (Ephesians 4:14-15)

Of course, some who want to promote the idea of "bound conscience" will point to sections of Scripture such as Romans chapters 14 and 15 or 1st Corinthians chapter 8 as evidence that we must be willing to respect and validate the views of others who understand Scripture differently than we do.

But if you examine those sections of Scripture you will quickly discover that Paul is there dealing with what theologians call *adiaphora* – which means "matters of indifference." Simply put, there are some behaviors that Scripture teaches we are free to do or not do with a clear conscience.

One example of an adiaphoron is eating pork. Even though the Jews were not allowed to eat pork in the Old Testament, this ceremonial law was never given to the Gentiles. In addition, now that Christ has fulfilled his work, the Old Testament ceremonial laws – including the food laws given to the Jews only – have been abolished. We are now free to eat pork chops!

However, some people may not understand this. Some may read the Old Testament and wrongly conclude that God's temporary ceremonial food laws for the Jews apply to ALL people of ALL times and places. Therefore, out of love for Christ, these same people refuse to eat pork because they believe that this is God's will for us. *How does Paul respond to this situation?*

First, Paul teaches that those of us who know better, that is, we who understand that we are free to eat pork - we should not immediately judge those who think eating pork is wrong because they are refraining from eating pork out of love for Christ. Those who refuse to eat pork are doing nothing wrong because God never said that it is sinful NOT to eat pork. Therefore, such people are not "caught in a sin" by not eating pork. They simply misunderstand what Scripture teaches concerning this issue.

Second, Paul teaches that those of us who know that we are free to eat pork should NOT eat pork if this would lead our "No pork!" brothers to conclude that it is permissible to rebel against God's will. In other words, if they believe it **is** sinful to eat pork – then for them to eat pork WOULD be a sin because the essence of sin is a heart of rebellion against God. As Paul says: "...everything that does not come from faith is sin." (Romans 14:23) Of course, the eventual goal would be lovingly to instruct our "No pork!" brothers about the abolition of ceremonial food laws so they will finally understand the correct teaching of Scripture on this issue.

But what if the "No pork!" brothers find out that some Christians are eating pork in the privacy of their homes? And then instead of concluding that it is permissible to rebel against God's will they rebuke the "pork loving" brothers and insist that they must stop eating pork or risk damnation. In this case, Paul would say: "...the man who does not eat everything must not condemn the man who does ... As one who is in the Lord Jesus, I am fully convinced that no food is unclean in itself ... Do not allow what you consider good to be spoken of as evil..."

In other words, if the "No pork!" brothers are making a matter of adiaphora equal to a universal moral law of Scripture and use that error to insist that the "pork loving" brothers are going to hell unless they repent and stop eating pork – then Paul would insist that we who know better continue to eat pork for the sake of the Gospel, and do our best to correct our erring "No pork!" brothers.

Please understand! When Paul says "Do not allow what you consider good to be spoken of as evil" he is speaking of behaviors that Scripture clearly classify as adiaphora!

In contrast, Paul would NEVER say to someone involved in homosexual behavior: "Do not allow what you consider good to be spoken of as evil." The distinction is that eating pork (or not) is a matter of adiaphora whereas homosexual behavior (and other sexual sins) is a violation of a universal moral law clearly taught in Scripture!

The ELCA's teaching about "bound conscience" regarding homosexual behavior results in us replacing the authority of Holy Scripture on this issue with subjective personal opinion. This view of "bound conscience" ends up denying the clarity of Holy Scripture on any issue of doctrine or life.

Martin Chemnitz, one of the great Reformation Lutheran theologians, faced a similar problem when some Roman Catholics in his day claimed that Scripture was a vague book and difficult to interpret – and that is why the people needed to rely on the inherited traditions of the Church and especially the Papacy for a proper understanding of God's will.

In response to this, Martin Chemnitz wrote these words: "Lest I take more time reciting the abusive words of individual papalists against Holy Scripture, the sum and substance is this: They maintain that Holy Scripture is not canon, norm, measuring instrument, or rule, according to which all disputes concerning matters of faith are to be adjusted ... because ... in those things which it does contain it is obscure and ambiguous..."[231]

In addition, in response to Roman theologians who used 2nd Peter 3:16 as evidence that Scripture is obscure, Martin Chemnitz wrote these words: "But they say: 'Peter ... affirms that the epistles of Paul are hard to understand ... Therefore it is dangerous to use the Scriptures, and it is safer to be satisfied with the traditions.' I reply: Peter does not say ... that all the dogmas in Paul's epistles are 'hard to understand,' but some ... And he does say that ... unlearned and unstable men twist them to their own destruction ... Of itself, therefore, unless it is twisted, [Scripture] does not give any but one, simple, true, and salutary meaning. And this fate, Peter says, the epistles of Paul have in common with the rest of Scripture, for he says: 'as they do the other Scriptures.' But does Peter for this reason warn against the reading of the Scripture? By no means! Rather he gives the reason and purpose of this reminder when he says: 'You therefore, beloved, knowing this beforehand, beware lest you be carried away with the error of lawless men and lose your own stability, etc.' We have therefore Peter's judgment concerning his own, concerning Paul's, and concerning the rest of the Scripture, from what considerations, for what reasons, and to what end they were transmitted and commended to the church."[232]

---

[231] *Examination of the Council of Trent: Part 1* by Martin Chemnitz (translated by Fred Kramer), 46.

[232] *Examination of the Council of Trent: Part 1* by Martin Chemnitz (translated by Fred Kramer), 143-144.

The words of Martin Chemnitz quoted above apply very well to the ELCA's idea of "bound conscience." Rather than relying on traditions and the Papacy as their source of doctrinal truth (as did Chemnitz's Roman Catholic opponents), the ELCA has now created a new "Papacy" in the form of the authority of the individual's subjective "bound conscience." The ELCA is essentially teaching that no one can challenge the authority of another's "bound conscience" without being guilty of sin and causing division within the body of Christ![233]

In addition to replacing the authority of Holy Scripture with the individual's "bound conscience," the actions of the August 2009 ELCA national convention also ignored the witness of the Church "catholic," that is, the universal Christian Church.

Not only does the ELCA's decision to affirm homosexual behavior ignore and reject the witness of the Christian Church since the time of the apostles – thereby ignoring the "Great Tradition" which gives witness to the clear teaching of Holy Scripture regarding homosexual behavior. The ELCA decision to affirm homosexual behavior also negatively affects ecumenical relations with other Protestant, Roman Catholic and Orthodox church bodies around the world – most of whom agree with Holy Scripture that homosexual behavior is sinful and contrary to God's will for us.

The LCMS has also responded to this problem with the following words:

---

[233] We find the same problem in the United Church of Christ's (UCC) "God is Still Speaking!" movement. A common slogan connected to this movement is: "Never place a period where God has placed a comma!" ***Of course, the problem is that many in the UCC end up placing <u>commas</u> where God has placed <u>periods</u>!*** Not only does the "God is Still Speaking!" movement validate any number of contradictory interpretations of Scripture. In addition, the "God is Still Speaking!" movement allows for other subjective revelations besides Holy Scripture as valid "words of God." The result is that there is no objective "Thus says the Lord!" possible among those in the UCC who promote the "God is Still Speaking!" movement. This helps us understand why the UCC refers to the universal Creeds (The Apostles', Nicene and Athanasian) as <u>testimonies</u> (not <u>tests</u>) of faith. In other words, the Faith confessed in the universal Creeds is reduced to just one testimony among many other – even contradictory! – testimonies. ***This explains why the UCC allows their ordained clergy to reject such basic Christian doctrines as Creation, the Trinity, the Deity of Christ and even the Atonement!*** Obviously, those in the UCC who promote the "God is Still Speaking!" movement usually affirm homosexual behavior because the passages of Scripture that clearly condemn such behavior as sinful are either reinterpreted or simply rejected.

"As evangelical Christians we are grounded in the Bible, God's written and infallible Word. The Bible, and not human traditions (even laudable church traditions), provides the final assurance about what is true and what the church is to believe and do.

We are also 'catholic' Christians. We confess with Roman Catholics the ecumenical Creeds of the western catholic tradition. Catholic means universal and complete. We believe that there is only one true faith and all who share it belong to Jesus Christ (Eph. 4:4-6). This one faith is faith in the Triune God, who is only known through Jesus, the Son of God who reveals the Father and who sends the Holy Spirit (Matt 28:19). The Athanasian Creed calls this the 'catholic' faith. This means we cannot compromise doctrinal convictions, nor can we forget that all those who confess faith in the Triune God are fellow Christians ...

The controversy over human sexuality is a case in point. Across the spectrum of Christianity, including both Evangelical and Roman Catholic churches (as well as Christians from virtually every denominational tradition throughout the world), church bodies and their leaders have declared their firm conviction that same-gender sexual relationships are contrary to God's will. Evangelical (and classical Protestant) leaders have emphasized that the contrary view contradicts the Scriptures. Roman Catholic (and Orthodox) churches have pointed out that the contrary view contradicts the 'Great Tradition' of Christian thought that has endured throughout millennia. As a Christian church body that seeks to be both evangelical and catholic, we are fully at home with this consensus and find in it a confirmation of Lutheran theology and identity.

The ELCA's decisions stand in sharp contrast to this genuinely ecumenical Christian consensus. The foundational document for the ELCA's controversial approval of same-gender genital sexual relationships describes itself as 'a distinctively Lutheran approach' to human sexuality. As Lutheran Christians, we find this claim to be deeply troubling ... we strongly disagree that 'a distinctly Lutheran approach' to Christian teaching should separate us either from the evangelical consensus regarding the teachings of Holy Scripture about human sexuality or from the catholic

tradition's perspective on Holy Marriage and its belief in the incompatibility of openly homosexual activity with Christian life."[234]

Simply put, not only does the ELCA's view of "bound conscience" undermine the clarity and ultimate authority of Holy Scripture. In addition, their view of "bound conscience" also ignores the nearly unanimous witness of the Church catholic on the issue of homosexual behavior.

Once again, I quote from the LCMS document *Theological Implications of the 2009 ELCA Decisions*:

"They assert that ... So long as differing moral perspectives on homosexual acts are held in good conscience, other Christians and the church ought to respect the validity of a variety of perspectives. The LCMS cannot and does not share this conclusion or the understanding of Scripture on which it is based. We believe that the Holy Scriptures of the Old and New Testament are the living Word of God, through His prophets and apostles. We affirm the infallibility of the Scriptures because they are 'God-breathed' (2 Tim 3:16 NIV) – that is, though they were written by men, God is their primary author and every word of Scripture is His word. Therefore they are not subject to all the same assumptions which apply to other ancient literature. We also hold the Scriptures to be understandable and truthful in their plain or simple meaning and that no other writing, understanding, or experience may call into question that meaning ... This view of scriptural authority leads us to affirm that where the Bible speaks clearly regarding matters of human values, conduct, or behavior, such teachings may not be denied or qualified, but must have continuing relevance in every era of the Church. Teachings contrary to the Scriptures must not be tolerated in the Church. For example, while some may debate whether the Bible specifically addresses the matter of same-sex attraction as it is understood and experienced

---

[234] *Italic* emphasis is mine. This quote is taken from *Theological Implications of the 2009 ELCA Decisions, 6-7.*

today, nevertheless, the Bible plainly and simply forbids same-sex genital activity as contrary to the will of God."[235]

Therefore, the ELCA's view of the "bound conscience" must not be used to undermine what Holy Scripture clearly teaches about the sin of homosexual behavior. Christians are called to bind their consciences to the Word of God, Holy Scripture, which clearly reveals God's will for us regarding what we are to believe and how we are to live. We are to use Holy Scripture to proclaim repentance and forgiveness of sins in Jesus' Name for the salvation of lost sinners – including those who bear the burden of homosexual orientation and behavior.

Finally, I offer once last quote in this section of my book from the article titled *How Did We Come to This?* by Robert Benne who was a voting member of the Virginia Synod at the August 2009 convention of the ELCA. Benne writes:

"The radicals wanted many voices and perspectives, especially those of the 'marginalized,' put forward in the ongoing deliberations of the ELCA. They were so successful that now after twenty years there is no authoritative biblical or theological guidance in the church. There are only many voices. The 2009 Assembly legitimated those many voices by adapting a 'bound-conscience' principle in which anyone claiming a sincerely-held conviction on about any doctrine must be respected. The truth of the Word of God has been reduced to sincerely-held opinion ... The ELCA has formally left the Great Tradition for liberal Protestantism." [236]

I want to stress that there are many faithful laypeople and pastors in the ELCA who are very disturbed by the "bound conscience" view officially adopted at the 2009 ELCA convention. They are doing their best to give a faithful biblical witness within the ELCA on the issue of homosexual behavior. We need to keep them in our prayers and support them in any way we can.

---

[235] *Theological Implications of the 2009 ELCA Decisions, 2.*

[236] *Concordia Theological Monthly: Volume 73 / Number 4, October of 2009, 366-367.*

We must also pray for those in the ELCA who have been misled into affirming homosexual behavior because of false teaching and their own self-deception. We must strive to speak the truth in love to them so that they may repent and rejoice in the forgiveness of Jesus Christ.

Back to the "Anonymous Letter"

At the beginning of this chapter I quoted an entire article I received in the mail from an anonymous person (see pp. 121-122 of this book). This article uses a very sarcastic tone to suggest that those who use Scripture to show that homosexual behavior is sinful simply don't know Scripture very well or they would realize that they don't obey many other laws found in Holy Scripture. Of course, the author's point is that we don't have to take Scripture seriously when it clearly condemns even consensual homosexual behavior.

However, as I have shown in this chapter, it is the author of this article (whose name I do not know because the anonymous person who mailed the article to me did not give me the name of the author) who has an extremely limited understanding of Scripture and how it applies to us today.

For example, the article suggests that the female engineering professor is violating 1st Peter 3:1 by pleading with her husband to shave off his beard. But 1st Peter 3:1 never says that wives can't ask their husbands to do them a favor or that wives can't offer their husbands good advice. Of course, if she were nagging her husband in a manipulative and selfish manner, then this would have been sinful and 1st Peter 3:1 would apply very well! She would need to repent!

The article also suggests that the female professor is violating 1st Timothy 2:12 because she very likely taught some men in her engineering classes. But this point only shows the author's biblical ignorance. As we will see in the next chapter, 1st Timothy 2:12 does not prohibit ALL forms of teaching done by women. Instead, 1st Timothy 2:12 only forbids a woman to engage in a ***very particular kind*** of teaching – the authoritative teaching done by the pastor in the context of the public Service. Not only does Scripture allow women to teach Scripture in the same manner that any layperson (male or female) is allowed to teach. In addition, Scripture has absolutely no problem with women teaching non-Scriptural secular information. Therefore, the female professor in the article is NOT violating 1st Timothy 2:12 by teaching engineering to men in her classes. The author of this article shows his limited understanding of Scripture by even suggesting that she did violate 1st Timothy 2:12.

In addition, the author of the article suggests that the female also violates 1st Timothy 2:9 by wearing gold and pearls. But this is ridiculous. 1st Timothy 2:9 does not condemn the wearing of gold, pearls (or any other jewelry) per se. Instead, 1st Timothy 2:9 condemns the sinful MOTIVES that some women can have for wearing outward adornments. In other words, in the culture of that day many women put their entire focus on outward beauty – not unlike some women and *even men* today! Paul's point in 1st Timothy 2:9 is that true beauty is found in a mature Christian character.[237]

So, Paul's point is NOT that wearing gold or pearls is sinful. His point is that women should not be shallow, self-centered people who care more about cultural fads than they do about pleasing the Lord. As long as women know what true beauty is, they can wear gold or pearls (or any other jewelry) in good conscience! Again, the author of this article shows his ignorance of Scripture by even suggesting that 1st Timothy 2:9 condemns the wearing of goal and pearls per se.

The article also points out that the female is violating Deuteronomy 22:5 because she is wearing slacks. Nonsense! Deuteronomy 22:5 is condemning those who deliberately despise the fact that God created them as male or female - and so they wear opposite sex clothing in order to try to be more like the opposite sex.[238] Obviously, if men or women in our modern culture wear opposite sex clothing because they despise their own sex and want to be the opposite sex – then they ARE violating Deuteronomy 22:5 and should repent! However, just because a woman wears slacks does not mean she is violating Deuteronomy 22:5. The fact is that even though both men and women wear slacks in our culture, we understand that this does not mean that such men or women are trying to be the opposite sex. For example, there are slacks specifically made for women and slacks specifically made for men – which is why we have different clothing sections (male and female) in our department stores!

---

[237] Also see 1st Peter 3:3-4.

[238] An extreme version of this rebellion against God's creation is when men or women choose to have "sex change" operations. Of course, such operations do NOT actually change men into women or women into men. Instead, male and female sex organs are mutilated or cut off and false body parts are added to give the illusion of "sex change."

The next "violation" of Scripture the author of this article mentions is that the couple may have ordered "shellfish or pork" (although the article doesn't mention that they did) at the restaurant – in rebellion against Leviticus 11:7, 10. However, this point especially shows the author's ignorance of Holy Scripture and his or her inability to make the proper distinction between the civil and ceremonial laws given only to Israel for a temporary period of time (the food laws are included in this!) versus the universal moral laws that apply to all people of all times and places. I responded thoroughly to this misunderstanding of Scripture in the section of this chapter titled **Red Lobster fans can't take Leviticus seriously!** *Read that section of this chapter again and you will see how ridiculous and biblically illiterate the author of this article is by suggesting that eating "shellfish or pork" in today's culture is a violation of Leviticus 11:7, 10.*

The author of the article next suggests that the man is violating Deuteronomy 23:19 by being a loan officer. Once again, the author fails to understand that Deuteronomy 23:19 was a civil law given only to Israel. Second, the Old Testament never prohibits charging interest per se, but only charging excessive interest. In other words, we should not be greedy and put unfair financial burdens on people simply because the law allows us to do so. In other words, we should treat others fairly in our business practices. In this sense, the spirit of Deuteronomy 23:19 DOES apply to us today.

Therefore, if someone is being greedy and is taking advantage of someone in a financial way, such a person should repent! On the other hand, the Bible never condemns charging interest per se – especially when the one giving the loan and the one taking the loan freely agree to the terms! In fact, most people would not be able to own a home or a car if it were not for the option of getting a loan and then paying interest on that loan. So, a person can be a loan officer in good conscience!

Simply put, Deuteronomy 23:19 does NOT condemn the charging of interest when the parties involved freely agree to the terms. Instead, Deuteronomy 23:19 condemns excessive interest being placed on people who have no other options. Again, the author of this article shows that he or she simply does not understand Scripture very well at all.

The author of the article then mentions that the man violates Leviticus 19:27 by shaving his beard and that both of the man and the woman violate Leviticus 19:19 by wearing clothing of more than one fabric. Once again, the author fails to distinguish between the civil and ceremonial laws given only to the Jews for a temporary period of time versus the universal moral laws that apply to all people of all times and places. The law about shaving was only given to Jewish men, and this law was abolished when Christ finished His work. The law about clothing with two fabrics was also given only to the Jews, and this, too, was abolished when Christ finished His work.

Neither the shaving nor the "two kinds of fabric" laws are ever mentioned in the New Testament as being binding on us. *In contrast, the universal moral laws (including the sexual prohibitions, such as homosexual behavior!) are clearly taught in the New Testament as binding on all people today!*

Next, the author of the article mentions the fact that this couple was "committing adultery" because the woman had been divorced from her previous husband (suggested by Matthew 19:9) - and then the author suggests that they should be stoned to death if we are going to take Deuteronomy 22:22 seriously. There are several problems with this argument.

First, the author never mentions if the woman had a legitimate reason for getting the divorce. If her previous husband had committed adultery and refused to repent, had deserted her or was abusing her, then she had a biblical reason to get a divorce and she was free to get married again. On the other hand, if she divorced her previous husband because she simply didn't take her vows seriously or because she herself committed adultery and wanted to marry the man with whom she had an affair – then she IS guilty of sin and needs to repent!

Second, regarding the death penalty for adultery, in chapter two of this book under the section on Leviticus I clearly explained that the Levitical prohibitions against adultery, incest, homosexuality and bestiality still apply because they are universal sexual laws. However, I also explained that the Old Testament death penalties for those sins no longer apply because those death penalty laws were given to Old Testament Israel when they functioned as a theocracy – both Church and State. But since this is not the case for Christians today who live under the laws of the nations where they live, the Levitical death penalty for adultery does NOT apply. Nevertheless, the Levitical condemnation of adultery as being sinful DOES still apply to us today. *Those who commit adultery need to repent or face something far worse than capital punishment!*

Finally, many who wish to affirm homosexual behavior will point out the fact that some churches today turn a "blind eye" to divorce.

They then suggest that if we are willing to ignore what Scripture teaches about divorce we should at least be willing to ignore what Scripture teaches about homosexual behavior. There are huge problems with this analogy. First, we should NOT turn a "blind eye" to divorce today. We should strive to keep marriages together and call people to repentance when they are guilty of unbiblical reasons for getting a divorce. Just because some churches turn a "blind eye" to what Scripture teaches about divorce does not mean we should turn a "blind eye" to what Scripture teaches about homosexual behavior. *Two wrongs don't make a right!* Second, most Christians who have been through a divorce are repentant, they trust in Jesus for forgiveness, and they rely on God for the strength to never get divorced again. This is not a good analogy for those who want to affirm homosexual behavior. In order for divorce to be a good analogy for the pro-gay argument one would have to say: "I think divorce is a good thing. I believe we should affirm this behavior, and encourage people to get divorced as often as possible!" But who would ever make this argument for divorce? Just as people who are guilty of the sin of divorce should repent, trust in Jesus for forgiveness and strive to never get divorced again. In the same way, someone who is guilty of homosexual behavior should repent, trust in Jesus for forgiveness and strive to never engage in homosexual behavior again.

The author of this article tells his or her little story about this man and woman, and all the biblical laws they are supposedly violating, in order to suggest that Christians who use Scripture to teach that homosexual behavior is sinful are biblically illiterate bigots! But this author's uneducated and willy-nilly use of Bible passages shows that he or she has a very limited understanding of Scripture's teaching.

For instance, the author of this article goes on to show how Scripture has been used in the past to justify slavery. But I have already shown in this chapter under the section on slavery that those who use the Bible to condone slavery are guilty of misinterpreting it! Not only does the Bible NOT condone slavery (especially not the raced based slavery in the American South!). Even more, the proper interpretation of the Bible on this issue is the primary reason for the abolition of slavery in America and in many parts of the world!

Simply put, the Bible teaches that all humans are descended from Adam. There's only one race – the HUMAN race![239] (This truth is

[239] See the book *One Blood* by Ken Ham, Carl Wieland and Don Batten.

based on a LITERAL reading of the creation account in Genesis!) Even though certain types of slavery were regulated in the Bible, slavery itself was never commanded must less condoned! *In contrast, various sexual sins – including consensual homosexual behavior – are clearly condemned in both the Old and New Testaments.*

The author of the article also mentions the oppression of woman – as though the Bible itself condones this! The author even mentions that some pastors used Genesis 3:16 to teach that women today should not use anesthesia during childbirth! However, the author fails to mention that the few pastors who may have done this were guilty of misinterpreting Holy Scripture and applying it improperly!

As I clearly pointed out in this chapter of my book, the Bible does NOT condone the oppression of women. In fact, the Bible CONDEMNS the oppression of women! Those who use the Bible to justify the oppression of women only show their ignorance of Scripture and their failure to interpret it properly.

In addition, even though Genesis 3:16 teaches that one result of the fall will be that women will have pain in childbirth. This same text does NOT teach that it is sinful for us to try to avoid the pain of this fallen world. In other words, Genesis 3:16 does NOT teach that it is sinful for women to use anesthesia during childbirth!

In His mercy, God allows us relief from the pain we deserve because of our many sins. We give God thanks and praise for these undeserved blessings! Nevertheless, in spite of our best efforts at relieving pain, we still must face suffering and eventual death. This reminds us that we live in a world broken by our sin against God. Only Jesus' death and resurrection for us gives us hope in the face of these things.

Finally, based on his or her misinterpretation of Genesis 3:19, the author ends the article by making fun of pastors who enjoy air conditioning while preaching that the Bible condemns homosexual behavior. Once again, this author shows his or her complete ignorance of Scripture and his or her total inability to apply it properly!

Even though Genesis 3:19 does teach that man will produce food by "the sweat of his brow," this does NOT mean – as noted above – that it is wrong for us to alleviate the pain and suffering we face in this fallen world. In fact, God in His mercy grants us much relief from the suffering and pain we deserve – and we should never cease to give Him thanks and praise for this!

I willingly confess that I have enjoyed God's gift of air conditioning while preaching sermons on any number of issues – and I can do this without being inconsistent at all!

However, I must admit, that in spite of God's gift of air conditioning, I still produce "sweat on my brow" when I give sermons on hot summer days. But this only makes me long for the New Creation where we will once again walk with God "in the cool of the day!" (Genesis 3:8)

Seriously! My prayer is that the author of this article will realize how his or her twisted and uneducated use of Scripture has misled many people into wrongly thinking that homosexual behavior can be affirmed.

I wonder if the author of this article would be willing to use his or her same silly arguments to justify the affirmation of adultery, incest or bestiality. I hope not! **But if this author is willing to admit that Scripture's condemnation of adultery, incest and bestiality still applies to us today, then maybe he or she will also eventually realize that the same Scripture's condemnation of homosexual behavior still applies to us today as well.**

╬ *CHAPTER FOUR* ╬

Bearing Their Burden

The subtitle for this book is: "Speaking the Truth in Love to People Burdened by Homosexuality." I believe the best way we can bear the burden of those who are burdened by homosexual desire and behavior is to proclaim God's Truth to them in a loving manner.

Therefore, the previous pages of this book clearly show what Scripture teaches about God's institution of marriage being between one man and one woman, God's will for sex being only within marriage, and God's condemnation of various sexual sins – including homosexual desire and behavior. Regarding Scripture's prohibitions of homosexual desire and behavior, I also answered arguments that attempt to 1) reinterpret those prohibitions in order to justify consensual, monogamous homosexual behavior *or* attempt to 2) discredit the authority of Holy Scripture with the goal of ignoring its clear prohibitions against homosexual desire and behavior.

If our intention is to bear the burden of those who are burdened by homosexual desire and behavior, then we must be sure that we are not merely imposing our opinions about homosexuality upon them. Instead, we must show such people what God Himself says about their homosexual desire and behavior. **But even more than this, we must proclaim to people the forgiveness, love, and hope we have through Jesus, the Savior of sinners!**

Acknowledge Our Guilt!

The Scripture text that is the theme for this book is Galatians 6:1-2, which reads: "Brothers, if someone is caught in a sin, you who are spiritual should restore him gently. But watch yourself, or you also may be tempted. Carry each other's burdens, and in this way you will fulfill the law of Christ." I have examined the meaning of this text earlier in this book. For now, I want to focus Paul's words "But watch yourself, or you also may be tempted."

Before any Christian attempts to proclaim repentance and forgiveness to another Christian, one must be aware of one's own complete and total sinful state before God. Even though believers are new creations in Christ who have been given hearts of repentance and faith, we Christians still have our sinful nature which we inherited from Adam – *and that sinful nature is NEVER decreased or reformed in this life!* In fact, no Christian will be free from his or her sinful nature until it ceases to exist at the time of death. Our hope this side of heaven is NOT our supposed "progress" in sanctification. Our only hope is Jesus – the righteousness, forgiveness and eternal life that only He can give us.

Therefore, we must acknowledge our own guilt before God before we attempt to confront a brother or sister who is caught in a sin. This is what Jesus means when He says: "Do not judge, or you too will be judged. For in the same way you judge others, you will be judged, and with the measure you use, it will be measured to you. Why do you look at the speck of sawdust in your brother's eye and pay no attention to the plank in your own eye? How can you say to your brother, 'Let me take the speck out of your eye,' when all the time there is a plank in your own eye? You hypocrite, first take the plank out of your own eye, and then you will see clearly to remove the speck from your brother's eye." (Matthew 7:1-5)

Sadly, these words of Jesus have been misinterpreted by those who affirm homosexual behavior. They suggest that Jesus means that we should NEVER confront anyone about his or her sin. In other words, the only real sin is rebuking someone else for his or her sin. Therefore, they use Jesus' words to condemn Christians who attempt to love and serve those who are caught in the sin of homosexuality by confronting them with their sin.

But Jesus is NOT condemning the act of confronting others about their sin! For example, in Luke 7:3 Jesus Himself says: "If your brother sins, rebuke him, and if he repents, forgive him." Instead, in Matthew 7:1-5 Jesus is condemning *sinful, self-righteous judgment* – the kind that was often done by the Pharisees.

Simply put, self-righteousness judgment can be summed up by three points: 1) Pointing out the sin of other people as though you yourself were sinless. 2) Using human opinion and tradition to judge other's behavior instead of using Scripture alone. 3) Pointing people to their own works as the source of their salvation instead of proclaiming forgiveness in Christ's Name.

However, even though we must repent of self-righteous judgment, Matthew 7:1-5 and the rest of Scripture is clear that we Christians MUST engage in Christ-righteous judgment! I can also sum up Christ-righteous judgment with three points: 1) Acknowledging one's complete and total guilt before God BEFORE one attempts to point out the sin in another person's life. 2) Using Scripture alone to point out the sin in a person's life and never imposing your mere opinion about morality on another person. 3) Proclaiming forgiveness and new life in Christ alone – a free gift for sinners who can not redeem themselves from their sinful desire or behavior.

We Must Acknowledge Our Sins of COMMISSION

If God is moving us to bear the burden of those who are burdened by homosexual desire and behavior, then we need to acknowledge the ways we have sinned against such people and then rejoice in the healing forgiveness of Jesus. How have we committed sins against those who bear the burden of homosexual desire and behavior? Here's a short list for starters:

- **We must repent of the times we have regarded homosexual desire or behavior as the WORST of all sins – or at least as being WORSE than our heterosexual lust and behavior.** Not only is such thinking in conflict with the teaching of Holy Scripture. Such thinking tempts us to condemn others (those burdened by homosexual desire and behavior) in order to somehow lesson the guilt of our own heterosexual sin. Many single heterosexual people - even Christians! – engage in sexual behavior before marriage. Many heterosexual people – even Christians! – are guilty of lustful thoughts and the use of pornography. Many heterosexuals – even Christians! - are guilty of the act of adultery. Our heterosexual sin is just as ugly and abominable before God as the homosexual sin of other people. We must repent!
- **We must repent of the times we have made fun of or mocked those who are burdened by homosexual desire and behavior.** I remember my days in high school. Some would make fun of the guys who had a more effeminate demeanor. Such young men were labeled as "fags," "sissies" or "queers." Some would also make fun of the girls who had a more masculine demeanor. Such young women were labeled as

"lesbians" and "dikes." But such sinful behavior is not limited to high school. Sadly, such behavior happens among adults in society – but usually behind the backs of those who are burdened with homosexual desire or behavior. Sadly, such sinful "behind the back" gossip even takes place in Christian congregations. We must repent!

- **We must repent if we have ever physically threatened or harmed a person simply because he or she is burdened by homosexual desire or behavior.** This doesn't happen as often as the media would like us to think – but it DOES happen. A few years ago, in my own community of Jamestown, ND, a young many was physically beaten by others. The reason? He was known as a practicing homosexual. We must repent of such evil behavior!
- **We must repent of the times we have thought or said that AIDS is God's specific judgment on those who practice homosexual behavior.** We do not have a revelation from God about this, and saying that AIDS is God's judgment on homosexual behavior only puts up walls between us and those with AIDS who are guilty of homosexual behavior. We must repent!

We Must Acknowledge Our Sins of OMISSION

We sinners tend to focus only on our sins of COMMISION – the evil things we do. But we must recognize that God also condemns our far more numerous sins of OMISSION – the good things we fail to do. We need to acknowledge our sins of omission against people who are burdened by homosexual desire or behavior, and then rejoice in the healing forgiveness of Jesus. Allow me to offer a short list of sins of omission:

- **We must repent of the times we have failed to confront others who are caught in the sin of homosexuality. We must repent of the times we have failed to show such people what Scripture clearly teaches about the sin of homosexual desire and behavior.** One reason we fail to do this is that we are simply apathetic about the spiritual dilemma of others. We care only about our own spiritual state. Another reason we fail to do this is that we don't want to risk being persecuted or rejected. Once again, we are being selfish and we lack genuine concern for others who are caught in sin. Still another reason we fail to do this is that we have allowed ourselves to be deceived by those who wrongly teach that Scripture does not condemn homosexual behavior. We gather around ourselves teachers who will say what our sinful, itching ears want to hear. Once again, we are being selfish. We must repent!

- **We must repent of times we <u>have</u> clearly and correctly used Scripture to condemn the sin of homosexual desire and behavior, *but then have FAILED to clearly and lovingly proclaim forgiveness of sins and new life in Jesus' Name.*** Sometimes we are all too eager to rebuke those who are caught in the sin of homosexuality. However, if we also FAIL to proclaim the Gospel; if we fail to point them to Jesus in Whom they have forgiveness and new life, then we have sinned horribly! Rebuking a person with God's law can often leave them in utter despair. We are guilty of great sin if we leave them in such despair and fail to proclaim forgiveness and new life with God in Jesus. *Yes, of course, we must proclaim God's law in order to convict people of their sin. But we must never, ever fail to proclaim the GOSPEL – the only hope for sinners who are burdened by the guilt of their rebellion against God.* We must repent!

- **We must repent of the times we have remained silent and failed to speak in defense of those who were being made fun of or mocked simply because they had the burden of homosexual desire or behavior.** In Martin Luther's Small Catechism he gives the following explanation to the Eight Commandment: "We should fear and love God so that we may not deceitfully belie, betray, slander, or defame our neighbor, *but defend him, think and speak well of him, and put the best construction on everything.*" [240] Even though Scripture clearly teaches that homosexual desire and behavior is sinful, this does not mean we should turn a blind eye and a deaf ear to situations when those who bear the burden of homosexual desire and behavior are being made fun of or mocked. We should be willing to defend such people and reach out to them in love. We sin when we fail to do this. We must repent!

---

[240] The *italic* emphasis is mine. Quotation is found on page 350 in *Concordia: The Lutheran Confessions (A Reader's Edition of the Book of Concord).*

- **We must also repent of the times we have failed defend and protect from physical harm those who are burdened by homosexual desire or behavior.** In Martin Luther's Small Catechism he gives the following explanation to the Fifth Commandment: "We should fear and love God so that we may not hurt or harm our neighbor in his body, *but help and befriend him in every bodily need [in every need and danger of life and body].*"[241] Even though Scripture clearly teaches that homosexual desire and behavior is sinful, this does not mean we should turn a blind eye and a deaf ear to situations when those who bear the burden of homosexual desire and behavior are being physically harmed. We should report such actions to the police or, if they are not available, do whatever is within our means to help a person in such a situation. We sin when we fail to do this. We must repent!
- **We must repent of the times we have failed to reach out in love and compassion to those with AIDS who have engaged in homosexual behavior.** We are often tempted to avoid those guilty of homosexual behavior who are dying of AIDS because we have convinced ourselves that they are "getting what they deserve." *We must remember that if God were to give us what we deserve, we would be in hell right now!* Even though Scripture clearly condemns homosexual desire and behavior, we must not fail to reach out to those who bear this burden and are dying of AIDS when God gives us the opportunity to do so. We must repent!

Simply put, we are guilty of many sins of commission and omission regarding those who bear the burden of homosexual desire and temptation. If you are guilty of any of these sins (and we all are, in one way or another), *then you need to know that you are completely forgiven and holy in God's sight through Jesus Who died in your place of damnation and conquered death for you by His resurrection.*

Christ has rescued you from sin and death, and now you are free to fulfill the law of Christ by bearing the burden of those who are caught in the sin of homosexuality.

---

[241] The *italic* emphasis is mine. Quotation is found on page 347 in *Concordia: The Lutheran Confessions (A Reader's Edition of the Book of Concord).*

Acknowledge Their Pain!

One way or another, sooner or later, we all experience suffering and pain in this fallen world. Sometimes we suffer as direct consequence of our sinful choices. Other times we suffer simply because we live in a broken world where violent and unloving acts by others, natural catastrophes, poverty, hunger, war and disease are all too common.

There are also times when faithful Christians will suffer precisely because they are living and speaking as faithful Christians – Jesus Himself said we who believe in Him should not be surprised when this happens. (Matthew 5:10-12; also 1st Peter 3:8-14 and 4:12-19)

Sometimes people wonder why God allows us to suffer. We must remember that suffering and death did not exist in God's original very good creation. Suffering and death is the result of our sin against God.

However, in His mercy, God chooses to use even our suffering and death to bless us. We don't know all the reasons God allows us to suffer, but He has revealed *some* reasons for our suffering in Holy Scripture.

Sometimes God will use suffering to humble us so that we will stop trusting in our own strength, take our sin seriously and recognize our need for God. Other times God will allow even faithful Christians to suffer in order to strengthen our faith in Him. In addition, God will also allow even faithful Christians to suffer in order to give us opportunities to witness to others about the hope we have in Christ.

However, sometimes we respond to suffering in sinful ways. Sometimes respond to suffering by blaming God and justifying ourselves. Sometimes we respond to suffering by playing the victim so that others will feel sorry for us and excuse our sinful behavior.

Sadly, some who are involved in homosexual behavior will sometimes play the victim in order to get sympathy and move others to tolerate or even affirm their homosexual behavior. We must never allow such people to use their pain as a way of keeping us from loving them by proclaiming the Truth of God's Word regarding the sin of homosexual behavior as well as the forgiveness and new life we have in Jesus.

However, we must recognize that there is some very legitimate suffering and pain in lives of those who bear the burden of homosexual desire and behavior. If we wish to bear the burden of those who are caught in this sin, we must be willing to acknowledge their legitimate pain. Allow me to give a list of the various types of pain experienced by those who are burdened by homosexual desire and behavior:

- **Those who bear the burden of homosexual desire did NOT choose to have this desire!** Even though *acting* on our desires is always a choice, we did not choose to *have* the sinful desires that we have – just as we did not choose to be conceived with a sinful nature that is completely opposed to God. Sometimes people say: "People who have homosexual desires can change if they really want to change. They can experience heterosexual desire just like the majority of humans if they would just put their minds to it and get their lust under control!" But this is not fair! Imagine saying to a married man who has heterosexual desires: "If you just try real hard you can stop having desires for women other than your wife! You're just choosing to have desires for other women. You can get rid of those desires if you really want to do it." The fact is, we sinners have many sinful desires that we did not ask for – and to suggest that we can eliminate these desires by an act of our will is not only unrealistic but it also denies what Scripture clearly teaches about our sinful nature. We must struggle with the desires of our sinful nature until the day we die! Therefore, we must understand that those who bear of the burden of homosexual desire did not choose to have this desire. Of course, this does not mean they should *act* on their homosexual desires (just as we should not act on any number of sinful desires that we may have). Nevertheless, we must acknowledge that those who bear the burden of homosexual desire did not choose to have this desire. In many cases such people truly do wish that they did not have homosexual desires, and in some cases they have done their very best to eliminate these desires – but to no avail. We need to understand that such people will very likely bear the burden of homosexual desire until the day they die – *and we need to do what we can to help them bear that burden.*

- **Some who bear the burden of homosexual desire and behavior experienced a very negative or distant relationship with the same-sex parent.** As noted earlier in this book, most now agree that the cause of homosexual orientation is not *merely* genetic. Those who bear the burden of homosexual orientation likely have this problem as the result of many factors at work in their lives.[242] With that said, a popular belief among experts about *one* possible cause for homosexual orientation is a negative or distant relationship with one's same-sex parent – *whether this negative or distant relationship was real or merely perceived to be real by the one who now has a homosexual orientation.*[243] Many people burdened by homosexual desire and behavior have a lot of unresolved pain regarding their relationship with their same-sex parent. As a result, such people may never have learned how to have intimate, non-sexual relationships with members of the same sex. The pain caused by this unmet need may have been one of the causes of their desire for intimacy with members of the same sex – a desire for intimacy that has been sexualized. Even though this pain is not a reason to affirm homosexual behavior in a person's life, we must be willing to acknowledge the emotional pain caused by a negative or distant relationship with one's same-sex parent – and then do what we can to help people who experience this pain.

- **Some who bear the burden of homosexual desire and behavior have often been made fun of and mocked because they share some aspects of demeanor in common with the opposite sex.** Some men have some effeminate characteristics. Some women have some masculine characteristics. This does not mean that all men with an *effeminate* demeanor have homosexual desires nor does this mean that all women with a *masculine* demeanor have homosexual desires. However, some who bear the burden of homosexual desire and behavior do

---

[242] On page 211 of *The Complete Christian Guide to Understanding Homosexuality* Joe Dallas writes: "It seems we are on the most solid theoretical ground when we resist holding to any one theory on the development of homosexuality as being always true in all cases, and instead hold to an interactive approach stating, in essence, that homosexuality is probably caused by a constellation of factors, some known and some unknown, including physical and emotional ones. The interactive theory considers both the inborn and developmental theories as having merit, with each of them contributing to the formation of attractions to the same sex."

[243]For more information about a negative relationship with one's same-sex parent being one possible cause of homosexual orientation, see: *The Complete Christian Guide to Understanding Homosexuality* by Joe Dallas and Nancy Heche, 197-218; *Homosexuality: The Use of Scientific Research in the Church's Moral Debate* by Stanton Jones and Mark Yarhouse, 47-92; *Homosexuality and the Politics of Truth* by Jeffrey Satinover, 93-108 & 221-228; *Desires in Conflict* by Joe Dallas, 91-120; *Counseling the Homosexual* by Michael Saia, 39-58.

share some characteristics of demeanor common to the opposite sex – *and they have experienced much torment and pain because of a demeanor that they did not choose.* This fact may have led some of these people to become loners who do not have many friends. We need to understand how these people have been hurt, and how much they need our love and friendship.

- **Some who bear the burden of homosexual desire and behavior have been sexually abused.** Not all people who experience sexual abuse end up having a homosexual orientation. In the same way, not all people who bear the burden of homosexual desire or behavior have experienced sexual abuse. However, some who bear the burden of homosexual desire and behavior HAVE been sexually abused – *often by members of the same sex!* Whether this sexual abuse happened only once or multiple times – the result is a great deal of pain and shame. For reasons not completely understood, some who have been sexually abused by members of the same sex end up bearing the burden of homosexual desire and behavior. One possibility is that they are trying to erase the pain of the sexual abuse from a member of the same sex by attempting to find love and acceptance within a CONSENSUL sexual experience with a member of the same sex. In any case, we need to acknowledge the pain of those who have been sexually abused by a member of the same sex and do what we can to help and heal them.

- **Some who bear the burden of homosexual desire and behavior have been spiritually damaged by false teaching about Christian sanctification.** I have visited with people who bear the burden of homosexual desire and behavior who have told me the following: "A pastor once told me that if I just confessed my sin of homosexual desire and behavior, trusted in Jesus, studied the Bible, attended Church and prayed for healing every day – then I would be healed of my homosexual desire and I would become a heterosexual! But no matter how hard I tried to be a faithful Christian, I never stopped having these homosexual desires. So, I concluded that either I must not be a real Christian or that God simply didn't want me. Either way, I gave up on Christianity!" This is so tragic. Imagine the spiritual pain of thinking that you are not a "real Christian" simply because you can not completely eliminate a particular sinful desire or behavior in your life. Imagine the spiritual pain of thinking that God must not want you if He does not completely eliminate a particular sinful desire or behavior in your life. Some who bear the burden of homosexual desire and behavior are in deep spiritual pain because of someone's false teaching about Christian sanctification. We must acknowledge their pain and proclaim the pure Gospel to them. They need to know that Christ's forgiveness and love for us does not depend on us eliminating all sinful desires or behaviors in our lives. We Christians must struggle with sinful desires and behaviors until the day we die. Even though the Spirit moves us to repent of our sinful desires and behaviors as well as resist them – we still may fall during times of weakness and temptation. During such times we need to know that we are completely forgiven and loved because of Christ who died in our place of damnation and thereby took away the guilt of all our sins – not just our PAST sins, but also our PRESENT and FUTURE sins!

Meeting Them Where They Are At!

Even though we should be willing to bear of the burden of those caught in the sin of homosexual behavior by proclaiming repentance and forgiveness of sins in Jesus' Name, we need to realize that such people are not all the same. In fact, people who bear the burden of homosexual behavior are at different places in their spiritual lives. This means that we must be willing to meet them where they are at, and this also means that dealing with the issue of their homosexual behavior may NOT be the first thing on our "to do" list.

First of all, whatever a person's spiritual state may be, we must first be willing to build a trusting friendship with him or her. If we meet a person who is involved in homosexual behavior but we don't even know that person, we should not introduce ourselves by saying: "Hi! My name is Tom. My desire is to speak God's Truth in love to you. Do you know that God condemns homosexual behavior? Do you know that you can have forgiveness and a new life in Jesus?" Even though these words are sincere and true, we probably won't get very far in bearing the burden of someone caught in the sin of homosexuality if we begin our relationship in that manner.

Instead, whatever a person's spiritual state may be, we must first get to know that person, become that person's friend, earn that person's trust – and then pray that God will give us an opportunity to speak His Truth in love to that person.

Now, there is no set timeline for how long this process must take. In some cases you might be able to begin a loving conversation about homosexual behavior in a few days after or even the same day you meet someone. In other cases you might not be able to have such a conversation for a year or several years. Or maybe you will never be able have a conversation about homosexual behavior with a person if that person refuses to allow you to share God's Truth with them. In the latter case, all you can do is pray for that person. The point is that we must be willing to build relationships with people before we attempt to speak God's Truth in love to them.

At this point I would like to offer five examples of "spiritual states" that people who bear the burden of homosexual behavior may be living in at any given time in their lives. I will then give advice on how we should attempt to witness to a person in each of these five "spiritual states."

1. **Some people are non-Christians who know nothing or very little about the Christian Faith.** If such a person is also a practicing homosexual, we should NOT begin our witness to such a person by dealing with the issue of his or her homosexual behavior. In fact, our ultimate goal with any people who bear the burden of homosexual behavior is NOT merely to get them to stop their homosexual behavior. Instead, our ultimate goal is to proclaim the Gospel of Jesus Christ through which the Holy Spirit creates faith in our hearts so that we can receive and believe in the forgiveness and new life that the Father gives us in His Son, Jesus. Without faith in Christ, ceasing from any type of sinful behavior does nothing to save us from our sinful condition!

   Therefore, if a person engaged in homosexual behavior is a non-Christian, after building a trusting relationship with him or her, you will want to begin your witness with basic information about God, creation, the Fall of Adam and Eve, original sin and our need for the person and work of Christ, God's Son. Help this person to see how God's plan of salvation unfolds throughout the history recorded in Holy Scripture – finding its fulfillment in the birth, life, death, resurrection and ascension of Jesus Christ. Once this person understands the nature of original sin and the hope we have in Jesus, you will then be in a position to deal with particular sin issues in his or her life – including his or her homosexual desire and behavior. The last impression we want to give to a non-Christian is that Christianity is just one more performance based religion which requires us to obey certain rules and live a certain way in order to be worthy of God's love. Instead, we want to show people the True God who reveals Himself to us in the cross where He sacrificed Himself to save His enemies and make them His children.

2. **Some people who were raised as Christians and once believed in Christ have fallen into unbelief and now are very skeptical about the teachings of the Christian Faith.** Some who have lost their faith in Christ and have fallen into unbelief also bear the burden of homosexual desire and behavior. Such people may be willing to admit that Holy Scripture condemns all forms of homosexual behavior, but they dismiss Scripture's teaching about homosexual behavior because they now believe that Holy Scripture need not be taken seriously. They have many objections about the doctrines of Christianity. They have many arguments that supposedly prove that the Bible is full of contradictions and shouldn't be trusted.

Before we attempt to speak God's Truth in love to such people regarding their homosexual behavior, we must first deal honestly with their objections to the Christian Faith and their arguments against the authority of Holy Scripture. We may not have to discuss the basic teachings of Christianity since such people may already be aware of such teachings due to being raised as Christians and having once believed in Christ. However, we must be willing to engage in some apologetics with such people and help them to recognize that their objections to and arguments against the Christian Faith are unfounded.

However, we must also remember that apologetics can only take us so far. Apologetics is a useful tool to expose the falsehood of people's objections to the Christian Faith and arguments against taking Holy Scripture seriously. But we can never bring people to faith in Christ through rational discussion. Therefore, at some point in the apologetics process we need to ask such people if we can simply share what we believe with them. If they give us permission, then we tell them God's story of salvation as recorded in Holy Scripture. We should not attempt to defend God's plan of salvation nor should we try to make God's plan of salvation sound rational (as though we could ever do that!). Instead, we must simply proclaim the Gospel and allow the Holy Spirit to create faith in their hearts.

Once the Holy Spirit gives people new hearts of faith, all their objections to and arguments against God's Word will fall away. They will now live by faith and not by sight. Once we have gone through this process we can then address particular sin issues in their lives – including their homosexual behavior. Remember! Our ultimate goal is not to get such people to stop their homosexual behavior. Our ultimate goal is for them to trust in Jesus as their Lord and Savior!

3. **Some people who are currently involved in homosexual behavior say that they believe in Christ and that they agree with every teaching of the Christian Faith. They even stress that they submit to the authority of Holy Scripture.** However, they justify their homosexual behavior because they believe that Christians have misinterpreted the Bible's prohibitions against homosexual behavior. They have been led to believe that God does not condemn homosexual behavior as long as it takes place within a loving, committed, consensual, monogamous relationship.

   Once we build a trusting friendship with such people, we should ask if they would be willing to study Holy Scripture about this issue. We should say to such a person: "We both believe that salvation comes through faith in Christ alone. Also, we both agree that we should submit to the authority of Holy Scripture. Can we study Holy Scripture together so we can learn what God truly teaches about homosexual behavior within a loving, committed, consensual, monogamous relationship? If you can show me from Scripture that I am wrong about God condemning even such homosexual behavior as this, then I will repent of my error and affirm your homosexual behavior within a loving, committed, consensual, monogamous relationship. However, if I can convince you from Holy Scripture that God does condemn even your type of homosexual behavior, then will you be willing to acknowledge your error, repent of your sin and rejoice in the forgiveness and healing that Jesus longs to give you?" If such a person is honest about his or her respect for the authority Holy Scripture and his or her desire to live according to God's will, then such a person should be willing to study Holy Scripture and be willing to submit to what it says about homosexual behavior.

If such a person does study Holy Scripture with you and is convinced that his or her type of homosexual behavior is also condemned by God's Word, *then you must assure this person that he or she is completely forgiven and holy in God's sight because of Jesus and His work on our behalf. You will need to surround such a person with Christian love and support as well as prayer, because it will be a difficult struggle for him or her to turn away from his or her homosexual behavior – especially if he or she has been in a long term relationship with his or her partner.*

4. **Some people who practice homosexual behavior are involved in liberal Christianity.** Unlike the former Christians described in #2 above, these people still consider themselves to be Christians – but their liberal form of Christianity has led them to deny some or all of the basic teachings of the Christian Faith. Very often such liberal Christians do not believe that Scripture is the inspired and inerrant Word of God. Instead, they believe the Bible *contains* "teachings from God."

   One example of these "teachings from God" is the unconditional love of Jesus who, because He loves unconditionally, therefore supposedly affirms or least tolerates many behaviors that the Bible clearly condemns as being sinful – and usually such behaviors that Jesus supposedly affirms or at least tolerates are of a <u>sexual</u> nature.

   Of course, such liberal Christians are being selective about which sins Jesus supposedly affirms or tolerates because most liberal Christians would not be willing to assert that Jesus would affirm or tolerate murder, theft and gossip. Therefore, their Jesus ends up affirming whatever sins <u>they</u> believe ought to be affirmed. In addition, such liberal Christians usually believe that the "Holy Spirit" (however they define "him, her or it") does not only speak to us in Holy Scripture but also inspires us directly in our individual "hearts" – and if they believe the "Spirit" is leading them to affirm their homosexual behavior, then you must affirm their subjective experience of the "Holy Spirit."

The fact is that some liberal Christians are willing to admit that Holy Scripture clearly condemns even homosexual behavior within loving, committed, consensual, monogamous relationships – *they simply deny that Scripture's teaching on this issue has any authority over us today.* Therefore, quoting them the Scripture's prohibitions against all forms of homosexual behavior usually does not make an impact on them.

Many who are involved in liberal Christianity embrace "relativism" – a philosophy that asserts that truth is subjective and that there are no moral absolutes that govern all people of all times and places. Ironically, such liberal Christian relativists, who deny moral absolutes, usually insist that those who believe all forms of homosexual behavior are sinful are absolutely wrong! If they are NOT willing to go so far as to assert that people like me are absolutely wrong to believe that homosexual behavior is sinful for those who believe it to be sinful, they will at least insist that it IS absolutely wrong for people like me to believe that homosexuality is sinful *even* for people like THEM who believe that it is not. But then they are stuck with an absolute moral truth in either case. The problem with liberal Christian relativists is that they are not able to have a logical, intelligent either/or discussion without deconstructing their own world view!

Simply put, just like the former Christian described in #2 above, we need to be willing to engage in some rational discussion and apologetics with liberal Christians in order to show them the inconsistency of their thinking and the errors that result from their liberal view of Holy Scripture. However, as with the former Christians in #2 above, rational discussion and apologetics alone will not bring them back to the Truth.

Once again, at some point in our discussions with such people, we must ask permission to share with them what we believe. If they agree, we simply speak the Truth in love to them – without trying to defend it or make it sound rational – and allow God's Holy Spirit to lead them out of the bondage of liberal Christianity into the true liberty that flows from child-like faith in God's inspired and inerrant Word which is fulfilled in the person and work of Christ for us! Once the Holy Spirit works through the Gospel to give such people faith in the authority of God's Word, we will then be in a position to discuss the issue of their homosexual behavior and their need to repent and trust in the forgiveness and new life that only Jesus can give them.

5. **Some people who are burdened by homosexual desire agree with Holy Scripture that all forms of homosexual behavior are sinful.** However, *some* of these same people have never heard the true Gospel and so they are in despair under God's wrath. If we ever meet such a person we must understand that the last thing he or she needs to hear is that homosexual behavior is sinful! God's Word has already convicted him or her of sin. God's law has done its job and His law has taken this person as far as it can. God's law can only lead us sinners to despair under His wrath. God's law can never comfort a despairing heart nor can God's law move us to cease our sinful behavior for godly reasons.

Therefore, if we meet a person who is convicted of the sin of his or her homosexual behavior and knows that he or she deserves God's wrath, then we must proclaim the Gospel. By the way, the Gospel is NOT: *"Believe in Jesus and then God will forgive you!"* Such a statement sounds like the Gospel, but we are actually pointing the person to something he or she must do in order to get God's forgiveness! An unbeliever crushed by God's law is not able to trust in Jesus by his or her own strength. If an unbeliever thinks that he or she is saved because of his or her work of faith, then he or she is still an unbeliever!

With the above understood, when we proclaim the Gospel to unbelievers crushed by God's law, we must say to them: *"In Jesus' Name I say to you: 'Your sins are forgiven! You are holy and innocent in God's sight. God loves you here and now! He will help you to resist your homosexual desires and live a pure life. If you do fall back into homosexual behavior during a moment of weakness, then you will fall into Christ's loving arms! He will pick you up and help you to live as His dearly loved and forgiven child!'"*

Lutheran's confess the Scriptural doctrine known as **objective justification**. When Jesus said "It is Finished!" the sins of all people were forgiven! You see, the problem with unbelievers is not that they have not done something to get God's forgiveness. The problem with unbelievers is that they don't believe in the forgiveness that they already have in Christ. They have the gift, but they don't believe it! They don't trust God because they believe He won't love them or forgive them until they are worthy. Therefore, when unbelievers are crushed by God's law and despair under God's wrath, the only way they can subjectively believe that they are already forgiven is if we proclaim the objective Gospel that is a present reality for them because of Christ's finished work on the cross for all sinners. We must remember this whenever we meet someone who is in despair under God's wrath because he or she agrees with God's Word that his or her homosexual behavior is sinful. Such a person needs to hear the GOSPEL!

The Importance of Creeds!

Even though it is very important for us to express deeds of love toward those who are burdened by homosexual desire and behavior (I'll address "the importance of deeds" in the next section), it is even more important for us to proclaim to them the teachings of God's Word which are united as one Teaching in the person and work of Christ. Human love for other humans is wonderful, but apart from Christ's love human love is nothing! (John 15:5) The best way we can love people burdened by homosexual desire and behavior is by giving them the Truth that sets them free (John 8:31-32) and by feeding their faith with the Word of God (1st Peter 2:2-3).

There is a popular quote from St. Francis that I absolutely *despise* because of how many people misuse it. The quote is: "Preach the Gospel always! Use words if necessary." Now, to put the best construction on the intentions of St. Francis, I assume he was using hyperbolic language to stress the importance of loving deeds toward one's neighbor. That's fine, as far as it goes. But many people today use that quote from St. Francis to suggest that our deeds of love for others are MORE important than the Word of God we proclaim to them. This is utter heresy!

In fact, some within liberal Christianity have completely replaced the true Gospel of Christ's work for us with the social "gospel" of human deeds of love toward one's neighbor.

I remember once hearing a Christian man say to me: "I don't have to tell people about Jesus. I proclaim the Gospel every time I hand out sandwiches to hungry people at the homeless shelter!" I then responded: "You most certainly do NOT proclaim the Gospel merely by handing out sandwiches! The Gospel of Christ may move you to give sandwiches to hungry people – but that action is the fruit of the

Gospel in your life. However, you giving sandwiches to hungry people is NOT the Gospel of Christ for them!" After examining the Scriptures together, I think he finally agreed with me. Sadly, he had been influenced by the false teaching of the liberal Christians who worked at the homeless shelter with him.

Yes, I'm aware of what it says in the book of James: "...faith without deeds is dead." (James 2:26b) However, James' point is NOT that faith in Christ's work alone is not enough to save us unless we do enough works to be worthy of His mercy. NOR is James teaching that our deeds of love are more important for people than the Truth of Christ's work for them. Instead, James IS teaching that the same Gospel of Christ that creates faith in us will also produce good works in our lives. If we deny that we should perform deeds of love for our neighbor, then we are in rebellion against God's teaching in Holy Scripture and we are unbelievers, that is, our "faith" is dead! In contrast, those who have faith in Christ will be moved to agree with God's Word that we should perform deeds of love for our neighbor – not in order to make ourselves worthy of salvation, but because the forgiveness and love of Christ for us moves us to love and serve our neighbor!

With the above understood, I will now continue to discuss the importance of creeds for giving comfort and hope to those who are burdened by homosexual desire and behavior. The English word "creed" comes from a Latin verb that means "I believe." Therefore, creeds are brief summaries of what we believe based on God's teaching in Holy Scripture. In order to give some structure to this section of my book, I will use articles I-VI and IX-XII of the Augsburg Confession – a creed used by Lutherans to sum up the teaching of Holy Scripture on the particular issues addressed in those articles.

Article I of the Augsburg Confession: "God"

"Our churches teach with common consent that the decree of the Council of Nicaea about the unity of the divine essence and the three persons is true. It is to be believed without any doubt. God is one divine essence who is eternal, without a body, without parts, of infinite power, wisdom, and goodness. He is the maker and preserver of all things, visible and invisible (Nehemiah 9:6). Yet there are three persons, the Father, the Son, and the Holy Spirit (Matthew 28:19). These three persons are of the same essence and power. Our churches use the term *person* as the Fathers have used it. We use it to signify, not a part or quality in another, but that which subsists of itself. Our churches condemn all heresies (Titus 3:10-11) that arose against this article, such as the Manichaens, who assumed that there are two 'principles,' one Good and the other Evil. They also condemn the Valentinians, Arians, Eunomians, Muslims, and all heresies such as these. Our churches also condemn the Samosatenes, old and new, who contend that God is but one person. Through sophistry they impiously argue that the Word and the Holy Spirit are not distinct persons. They say that *Word* signifies a spoken word, and *Spirit* signifies motion created in things."[244]

On one occasion I was walking in a shopping mall in the St. Louis area. There was a young man wearing a shirt with the following written on the front: "There is only ONE God…" Then he turned around, and on the back of his shirt was written the following: "…and you're not Him!"

Yes, there is only ONE God! How do I know that? The ONE God has revealed Himself to us. (John 1:1-3, 14; Hebrews 1:1-3; 1st John 1:1-4) But we sinners love to make gods for ourselves – gods who will say what we want them to say; gods who will do what we want them to do. At the heart of all idolatry is the fact that we actually worship OURSELVES. We want to be in control – even if it means serving an idol of our own making! As the devil said to Eve: "…you will be like God, knowing good and evil." (Genesis 3:5; also 2nd Corinthians 11:3)

We live in a culture where people say that there is "One God" who is known by many names – but these names are invented by people who have invented the god or gods whom they have named. The only way for us sinners to know the True God is for Him to give us His Name – and He has done that through His Word: His written Word (Holy Scripture) *and* the Word made Flesh (The Son of God).

The One God has revealed Himself to us as Father, Son and Holy Spirit: Three Persons; One God. The Augsburg Confession asserts this truth about God not because they want to teach some abstract, academic speculation about the nature of God. Instead, those who wrote the Augsburg Confession understood that the only God who exists has revealed Himself to us and only He can save us sinners from the damnation we deserve. All false gods of our creation whom we have named are gods that can not save us. Our false gods are products

---

[244]See *Concordia: The Lutheran Confessions (A Reader's Edition of the Book of Concord)*, 57.

of our sinful understanding of God and His ways with us. Our false gods do not say to us from the cross: "Father, forgive them!"

Those who bear the burden of homosexual desire and behavior need to be reconciled to the One God who is Father, Son and Holy Spirit. They need to be set free from the false gods that blind them to the love that the True God has for them – a love that radiates from the face of God's Son who died on the cross in our place of damnation; a love that radiates from the face God's Son who conquered death for us by His resurrection; a love that radiates from the face of God's Son who ascended to the Father and now reigns over all creation for us; a love that radiates from the face of God's Son who, with the Father, has given us the Holy Spirit who calls us to faith in Christ through the Gospel! However, before they can understand their need for such a God, those who bear the burden of homosexual desire and behavior need to realize that their homosexuality is merely a symptom of their real problem: WE ARE ALL <u>ENEMIES</u> OF THE ONE TRUE GOD WHO LOVES US!

Article II of the Augsburg Confession: "Original Sin"

"Our churches teach that since the fall of Adam (Romans 5:12), all who are naturally born are born with sin (Psalm 51:5), that is, without the fear of God, without trust in God, and with the inclination to sin, called concupiscence. Concupiscence is a disease and original vice that is truly sin. It damns and brings eternal death on those who are not born anew through Baptism and the Holy Spirit (John 3:5). Our churches condemn the Pelagians and others who deny that original depravity is sin, thus obscuring the glory of Christ's merit and benefits. Pelagians argue that a person can be justified before God by his own strength and reason."[245]

I once heard a pastor say: "We are basically good people. We just do bad things sometimes." As long as we convince ourselves that we are basically good people, we will believe the lie that there is something in us that God ought to love. Only when we recognize the truth that we are enemies of God who do not love Him and do not trust Him, and that even our GOOD works, apart from Christ, are an abomination before Him – only then will we be in a position to see our

---

[245] See *Concordia: The Lutheran Confessions (A Reader's Edition of the Book of Concord)*, 57-58.

need for God's Son who suffered and died in our place of damnation. As long as we think there is some small part in us that God *ought* to love, we will not rely on Christ alone for salvation – and if we do not have ALL of Jesus, we have NONE of Him!

The doctrine of "original sin" teaches us about our sin's origin – we have inherited a sinful nature from Adam (see John 3:6a and Romans 5:12-14). Only God can create in us a *new nature* – and He does that through the Gospel! The Augsburg Confession says that original sin "damns and brings eternal death on those who are not born anew through Baptism and the Holy Spirit (John 3:5)."

This does NOT mean that Baptism is the ONLY way that God creates in us a heart of faith. The Holy Spirit can also create faith in our hearts through the spoken and written Word of God. Therefore, the Augsburg Confession is NOT teaching that a believer, who has been given faith through the spoken or written Word, will be damned if he or she dies before being baptized. When Jesus says "Unless you are born again of water and the Spirit" He is speaking to the unbelieving Pharisee, Nicodemus, who refused the baptism of John because he saw no need for a baptism of repentance for the forgiveness of sins (see John 3:1-6; also Mark 1:4 and Matthew 21:23-32). In contrast, a person who is convicted of sin by the preaching of God's Word will rejoice in receiving the salvation of Christ that God delivers to sinners in the waters of Holy Baptism (see Acts 2:36-41 and 22:6-16).

The "new birth" that the Holy Spirit gives us through the Gospel – Holy Baptism and the preaching of forgiveness in Christ – gives spiritual life to those who are spiritually dead because of original sin (see Romans 6:3-4, Ephesians 2:1-10, Titus 3:3-7 and James 1:18).

Scripture's teaching about original sin keeps people burdened by homosexual desire and behavior from searching for something good in themselves as the basis for their salvation before God. Scripture's teaching about original sin keeps our focus on God's Son, Jesus the Christ, who alone gives us life and salvation.

Article III of the Augsburg Confession: "The Son of God"

"Our churches teach that the Word, that is, the Son of God (John 1:14), assumed the human nature in the womb of the Blessed Virgin Mary. So there are two natures – the divine and the human – inseparably joined in one person. There is one Christ, true God and true man, who was born of the Virgin Mary, truly suffered, was crucified, died, and was buried. He did this to reconcile the Father to us and to be a sacrifice, not only for original guilt, but also for all actual sins of mankind (John 1:29). He also descended into hell, and truly rose again on the third day. Afterward, he ascended into heaven to sit at the right hand of the Father. There He forever reigns and has dominion over all creatures. He sanctifies those who believe in Him, by sending the Holy Spirit into their hearts to rule, comfort, and make them alive. He defends them against the devil and the power of sin. The same Christ will openly come again to judge the living and the dead, and so forth, according to the Apostles' Creed."[246]

At least once a year there seems to be some popular magazine that hopes to sell many copies by putting a picture of Jesus on the front cover with a question like this: "Who was Jesus?" First of all, note the word "was" – as though Jesus is no longer alive! Also, the answers such a magazine article gives to the question "Who was Jesus?" are many and varied – but most of them agree that Jesus was just a man, not God in human flesh.

There is nothing new under the sun. Jesus asked His apostles: "Who do people say that I am?" They gave multiple answers based on the opinions of various people. All of them were wrong. However, by the grace of the Father, Peter spoke the Truth about Jesus: "You are the Christ, the Son of the living God!" Not only did Peter believe that Jesus was the Messiah – the Savior of all nations promised in the Old Testament (Genesis 3:15 & 12:1-3; also Isaiah 7:14 & 9:1-7). Even more, Peter believed that Jesus was the very Son of God – the Lord in human flesh! (Matthew 1:21-23; also Luke 1:29-37 & 2:10-11)

I've often said the following to the Christians at Concordia Lutheran: "If the Jesus who hung on the cross was only a man, then his death was no big deal – because the Romans crucified thousands of people! What makes the death of Jesus unique is that in His case, God Himself was hanging on the cross. If Jesus is God, why did He allow Himself to be nailed to the cross? He allowed Himself to be nailed to the cross FOR YOU! He did it for those who nailed Him there with their sins. Only God's death can give life to us sinners! Jesus lives to give life to YOU!"

---

[246] See *Concordia: The Lutheran Confessions (A Reader's Edition of the Book of Concord)*, 58.

We can't separate the PERSON of Christ from the WORK of Christ – the TWO go together! If Jesus is NOT God, then His death is NOT good news for us sinners. If Jesus did NOT die for our sins, then His being God is NOT good news for us sinners. The only God who can save sinners is the One who died on the cross for us.

Scripture's teaching about the person and work of Christ gives hope to the person who is burdened by the guilt of homosexual desire and behavior. Because of Jesus, we who are guilty before God can hear Him say to us: "Not guilty!"

Article IV of the Augsburg Confession: "Justification"

"Our churches teach that people cannot be justified before God by their own strength, merits, or works. People are freely justified for Christ's sake, through faith, when they believe that they are received into favor and that their sins are forgiven for Christ's sake. By His death, Christ made satisfaction for our sins. God counts this faith for righteousness in His sight (Romans 3:21-26; 4:5)."[247]

When the judge in a courtroom lowers His gavel and says "Not guilty!" the person to whom the judge is speaking is declared innocent of all crimes and set free. This is true even if the person is actually guilty of the crimes of which he or she was accused. The judge's word is final! Christians will often use this courtroom analogy to describe what happens when God justifies us. When God declares us "Not guilty!" His Word creates the reality of our freedom from guilt even though we are guilty of sin and deserve eternal hell!

Of course, the analogy of an earthly courtroom breaks down at various points. Some people in this world actually ARE innocent of the crimes of which they are accused and yet they are sometimes declared to be guilty by the judge in an earthly courtroom. In contrast, ALL people without exception are guilty before <u>God</u> in His heavenly court and so we ALL <u>deserve</u> the judgment "Guilty!"

In addition, when the judge in an earthly court declares someone "Not guilty!" that judgment is based on the fact that a jury found the person to be innocent. In contrast, when God declares sinners "Not

---

[247]See *Concordia: The Lutheran Confessions (A Reader's Edition of the Book of Concord)*, 59.

guilty!" that judgment is based on the fact that God's own Son took our guilt upon Himself and suffered the punishment we deserved.

Finally, when the judge in an earthly courtroom declares a person "Not guilty!" that verdict does not necessarily change the person or create a relationship between that person and the judge. In contrast, when God declares sinners "Not guilty!" that judgment actually creates a new reality. God's Gospel actually creates in us a new heart that longs to please the judge with our lives of obedience to His laws.

When the New Testament Scriptures talk about "justification" they use a Greek word that means "to declare righteous." The authors of the Augsburg Confession are stressing in article IV that God declares sinners righteous for Christ's sake and not because of our strength, merits or works.

We can't do anything to make ourselves worthy of God's salvation. In fact, if we try to make ourselves worthy of God's salvation by obeying His laws we thereby actually remain guilty before God! (Galatians 3:10) Therefore, the Holy Spirit works through the Gospel of Christ's person and work for us to create faith in our hearts which clings to Christ alone for salvation.

If people who are burdened by homosexual desire and behavior attempt to be justified before God by ceasing their homosexual behavior, then such people will *either* eventually despair because of their inability to completely conquer this sin in their lives *or* they will boast before God because they have been successful in avoiding homosexual behavior and think they have thereby merited God's salvation by their obedience. Either way, they remain in unbelief!

Scripture's teaching about justification nurtures saving faith in those who are burdened by homosexual desire and behavior by convincing them that they are justified before God based on the person and work of Christ alone! Scripture's teaching about justification delivers us from both despair and self-righteousness before God. Scripture's teaching about justification keeps our focus on Christ.

But how do people who are spiritually dead receive the faith they need to believe that they are justified before God because of Christ? Article V of the Augsburg Confession uses Scripture to answer that question.

Article V of the Augsburg Confession: "The Ministry"

"So that we may obtain this faith, the ministry of teaching the Gospel and administering the Sacraments[248] was instituted. Through the Word and Sacraments, as through instruments, the Holy Spirit is given (John 20:22). He works faith, when and where it pleases God (John 3:8), in those who hear the good news that God justifies those who believe that they are received into grace for Christ's sake. This happens not through our own merits, but for Christ's sake. Our churches condemn the Anabaptists and others who think that through their own preparations and works the Holy Spirit comes to them without the external Word."[249]

Almost 2000 years ago the Son of God accomplished our salvation by His life, death and resurrection for us in a small area of the earth near the eastern shores of the Mediterranean. So, how does what Jesus accomplished for us almost 2000 years ago in that small area of the earth get applied to us personally here and now? The answer is that God uses certain "means," "tools," "channels" or "instruments" to give to us personally the salvation that Christ accomplish for us.

God calls pastors to baptize in Christ's Name, to forgive sins in Christ's Name, to preach and teach God's Word in Christ's Name, and to administer the Lord's Supper in Christ's Name. These are all various means that God uses to deliver Christ's salvation to people. Through these means God creates and sustains faith in sinners who, by this gift of faith, cling to Christ who has saved them.

Those who attempt to find God and His mercy apart from the means His has instituted will either end up in despair or will falsely conclude that they are believers when in fact they are actually unbelievers. Some

---

[248] By the word "Sacrament" Lutherans mean a Church practice that has been 1) instituted by Christ 2) Who conveys the forgiveness of sins 3) through earthly means that He has selected (for example, water; bread and wine). According to this definition, the Sacraments refer to Baptism and the Lord's Supper. Lutherans also understand ordination (or better, the pastoral office) as a Sacrament in the sense that called pastors are used by Christ to bestow His gifts to His people. In paragraph 11 of article XIII of *The Apology of the Augsburg Confession* we read: "But if ordination is understood as carrying out the ministry of the Word, we are willing to call ordination a Sacrament. For the ministry of the Word has God's command and has glorious promises…"

[249] See *Concordia: The Lutheran Confessions (A Reader's Edition of the Book of Concord)*, 59.

try to find God in nature or in various man-made religions, but all of these lead us away from Christ.

The Holy Spirit moves us to focus on Holy Baptism, the preaching of forgiveness, the teaching of God's Word and the Lord's Supper for the assurance that we worship the True God and have received His salvation. Those who are burdened by homosexual desire and behavior will find great comfort from God's "means of grace" – through which their faith in Christ is nurtured with the result that they desire to turn from sin (including their homosexual behavior) and conform to God's loving plan for their lives.

Article VI of the Augsburg Confession: "New Obedience"

"Our churches teach that this faith is bound to bring forth good fruit (Galatians 5:22-23). It is necessary to do good works commanded by God (Ephesians 2:10), because of God's will. We should not rely on those works to merit justification before God. The forgiveness of sins and justification is received through faith. The voice of Christ testifies, 'So you also, when you have done all that you were commanded, say, "We are unworthy servants; we have only done our duty"' (Luke 17:10). The Fathers teach the same thing. Ambrose says, 'It is ordained of God that he who believes in Christ is saved, freely receiving forgiveness of sins, without works, through faith alone.'"[250]

In Romans chapter 6 the apostle Paul asks a question that some who doubt God's Word about salvation being a free gift to unworthy sinners are tempted to ask: "What shall we say, then? Shall we go on sinning so that grace may increase?" (Romans 6:1)

In other words, if God loves to forgive, and I don't have to do anything to earn His forgiveness, then I might as well sin all I want, right? Wrong! The apostle Paul answers that sinful question with these words: "By no means! We died to sin; how can we live in it any longer? Or don't you know that all of us who were baptized into Christ Jesus were baptized into his death? We were therefore buried with him through baptism into death in order that, just as Christ was raised from the dead through the glory of the Father, we too may live a new life." (Romans 6:2-4)

---

[250] See *Concordia: The Lutheran Confessions (A Reader's Edition of the Book of Concord)*, 59-60.

Simply put, when the Holy Spirit creates faith in the heart of us sinners, that faith in Christ moves us to grieve over the sin in our lives and to long to live according to God's loving will for us. So, if someone claims to be a Christian but does not grieve over the sin in his or her life and sees no need to repent, then such a person is an unbeliever who is resisting the Holy Spirit – because one of the works of the Holy Spirit is to convict us of sin! Such a person needs to hear the condemnation of God's law. If such a person then takes his or her sin seriously and despairs under God's wrath, we then proclaim the Gospel through which the Spirit creates faith as well as the desire to turn from sin and live according to God's will. (Romans 8:1-17 & 12:1-2; also Galatians 5:16 and Titus 2:11-14)

However, even though the Holy Spirit will move Christians to turn from sin and do good works, we will still struggle with the desires of our sinful nature that remains with us. As Paul says: "For the sinful nature desires what is contrary to the Spirit, and the Spirit what is contrary to the sinful nature. They are in conflict with each other, so that you do not do what you want. But if you are led by the Spirit, you are not under law." (Galatians 5:17-18) What does Paul mean? He means that we Christians want to obey God because of His love for us in Christ, but our sinful nature often leads us to do the very things we don't want to do. In other words, we sin every day by thought, word and deed!

However, if we are led by the Spirit, that is, if the Spirit moves us to repent of our sin and trust in Christ, then we are not "under law," that is, we are not under the condemnation of God's Law. Even though we Christians will never be free from sin in this life, we are free from condemnation through faith in Christ through whom we have God's free gift of forgiveness and the hope of eternal life in His love.

Therefore, the "new obedience" or "sanctification" has nothing to do with salvation – as though we can obtain or maintain our salvation before God by our good works. Instead, the "new obedience" or "sanctification" means that Christ lives in us and does good works through us who trust in Him for salvation – and this salvation is complete, sure and certain even while we continue to struggle with the desires and behaviors of our sinful nature.

"New obedience" or "sanctification" does NOT mean that we become more holy and less sinful over time – because our sinful nature is never diminished or reformed this side of heaven, and our new nature is whole and complete in Christ. Instead, "new obedience" or "sanctification" means that we ARE New Creations in Christ

(2nd Corinthians 5:17) who live by faith and not by sight (2nd Corinthians 5:7). The Spirit moves us to resist sin and do good works, and in spite of our struggle with our sinful nature, we trust God's Word that we are saints in Christ!

Scripture's teaching about "new obedience" or "sanctification" gives great comfort to people who are burdened by homosexual desire and behavior. Such people can know that they are TOTAL saints before God in Christ even as they continue to struggle with their sin of homosexual desire and behavior. They can be at peace knowing that God does not expect them to eliminate their sinful desires – including their homosexual desires! – before He will love them or forgive them. Instead, Scripture teaches that we are already forgiven in Christ – and that Good News moves us to live lives of "new obedience" or "sanctification."

Article IX of the Augsburg Confession: "Baptism"

"Concerning Baptism, our churches teach that Baptism is necessary for salvation (Mark 16:16) and that God's grace is offered through Baptism (Titus 3:4-7). They teach that children are to be baptized (Acts 2:38-39). Being offered to God through Baptism, they are received into God's grace. Our churches condemn the Anabaptists, who reject the Baptism of children, and say that children are saved without Baptism."[251]

There is a lot of confusion about God's gift of Baptism among Christians today. Therefore, I believe it would be helpful for me to dedicate some space explaining what Lutheran's believe Scripture teaches about the nature of Baptism and the practice of Infant Baptism.

First, we must understand what Lutherans DO NOT believe about Baptism and Infant Baptism. We do NOT believe that all infants who have not been baptized are going to hell! Some wrongly think Lutherans teach this. Even though Baptism is one important way that God brings Christ and His gifts to infants, Baptism is not the only way that God does this. God also uses His spoken Word to bring infants to faith in Christ. (I will discuss what Scripture teaches about infant faith below.)

---

251 See *Concordia: The Lutheran Confessions (A Reader's Edition of the Book of Concord)*, 61.

In addition, Lutherans do NOT believe that Baptism is a magical work of humans that guarantees salvation even if a person later rejects Christ and lives as an unbeliever. Sadly, some who were baptized as infants were not nurtured by God's Word over the years and in certain cases they eventually lost their faith in Christ. (Below I will explain in more detail how those who are baptized also must have their faith in Christ nurtured by God's Word throughout life.)

Now that we know what Lutherans do NOT believe about Baptism and Infant Baptism, I would like to explain what Lutherans DO believe Baptism actually is. Simply put, some Christians view Baptism as only an outward symbol of an adult's conscious decision to trust in Jesus. However, Lutherans do not have this understanding of Baptism because in no place does Scripture ever speak of Baptism in this way! Instead, Scripture always defines Baptism as something much more than a mere symbol. According to Scripture, Baptism is the work of God through which He gives us various gifts.

God uses Baptism to put His Name on us (see Matthew 28:19). God uses Baptism to give us "new birth," that is, faith in Christ (see John 3:5 and Titus 3:5). God uses Baptism to give us forgiveness of sins and the Holy Spirit (see Acts 2:28 and 22:16; Ephesians 5:26). God uses Baptism to connect us to the death and resurrection of Jesus (see Romans 6:3-4 and Colossians 2:11-12). God uses Baptism to clothe us with Christ (see Galatians 3:27). God uses Baptism to save us by the power of Jesus' death and resurrection (see 1st Peter 3:18 & 21).

Now that we understand what Lutherans DO and DO NOT believe about Baptism and Infant Baptism, I will give a brief response to the seven most common objections to Infant Baptism.

The **first** objection is: *"But we're saved by Jesus, not by our work of Baptism!"* This objection wrongly thinks that Baptism is a human work. If that were the case, then Baptism could not save us. However, Scripture teaches that Baptism DOES save us (see 1st Peter 3:21) because Baptism is GOD'S WORK! In addition, this objection fails to understand that Baptism is one of the means God uses to give us the salvation of Christ. In other words, Jesus ACCOMPLISHED our salvation by His life, death and resurrection for us. However, this salvation is GIVEN and DELIVERED to us through God's "means of grace" – and one such "means of grace" is Holy Baptism! (See Acts 2:38-39 and Titus 3:5)

The **second** objection is: *"But infants are not sinners! Therefore, Baptism is not for infants because Baptism is for those who have* *consciously sinned."* On the contrary, Scripture clearly teaches that we are sinners from the time of our conception (see Psalm 51:5) because we inherit a sinful nature from Adam (see Romans 5:12-14). The fact that infants die is God's sign that they are sinners (see 1st Corinthians 15:22). We sin BECAUSE we are sinners, and we have this condition even as infants and little children (see Genesis 8:21 and John 3:6). Also, Romans 3:23 clearly shows that ALL have sinned and need the salvation that only Jesus gives.

The **third** objection is: *"But infants can't have faith!"* First, Scripture clearly teaches that infants and children CAN have faith. In Psalm 8:2 we see that infants can give praise to God. In Psalm 22:9 we see that David trusted in the Lord when he was a breast-feeding infant. In Matthew 18:6 Jesus teaches that "little ones" can believe in Him. Jesus is speaking about the "child" mentioned in Matthew 18:2. The Greek word for child is *paidion* which can also refer to infants. For example, the plural form of *paidion* is used in Matthew 2:16 for the children who were 2 years old and younger. Also, in Luke 18:15-17 we see that Jesus uses babies as examples of sincere faith. The Greek word for babies in Luke 18:15-17 is *brephos* which means infant. In addition, John the Baptist was filled with the Holy Spirit in the womb (Luke 1:15 & 39-45). The fact is that Jesus holds up infants as ultimate examples of faith (Matthew 18:5-6 and Luke 18:16-17). Second, Scripture clearly teaches that faith is MORE than a conscious knowledge of facts about God. Faith is trust in God that flows from a heart made new by the Holy Spirit. If faith is ONLY a conscious awareness of God's Word, then does one lose his or her faith when asleep or in a coma? What about those with mental disabilities? Third, those who say "Infants can't have faith!" must either 1) say that infants who die are damned or 2) say that faith in Christ is not necessary for salvation.

The **fourth** objection is: *"Jesus was baptized as an adult!"* If one takes this assertion to its logical end, then you must say: "Jesus wasn't baptized until he was about 30, so no one should be baptized BEFORE that age! In addition, Jesus was baptized in the Jordan, and so all baptisms must take place in the Jordan or they are not valid. In fact, Jesus was a man and so women should not be baptized!" This is ridiculous, of course! One must note that Jesus was baptized for reasons completely different than why we are baptized. First, Jesus was sinless and so He did not need the forgiveness delivered in Baptism. Second, Jesus' Baptism was God's way of showing that Baptism saves us because Jesus has made Himself part of it. In other words, Jesus was not baptized to give us an example to follow – as though being baptized is something we do merely as an act of obedience to God. Instead, He was baptized to show us the source and power behind the salvation given in Baptism. This becomes obvious when God uses Jesus' Baptism as a public witness to show us that Jesus is His Son, our Savior!

The **fifth** objection is: *"The Bible never says that we should baptize infants!"* How do we answer this objection? First of all, the entire Old Testament assumes that infants were always part of the salvation acts of God. For example, God gave Abraham the ritual of circumcision as an outward sign that the Savior would come from his family line (see Genesis 12:1-3 and Galatians 3:6-9). The sign of circumcision was given to infant boys when they were only 8 days old! In Colossians 2:11-13 the Apostle Paul shows that circumcision has been replaced with Baptism through which Christ Himself works to give spiritual life to those who are dead in sin. The Jews who became Christians would have assumed that Baptism was for infants because infants had also received the Old Testament ritual of circumcision. In addition, the infants and children of Israel participated in many of the Old Testament rituals (the Passover, the Sabbath, the Day of Atonement, etc.). The infants and children of Israel were included in the high priest's blessing which God used to put His Name on His people (see Numbers 6:22-27; also Matthew 28:19). The infants and children of Israel took part in the crossing of the Red Sea which was a picture of the New Testament gift of Baptism (see 1st Corinthians 10:1-4).

Secondly, Jesus says that we should MAKE disciples by baptizing them. He says to do this for ALL nations, and he gives no exceptions as to age. Then in Acts 2:38-39 Peter tells the crowd who had been convicted by his preaching: "Repent and be baptized EVERY ONE of you in the name of Jesus for the forgiveness of your sin and you will receive the gift of the Holy Spirit. The promise is for you AND YOUR CHILDREN."

Simply put, the bible assumes (especially based on the practice of the Old Testament!) that infants will be baptized, and Matthew 28:19 and Acts 2:38-39 confirm this. Therefore, the burden of proof is not on Lutherans to find yet ANOTHER text that says infants should be baptized. Instead, the burden of proof is on those who deny infant baptism. They must find just ONE passage that says infants should NOT be baptized. However, there is no such passage! The reason there is no such passage is that Scripture assumes that infants will be baptized!

The **sixth** objection is: *"Adults were taught first and then were baptized later. So we should wait for infants to grow up so we can teach them before we baptize them."* This objection fails to distinguish the difference between infants and adults. Scripture clearly teaches that humans are conceived in sin. However, unbelieving infants have one advantage over unbelieving adults. Infants do not yet have a rebellious reason! Scripture teaches that we are conceived in sin and if we grow up as unbelievers we develop a conscious reason that is hostile to the Gospel. So, unlike infants who are in a position to receive the Gospel, adults need to have their reason humbled through the preaching of God's Word. Adults must become like "little children" or "spiritual infants" before they can receive Holy Baptism. I like to use the following analogy: Unbelieving infants are like a plowed field. They do not have the "seed of life" but they are in a position to receive it. In contrast, unbelieving older children and adults are like a field with hard soil (covered by weeds and rocks) that needs to be broken up and cleared out before it can receive the "seed of life." This explains why infants are baptized and then taught, whereas older children and adults are taught and then Baptized.

Finally, the **seventh** objection is this: *"Joe Lutheran was baptized as an infant. But now as an adult he never attends church and he lives a life of unrepentant sin!"* The Bible teaches that our faith must be nurtured by God's Word, or it will die! Sadly, some who were baptized as infants are now living as unbelievers because their faith was not nurtured by hearing and reading God's Word and receiving the Lord's Supper. Such people should be called back to faith in Christ by the preaching of God's Word! However, the fact that some fall away after Baptism does NOT mean we should stop baptizing infants! For example, some adults are brought to faith in Christ through the preaching of God's Word, but then later fall away. Does this mean we should never preach God's Word to adults because some later fall away? Of course not! In the same way, we still baptize infants even though, sadly, some later grow up and fall away from the Faith.[252]

When article IX of the Augsburg Confession says that Baptism is "necessary for salvation" is does NOT mean that those who die without Baptism are damned even if they believe in Christ. Instead, the Augsburg Confession is teaching that Baptism is "necessary for salvation" because it is one of the means God uses to give us Christ and

---

[252] For a much more thorough study of this issue, read the book ***Baptized into God's Family (The Doctrine of Infant Baptism for Today)*** by Dr. A. Andrew Das.

His gifts – and if we *despise* God's gift of Holy Baptism, we thereby *despise* CHRIST!

If the person who bears the burden of homosexual desire and behavior understands that Baptism is NOT a mere symbol of his or her "commitment to Jesus" but the work of God whereby He adopts us as His children and gives us Christ and His gifts – then Baptism becomes not only a source of comfort and peace as this person continues to struggle with homosexual desire and behavior, but God's gift of Baptism also defines this person's identity as a CHILD OF GOD IN CHRIST!

If the person who bears the burden of homosexual desire and behavior was baptized as an infant, he or she can know that his or her identity as God's child in Christ was sealed by Him in the waters of Holy Baptism before he or she ever began to view his or her identity in terms of homosexual desire. Such a person can see himself or herself as God sees him or her: *a forgiven child of God set free to live according to His loving plan for our lives!*

Very often, those who bear the burden of homosexual desire and behavior tend to base their identity on their sexual orientation. "I'm a homosexual!" they learn to say to themselves – and our culture is all to willing to affirm them in that identity! But people who bear the burden of homosexual desire and behavior can be liberated from this false identity when they realize that God's gift of Baptism is what truly defines their identity! In Holy Baptism God says to you: "You are my beloved child! You are a New Creation in Christ! You get to live in my love forever! You get to live to my glory as I glory in you!"

The devil does his best to convince us that our identity is wrapped up in our various sinful desires. But God's gift of Holy Baptism tells us that we are God's forgiven and dearly loved children – and that we are free to live to His glory.

Article X of the Augsburg Confession: "The Lord's Supper"

"Our churches teach that the body and blood of Christ are truly present and distributed to those who eat of the Lord's Supper (1 Corinthians 10:16). They reject those who teach otherwise."[253]

---

[253] See *Concordia: The Lutheran Confessions (A Reader's Edition of the Book of Concord)*, 61.

If you love a person dearly and long to be close to that person, which of these would you choose: 1) A *picture* of the person you love. 2) The person you love *in the flesh.* I don't know of many people who would choose a *picture* of the person they love over the person *in the flesh.*

During the final plague on Egypt, the death of the first born male child, God provided a protection for His people called the Passover. God told them to take male lambs without defect, kill them, and smear their blood on the doorframes of their homes. They were then to eat those lambs for their meal that evening. When the angel of death came and saw the blood of the lamb, he would "pass over" that home.

Why did God ask His people to do this? He didn't want them to think that they were being spared because they were better or more worthy of God's mercy than the Egyptians. God wanted them to know that they were being spared because of the blood of the lamb – a picture of THE LAMB OF GOD who takes away the sins of the world.

On the night before Jesus would die on the cross for our sins, He celebrated the Passover with His apostles. But they were about to experience a Passover like no other. Jesus said: "Take, eat. This is My Body given for you. Take, drink. This is My Blood shed for you for the forgiveness of your sins." The *picture* of the Savior had now been replaced by the Savior *in the flesh*!

In 1st Corinthians 10:14-17 and 11:23-32 the apostle Paul clearly teaches that Jesus' words "This is My Body! This is My Blood!" are much more than mere symbolism. These words of Jesus give us what they say: His very Body and Blood to eat and drink for the forgiveness of our sins!

However, those who *refuse* to repent of their sins that are condemned by God's Word and/or *refuse* to trust in Christ alone for forgiveness and new life – such as these should NOT receive the Lord's Supper lest they receive it to their judgment. As Paul writes: "Therefore, whoever eats the bread or drinks the cup of the Lord in an unworthy manner will be guilty of sinning against the body and blood of the Lord." (1st Corinthians 11:27)

In the bread consecrated by Christ's Words we receive His Body given for us. In the wine consecrated by Christ's Words we receive His Blood shed for us. We don't attempt to comprehend this mystery with our limited reason. Instead, we say with Peter: "Lord, to whom shall we go? You have the words of eternal life." (John 6:68)

Before Jesus ever instituted the Lord's Supper He said to His disciples: "Whoever eats my flesh and drinks my blood has eternal life, and I will raise him up at the last day. For my flesh is real food and my blood is real drink." (John 6:54-55)

Later Jesus would say: "The Spirit gives life; the flesh counts for nothing." (John 6:63a) When Jesus said "the flesh counts for nothing" He was NOT speaking of His flesh – which counts for EVERYTHING! Instead, by "the flesh" Jesus was speaking of our *sinful flesh* that doubts His Words. But the Holy Spirit gives us the faith to trust Jesus' Words: "The words I have spoken to you are Spirit and they are life." (John 6:63b)

Jesus' disciples very likely did not understand His words at that time. But later, on that night before His death for us, they would hear Him say: "Take, eat. This is My Body. Take, drink. This is My Blood!" Those who are baptized and trust in Jesus as their Savior also get to eat and drink His Body and Blood in the Lord's Supper. Jesus IS with us always – just as He promised!

Those who are burdened by homosexual desire and behavior can approach the Lord's Table in repentant faith and know that they will receive their Savior *in the flesh*. In spite of our ongoing struggle with our sinful flesh, Jesus puts His Flesh and Blood into us to assure us that we are forgiven and that He is with us always – and that we will live with Him forever. As Paul writes: "For whenever you eat this bread and drink this cup, you proclaim the Lord's death until he comes." (1st Corinthians 11:26)

Article XI of the Augsburg Confession: "Confession"

"Our churches teach that private Absolution should be retained in the churches, although listing all sins is not necessary for Confession. For, according to the Psalm, it is impossible. 'Who can discern his errors!' (Psalm 19:12)."[254]

The Augsburg Confession titles article XI simply as "Confession" – which entails two things: **1)** Agreeing with Scripture about the evil of your sinful nature as well as the particular sins it exposes in your life, and the fact that you deserve God's wrath because of these.

---

[254] See *Concordia: The Lutheran Confessions (A Reader's Edition of the Book of Concord)*, 61 & 63.

2) Receiving "absolution," that is, the forgiveness of sins from the pastor who is used by God to declare that you are forgiven for Christ's sake. Most Services in Lutheran congregations begin with public confession and absolution. For example, the liturgy for Divine Service: Setting Two in *Lutheran Service Book*[255] begins as follows:

P: In the name of the Father and of the Son and of the Holy Spirit

C: Amen.

P: If we say we have no sin, we deceive ourselves, and the truth is not in us.

C: But if we confess our sins, God, who is faithful and just, will forgive our sins and cleanse us from all unrighteousness.

P: Let us then confess our sins to God our Father.

C: Most merciful God, we confess that we are by nature sinful and unclean. We have sinned against You in thought, word, and deed, by what we have done and by what we have left undone. We have not loved You with our whole heart; we have not loved our neighbors as ourselves. We justly deserve Your present and eternal punishment. For the sake of Your Son, Jesus Christ, have mercy on us. Forgive us, renew us, and lead us, so that we may delight in Your will and walk in your ways to the glory of Your holy name. Amen

P: Almighty God in His mercy has given His Son to die for you and for His sake forgives you all your sins. As a called and ordained servant of Christ, and by His authority, I therefore forgive you all your sins in the name of the Father and of the Son and of the Holy Spirit. Amen.

Some people who are not familiar with this order of confession and absolution are shocked to hear the pastor say: "I therefore forgive you all your sins." Some people will then respond: "Who does the pastor think he is? Only GOD can forgive sins!" They are correct, of course. Only God has the authority to forgive sins. But notice what the pastor says: "As a called and ordained servant of Christ, *and by His authority...*"

As you can read in the beginning section of Appendix I in this book, pastors are God's ambassadors whom He uses to proclaim His Word to His people. Therefore, when the pastor says "I forgive you..." he is actually speaking the words of CHRIST.[256] This is why we read the

[255] See *Lutheran Service Book* (Concordia Publishing House), 167.

[256] When a pastor performs a baptism he says: "I baptize you in the Name of the Father and of the Son and of the Holy Spirit." Properly understood, the pronoun "I" does not refer to the pastor but to CHRIST who alone has the authority to baptize (Matthew 28:18) and uses the pastor's hands and voice to perform the baptism. In the same way,

following in a later edition of Luther's *Small Catechism*: "I believe that when the called ministers of Christ deal with us by His divine command, in particular when they exclude openly unrepentant sinners from the Christian congregation and absolve those who repent of their sins and want to do better, this is just as valid and certain, even in heaven, as if Christ our dear Lord dealt with us Himself."[257]

Jesus Himself says: "He who listens to you listens to me…" (Luke 10:16a) Jesus also says: "If you forgive anyone his sins, they are forgiven; if you do not forgive them, they are not forgiven." (John 20:23)

Simply put, if a person is crushed by God's law and despairs because he or she knows that he or she deserves God's wrath, then the pastor is to say what Christ Himself says: "Your sins are forgiven!" But if a person refuses to acknowledge his or her sins exposed by God's Word and/or refuses to trust in Christ alone for salvation, then the pastor is to say what Christ Himself says: "Your sins are NOT forgiven!" *Please understand.* The reason an unbeliever's sins are not forgiven is NOT because Jesus did not atone for those sins! Instead, the reason an unbeliever's sins are not forgiven is that he or she rejects Christ's forgiveness by his or her unbelief.

Lutherans do not require their people to utilize PRIVATE confession and absolution – it is a matter of "get to" and not "got to." The purpose of private confession and absolution is that it gives a person who is burdened by a particular sin an opportunity to share that burden with the pastor and then to hear Christ's words of forgiveness from the pastor's own mouth: "Your sin of ________________ has already been forgiven! Go in peace!"

Many years ago I was in my office at the congregation I was serving at that time. I was the only one in the building – but that was about to change. I heard a knock on my door, and welcomed into my office a man whose face looked anxious and tired.

To make a long story short, this man confessed to me that he was burdened by the sin of homosexual desire and behavior. He agreed with God's Word that his homosexual desire and behavior was sinful.

---

when a pastor speaks the words of institution for the Lord's Supper ("This is My Body given for you. This is My Blood of the New Testament shed for you for the forgiveness of sins.") he is speaking the words of CHRIST who is using the pastor's voice to consecrate the bread and the wine used in the Lord's Supper.

[257] See *Lutheran Service Book* (Concordia Publishing House), 326.

He agreed with God's Word that he deserved nothing but His wrath. This man needed to hear the GOSPEL! So, I encouraged him to use the order of private confession and absolution with me. The liturgy for this was very similar to what now follows:

Pastor, please hear my confession and pronounce forgiveness in order to fulfill God's will.

Proceed.

I, a poor sinner, plead guilty before God of all sins. I have lived as if God did not matter and as if I mattered most. My Lord's name I have not honored as I should; my worship and prayers have faltered. I have not let His love have its way with me, and so my love for others has failed. There are those whom I have hurt, and those whom I have failed to help. My thoughts and desires have been soiled with sin. What troubles me particularly is that ________________________ . I am sorry for all of this and ask for grace. I want to do better.

God be merciful to you and strengthen your faith.

Amen.

Do you believe that my forgiveness is God's forgiveness?

Yes.

Let it be done for you as you believe. In the stead and by the command of my Lord Jesus Christ I forgive you all your sins in the name of the Father and of the Son and of the Holy Spirit.

Amen.

Go in peace.

Amen.[258]

That man came to my office with a heavy burden of guilt and fear because of his battle with homosexual desire and behavior. He left my office with God's promise that his sin was forgiven and that he was at peace with God.

Before he left, I encouraged him to remember his baptism and what God did for him there. I encouraged him to attend Services on a regular basis so that He could be comforted and strengthened in his faith by God's Word. I encouraged him to receive the Lord's Supper as often as possible that so the Body and Blood of Christ would assure him that he was forgiven and that Christ would be with him always.

---

[258] See *Lutheran Service Book* (Concordia Publishing House), 292-293.

Article XII of the Augsburg Confession: "Repentance"

"Our churches teach that there is forgiveness of sins for those who have fallen after Baptism whenever they are converted. The Church ought to impart Absolution to those who return to repentance (Jeremiah 3:12). Now, strictly speaking, repentance consists of two parts. One part is contrition, that is, terrors striking the conscience through the knowledge of sin. The other part is faith, which is born of the Gospel (Romans 10:17) or the Absolution and believes that for Christ's sake, sins are forgiven. It comforts the conscience and delivers it from terror. Then good works are bound to follow, which are the fruit of repentance (Galatians 5:22-23). Our churches condemn the Anabaptists, who deny that those who have once been justified can lose the Holy Spirit. They also condemn those who argue that some may reach such a state of perfection in this life that they cannot sin. The Novatians also are condemned, who would not absolve those who had fallen after Baptism, though they returned to repentance. Our churches also reject those who do not teach that forgiveness of sins comes through faith, but command us to merit grace through satisfactions of our own. They also reject those who teach that it is necessary to perform works of satisfaction, commanded by Church law, in order to remit eternal punishment or the punishment of purgatory."[259]

I recently heard a pastor on the radio who gave a sermon about repentance. In one part of his sermon he said: "It is not enough to agree with God that you have sinned and agree that you deserve His wrath. You also need to stop your sinful behavior before you can be forgiven!"

Now, I'm sure that pastor had very good intentions when he said that. I'm sure he was trying to explain that the Holy Spirit moves us to turn from our sin and live according to God's will. I'm sure that he was trying to stress that we can't deliberately and intentionally remain in our sin without regret and at the same time have saving faith in the forgiveness that Christ has provided for that sin.

However, when he said that we must stop our sinful behavior BEFORE we can be forgiven he was suggesting (probably not intentionally) that we must perform some action in order to be worthy of Christ's forgiveness. But this is false teaching!

---

[259] See *Concordia: The Lutheran Confessions (A Reader's Edition of the Book of Concord)*, 64.

If I can't receive Christ's forgiveness until I cease all sinful behavior in my life, then I will NEVER have Christ's forgiveness. Yes, I should resist the desires of my sinful nature. Yes, I should strive to do the good things that God would have me do. But my life of sanctification is the RESULT of having been forgiven and not the CAUSE or the BASIS for receiving Christ's forgiveness!

Imagine if a person burdened by homosexual desire or behavior had heard that radio sermon on repentance and concluded: "If I can just stop having these homosexual desires and cease my homosexual behavior, then I will be worthy of God's forgiveness." Such a person will very likely end up in despair.

In article XII of the Augsburg Confession it says the following: "Now, strictly speaking, repentance consists of two parts. One part is contrition, that is, terrors striking the conscience through the knowledge of sin. The other part is faith, which is born of the Gospel (Romans 10:17) or the Absolution and believes that for Christ's sake, sins are forgiven."

Did you notice what this does NOT say? It does NOT say that the first part of repentance includes ceasing one's sinful behavior BEFORE one can be forgiven. Instead, the first part of repentance – "terrors striking the conscience through the knowledge of sin" – is the state of all sinners who are crushed by the judgments of God's Law.

If a person is left under the judgment of God's law and does not hear the Gospel ("Your sins ARE forgiven!"), then that person will not have the power to cease his sinful behavior nor will that person be able to cease from his or her sinful behavior for godly reasons.

You see, if we actually succeed in ceasing from a particular sinful behavior but then think that we have thereby made ourselves worthy of God's mercy because of our lack of sin – then we are still under the curse of the law and are in bondage to unbelief!

Therefore, when a person is convicted of his or her sin by God's law and fears God's wrath, that person needs to hear the GOSEPL! Only then will that person have the power and the proper attitude to turn from his or her sinful behavior. In other words, the Christian strives to turn from sin because of the peace and joy that flows from knowing that our sins are forgiven for Christ's sake. In other words, "sanctification" is the RESULT of having been forgiven and not the CAUSE of being forgiven!

The Scripture's teaching about repentance will be a huge comfort to people who are burdened by homosexual desire and behavior. As they continue to struggle with homosexual desire and behavior they will not have to believe the lie that they are not yet worthy of God's mercy. The fact is that we are NEVER worthy of God's mercy. Nevertheless, He freely gives mercy to unworthy sinners who long for it because Christ has already suffered the full weight of God's wrath for all our sins – past, present and future!

The Good News of complete and total forgiveness in Christ will give those burdened with homosexuality the desire to turn from their sin and live according to God's will. As it says in article XII of the Augsburg Confession: "Then good works are bound to follow, which are the fruit of repentance (Galatians 5:22-23)."

Obviously, there are many more "creeds" – many more doctrines of the Christian Faith – I could share with you in this section of my book. But what I have already offered will have to suffice.[260] The point is that the best way we can show love to those who are burdened by homosexual desire and behavior is to speak God's Truth to them. The words and promises of God in Christ are the only hope for us who are burdened by original sin and numerous actual sins. *Now we're ready to hear about the importance of DEEDS.*

The Importance of Deeds!

Someone once said: "People won't care how much you know until they know how much you care." How we treat people is so important. Please understand! I'm not suggesting that our loving deeds toward people somehow add to the power of God's Word that we proclaim to them. We can't add anything to the power of God's Word. But we CAN get in the way of God's Word being heard by other people!

In Ephesians chapter 5 the apostle Paul says that we should speak the Truth in love. Sadly, many in our culture have abandoned God's Truth and have replaced it with human "love." However, those who preserve the Truth of God's Word in all its purity are sometimes guilty of proclaiming that Word in an unloving manner.

---

[260] I encourage you to read all the Lutheran confessional writings as found in *Concordia: The Lutheran Confessions (A Reader's Edition of the Book of Concord)* by Concordia Publishing House.

We may be proclaiming the pure Truth of God's Word, but if we are apathetic about people's pain; if we have an arrogant "I know more about God's Truth than you do!" attitude; if we have an obnoxious and cold personality, then this sin may put up a barrier that will prevent people from hearing the pure Truth of God's Word that we are proclaiming.

We need to be sensitive to people's emotional and physical needs not only because God wants us to love the WHOLE person but also because our failure to do this may keep our proclamation of repentance and forgiveness of sins from being heard.

In Galatians chapter 6 Paul teaches that we must bear the burden of those caught in sin by restoring them "gently." This does not mean that we ignore their sin. There are times we must confront people with God's law. However, we need to do this in a spirit of humility, love and gentleness. If people are going to reject God's Word then let's be sure that it is GOD'S WORD they are rejecting and not our offensive, obnoxious, unloving attitudes and behaviors that keep them from hearing God's Word in the first place.

I must confess that as I look back on my 20 years of pastoral ministry, there were times when my sinful nature got in the way of people hearing God's Word. I am guilty and I deserve nothing but God's wrath for my behavior. But I also believe that I am completely and totally forgiven for Christ's sake, and His unconditional love for me moves me to proclaim His Word to others in a spirit of humility, love and gentleness.

Of course, I will never be able to love people perfectly. I'm sure I will sin against people many more times in the future years of ministry that God may give to me. Therefore, we must be willing to repent on a daily basis and ask people to forgive us if we have wronged them in any way. Such repentant humility goes a long way in opening doors for others to hear God's Word that is proclaimed by us.

The apostle Peter writes: "Always be prepared to give an answer to everyone who asks you to give the reason for the hope you have. But do this with gentleness and respect..." (1st Peter 3:15) Did you notice what Peter wrote? He said that we should be prepared to witness to people when they ASK!

Simply put, the best witness is the one asked for – and people will be willing to ask us about what we believe if we first love them and care for them as human beings.

Please understand! I'm NOT saying there aren't times when we need to take the initiative and confront people about their sin – *especially if such people are members of your congregation and claim to be professing Christians while living openly in unrepentant sin.*

However, if your goal is to speak God's Truth to someone you don't even know who may not even understand the basics of the Christian Faith, then it would be best to first build a relationship with that person before you attempt to witness to him or her.

Be a friend! Earn Their Trust!

If you want to bear the burden of people who are burdened by homosexual desire and behavior by proclaiming the Truth of God's Word to them, then be their friend and earn their trust. Build a relationship with such people. Invite them to your home for coffee or lunch. Offer to help them with any needs they may have.

In fact, if you have the opportunity, spend time with people who are burdened by homosexual desire and behavior. Very often homosexuals are lonely and they actually do crave *non-sexual* intimacy with other people – especially from members of the same sex. It's just that they have not learned how to find that kind of intimacy, and so they have replaced it with SEXUAL intimacy.

If you have the opportunity, visit homosexuals who are suffering from AIDS. Show them compassion and love. Let them know that you care. Even more, tell them how much God loves them – so much, in fact, that He sent His only Son to be their Savior.

Of course, if you ever **do** have a chance to speak God's Truth in love regarding the sin of people's homosexual behavior, there are times when they will reject you and your witness – *no matter how lovingly and gently you speak the Truth to them.* You must not condemn yourself when this happens. Sinners are able to resist the Holy Spirit. If you speak the Truth in love, then you have done what you can and you must allow the Holy Spirit to create repentance and faith where and when it pleases Him.

Invite Them to Your Congregation's Services!

If God opens the door in your relationship with people who are burdened by homosexuality, invite them to your congregation's public

Services – and then make sure that they feel welcome, loved and accepted.

However, if you are going to invite your homosexual friends to your congregation, and you know that your pastor addresses the issue of homosexuality in his sermons from time to time (which he ought to do!), let them know this in advance and make it clear to them that your congregation teaches that we are ALL sinners before God and that no one particular sin is worse than another.

Stress to your homosexual friends that our real problem is not our particular sin issues but the fact that we are by nature enemies of God who deserve nothing but His wrath. Also stress to them that we sinners have complete forgiveness of sins through faith in Christ even in the midst of our struggle with sinful desires and behaviors.

In some cases, those who are burdened by homosexual desire and behavior have never heard preaching about the sin of homosexuality within the context of all people being equally sinful and yet having the hope of complete and total forgiveness through faith in Christ.

However, if your congregation does NOT preach God's Word in its purity regarding homosexuality – either because it affirms homosexual behavior or because it teaches that homosexual behavior is somehow worse than other sins - then find a congregation that DOES teach God's Word purely on this issue and invite your homosexual friends to attend with you there.

Don't Forget About Their Families!

For every person who bears the burden of homosexual desire and behavior, there are other people who also bear that burden – especially family members who agree with God's Word that homosexual behavior is sinful and therefore grieve for their loved ones who are caught in this sin.

I think of the wife or husband whose spouse has just announced that he or she is homosexual and wants out of the marriage. I think of the mother and father who find out that their son or daughter is involved in homosexual behavior. I think of the children who find out that their father or mother is a practicing homosexual. Very often these family members feel alone and isolated because they don't know where to find help.

If someone's family member is involved in alcohol or drug abuse, very often such people will receive a great deal of support from their congregations. But what about family members whose loved one is living the gay lifestyle? Very often they don't mention this issue because they are too ashamed.

We need to be willing to bear the burden of family members who have pain and grief because a member of their family is living the gay lifestyle. We need to love them, support them, comfort them and pray for them.

Start a Support Group!

When I was a pastor in the St. Louis area I served on the board of directors for "FirstLight" – an organization that offered support groups for people who struggled with unwanted same sex attractions. They eventually expanded their services to offer support groups for wives and husbands whose spouse was homosexual as well as for parents who had a child who was homosexual.

During the time I've served as a pastor in Jamestown, ND, I've given some pastoral care to individuals who struggle with unwanted same sex attraction and behavior. I've also worked with parents whose children are involved in the gay lifestyle.

Starting support groups for homosexuals and their families can seem overwhelming for a congregation. But this is a wonderful way to reach out to those in your community who are burdened by their homosexual desire and behavior and would seek help if it were available.

In Appendix V of this book I will provide information about various resources that are available for those who are being led to bear the burden of those who are caught in the sin of homosexual desire and behavior. Be sure to read that section of this book and spend time in prayer regarding how you might show deeds of love to someone you know who bears the burden of homosexual sin.

╬ *APPENDIX I* ╬

"To Refer or NOT to Refer?"

As pastors and laypeople strive to bear the burden of those caught in the sin of homosexuality, we may discover that some of these people have various emotional and psychological issues that are beyond our ability to handle. During such times we may need to refer such people to those who practice psychiatry or psychotherapy.

But how do we know that such professionals will not lead these people astray with teaching or philosophy that is contrary to the teaching of Holy Scripture? Therefore, it is important for us to have a basic understanding of the various psychological schools of thought that serve as the paradigm for how various professionals perform their services.

In this section I will summarize three common psychological schools of thought and point out the concerns in each for Christians as well as some of the positive aspects of these schools of thought that Christians can use in good conscience. This brief treatment of these three psychological schools of thought is very basic and by no means exhaustive – but it does offer a beginning to help people understand how some professionals my seek to deal with those who struggle with homosexual desire and behavior.[261]

So, what is the origin of modern psychotherapy? Most scholars concur that modern psychotherapy as we know it can be traced back to the pioneering work of Wilhelm Wundt who founded the first laboratory of psychology at the university of Leipzig in 1879.[262] However, one must recognize that Wundt's views about psychology were not completely new in the history of the world as though various people and events did not influence the development of psychological

---

[261] For a thorough treatment of the various models of psychotherapy from a Christian point of view, see *Modern Psychotherapies* by Stanton Jones & Richard Butman.

[262] For a brief summary of Wundt, his views and work, see *Baker Encyclopedia of Psychology* by David Benner, 1219.

thought up to the time of Wundt. Therefore, the pastor will find it helpful to read some books that treat the history of psychology and the various people and events that have contributed to the evolution of this social science over the years.[263]

Secular Psychological Schools of Thought

SIGMUND FREUD AND PSYCHOANALYSIS

Sigmund Freud is one of the giants of what can be called modern psychotherapy. Freud was born in Moravia on May 6th, 1856. His family moved to Vienna when he was four. Freud entered the University of Vienna in 1873 and became a psychiatrist. Freud later did work with other famous psychiatrists such as Joseph Breuer, but Freud eventually parted company with Breuer because of Freud's stress on sexual conflict as the cause for neurosis.

Freud's theory of personality is based on his concepts of the **id**, **ego** and **superego**. The id is the unconscious which contains basic human instincts guided by what Freud called the **pleasure principle** (the reduction of anxiety) and the **primary process** (the means of reducing anxiety by producing mental images of various needs[264]). Because the primary process reduces anxiety only to a limited degree, the ego takes over the process. The ego leads a person to satisfy his or her needs through contact with an object of desire in the outside world. However, the ego uses what Freud called the **reality principle** which uses the **secondary process** (that is, realistic thinking verses the fantasy of the dream world) that restrains the fulfillment of need until an appropriate object is found. Finally, the superego consists of the moral standards imposed upon a person primarily by his or her parents but also from society. Therefore, the superego can be understood as "the conscience". The ego is constantly working to balance the basic desires of the id with the rules of the superego. This struggle causes anxiety which can lead to psychological distress if not handled properly.

---

[263] For an excellent survey of the historical development of psychology, see *The Story of Psychology* by Morton Hunt as well as *A History of Psychology* by Thomas Leahey.

[264] For example, a person who has sexual tension may dream about an object of sexual attraction.

Obviously, there is much more that could be said about Freudian psychological theory. However, one more thing we will consider is what Freud called the **life instinct**. The life instinct has to do with a person's basic needs for survival and the desire to propagate the human species. Freud believed that sex (along with hunger, thirst, etc.) is one of the strongest life instincts. Freud used the word **libido** to define the drive that motivates one to satisfy his or her life instincts. Because Freud focused so heavily on sex, the word libido is often associated with this.

Freud believed that there were various **psychosexual stages** that are part of the development of every human from infancy through adulthood. The stages are the **oral, anal, phallic, latency** and **genital.** During the genital stage (about 3 to 6 years of age) both boys and girls must deal with what Freud called the **Oedipus complex** and the **castration complex**. In order to properly understand both of these complexes, it would be helpful to quote here the following concise definitions from Hall and Nordby:

> **"[The Oedipus complex], name for the Greek king who killed his father and married his mother, differs for males and females. The boy has sexual desires for the mother and aggressive feelings toward his father. The girl develops hostility toward the mother and becomes sexually attracted to the father. The girl's complex is sometimes called the *Electra complex* . The Oedipus complex lays the foundation for a person's attitudes toward persons of the same sex and of the opposite sex ... As a consequence of the Oedipus complex, the boy is afraid that his father will castrate him for loving the mother. The girl's castration complex takes the form of her envying the male because he has prominent genitals which she lacks. Her jealousy makes her want to deprive him of his genitals. Having a baby is supposed to be a compensation for the female's not having a penis."** [265]

The above quotation helps us understand the context that Freud believed was foundational for the psychological development of one's

---

[265] *A Guide to Psychologists and Their Concepts* by Calvin Hall and Vernon Nordby.

sexual identity. If one is able to properly process the sexual tension prevalent during the genital stage, one will develop a normal[266] attraction for members of the opposite sex when one reaches adulthood. However, if a person did not properly process the sexual tension during this stage, one's relationship with members of the opposite sex could be adversely affected. At this point we are now ready to consider how Freud understood homosexuality.

Even though Freud considered homosexuality to be an abnormal form of human sexual expression, he did not mean to suggest that homosexuality was sinful or immoral. By the word "abnormal" Freud meant that homosexuality did not represent the majority of human sexual behavior.

Because many people have not understood what Freud meant by "abnormal", some have wrongly assumed that Freud was opposed to homosexuality and might even seek to cure people of this problem. As a result, some within the pro-homosexual movement over the years have reacted negatively to Freudian psychoanalysis. However, some scholars have pointed out that not only did Freud see no point in trying to cure people of their homosexuality. Even more, Freud had absolutely no negative moral judgments about homosexuality. In fact, many pro-homosexual scholars will often refer to a letter that Freud wrote in 1955 to the mother of a homosexual son in which Freud clearly states that he has no moral reservations about homosexuality nor does he believe that treatment will likely help. Following is a brief quotation from this letter:

> **"Homoeroticism … is nothing to be ashamed of, no vice, no degradation, it cannot be classified as an illness; we consider it to be a variation of the sexual function produced by a certain arrest of sexual development … By asking me if I can help … If he is unhappy, neurotic, torn by conflicts, inhibited in his social life, analysis may bring him harmony, peace of mind, full efficiency, whether he remains a homosexual or gets changed … "**[267]

---

[266] By "normal" Freud means that which is represented by the majority of the human population. Therefore, "normal" is a statistical term and not meant to convey a moral judgment about one's sexual identity.

[267] See the full letter in *Sexualities and Homosexualities* by James Stubrin, 90-91.

In view of the forgoing, it is obvious that Christians who take Scripture seriously should have some concerns when referring a person who struggles with homosexuality to a psychiatrist or psychologist who practices from a Freudian model. Not only is psychoanalysis a long, drawn out process that is emotionally exhausting and financially costly. Of even greater concern is the fact that many modern scholars believe that Freud's focus on sex and its connection with the Oedipus and Castration complexes during the genital stage as the basis for most neurotic behavior is far too narrow and fails to consider the complexities of the human psyche. Most important of all, a pastor will want to discover whether or not the counselor shares Freud's views about homosexuality.

However, this does not mean that there is nothing from Freudian theory that can benefit those who struggle with homosexuality.[268] In fact, considering that some models of psychotherapy completely ignore the affect that one's past has on present psychological issues, a Christian can appreciate Freud's focus on the past and how it certainly can, in certain ways, affect one's psychological health in the present. Having said that, it must be stressed once again we will need to use great discernment when considering a referral to a counselor who uses the Freudian model.

B. F. SKINNER AND BEHAVIORISM[269]

B. F. Skinner was born was in Pennsylvania on March 20th, 1904. Skinner received his Ph.D. from Harvard in 1931 and worked for 5 years with the experimental biologist W. J. Crozier. Skinner was also influenced by earlier behaviorists such as Pavlov, Watson and Thorndike.[270] Skinner ended up teaching at the University of Minnesota during which time he wrote two popular books - *The*

---

268 For example, see *Modern Psychotherapies* by Stanton Jones & Richard Butman, 76-88.

269 For an excellent treatment of other models of psychotherapy that are related in various ways to behaviorism (e.g., the Rational Emotive Therapy of Albert Ellis, Cognitive-Behavioral Therapy, the Reality Therapy of William Glasser, and Alderian therapy), see *Modern Psychotherapies* by Stanton Jones & Richard Butman, 173-252.

270 See *A Guide to Psychologists and Their Concepts* by Calvin Hall and Vernon Nordby, 135-138, 168-170, 177-179.

Behavior of Organisms (1938) and the novel *Walden Two* (1948). In 1971 Skinner wrote the book *Beyond Freedom and Dignity* in which he gives opinions about how human society should ideally be shaped and controlled by imposed systems of rewards and reinforcements.

Simply put, whereas Freud believed people were influenced in part by unresolved issues in the id, Skinner believed that people responded like machines when influenced by certain stimuli from the environment. Skinner distinguishes between two types of behavior -- **respondent** and **operant**. Respondent behavior refers to a stimulus that produces a certain behavior in an organism. Operant behavior refers to the action of an organism that is triggered by a physical need. Therefore, operant behavior acts upon the environment in order to obtain the thing desired. However, such operant behavior can be easily influenced and controlled by **reinforcement**, which is any applied stimulus that can change the response of an individual. In this way, the behavior of humans can be manipulated, guided and eventually changed through a series of planned reinforcements.

As with Freudian theory discussed earlier, the above is a very simple summary of Skinner's behaviorism. What needs to be stressed at this point is that Skinner viewed human beings as machines who would automatically respond to particular stimuli and reinforcements depending on their needs or desires. Behaviorism does not ask whether a particular desire behavior is moral or not. Instead, the goal of therapy based on the behaviorism model is pure pragmatism. Various reinforcements are used to obtain the desired behavior -- whatever that behavior may be. *Therefore, one acceptable goal of behaviorism therapy could be to develop a system of reinforcements that would help a person feel more comfortable about his or her homosexual identity.*

This does not mean that the techniques of the behaviorism model can not be used to benefit those who struggle with homosexuality.[271] In fact, even though behaviorism ignores the inner psychological aspects of humans as well as their spiritual aspirations, Christians can appreciate the focus that behaviorism places on the way humans are affected by various stimuli and reinforcements in our environment. In fact, Christians can accept that certain elements of behaviorism therapy could be used by God to curb evil behavior and keep order in society.

---

[271] For a treatment of some of the positive benefits of behaviorism therapy, see *Modern Psychotherapies* by Stanton Jones & Richard Butman, 154-170. Also see *Behavioral Sciences: A Christian Perspective* by Malcolm Jeeves.

In other words, behaviorism therapy could be one of God's gifts used by homosexuals to help curb their behavior.

However, having said that, we Christians will want to avoid counselors whose use of behaviorism includes the naturalistic presuppositions inherent in Skinner's model. Not only will we want to protect people from the philosophy of moral relativism. We will also want to make sure that people understand that there is more to the Christian life than having one's behavior manipulated by external stimuli and reinforcements.

CARL ROGERS AND PERSON-CENTERED THERAPY[272]

Carl Rogers was born in Illinois on January 8th, 1902. After graduating from high school he enrolled at the University of Wisconsin, but during his sophomore year he decided to pursue a religious education. As a result, after receiving his B.A. in history from the University of Wisconsin in 1924, he then enrolled at the Union Theological Seminary in New York, which he chose to attend because of its liberal theological views. During this time he also took courses in psychology at Columbia University.

Roger's received his Ph.D. in 1931 and eventually wrote *The Clinical Treatment of the Problem Child* (1939). Later on he wrote *Counseling and Psychotherapy: Newer Concepts in Practice* (1942), in which he explained his theory of nondirective counseling. Over the next few years Rogers continued to develop his theories and presented them in one of his most influential books, *Client-centered therapy: Its Current Practice, Implications, and Theory* (1951).

Rogers taught the concept of the **organism**, which is the center of all human experience. The totality of a person's experience is called the **phenomenal field**, part of which splits off and forms the **self**. The relationship of one's self with his or her total experiences will result in either **congruence** (the ability to live according to one's own experience) or **incongruence** (the self being forced to conform to the expectations of others). In order to achieve a life of congruence,

---

[272] Carl Rogers is one of the more influential people within the humanistic psychotherapy models. Other models of psychotherapy that fall into this category, but are not treated in this paper, are Transactional Analysis, Gestalt Therapy and Existential Therapy. For an excellent treatment of these three models from a Christian point of view, see *Modern Psychotherapies* by Stanton Jones & Richard Butman, 278-346.

Rogers taught that every person needs two things: **unconditional positive regard** (the affirmation and complete acceptance of self from others) and, ideally, **self-regard** (self affirmation and acceptance *in spite of* the opinion of others).

Therefore, the goal of client-centered therapy is to reduce incongruence in an individual via an experience with a counselor who has unconditional positive regard for the counselee and affirms him or her with warmth and compassion. In addition, the counselor will facilitate the development of self-regard in the counselee by being non-directive and allowing the counselee to get in touch with his or her own feelings and desires - and then accept them as good and proper.

Obviously, we should have great concern if a counselor is using the client-centered model *apart from a Christian worldview* since he or she could lead clients to place all their trust in their own experience with the result that they either ignore or despise all critical authority outside of themselves. In the worst case, this would lead to self worship and total moral relativism. A counselor who accepts these presuppositions of client-centered therapy would likely encourage a counselee who is struggling with homosexuality to simply cease struggling and ignore the critical judgments placed upon them by the Christian Faith.

Of course, this does not mean that certain aspects of client-centered therapy are not useful.[273] For example, Roger's technique called "active listening" gives the counselor the ability to become a good listener and give the client the opportunity to express his or her true feelings without constantly being interrupted by an overly directive counselor. In addition, Christians can appreciate "unconditional positive regard" as putting into practice Christ's command that we love even our enemies. *However, we strive to love people unconditionally based on God's love for them in Christ - understanding that such love for others is not in conflict with Jesus' command that we also proclaim repentance and rebuke those who are caught in sin so that we might proclaim forgiveness as well.*

The Rogerian model, left unchecked and uncorrected by Christian Truth, has resulted in many people being counseled into a life of self-worship and total disregard for any objective truth that might call into question their experiences or choices. Even though we can appreciate and utilize some of the techniques of client-centered therapy, we must

---

[273] For example, see *Modern Psychotherapies* by Stanton Jones & Richard Butman, 261-275.

also use great discernment when referring a person to a counselor who uses this model.

Now that we have examined the theories of Freud, Skinner and Rogers, it should be noted that there are many Christian psychiatrists and psychologists who utilize aspects of these models in a responsible manner that is faithful to the teaching of Holy Scripture. Therefore, we should not hesitate to interview such counselors to determine what models of psychotherapy they use and how they relate these models to the Christian Faith. Pastors and laypeople who are working with those who struggle with homosexuality will especially want to make sure that such counselors will in no way justify or affirm homosexual desire or practice.

One other thing must be understood. There are many counselors who do not strictly conform their counseling to any **one** model. In other words, some have an *eclectic approach* to psychotherapy. This "eclectic approach" can be good or bad - depending on what certain counselors mean by an "eclectic approach".

For example, Butman and Jones suggest that there are four ways of understanding what it means to be an eclectic psychotherapist.[274] These four approaches are *Chaotic Eclecticism* (the unsystematic use of techniques without the controlling features of a particular model), *Pragmatic Eclecticism* (the use of whatever model of psychotherapy seems best for the individual client), *Transtheoretical Eclecticism* (the idea that a use of various models will eventually lead to the discovery of one, true, overarching model that can embrace all theories and techniques), and *Theoretical Integrationism* (holding to one model but overcoming its limitations by utilizing the techniques of other models).

Butman and Jones react negatively to Chaotic Eclecticism. Also, even though Butman and Jones see positive things about Pragmatic and Transtheoretical Eclecticism, they end up recommending that Christians pursue **Theoretical Integrationism.** The foundation model that Butman and Jones recommend is the nature of humans in their relationship to God as revealed in Holy Scripture. This biblical model of anthropology allows Christian counselors to work with assumptions about the sinful nature of human beings as well as our accountability before God and our need to receive the freedom and healing that only Christ can give us.

---

[274] See *Modern Psychotherapies* by Stanton Jones & Richard Butman, 379-400.

However, Butman and Jones go on to stress that the biblical teaching of anthropology in itself is not enough to deal with the various complexities of the human body, emotions and mind. Just as Scripture does not give us information about the development of corrective eyewear or the procedure one should follow in order to perform heart bypass surgery, the same Scripture also does not give us all the particular details we may need to deal with the various psychological issues that afflict human beings. Therefore, Butman and Jones encourage counselors to utilize the techniques of various psychotherapies while using Scripture's teaching as the foundational model for morality and anthropology so that discernment can be used to avoid those things that are contrary to God's will.[275]

Can Homosexuals Become Heterosexuals?

Many people who were once practicing homosexual behavior have "changed."[276] But what do we mean by that word "changed?" If we mean they ALL no longer struggle with same sex attractions and are now happily married to a person of the opposite sex with whom they experience a fulfilling sex life – then "No," all these people have NOT "changed."

Some of them continue to struggle with various degrees of same sex attraction. Some of them remain single and celibate. Others are married to a person of the opposite sex – but they acknowledge that they continue to struggle with same sex attraction.

In any case, with help from fellow Christians and counselors who believe that one does not have to be in bondage to homosexual behavior simply because one bears the burden of a homosexual orientation, many have found the strength to cease their homosexual behavior and live a new life. After receiving help, some confess they have little or no same sex desires. On the other hand, after receiving help, there are others who continue to have various levels of homosexual desire.

---

[275] For a very helpful summary of the core values that should make up a model of Christian counseling, see the section **Dimensions of a Comprehensive Christian Counseling Approach** in *Modern Psychotherapies* by Stanton Jones & Richard Butman, 397-398.

[276] See the web page for Exodus International (**www.exodusinternational.org**) where you will find many testimonies from both men and women who no longer practice homosexual behavior.

As with alcoholics, the success rate of helping people cease their homosexual behavior depends on whether they actually WANT to cease their behavior or not. If people are comfortable with their homosexual desires and do not want to change their behavior, then obviously all the counseling and therapy in the world is not going to "change" them. But if a person wants to be free of his or her homosexual behavior, then "change" is possible and help is available!

Dr. Joseph Nicolosi and many other respected psychiatrists and psychologists are part of an organization known as NARTH (National Association of Research & Therapy of Homosexuality). They have helped many people overcome their bondage to homosexual desire and behavior – with varying degrees of success.[277]

Many involved in the pro-gay movement will accuse organizations such as NARTH and Exodus International of causing harm to those whose homosexual orientation they think should be affirmed and encouraged. But many people burdened by homosexual desire and behavior have been helped by them and other organizations like them.

Just because such organizations as NARTH and Exodus International do not have a 100% success rate with all the people they strive to help is no reason to discredit their efforts. Most people praise the efforts of groups like Alcoholics Anonymous and Narcotics Anonymous even though their efforts don't result in anything close to a 100% success rate.

At this point I would like to quote from the book *Homosexuality: The Use of Scientific Research in the Church's Moral Debate* by Stanton Jones and Mark Yarhouse in which they summarize the findings of their intensive study of therapies that attempt to help people change their homosexual behavior and orientation. They write:

- **The research on change of sexual orientation is intensely debated today. Most of the research was conducted and published between the 1950s and the 1970s, with an average positive outcome of approximately 30%.**
- **Definitions of "positive outcome" vary across studies. Positive outcome has been defined in the following ways: reduced preoccupation with homosexual thoughts, reduced homosexual activity, reduced anxiety about heterosexual functioning,**

[277] See their web page: **www.narth.com**

increased heterosexual activity, increased heterosexual fantasy, celibacy, heterosexual marriage and reports of change of sexual orientation from homosexual to heterosexual.

- **There are a number of methodological limitations to the early studies published on change, including small sample sizes, the reliance on self-report and therapist-report of change, and lack of control groups. However, many of the these same methodological limitations plague studies conducted today, so critics should be consistent across all efforts to provide professional interventions to human concerns.**
- **There may be tremendous value in publishing outcome studies of higher quality than have been published to date. Along these lines, collaboration between religion-based ministries and researchers would provide empirical evidence for what homosexual persons can expect upon entering these programs.**
- **Research on change of orientation is not formally relevant to the moral debate in the church, as the church's moral concern is not with changing experiences or same-sex attraction but with how a person chooses to express those inclinations across relationships.[278]**

Regarding their final bullet point (above), Stanton and Yarhouse write the following: "As a 'worst case' scenario let us suppose that change from homosexual preferences or experiences of same-sex attraction by human effort is found to be impossible. Such a finding would not necessarily change fundamental Christian teaching at all, in that God's standard for homosexual persons would continue to be the same as that for all persons. That standard is chastity in heterosexual marriage or celibacy outside of marriage. It may be that the church can no more guarantee healing to homosexuals than it can guarantee marriage to disconsolate single heterosexuals. There are many more single Christian heterosexuals 'doomed' to sexual abstinence by the church's 'narrow' sexual morality than there are homosexual persons similarly constrained. The core issue is that the church's stance on homosexual behavior requires only that individuals be able to refrain from homosexual action and find a life of fulfillment in God's own provision in meeting their personal needs and not that they necessarily be able to become heterosexuals. Certainly behavior change is within

---

[278]See pages 150-151.

the realm of that which can be changed, as evidenced by … scientific findings that clearly support change of behavior methods."[279]

Simply put, those who wish to follow Christ are not expected to *eliminate* their various sinful **desires** – including their sinful sexual desires (whether heterosexual or homosexual). In fact, those who follow Christ are not even expected to *eliminate* all forms of sinful **behavior** from there their lives – as this is impossible! Certainly, those who follow Christ should fight against the desires of their sinful nature and avoid all forms of evil behavior – which is one thing it means for us to "take up our cross." But there is no Christian who has ever had 100% success at accomplishing this!

Therefore, Christ is not asking those burdened with homosexual desire and behavior to eliminate all homosexual desire and behavior from their lives before they can be worthy of His forgiveness and love. Instead, the forgiveness and love that Christ freely gives to those who carry the heavy burden of homosexual desire and behavior will move them to turn from their sin and strive to live lives of sexual purity to the glory of God who saved them!

[279] Ibid, 150.

☩ *APPENDIX II* ☩

Female Pastors *and* Homosexual Behavior:

Is the Affirmation of <u>Both</u> Connected?

From 1994 to 1998 I served a congregation in Bismarck, North Dakota. During that time I worked with a local ELCA pastor and an Association of American Lutheran Churches (AALC) pastor to establish a "Lutherans for Life"[280] chapter in the area.

We sent letters to all area Lutheran congregations inviting pastors and laypeople to our first organizational meeting. On the night of the meeting several Lutheran pastors showed up. Most of them were LCMS, but there were a few ELCA pastors – including one <u>female</u> ELCA pastor who served a rural parish in the area.

Even though I am convinced that Scripture does not allow women to serve in the pastoral office, I was very pleased to have a "pro-life" ELCA female pastor attend our meeting. After I got to know this female ELCA pastor, I discovered that we had total and complete theological agreement – EXCEPT ON THE ISSUE OF WOMEN SERVING IN THE PASTORAL OFFICE. However, as I grew to understand her respect for the authority of Holy Scripture, I realized that if she were to be convinced that the Scriptures prohibited her from serving in the pastoral office, she would have submitted to Scripture's

---

[280] For information about the pro-life teaching of "Lutherans for Life," see the web page: www.lutheransforlife.org .

teaching out of respect for the authority of Holy Scripture and out of love for Christ, her Savior.

Now, are there female Lutheran pastors who deny the authority of Holy Scripture and who reject basic doctrines of the Christian Faith? Sadly, yes.[281] Some female pastors even acknowledge that Scripture does not allow women to be pastors, but they dismiss this teaching of Scripture as outdated, patriarchal, male chauvinism that has no authority over us today. Are there female Lutheran pastors whose motive for being pastors flows from their sense of social justice and a desire for equal rights with men? Sadly, yes. ***However, it would be sinful to suggest that all female pastors are like this!***

I have met some female Lutheran pastors who respect the authority of Holy Scripture and who faithfully hold to the basic doctrines of the Christian Faith as confessed in the Book of Concord. They simply believe that the traditional biblical passages used to prohibit women serving as pastors have been misinterpreted. I have met some female Lutheran pastors whose desire to be a pastor flows not from a longing for "social justice" or "equal rights" but from a desire to serve others according to Christ's own example.

Nevertheless, even though some female Lutheran pastors believe that Scripture allows them to serve in the pastoral office, this does not mean that they are correct. They could be misled, which is what I believe is the case. I believe that such female Lutheran pastors, if convinced from Scripture that God prohibits them from serving in the pastoral office, would be willing to stop serving as pastors out of respect for the authority of Holy Scripture and out of love for Christ.

In chapter three of this book under the section *The Genesis creation account is a myth!* I suggested that those who deny the historicity of the creation account in Genesis must logically deny all the basic doctrines of the Christian Faith – and I gave evidence from a book by John Shelby Spong to show how at least one liberal theologian does that very thing.

This does not mean that all who deny the historicity of the creation account in Genesis end up denying all the other basic doctrines of the Christian Faith – *but their denial of the creation account in Genesis lays the foundation for them to do that very thing!* In other words, the same presuppositions that would lead one to deny the historicity of the

---

[281] For example, go to the web page: **www.herchurch.org** (an ELCA congregation in California).

creation account in Genesis can just as easily lead one to deny every other doctrine of the Christian Faith.

In this chapter of my book I hope to show that the same presuppositions and approach to Scripture that have led some to affirm the ordination of women into the pastoral office can just as easily, if not consistently, also lead to the affirmation of homosexual behavior and the ordination of practicing homosexuals into the pastoral office.

Obviously, not everyone who affirms the ordination of women to the pastoral office is in favor of affirming homosexual behavior. *In fact, there are many within the ELCA who affirm the ordination of women to the pastoral office and yet are very much opposed to the affirmation of homosexual behavior because they believe it is contrary to the teaching of Holy Scripture.* However, what I hope to point out in this chapter, in love and humility, is that those who affirm the ordination of women to the pastoral office and yet condemn homosexual behavior as being sinful are simply not being consistent.

In fact, my fear is that some Lutheran church bodies being newly formed as I write this book are only moving the theological train further back on the same track – and that theological train, because it is moving in the same direction, will eventually lead once again to the affirmation of homosexual behavior in their own newly formed Lutheran church bodies.

My prayer is that our brothers and sisters in the ELCA (and other newly formed Lutheran bodies) who agree with other Lutherans that homosexual behavior is sinful will be willing to revisit the issue of the ordination of women into the pastoral office by thoroughly studying the Holy Scriptures with us who believe Scripture prohibits this practice. I also pray that our Lutheran brothers and sisters who agree with other Lutherans that homosexual behavior is sinful will be willing to listen to the voice of the Church catholic, from the time of the apostles, on the issue of women in the pastoral office.

Before I offer my arguments for why I believe the ordination of women to the pastoral office and the affirmation of homosexual behavior are related, I will first offer ten points in favor of my arguments from an paper written by John Pless titled *The Ordination of Women and Ecclesial Endorsement of Homosexuality: Are They Related?*[282]

---

[282] This paper was offered at the Lutheran Theological Conference of South Africa in the FELS Retreat Center, August 11th – 14th, 2009.

In this article Pless offers the following ten points in support of the connection between the affirmation of the ordination of women to the pastoral office and the affirmation of homosexual behavior and the resulting affirmation of ordination of practicing homosexuals into the pastoral office:

1. **The advocacy for women's ordination and for the ordination of homosexuals and the blessing of same-sex unions is argued in the churches as a matter of social justice.**[283]
2. **Churchly acceptance of woman's ordination, the ordination of homosexuals and blessing of same-sex unions has been fueled by powerful liberationist movements within the culture rather than biblical understanding.**[284]
3. **In case for both the ordination of women and the ordination of homosexuals, Galatians 3:28 is used in such a way as to sever redemption from creation.**[285]
4. **Opponents of women's ordination and those who resist the acceptance of homosexuality as a moral equivalent to**

---

[283] On page 2 of *The Ordination of Women and Ecclesial Endorsement of Homosexuality: Are They Related?* Pless writes: "Church office and sexual fulfillment are seen as matters of entitlement. Just as barriers to women and homosexuals have been removed in other areas of civic life and the work place, the same demand is made on the church. This is especially true in church bodies where social justice is not seen as a work of God in the government of the left hand but where the promotion of social justice is seen as part, perhaps even the major part of the church's mission to the world. Here it is argued that the church must enact social justice in its own midst by removing barriers to equality. In fact, Krister Stendahl argues 'It seems to me almost impossible to assert – be it reluctantly or gladly – to the political emancipation of women while arguing on biblical grounds against the ordination of women.'"

[284] Pless writes: "While feminist theologies are variegated, they have in common a strong theme that women are oppressed by patriarchal structures and need to be emancipated from these restrictive, ideological paradigms and freed for access to all aspects of the church life including the pastoral office. While various gay liberationist movements are historically much more recent than feminism, they tend to have similar goals ... Both movements of feminist and gay liberation insist on a revisionist understanding of biblical texts that were previously held to be prohibitive and see the Gospel primarily as a means of empowerment and change." Ibid, pg. 3.

[285] I will treat Galatians 3:28 more thoroughly later in this chapter.

heterosexuality are labeled as fundamentalists and legalists.[286]

5. **In making the case for women's ordination and for the ordination of homosexuals and the blessing of same-sex unions, biblical texts once taken as clear are argued unclear or dismissed as culturally conditioned and time bound.**[287]
6. **Ordination of women and ordination of homosexuals is seen as a matter of necessity for the sake of the Gospel and mission.**[288]
7. **Arguments for both the ordination of women and the ordination of homosexuals along with churchly blessing of**

---

[286] Pless writes: "Taking 'the interpretation closest to hand' as that one 'which allows the text to say what it says most simply' to use the language of Herman Sasse is equated with fundamentalism. The labeling then becomes a weapon of defense from listening to what is said in the text. A simple reading of the text that yields an undesired result, i.e., that women can't be pastors or that homosexual acts lie outside of the realm of God's design is dismissed." Ibid, pg. 8.

[287] Pless writes: "Some assert that the contested texts relative to women in the office (I Corinthians 14:33-38 and I Timothy 2:11-14) and on homosexuality (Leviticus 18:22, 24; 20:13; Romans 1:24-27; I Corinthians 6:9-10; I Timothy 1:9-10) clearly reflect the theological worldview of the biblical writers but that these teachings are culturally conditioned and hence open to reassessment. Typical are the arguments that the Bible represents a patriarchal and or heterosexualist structure that may be abandoned without doing violence to the essential message of the Holy Scriptures. Others argue that the disputed texts are unclear and therefore incapable of providing a sure foundation for church practice." Ibid, pg. 9.

[288] Pless writes: "The case is made that a church that excludes women from the pastoral office … and/or renders a negative moral judgment on homosexual practice will not be attractive to a world that does not discriminate on the basis of gender or sexual orientation … Teachings that would exclude some Christians on the basis of gender or sexual identity from full participation in the mission of the church are seen as detrimental to effective missionary outreach and stumbling blocks to the proclamation of the Gospel which is meant for all people." Ibid, pg. 9. *Pless makes a good point! Do we compromise the teaching of Scripture regarding the prohibition of women serving in the pastoral office or the prohibition of homosexual behavior in order to make the Gospel more appealing to the people of this world? No! The Gospel* *__itself__* *is offensive to people unless the Spirit opens their hearts (see 1st Corinthians 1:18 & 2:9-16). John Shelby Spong has argued that Christianity must change or die. By this he means that such doctrines as creation, the virgin birth, the deity of Christ, the atonement and the resurrection are ridiculous to most modern minds. Therefore, such Christian doctrines must be rejected. But if we reject such doctrines in order to change Christianity to make it more appealing to the world, then Christianity* *__itself__* *DIES!*

same-sex unions are often made on the basis of what A. MacIntyre has identified as an "ethic of emotivism."[289]

8. **Women's ordination and the ordination of homosexuals are urged on the church for the sake of unity and inclusiveness yet both practices fracture genuine ecumenicity.[290]**

9. **Ordination of women, ordination of homosexuals and ecclesiastical recognition of same-sex unions are at first proposed as a matter of compromise or as a local option but they will finally demand universal acceptance.[291]**

10. **It is argued that by refusing to ordain women and homosexuals to the pastoral office the church is deprived of the particular spiritual gifts they possess and that these individuals are unjustly denied the opportunity for spiritual self-expression.[292]**

I will now go on to offer my own arguments for why I believe the Scripture prohibits women from serving in the pastoral office and why a rejection of this Scriptural teaching can easily and consistently lead to

---

[289] Pless writes: "The case is made for women's ordination and an ethic affirming of homosexuality on the basis of emotional appeal. The pain of exclusion, for example, is used by advocates to urge the church to respond with sympathy rather than restriction. With an 'ethic of emotivism' claims to biblical authority or creedal teaching are trumped by an appeal to the emotional well-being of those denied access either to the pastoral office or marriage." Ibid, pg. 10.

[290]Pless writes: "...such an approach will finally exclude from unity those who hold a traditional position on these matters. When truth is sacrificed for unity, unity will finally demand the exclusion of those who insist on truth." Ibid, pg. 10.

[291]Pless writes: "...such a situation of compromise will hardly satisfy either activist for change or those who believe that the Scriptural ethic precludes the placing in office of those who practice homosexuality. To paraphrase Richard John Neuhaus, where orthodoxy is made optional, orthodoxy will finally be proscribed." Ibid, pg. 11.

[292] Pless writes: "This argument relies on an understanding of the ministry that sees the ministry as an avenue for the expression of personal *charismata* rather than an office established by Christ and filled according to His mandates. Spiritual giftedness is confused with personal expression. Creativity and freedom to express oneself without boundary or restrict are celebrated in the name of autonomy. Given the spiritual climate of the postmodern context this becomes attractive as 'gifts of the Spirit' are set in contrast to a biblical/confessional understanding of office. Expressive individualism takes precedence over an understanding of an office instituted by Christ to serve His church with Word and Sacrament." Ibid, pg. 11.

the affirmation of homosexual behavior as well as the affirmation of the ordination of practicing homosexuals to the pastoral office.

We must distinguish ministry from Ministry!

If one does some research into the staff of many Protestant and Lutheran congregations one will find children's ministers, youth ministers, visitation ministers, music ministers, social ministers, stewardship ministers, administrative ministers, teaching ministers, evangelism ministers, worship ministers and preaching ministers. This has contributed to the confusion and misunderstanding that the pastoral office is just one more type of "ministry." The word "minister" simply means "servant." However, as we will see, according to Scripture there is a kind of "service" that is done by laypeople and another kind of "service" that is given for only pastors to do.

But even the word "pastor" is not understood in the same way by all Christians or even by all Lutherans. For example, I know of women in non-Lutheran denominations who perform functions similar to women in the LCMS who are known as "Directors of Christian Education" and yet these non-Lutheran women performing these same functions are often called "teaching pastors" or "youth pastors."

I remember on one occasion a non-Lutheran female "youth pastor" asked me: "I heard that you Missouri Synod Lutherans don't allow women to be pastors. So, do you only allow men to teach? Do only men work with your youth?" She assumed that since we do not ordain women into the pastoral office that this meant we do not allow women to do any kind of church work whatsoever.

What point am I trying to make? My point is that before we consider whether Scripture does or does not allow women to serve in the pastoral office, it would be good for us to agree on what we mean by the "pastoral office."

Based on the teaching of Holy Scripture, Missouri Synod Lutherans have usually understood the "pastoral office" not as defining any kind of professional church work but as referring to a specific office instituted by Christ Himself for the benefit of His Church. Simply put, even though any Christian can give witness to others of the person and work of Christ, the pastoral office was instituted by Christ so that Christ might serve His Church through those who are placed into that office.

In other words, pastors are called to represent Christ and be His instruments by baptizing in Christ's Name, forgiving and retaining sins in Christ's Name, preaching in Christ's Name, and speaking Christ's Word's of institution for the Lord's Supper in His Name – *and all of this especially within the context of the public Divine Service where God gives His gifts to His people.*

Even though all Christians are "a royal priesthood, a holy nation" (1st Peter 2:9a) who are called to offer "spiritual sacrifices acceptable to God through Jesus Christ" (1st Peter 2:5b) and to "declare the praises of him who called you out of darkness into this wonderful light" (1st Peter 2:9a), this does NOT mean that all Christians are thereby called and placed into the pastoral office instituted by Christ.

Scripture teaches that Christ chooses certain men to represent Him before His people – and these men are called by various names (elders, teachers, pastors, bishops, shepherds), but they all share the same office. This office was instituted by Christ Himself (Matthew 28:18-20; Luke 10:1-2, 16; John 20:21-23; Ephesians 4:7-13). Christ passed on this office through His pastors who placed into this same office other men who were called by God's people to serve them in Christ's stead (Acts 14:23; 1st Timothy 1:12, 3:1-10, 4:13-16; 2nd Timothy 1:6; Titus 1:5-9). Christians are to view pastors as instruments through whom Christ proclaims His Word and bestows His gifts (2nd Corinthians 5:20-21, 1st Thessalonians 5:12-13, Hebrews 13:17).

In The Apology of the Augsburg Confession [293] we read the following about pastors: "Because of the call of the Church, the unworthy still represent the person of Christ and do not represent their own persons, as Christ testifies, 'The one who hears you hears Me' (Luke 10:16) … When they offer God's Word, when they offer the Sacraments, they offer them in the stead and place of Christ … Ministers act in Christ's place and do not represent their own persons…"[294] In addition, The Augsburg Confession says the following about the pastoral office: "…the authority of the Keys (Matthew 16:19), or the authority of bishops – according to the Gospel – is a power or commandment of God, to preach the Gospel, to forgive and retain sins, and to administer the Sacraments. Christ sends out His apostles with this command, 'As the Father has sent Me, even so I am

[293] Quotations from The Book of Concord are taken from *Concordia: The Lutheran Confessions - A Reader's Edition of The Book of Concord* (Concordia Publishing House, 2005).

[294] Article VII, paragraphs 28 & 47.

sending you … Receive the Holy Spirit. If you forgive the sins of anyone, they are forgiven; if you withhold forgiveness from anyone, it is withheld' (John 20:21-22)."[295]

In article III of The Augsburg Confession we read about the person and work of Christ. In article IV we read that Christ's person and work result in the justification of sinners before God. The words of article IV are as follows: "Our churches teach that people cannot be justified before God by their own strength, merits, or works. People are freely justified for Christ's sake, through faith, when they believe that they are received into favor and that their sins are forgiven for Christ's sake. By His death, Christ made satisfaction for our sins. God counts this faith for righteousness in His sight (Romans 3:21-26; 4:5)."

But how is it possible for sinners to receive Christ's gifts and the faith that receives them? How does the justification made possible by Christ's person and work get applied to us personally? Article V of The Augsburg Confession answers that question with these words: "So that we may obtain this faith, the ministry of teaching the Gospel and administering the Sacraments was instituted. Through the Word and Sacraments, as through instruments, the Holy Spirit is given (John 20:22). He works faith, when and where it pleases God (John 3:8), in those who hear the good news that God justifies those who believe that they are received into grace for Christ's sake. This happens not through our own merits, but for Christ's sake."

Article V of The Augsburg Confession clearly teaches that the teaching of the Gospel and the administering of the Sacraments are to be given to God's people through the ministry that Christ instituted.

With the above in mind, Article XIV of The Augsburg Confession states: "Our churches teach that no one should publicly teach in the Church, or administer the Sacraments, without a rightly ordered call." When article XIV refers to "a rightly ordered call" it means that Christians must call men and place them into the pastoral office according to Christ's institution. These men must meet the biblical qualifications for pastors (see 1st Timothy 3:1-7 and Titus 1:5-9) and be placed into the office by the Word of God and prayer. God uses a local group of Christians to call a man to be their pastor who is then placed into that office by other pastors during a public Divine Service.

---

[295] Article XXVIII, paragraph 5.

The pastoral office has nothing to do with worldly authority and power. Instead, the pastoral office is used by Christ to bestow His gifts upon His people. In other words, pastors are servants of God's people!

In his article *The Office of the Holy Ministry* Joel Okamoto writes: "The New Testament teaches us that Christ is not only the one who authorizes the office and calls men to service but also serves as the paradigm for those whom he calls and sends: 'As the Father has sent me, even so I send you' (John 20:21). Those called to the office are called to continue the work that God gave his Son. Ministers do not merely speak about God's grace and salvation; they are called to convey God's grace and offer salvation. Their calling is to act, as our liturgical orders put it, 'in the stead and by the command' of the Lord. Their office is not simply to talk about God's reign or God's forgiveness or God's justification; their office is to announce the coming of God's reign, to forgive sins, and to justify sinners (see also John 15:18-16:15; 17:6-26). It is further reflected in the appointing and sending of the twelve (Matt 10:1-42; Mark 3:13-19; 6:7-13; Luke 9:1-6) and the seventy-two (Luke 10:1-20). Here Christ commissions them for work that he himself is doing…" Later on Okamoto writes: "This office of teaching, preaching, and administering the sacraments is held not simply as a matter of good order, but, as we have already seen, because the office has Christ's institution and command."[296]

We misunderstand Scripture's teaching about the pastoral office if we conclude that those in the pastoral office are merely working full time performing functions that laypeople could also perform if they were not busy doing something else. The idea that the pastoral office is nothing more than a human invention for the sake of order in the Church misses the fact that Christ Himself instituted the pastoral office in order to give gifts to His people – especially during the context of the public Divine Service!

Now, does all this talk about the pastoral office mean that a baptism performed by a layperson in an emergency situation is not valid or efficacious? No! The point is that baptism is normally done by the pastor who represents Christ in the context of the Divine Service. Does this mean that the Gospel spoken by a layperson to his or her neighbor can not be used by the Holy Spirit to convert an unbelieving heart? No! The point is that the pastor has been called to forgive sins and

[296] See *The Office of the Holy Ministry* by Joel Okamoto in the Concordia Theological Quarterly: Volume 70 / No. 2, 2006, 99-101.

teach Holy Scripture in the context of the Divine Service as the representative of Christ for the benefit of His people.

In other words, Scripture's teaching that all Christians are "priests" and Scripture's teaching that God calls some men from these "priests" to serve in the pastoral office are not in conflict with each other. All Christians can give witness to Christ! But God calls some into the pastoral office through which Christ bestows His gifts upon His people – especially during the context of the public Divine Service.

Joel Okamoto writes the following: "…we should acknowledge both that Christ instituted the office of the holy ministry and gave it the power of the keys (John 20:21-23; Matt 16:13-19), and also that Christ gave the power of the keys to the whole church (Matt 18:18-20). The Lutheran Confessions affirm both testimonies … The Confessions, moreover, testify to the keys granted to the whole church in other ways, notably when the Smalcald Articles speak about 'the mutual conversation and consolation of brothers and sisters' (SA III, iv) and when the Large Catechism identifies a 'secret confession that takes place privately before a single brother or sister' (LC Conf 13) … The assertion that Christ gave the keys to the whole church is significant also because it gives to the church the right and the responsibility to call and ordain ministers. The Confessions never use the truth that the whole church possesses the power of the keys to make the office of the holy ministry unnecessary or merely useful. On the contrary, this truth serves as the basis for the church's right to call, choose, and ordain ministers … Exercising this right by calling those who are placed in the office is one significant way that the church keeps Christ's institution and command."[297]

In addition, regarding emergency situations when laypeople baptize or absolve others, Okamoto writes the following: "…the fact that the whole church has been given the power of the keys makes ordination appropriate, not irrelevant. Persons who act in such emergencies are not thereby put into the office. Simply because one is thrust into such a situation … one should not be understood as being put into the office.

[297] See *The Office of the Holy Ministry* by Joel Okamoto in the Concordia Theological Quarterly: Volume 70 / No. 2, 2006, 105-108.

But the point is that the Treatise[298] does not imagine churches without ordained ministers of some kind, even in emergency situations…"[299]

Much more could be said about the pastoral office, but this subject is beyond the scope of this book.[300] The important thing is that we understand what we mean by the word "pastor." According to Scripture, women can serve in the Church and give witness to Christ in all the same ways that any layperson can. However, Scripture also teaches that the pastoral office is to be filled only by certain men and never women.

What must we ignore if we affirm female pastors and homosexual behavior?

As with the subject of the pastoral office, this short chapter of my book can not begin to do justice to the subject of the ordination of women into the pastoral office. Therefore, I encourage you to read the following excellent works on the subject:

- *Women Pastors? The Ordination of Women in Biblical Lutheran Perspective* edited by Matthew Harrison and John Pless.
- *Recovering Biblical Manhood & Womanhood* edited by John Piper and Wayne Grudem.

---

[298] The word "Treatise" refers to The Treatise on the Power and Primacy of the Pope. See *Concordia: The Lutheran Confessions - A Reader's Edition of The Book of Concord* (Concordia Publishing House, 2005), 317-332.

[299] See *The Office of the Holy Ministry* by Joel Okamoto in the Concordia Theological Quarterly: Volume 70 / No. 2, 2006, 109.

[300] For other excellent articles on the pastoral office see the following: *The Office of the Holy Ministry According to the Gospels and the Augsburg Confession* by David Scaer and *Augsburg Confession XIV: Does It Answer Current Questions on the Holy Ministry?* By Naomichi Masaki – both found in the Concordia Theological Quarterly: Volume 70 / No. 2, 2006. Also see *The Ministry: Offices, Procedures, and Nomenclature* (A report of the CTCR of the LCMS, September 1981).

- *Women in the Church: A Fresh Analysis of 1 Timothy 2:9-15* edited by Andreas Kostenberger, Thomas Schreiner and H. Scott Baldwin.
- *Two Views on Women in Ministry* edited by James Beck and Stanley Gundry.
- *Women in the Church: Scriptural Principals and Ecclesial Practice*, A Report of the Commission on Theology and Church Relations of The Lutheran Church – Missouri Synod.

At this point I would now like us to consider the following **three things that we must be prepared to ignore** if we wish to affirm the practice of ordaining women into the pastoral office as well as homosexual behavior.

The **first** thing we must ignore if we wish to affirm women serving in the pastoral office as well as homosexual behavior is that **there is not a positive affirmation** of either in the Old or New Testament.

I have provided evidence in the previous chapters showing that there is not one bit of evidence in all of Scripture for the positive affirmation of homosexual behavior within a consensual, monogamous relationship. If God does affirm such behavior we would expect to find such affirmation in Scripture – especially from Jesus, Who never hesitated confronting the sinful practices of His day. In other words, since the Jews of Jesus' day clearly condemned even consensual, monogamous homosexual behavior, it is surprising that Jesus never rebuked their view if, indeed, He had actually affirmed such behavior.

Some of those who affirm the ordination of women into the pastoral office are willing to admit that a positive affirmation of this practice can not be found in Holy Scripture.

Of course, others point out the fact that in both the Old and New Testament we find examples of female leaders, female prophetesses, female teachers, females who were fellow workers and laborers with male apostles and pastors, female deacons, and, according to some, even a female apostle!

However, none of these examples (except for the possibility of a female being an apostle) are equal to what the New Testament describes as the pastoral office. Instead, all of these examples of women serving in various positions (except for the possibility of a female being an apostle) are of a type that any layperson – male or female – could perform.

Before I give evidence to support my assertion that women mentioned in Scripture who served in various leadership and ministry roles did so as laypersons, I will first deal with the assertion that there is evidence of a woman serving as an apostle.

So, what are we to make of the possibility that a female served as an apostle on the same level as the twelve or Paul? The only evidence for this is Romans 16:7 where Paul writes: "Greet Andronicus and Junias[301], my relatives who have been in prison with me. They are outstanding among the apostles, and they were in Christ before I was." *However, there are several problems associated with using Romans 16:7 to "prove" that a woman served as an apostle on the same level as the twelve or Paul.*

First, scholars are not agreed about the gender of the name "Junias" – there is evidence that it could be either masculine or feminine.[302] If "Junias" was a <u>man</u>, then this text has nothing to say about women in the pastoral office!

Second, even if we assume that "Junias" were a woman, scholars are not agreed about the meaning of the words "outstanding among the apostles" (Greek = *oitines eisin episeimoi en tois apostolois*). Some think these words mean that these two were some of most well known and respected apostles. But this seems very unlikely, as these two are never mentioned anywhere else as being on an equal plain with the twelve or Paul - much less *more* well known and respected than they were! However, other scholars believe these words mean that "Junias" was respected <u>**by**</u> the apostles. In other words, the twelve and Paul respected "Junias" for his or her work as a Christian layperson.

Third, even if "Junias" were a woman *and* an apostle, the word "apostle" does not always refer to those placed into the pastoral office by Jesus. The word "apostle" could also be used in a more general sense to mean simply "messenger" (see Philippians 2:25). These "messengers" were laypeople who supported the primary apostles and pastors in their ministry. In other words, even if "Junias" were a woman *and* an apostle – her being an "apostle" could simply mean that

---

[301] The Greek for "Junias" is *Iounian* , which is the accusative case of *Iounias* .

[302] See *Recovering Biblical Manhood & Womanhood* edited by John Piper and Wayne Grudem, 79-81.

she was a "messenger," that is, a layperson who helped those who served in the pastoral office.

Fourth, and I believe this the strongest argument against "Junias" being an apostle on the same level as the twelve or Paul, Romans 16:7 needs to be interpreted in light of the rest of Scripture! The context of Romans 16:7 says nothing about the pastoral office or who should serve in that office. The apostle Paul who wrote Romans 16:7 is the same apostle Paul who wrote 1st Corinthians 14:34 and 1st Timothy 2:11-3:7. The wider context of Paul's writings shows that Paul's words in Romans 16:7 very likely do NOT suggest that "Junias," if a woman, would have served in the pastoral office when Paul clearly prohibits this practice elsewhere!

I find it interesting that some who promote the ordination of women to the pastoral office will often accuse those who oppose this practice of quoting passages out of context to prove their point. As we will see below, 1st Corinthians 14:34 and 1st Timothy 2:11-3:7 (along with other supporting passages!) are NOT being taken out of context when used to discuss the issue of whether women should serve in the pastoral office. *In contrast, however, those whose affirm the practice of women serving in the pastoral office are certainly guilty of quoting Romans 16:7 out of context in order to prove their point – as the evidence I've given above clearly shows!*

Now I will discuss the evidence for suggesting that women in Scripture who served in various leadership or ministry roles were doing so as laypersons.

For example, Deborah was both a judge and a prophetess (Judges 4:4-5). However, we must note that all other judges of Israel were men. Why the exception with Deborah? The men of Israel at that time had forsaken their leadership roles. Deborah even had to rebuke Barak because he was not willing to go into battle without her (Judges 4:8). Also, some aspects of the role of judges in Israel were more in line with a "State" role rather than a "Church" role in the theocratic nation of Israel. The Bible has no problem with women serving as leaders in secular positions (such as the CEO of a business, the mayor of a city or even the president of the United States). However, the Bible clearly shows that no woman ever served as a priest in Old Testament Israel nor does the New Testament give us any evidence of a woman ever serving in the pastoral office.

As for women who served as prophetesses – such as Deborah, Huldah (2nd Kings 22:14-20), Anna (Luke 2:36-38) and Philip's daughters (Acts 21:9) – we must make at least two distinctions.

First, just as we must distinguish general "ministry" (any kind of "service") from the "Ministry" (the pastoral office) we must also distinguish between general "prophecy" (the proclamation of God's Word that any Christian can do) and "Prophecy" (the word of God as proclaimed by God's chosen prophets and apostles – all of them MEN!).[303]

Second, we must note that women prophetesses clearly exercised their gifts differently from the men who used this gift. For example, even though Anna proclaimed God's Word, she was not a priest nor did she ever proclaim God's Word in a public Service as a pastor. Even though Philip's daughters prophesied, they did not do so in a public Service as pastors!

Thomas Schreiner writes about this fact: "Isaiah, Jeremiah, Ezekiel, and other male prophets exercised a public ministry where they proclaimed the word of the Lord. But note that Deborah did not prophesy in public. Instead, her prophetic role seems to be limited to private and individual instruction. Judges 4:5 says, 'And she used to sit under the palm tree of Deborah between Ramah and Bethel in the hill country of Ephraim; and the sons of Israel came up to her for judgment.' ... The difference between Deborah's prophetic ministry and that of male Old Testament prophets is clear. She did not exercise her ministry in a public forum as they did ... Huldah ... did not publicly proclaim God's word. Rather, she explained in private the word of the Lord when Josiah sent messengers to her. She exercised her prophetic ministry in a way that did not obstruct male headship."[304]

We find the same situation with female teachers in the New Testament. Those who affirm women serving in the pastoral office will often point to Priscilla, who, with her husband, Aquila, taught a man by the name of Apollos (see Acts 18:24-26). However, Priscilla was not teaching in the public Divine Service as an ordained pastor! She was simply teaching the word of God in private as any layperson can do.

---

[303]See *The Gift of Prophecy in the New Testament and Today* by Wayne Grudem (Crossway, 1988).

[304] See *The Valuable Ministries of Women in the Context of Male Leadership* by Thomas Schreiner in *Recovering Biblical Manhood & Womanhood*, 216.

One must also note the obvious fact that Jesus Himself chose only men for His twelve apostles – and then later Paul (Acts 9:1-19), James (the half brother of our Lord - 1st Corinthians 15:7 and Galatians 2:9) and Matthias (Acts 1:23-26), all of whom were men. This is significant, since Jesus did not do this for sexist reasons. First, Jesus is sinless – and so such sinful sexist views have no place in His life. Second, in contrast with the culture of His day, Jesus exalted women and many women supported His ministry.

Some attempt to argue that Jesus chose only men to be His apostles because He knew that female apostles would not have been accepted in His day. But this is a very weak argument! Jesus did not care if He offended the culture of His day. Jesus spoke the truth, regardless of the consequences. If Jesus had believed that it would have been proper for a woman to be an apostle, then He would certainly have chosen some of the women with whom He worked closely for such an office. Jesus never hesitated challenging the views of His culture on any other issues with which He disagreed. It's hard to imagine, if Jesus had been in favor of a woman serving as an apostle, that He would have not done so simply to avoid giving offense.

Thomas Schreiner comments on this point: "Not one single example of a female apostle can be given in the New Testament. G. Bilezikian says that Jesus chose twelve men to be His apostles because of the 'cultural constraints' that would have made the ministry of women 'unacceptable.' There are at least two problems with this view. (1) Nowhere else does Jesus give in to cultural pressures when a moral issue is at stake. To imply that He gave in for this reason impugns His courage and integrity. Jesus associated with tax-collectors and sinners, healed on the Sabbath, commended Gentiles who had great faith, and rebuked the scribes and Pharisees. All of these actions brought considerable cultural pressure on Jesus, and yet He continued to do what He thought was right. Thus, it is unlikely that Jesus did not appoint a female apostle because of merely cultural reasons. (2) If, as Bilezikian asserts, Junias was an apostle, then Jesus' reluctance to appoint a woman apostle becomes even more blameworthy. For just a few years after Jesus' resurrection, the church (according to Bilezikian) is willing to appoint female apostles.[305] Had the culture changed so

---

[305] The only "evidence" Bilezikian has for the notion that the apostolic church appointed female apostles is the reference to Junias in Romans 16:7. However, as I have already argued in this chapter, the evidence for Junias being an apostle on the same level as the twelve or Paul is non-existent.

dramatically in the few years since Jesus' ministry that now such appointments were feasible? Bilezikian's view suggests that the early church was even more courageous than Jesus, and this is surely incorrect."[306]

Finally, in 1st Timothy 3:1-7 and Titus 1:5-9 the apostle Paul lists the requirements for those who are willing to serve in the pastoral office – and we must note that Paul mentions only MEN in these lists! If Paul in Romans 16:7 was actually implying that Junias was a female apostle on the same level as himself and the twelve, then it seems very odd that this same Paul would not have mentioned women in his pastoral qualifications lists in 1st Timothy and Titus.

There are many other examples I could give to show that women who served as leaders, prophets and teachers in the Church did so in a private manner as laypersons. There is simply no evidence in either the Old or New Testament for a positive affirmation of women serving in the pastoral office. For a thorough treatment of this issue, see the article *The Valuable Ministries of Women in the Context of Male Leadership: A Survey of Old and New Testament Examples and Teaching* by Thomas Schreiner.[307]

Those who wish to affirm women serving in the pastoral office must ignore the fact that Scripture does NOT give a positive affirmation of this practice. In the same way, those who wish to affirm homosexual behavior within a consensual, monogamous relationship must ignore the fact that Scripture does NOT give a positive affirmation of this practice. *Therefore, it is not surprising that many church bodies who affirm the practice of women serving in the pastoral office are also now open to homosexual behavior and the ordination of practicing homosexuals into the pastoral office.*

Now, the **second** thing we must ignore if we wish to affirm women serving in the pastoral office as well as homosexual behavior is that **there are clear prohibitions against both practices** in the New Testament.

In chapters two and three of this book I examined the clear prohibitions against homosexual behavior in both the Old and New

---

[306] See *The Valuable Ministries of Women in the Context of Male Leadership* by Thomas Schreiner in *Recovering Biblical Manhood & Womanhood*, 221-222.

[307] This article appears in *Recovering Biblical Manhood & Womanhood*, 209-224.

Testaments. I responded to many revisionist arguments that either 1) attempt to reinterpret the prohibitive passages in such as way as to suggest that they do not condemn consensual, monogamous homosexual relationships or 2) admit that the prohibitive passages do condemn even consensual, monogamous relationships but then offer reasons why we need not take such texts as being authoritative for us today. In my responses to these revisionist arguments I offered solid evidence showing why they are not to be taken seriously.

As with those who affirm homosexual behavior, those who affirm the ordination of women into the pastoral office either 1) reinterpret the prohibitive passages in such a way as to suggest that they do not condemn the modern practice of women's ordination or 2) they admit that these prohibitive passages do condemn women's ordination but they offer reasons why we need not take such texts as being authoritative for us today.

I will now briefly examine the two prohibitive New Testament texts that we have against women serving in the pastoral office – these two texts are 1st Corinthians 14:33b-35[308] and 1st Timothy 2:11-15. After I briefly examine these two texts I will deal other texts of Scripture that help us understand the purpose behind these prohibitions.

1st Corinthians 14:33b-35 reads: "As in all the congregations of the saints, women should remain silent in the churches. They are not allowed to speak, but must be in submission, as the Law says. If they want to inquire about something, they should ask their husbands at home; for it is disgraceful for a woman to speak in church."

---

[308] Some who are in favor of women serving in the pastoral office will point out that a few ancient manuscripts do not contain 1st Corinthians 14:34-35 or that it appears at a different place in the text. However, the manuscript evidence is very strong in support of 1st Corinthians 14:34-35 being part of Paul's original letter as it appears in the received text. In fact, there is evidence that the few variant texts are likely the result of followers of Marcion – an early church false teacher who, among other things, promoted the ordination of women to the pastoral office in opposition to the apostolic tradition that only men should serve in the pastoral office. Such followers of Marcion may have omitted 1st Corinthians 14:34-35 from the copies they made of Paul's letters in order to support their affirmation of women serving in the pastoral office. Such an act would not be surprising since Marcion himself edited out other portions of the New Testament that did not support his heretical views. For a thorough treatment of the manuscript evidence for 1st Corinthians 14:34-35, see *"As in All the Churches of the Saints": A Text-Critical Study of 1 Corinthians 14:34, 35* by David Bryce found in *Women Pastors?* edited by Matthew Harrison and John Pless, 57-68.

A thorough examination of this text is beyond the scope of this book. Therefore, I encourage you to read pp. 503-544 of the Concordia Commentary *1 Corinthians* by Gregory Lockwood, *1 Corinthians 14:33b-38, 1 Timothy 2:11-14, and the Ordination of Women* by Peter Kriewaldt and Geelong North[309], and *"Silent in the Churches": On the Role of Women in 1 Corinthians 14:33b-36* by D. A. Carson.[310]

Now, as with any individual passage of Holy Scripture, we need to interpret it within its context - the immediate context (the surrounding chapters and even the entire letter of 1st Corinthians) and the wider context (the other letters of Paul and the rest of Holy Scripture).

In 1st Corinthians 14:33-34 Paul says that women should be "silent" as the Law says. By "the Law" Paul is speaking of the order of creation as reflected in Genesis chapters 1 & 2 - also see Ephesians 5:22-33. In other words, based on Paul's view of marriage in Ephesians 5:22-33, he is stressing that Scripture's teaching that only men should serve in the pastoral office is based on God's very good distinction between male and female in the pre-Fall creation.

Now, what does Paul mean when he says that women should be "silent" in the churches? Obviously, Paul does not mean that women can not say anything at all because in 1st Corinthians chapter 11 he says women can pray and prophesy. Nor does Paul mean that women can not vote at a congregational voters meeting![311]

Instead, Paul says that women are not allowed to "speak." The Greek word for "speak" is *lalein* which is often used for the authoritative preaching done by the apostles and pastors. This explains why Paul says that women should not "inquire" about something in the assembly. Some scholars believe that in Paul's day the pastor would

---

[309] Found in *Women Pastors?* edited by Matthew Harrison and John Pless, 45-56.

[310] Found in *Recovering Biblical Manhood & Womanhood* edited by John Piper and Wayne Grudem, 140-153.

[311] The modern phenomenon of the congregational voters assembly should not be imposed upon 1st Corinthians 14:34-35, which puts limits on what women can do during the Divine Service. In addition, the issues at a voters assembly usually deal with matters that have nothing to do with theology. But even if a voters assembly does deal with theological issues, then women should vote in order to voice their agreement or disagreement with such issues. This enables them to voice their confession, which they should do. Casting a vote to voice one's <u>opinion</u> <u>about</u> a doctrinal position is not the same as <u>establishing</u> a doctrinal position because establishing a doctrinal position is not accomplished by majority vote but by the study of Holy Scripture, which is our only authority for establishing doctrine.

often ask questions as a teaching device. The Greek word for "to inquire" in 1st Corinthians 14:35 is *eperotatosan* – a Greek word which can be used to refer to a teacher who asks questions for the purpose of instruction in a public setting.

For example, after asking a rhetorical question the pastor himself would then give the answers from God's Word! We see Jesus doing this very thing when He was teaching in the Jerusalem temple at age twelve (see Luke 2:46-47). In fact, in Luke 2:46 we find the same Greek word for "to inquire" or "to question" (*eperotanta*) that is found in 1st Corinthians 14:35.

So, when Paul says "women should ask their own husbands at home" he is NOT saying that it is wrong for women to ask the pastor questions about the teaching of Scripture. Instead, Paul is likely saying the following with a bit of sarcasm: *"If you women are going to rebel against God's order of creation by speaking as though you're a pastor, then please act that way with your husband at home and do not display such behavior in the public Service!"* In fact, in 1st Corinthians 11:22 & 34 we see a similar rebuke from Paul (with a bit a sarcasm) regarding the sinful behavior of both men and women during the Lord's Supper!

Some who affirm women serving in the pastoral office will suggest that in 1st Corinthians 14:34 Paul is merely asking women to stop having disruptive conversations during the Service. However, there are two problems with this view. First, the Greek word *lalein* is not normally used in the New Testament to refer to disruptive conversations but refers to the authoritative preaching done by apostles and pastors. Second, the context of 1st Corinthians 14:34 does not support the notion that *lalein* should be translated as "disruptive conversations." Why? There are two reasons.

First, 1st Corinthians 14:29 suggests that the "others" who judge the prophecies (which can be spoken by men or women) are the pastors whose job it is to refute error and teach the truth of Scripture.[312]

---

[312] Regarding the interpretation of 1st Corinthians 14:29, D. A. Carson writes: "Paul's point here … is that [women] may *not* participate in the oral weighing of such prophecies. That is not permitted in any of the churches. In that connection, they are not allowed to speak – 'as the law says.' … More broadly, a strong case can be made for the view that Paul refused to permit any woman to enjoy a church-recognized teaching authority over men (1 Timothy 2:12ff.), and the careful weighing of prophecies falls under that magisterial function … this interpretation makes sense not only of the flow but also of the structure of the passage … In verse 29, Paul turns to prophecy and writes, 'Two or three prophets should speak, and the others should weigh

Second, if Paul is merely forbidding disruptive conversation, why does he not also forbid the men to engage in this? Are we to think that only the women were guilty of disruptive conversation and not the men? The argument that Paul is merely forbidding women from engaging in disruptive conversation (and not authoritative preaching as a pastor) does not fit the context.

Finally, when Paul says "As in all the congregations of the saints" he is reminding the Corinthians (and us!) that his prohibition against women serving in the pastoral office is not a concession to their culture. *In fact, the Corinthian culture was accustomed to female priestesses serving in pagan idol temples!* Instead, Paul wants the Corinthian Christians (and us!) to remember that all Christian congregations – in whatever culture they may exist – must submit to Scripture's teaching that only men are to serve in the pastoral office.

At this point one must ask the following question: "Why would Paul need to give this prohibition against women serving as pastors?" The answer seems to be that some of the women in that congregation, possibly under the influence of pagan feminism in their city as well as the example of female priestesses in the city's idol temples, were attempting to mimic their culture by performing functions of the pastoral office – even though God's Word clearly forbids this!

Next we will consider 1st Timothy 2:11-15, which reads: "A woman should learn in quietness and full submission. I do not permit a woman to teach or to have authority over a man; she must be silent. For Adam was formed first, then Eve. And Adam was not the one deceived; it was the woman who was deceived and became a sinner. But women will be saved through childbearing – if they continue in faith, love and holiness with propriety."

As with 1st Corinthians 14:33b-35, a thorough examination of 1st Timothy 2:11-15 is beyond the scope of this book. Therefore, I encourage you to read *Women in the Church: A Fresh Analysis of 1 Timothy 2:9-15* edited by Andreas Kostenberger, Thomas Schreiner and H. Scott Baldwin, *1 Corinthians 14:33b-38, 1 Timothy 2:11-14,*

---

carefully what is said.' The two parts of this verse are then separately expanded upon: the first part ('Two or three prophets should speak') is treated in verses 30-33a, where constraints are imposed on the *uttering* of prophesies; the second part ('and the others should weigh what is said') is treated in verses 33b-36, where constraints are imposed on the *evaluation* of prophecies." See *"Silent in the Churches": On the Role of Women in 1 Corinthians 14:33b-36* by D. A. Carson in *Recovering Biblical Manhood & Womanhood* edited by John Piper and Wayne Grudem, 151-152.

and the Ordination of Women by Peter Kriewaldt and Geelong North,[313] *Ordained Proclaimers or Quiet Learners?* By Charles Gieschen,[314] and *What Does It Mean Not to Teach or Have Authority Over Man?: 1 Timothy 2:11-15* by Douglas Moo.[315]

The setting of 1st Timothy 2:11-15 is the public Service where Christians would gather to receive Christ's gifts. During the public Service pastors would preach, administer the Lord's Supper, and perform baptisms.

In 1st Timothy 2:11 Paul says that women should learn in quietness and full submission. By the word "quietness" Paul does not mean that women can not utter a sound during the Service. They can sing, pray and even prophesy (see 1st Corinthians 11:5). Instead, by the word "quietness" Paul means that women should be willing to learn in humble submission to the pastor who has been called to preach God's Word in Christ's stead. Women should NOT attempt to usurp the pastor's authority by teaching in public as though they were pastors themselves.

The above interpretation of 1st Timothy 2:11 is confirmed by Paul's next words in 1st Timothy 2:12 where Paul writes: "I do not permit a woman to teach or to have authority over a man; she must be silent." Once again, by the word "silent" Paul does not mean absolute silence but that women should not attempt to teach in the public Service as though they were pastors.

In the same way, when Paul says "I do not permit a woman to teach" he does not mean that women can not perform any kind of teaching[316] but that they should not strive to teach within the pastoral office.

---

[313] Found in *Women Pastors?* edited by Matthew Harrison and John Plessj, 45-56.

[314] Found in *Women Pastors?* edited by Matthew Harrison and John Pless, 69-90.

[315] Found in *Recovering Biblical Manhood & Womanhood* edited by John Piper and Wayne Grudem, 179-193.

[316] As I noted earlier in this chapter, women in both the Old and New Testament were allowed to teach other women and even men in the manner that any layperson can teach another. We see an example of this in Acts chapter 19 where Priscilla teaches Apollos in private.

When Paul says that women should not "have authority over a man" he does not mean that women can not have any authority over a man in any situation. The Bible does not prohibit women from serving in positions of authority over men in the secular realm (such as being a CEO of a business or even being the president of the United States). Instead, the context of 1st Timothy 2:11-15 is the public Christian Service where God's principle of male spiritual headship must be obeyed. In other words, a woman should not have authority over a man by teaching him as a pastor.

In 1st Timothy 2:13-14 Paul alludes to the creation account in Genesis to make his point. First Paul says: "For Adam was formed first, then Eve." This is a reference to Genesis chapter 2 where we not only learn that Adam was formed first chronologically (which is <u>not</u> really Paul's main point) but also that Adam was formed "first" (the Greek word is *protos*) in the sense that he was to be Eve's "spiritual head" – serving her by leading her in the ways of God's Word.

We find a similar use of the concept of "first" referring to "spiritual headship" in Colossians 1:15 where Paul writes: "[The Son] is the image of the invisible God, the firstborn over all creation." When Paul says that Christ, the Son of the Father, is the "firstborn" (the Greek word is *prototokos*) he does not mean that the Son was born first chronologically (because the Son exists from all eternity with the Father!) but that the Son is the "head" over all creation.

Therefore, when Paul says "Adam was formed first, then Eve" he means that Adam was created first as the "spiritual head" and then Eve was given to him to love as Christ loves His Bride, the Church!

Next, in 1st Timothy 2:14, Paul says: "And Adam was not the one deceived; it was the woman who was deceived and became a sinner." Paul does NOT mean that Adam was not deceived at all NOR does Paul mean that Adam did not sin! Paul's point is that the devil usurped God's order of creation by confronting Eve instead of Adam. In other words, even though Adam was present when the devil was deceiving Eve (see Genesis 3:6), Adam did nothing to protect Eve from the devil's lies. Instead, Adam forfeited his role as Eve's "spiritual head" and the consequences were tragic for ALL of us (see Romans 5:12-14 and 1st Corinthians 15:21-22).

In view of my above point about 1st Timothy 2:14, Kriewaldt and North write the following: "Paul's second appeal to Scripture concerns the fall. Paul does not assert that women alone are responsible for the fall or that they are more susceptible to deception by Satan than men.

But the woman ceased to be a disciple and became insubordinate by assuming authority in making the wrong decision and then pressing her decision onto the man. The man, who was meant to be leader and head, fell down on the job with eyes wide open. He deliberately and knowingly chose to listen to the woman and thereby sinned by following her teaching. If women at the church in Ephesus proclaim their independence from the male leaders, refusing to learn 'in quietness and full submission,' seeking roles that have been given to men in the church, they will make the same mistake Eve made. So today, Christian worship is to reflect the order established by God in creation, not followed in Eden, in which males have the responsibility for teaching God's Word."[317]

However, what are we to make of 1st Timothy 2:15 where Paul writes: "But women will be saved through childbearing – if they continue in faith, love and holiness with propriety." As Luther loved to ask in his Small Catechism: "What does this mean?"

First of all, I want to point out that the NIV translation of 1st Timothy 2:15 (above) is not the best. The original Greek is: *sotheisetai de dia teis teknogonias, eav meinosin en pistei kai agapei kai agiasmo meta sophrosuneis* . A more accurate translation would be: "She will be saved through the childbearing, if they continue in faith, love and holiness with propriety."

The Greek word *sotheisetai* is singular (which the NIV translation ignores), which is why I translate it as "She will be saved." In addition, the Greek word *teknogonias* is preceded by the definite article *teis* (which the NIV translation leaves out), which is why I translate those words as "the childbearing."

Now that we have a more accurate translation of 1st Timothy 2:15, the question still remains: "What does this mean?"

One interpretation suggests that Paul is teaching that the Greek word *sotheisetai* should be understood as "kept safe" or "preserved" – meaning that women will not suffer physical harm during childbirth if they continue in "faith, love and holiness with propriety." But there are huge problems with this interpretation.

First, the Greek word *sotheisetai* in normally used by Paul to refer to the salvation – the forgiveness and eternal life with God – that we

---

[317] See *1 Corinthians 14:33b-38, 1 Timothy 2:11-14, and the Ordination of Women* by Peter Kriewaldt and Geelong North in *Women Pastors?* edited by Matthew Harrison and John Pless, 54.

receive through faith in Christ. The immediate context strongly suggests that *sotheisetai* should be understood in this way because Paul uses the Greek word *sotheinai* (a different form of the Greek verb *sotheisetai*) in 1st Timothy 2:4 to stress that God wants all people to be saved through Christ! Second, the idea that women will be "kept safe" during childbirth does not fit the subject matter of the context. Finally, it is simply false that faithful Christian women will always be "kept safe" during childbirth because many faithful Christian women have died while giving birth.

Another interpretation suggests that Christian women should "give evidence of their salvation" that they have through faith in Christ by refusing to serve as pastors and, instead, fulfilling one of the roles that God has given to women – bearing children! But this view, although much better than the previous interpretation above, also has problems.

First, Paul does not say that women should "give evidence of their salvation" but that "they will be saved." Second, even though giving birth to children is one of the roles God has given to women, it does not seem to fit with the subject matter of the immediate context.

One last interpretation, the one I prefer, is that Paul is teaching that women who have sinned against God, like Eve, by rebelling against God's order of creation by trying to teach as pastors can receive salvation as a result of "the childbearing" – the birth of Christ!

This fits with the immediate context because Paul refers to Genesis chapter 3 in 1st Timothy 2:14. Even though Eve was guilty of sinning against God, she could be saved by trusting in the child who would be born of "the woman" and crush the "serpent" (the devil) – see Genesis 3:15 and Galatians 4:4.

In the same way, just as Eve has salvation in Christ, ALL women who have sinned against God by striving to be pastors and thereby rebelling against His order of creation can also be saved through "the childbearing" – if they continue in faith, love and holiness with propriety. In other words, if such women continue to live in repentance and faith in Christ and do not cling to their sin and deny Christ, they will be saved!

Some are uncomfortable with the interpretation of 1st Timothy 2:15 that I have offered. Their reason is that they think Paul would have used more explicit and direct language if he had intended "the childbearing" to refer to Christ and the salvation He gives. But what does it mean for Paul to use "explicit and direct" language?

Many who are uncomfortable with my interpretation of 1st Timothy 2:15 have no problem thinking that Paul is speaking of the Virgin Mary in Galatians 4:4 even though Paul never mentions her!

In addition, many who are uncomfortable with my interpretation of 1st Timothy 2:15 would have no problem confessing that Genesis 3:15 alludes to the Virgin Mary and the birth of Christ – even though Moses does not speak of either with explicit or direct language in Genesis 3:15!

There are many other examples of statements from Paul that are obscure if read in isolation but become clear when interpreted in light of the rest of Holy Scripture. When 1st Timothy 2:15 is interpreted in light of 1st Timothy 2:13-14 as well as Genesis 3:15 it is not hard to see how Paul is proclaiming the Gospel to women by pointing them to "the childbearing."

Now that I have briefly examined 1st Corinthians 14:33b-35 and 1st Timothy 2:11-15, I will attempt to use other Scriptures to show the purpose behind these prohibitions.

In 1st Corinthians 11:1-16 Paul discusses male headship in the context of the public Service. The women must wear clothing – specifically, "head coverings" – that reflect their willingness to submit to their husbands' headship. *However, we must note that Paul discusses male headship as flowing from God's very being!* Paul writes: "Now I want you to realize that the head of every man is Christ, and the head of woman is man, and the head of Christ is God." What do we learn from this?

First, male headship is not the product of Paul's male chauvinist, patriarchal culture. Instead, Paul clearly teaches that even though the Father and the Son are equals there is an order of "authority" within the Trinity. Paul says that the Father is the "head" of Christ. In other words, the Father loves and serves the Son, and the Son willingly and joyfully submits to the headship of the Father. In the same way, the husband is the "head" of his wife (see Ephesians 5:22-33).

Second, when Paul tells the men NOT to wear something on their heads during the Service and then tells the women that they MUST wear something on their heads during the Service, Paul is simply telling them that they must act like men and women by wearing the clothing that pertained to men and women in that culture.

For example, in most Christian churches it would be shameful for a man to attend a Service dressed as a woman. In the same way, it would be shameful for a woman to attend a Service dressed as a man. But why would the women in Corinth attend Services with hair styles common to men? As we learned in our study if 1st Corinthians 14:33b-35, there were some women who were attempting to serve as pastors. One way they may have flaunted their authority to do this could have been by appearing at Services with hair styles common to a man. Therefore, in 1st Corinthians 11:1-16 Paul stresses that both men and women should submit to God's order of creation and not rebel against it in any way – including appearing in public as the opposite sex!

Now, some point out that we no longer require women to wear hats in church Services today. They then infer from this that we are also free to ignore what Paul says about women not serving in the pastoral office. However, this argument fails to distinguish between cultural expressions of what is means to be male and female (which can vary in different times and places) and the universal principle that we should respect God's order of creation.

In other words, even though our culture today does not view head coverings as a common expression of female attire. Nevertheless, our culture still does expect men to dress a certain way and women to dress a certain way. For example, men do not wear skirts in our culture – unless they are doing so as a joke! But if men dress in skirts as a way of denying their male gender, this is not acceptable – at least not to Christians to who take Scripture seriously. In the same way, even though women in our culture commonly wear slacks or pants as well as skirts – the slacks or pants they wear are not intended to deny their female gender! In fact, women usually buy their slacks and pants in the WOMEN'S section of stores!

Therefore, we still submit to Paul's teaching in 1st Corinthians 11:1-16 by wearing clothing that affirms our male or female genders as expressed in our particular culture. This practice allows us to remember that God created us as male and female, and so we should be willing to submit to God's order of creation as reflected in the husband's spiritual headship over his wife.

Regarding Paul's teaching in 1st Corinthians 11:1-16, Gregory Lockwood writes: "From the outset it should be noted that Paul does not wish to set in concrete a rule *about specific practices* for all places and all times regarding head-coverings. (When he does state a universal and permanent rule for practice, he often refers to a direct command from God, as in 14:37, or to the teaching or practice 'in every church' or 'in all the churches,' as in 4:17; 7:17; 14:33.) Rather, he is establishing the *universal and permanent principle* that men and women at worship should conduct themselves modestly and sensibly (1 Tim 2:9; cf. 1 Pet 3:1-6), in keeping with whatever happen to be the *customs* of the time. In a similar way, Jesus laid down the permanent principle ('a new commandment') that his disciples should love one another (Jn 13:34) and, in keeping with the custom of his day, exemplified that principle by washing the disciples' feet (Jn 13:3-17), but Jesus did not command the specific *practice* of foot-washing for all Christians of all times. The universal and binding principle of love finds expression today in different ways of showing consideration and courtesy to one another."[318]

In 1st Corinthians 11:8-9 and 11-12 Paul stresses that even though men and women have been created with different roles they are still completely equal before God. In other words, male headship reflected in marriage and in the pastoral office (the pastor representing Christ Who serves His Bride) is not a product of Paul's male chauvinist culture. Instead, male headship as reflected in marriage and the pastoral office is rooted in God's very good distinction between male and female in the pre-Fall creation as recorded in Genesis chapters 1 and 2. In fact, this headship principle flows from God's very being!

In Ephesians 5:22-33 Paul quotes from Genesis chapter 2 (pre-Fall!) as the foundation for his teaching that the husband is the head of his wife. The husband's role as head of his wife reflects the ultimate marriage that exists between Christ and His Bride, the Church!

Just as the wife can never be the spiritual head of her husband, a woman can never represent Christ in the pastoral office as the spiritual head of His Bride, the Church. Contrary to what some teach in our culture, the roles of the husband and wife are NOT interchangeable! A wife can NEVER be the spiritual head of her husband. In the same way, a woman can NEVER represent Christ's headship over His Bride in the pastoral office!

In his article *"It Is Not Given to Women to Teach"* William Weinrich does an excellent job showing how Paul's prohibitions against women serving in the pastoral office (1st Corinthians 14:33b-35 and 1st Timothy 2:11-15) are based on Christ's relationship to the Father and Christ's relationship with His Bride, the Church. Weinrich writes: "...those figures, both in the Old Testament and in the New Testament, who serve as fundamental representatives or types of the redemptive purposes of God in Christ are male figures ... It is not that

---

[318] See the Concordia Commentary *1 Corinthians* by Gregory Lockwood, 362.

Christ was a male human person because in the 'order of creation' God had given headship and authority to the man, Adam. Rather, God who created humankind in order that He might have communion with it in and through His Word gave the headship of humanity to the man, Adam, *in view of* the eschatological goal of humanity, which is Christ and His church. Because in the final purpose and *telos* of God for the world the man Jesus Christ was to be the head of His Body, the church (which relates to Christ as bride to bridegroom), God in the beginning gave Adam to be the head of Eve. As Paul says, 'the head of woman is the man' (1 Cor 11:3), and 'Adam was created first [or perhaps 'as the first'], then Eve' (1 Tim 2:13) ... in Ephesians 5 Paul's point is not that Christ's love for His Bride, the church, is patterned after what was to be the case between Adam and Eve in the garden. Rather, it is in view of Christ's love for His Bride, the church, that husbands are to love their wives and that wives are to be subject to their husbands as to their head. The true marriage was not that marriage in the garden. The true marriage is that between Christ and the church. All other marriages (including that first one in the garden) – and this is true the more marriages are blessed by love – are faint images and icons of that marriage of the Lamb with His Bride, the church."[319]

Finally, many who affirm women serving in the pastoral office attempt to ignore Paul's prohibitions by using Paul's own words in Galatians 3:28, which read: "There is neither Jew nor Greek, slave nor free, male nor female, for you are all one in Christ Jesus."

The context of this passage clearly shows that Paul is teaching that salvation in Christ is an undeserved, free gift and is not merited because of one's work or person. In other words, one is not "more worthy" of salvation because one is a Jew or a free person or a male. We are all equally condemned sinners before God under the Law (see Galatians 3:10). We are all equally forgiven saints before God in Christ (see Galatians 2:20-21 & 3:13-14).

Certainly, the Gospel sets us free from various <u>sinful</u> human distinctions, such as racism or sexism, that are based on salvation by one's person or work. Such things as slavery or the distinction between Jew and Gentile are also aspects of this fallen world.

In contrast, God's very good distinction between male and female was intrinsic to God's pre-Fall creation! Simply put, the free gift of

---

[319] See *"It Is Not Given to Women to Teach"* by William Weinrich in *Women Pastors?* edited by Matthew Harrison and John Pless, 370 & 376.

salvation we have in Christ does not remove the very good distinctions that exist between male and female as part of God's pre-Fall created order. In fact, the Gospel restores the very good distinctions between male and female that God created "In the beginning." Paul makes this very point in Ephesians 5:22-33 where he quotes from Genesis 2:24, which reads: "For this reason a man will leave his father and mother and be united to his wife, and they will become one flesh."

Therefore, Galatians 3:28 can not be used to eliminate God's very good distinction between male and female – whether the goal is to affirm the ordination of women to the pastoral office (a practice clearly prohibited in the New Testament) or to affirm homosexual behavior or even homosexual marriage (practices clearly prohibited in both the Old and New Testaments).

Finally, the **third** thing we must ignore if we wish to affirm women serving in the pastoral office as well as homosexual behavior is that **the witness of the Church catholic is opposed to both practices.**

I do not need to devote much space to this third point. Virtually everyone familiar with the historical evidence is willing to admit that the witness of the Church catholic is opposed to even consensual, monogamous homosexual behavior.[320] In the same way, virtually everyone familiar with the evidence is willing to admit that the witness of the Church catholic is opposed to the ordination of women into the pastoral office.[321]

Not until recently (the last 100 years) have a minority of Christians around the world ignored the witness of Scripture and of the Church catholic by ordaining women into the pastoral office. I find it odd that some in the ELCA will point to the witness of the Church catholic in support of their opposition to homosexual behavior and yet ignore the same witness of the Church catholic when it comes to the practice of women serving in the pastoral office.

My hope and prayer is that those in the ELCA or in newly formed Lutheran bodies (for example, the LCMC) who are giving a faithful witness from Scripture regarding homosexual behavior would be willing to reconsider their practice of ordaining women into the

[320] For example, see *Homosexuality & Civilization* by pro-gay scholar Louis Crompton. Also *Love Between Women* by the lesbian New Testament scholar Bernadette Brooten, 303-358.

[321] For example, see *Women in the History of the Church* by William Weinrich in *Women Pastors?* edited by Matthew Harrison and John Pless.

pastoral office by engaging in a careful study of Holy Scripture on this issue with other Lutherans who are convinced by Holy Scripture and the witness of the Church catholic that the ordination of women into the pastoral office is opposed to God's loving will for His Church.

╬ *APPENDIX III* ╬

Creation versus Evolution:
"Whose Word Do We Trust?"

Why am I offering this appendix about the Creation versus Evolution debate? If you have read the chapters of this book you will know that the biblical teaching about marriage, sexuality and the issue of homosexual behavior is based on the historicity of the creation account in Genesis. In fact, other basic doctrines of the Christian Faith (for example, original sin, the origin of death and suffering, the purpose of Christ's atoning work on the cross) are based on the historicity of the creation account in Genesis.

Sadly, those who attempt to speak God's truth in love regarding Scripture's teaching about the historicity of the creation account in Genesis are often mocked and rebuked as biblical illiterates. However, I will show in this appendix that those who suggest that Darwinian macro-evolution is compatible with the Hebrew text of Genesis (and the rest of Scripture, for that matter) are the ones who do not understand the Bible. In addition, I will show why it is so important for us to take Holy Scripture seriously regarding what it says about the historicity of the creation account in Genesis and how it applies to all the other doctrines of the Christian Faith.

However, I will not cover much of the variety of scientific evidence for Creation versus Evolution in this appendix. The reason is that we all observe the same data, but we interpret that data through our various presuppositions about reality. The Creation versus Evolution debate covers many areas of science. *Therefore, I encourage you to read the books on the suggested reading list provided at the end of this appendix. These books will give you arguments from very intelligent scientists who offer new interpretations of the same data observed by those who hold to Darwinian Evolution.*

Simply put, many scientists today assume that there must be a naturalistic cause for all of life. But when considering the question of *how* life could have come from inorganic matter, even scientists who hold to purely naturalistic Darwinian macro-evolution (e.g., Richard Dawkins) will admit that we simply do not know how this took place.

Nevertheless, most scientists assume that once biological life came into existence it began to evolve from the simple to the complex – often defined simply as "descent from a common ancestor" or "macro-evolution." Even though we obviously have not been able to observe the process of macro-evolution, most scientists believe that macro-evolution best explains various phenomena - such as the fossil record, comparative anatomy, and recent research in DNA and the genomes of various animals.

As for the ***mechanism*** behind macro-evolution (HOW macro-evolution took place), most modern scientists assume that micro-evolution (small biological changes that we observe within modern life forms) best explains how this could have happened.

Micro-evolution is usually defined as natural selection working on random biological mutations that are passed down to future generations. *In other words, macro-evolution (evolution from one-celled life forms into complex multi-celled life forms) is simply a description of micro-evolution (small changes within modern life forms) at work over vast periods of time (billions of years).*

However, not all scientists agree with the macro-evolutionary theory of how life developed on earth. Some believe that the micro-evolution we observe today simply cannot produce the massive amounts of genetic information necessary for macro-evolution to have occurred over billons or even trillions of years.

For example, micro-evolution can be observed in the present by watching bacteria develop immunities to antibiotics (either through a loss of genetic information or a reorganization of existing genetic information). But the changes that occur even over the course of millions of generations of bacteria result in only more bacteria. No other complex biological features have been added that would allow bacteria to become anything else than bacteria.

Micro-evolution explains how some bacteria can survive to live another day. **However, micro-evolution does not seem to be able to produce the information necessary for a bacterium to eventually evolve into a biologist!** *But most scientists today assert that micro-evolution can accomplish that very thing! However, more and more scientists see problems with the theory of macro-evolution.*

For example, in his book *The Edge of Evolution* Michael Behe shows the limits of micro-evolution and its failure to account for irreducibly complex biological systems. Michael Behe still assumes that descent from a common ancestor took place, but he believes that natural selection working on random mutations simply can not explain how this could have happened. **In other words, purely random, naturalistic processes alone can not account for the evolution of simple life into complex life.** Behe, along with many other scientists, believes the complexity of biological life is best explained by Intelligent Design.

In fact, some scientists who agree with Intelligent Design even question whether descent from a common ancestor (MACRO-evolution!) is the best explanation of the fossil record, comparative anatomy and the genome of biological life. They suggest that common design can also be an explanation of the data.

For example, the pentadactyl pattern found in most mammals is usually explained by descent from a common ancestor. But the pentadactyl pattern can also be explained by common design. Also, human endogenous retroviruses are usually explained by descent from a common ancestor. But there are some who argue that common design can also explain this phenomenon. Common design may not answer all questions or predict everything perfectly, but then descent from a common ancestor does not answer all questions and predict everything perfectly, either! *Simply put, one's presuppositions will determine how one chooses to explain the data.*

However, many scientists who hold fast to Darwinian macro-evolution will accuse Intelligent Design (ID) scientists of being **un**scientific when they suggest that a Designer is necessary to explain complex biological life. Even though many Darwinists admit that biological life has the appearance of being designed, they charge ID scientists of invoking a "God of the gaps" argument - that is, using God to explain something that science will eventually explain in terms of naturalistic processes.

For example, in the 1800's William Paley made himself famous with his watchmaker argument. Simply put, if you find a watch on the ground you will immediately assume that you have just found something that had to be made by an intelligent being. Nothing so complex as a watch could come together and function by sheer accident. *Therefore, Paley argued that the even more complex biological life of this world is best explained as being the result of a Creator.*

Richard Dawkins wrote a book titled *The Blind Watchmaker* in which he admitted that Paley had a point. Biological life does appear to be designed! But then Dawkins went on to argue that Paley simply did not have the information we now have about natural selection working on random mutations. Dawkins argued that micro-evolution is a "Blind Watchmaker" and so we do not need a Creator to explain complex biological life.

However, Dawkins' assertion that micro-evolution can account for such complexity is the very thing that is being challenged by more and more scientists today! In other words, Paley's argument still holds true even more today as we have come to understand the immense complexity of the cell and DNA.

But what of the accusation that ID scientists are invoking a "God of the gaps" argument? Is such an accusation really fair? For example, Carl Sagan is famous for helping to establish the SETI project. SETI scientists would listen for signals from space that had the appearance of being non-random. If such a non-random signal were ever heard, Sagan suggested this would be evidence of intelligent alien life!

Carl Sagan's SETI project influenced the 1997 movie *Contact* in which actress Jodie Foster hears a signal from space – and this signal was a series of prime numbers that repeated itself. This simple signal of prime numbers was seen as evidence of intelligent alien life!

Now, did anyone accuse Carl Sagan of being guilty of invoking an "aliens of the gaps" argument? No! Why not? The reason is that most scientists believe that inferring an alien intelligence as the source of such a signal is a logical scientific conclusion.

Let's consider another example. Let's say we finally put some people on Mars. When they get there they find structures similar to our pyramids on earth. They then immediately signal earth and announce that they have found evidence of an ancient intelligent civilization on Mars. Can you imagine NASA responding: **"Nonsense! You are lazy scientists! You are simply invoking an 'ancient intelligent civilization of the gaps' argument. No more of this nonsense. Keep hard at it until you find a naturalistic cause for your discovery!"** You know this would never happen.

Yet modern scientists who infer the possibility of a Designer to explain biological systems that are a million times more complex than any pyramid are told to recant and continue to look for purely naturalistic explanations for biological complexity.

Some scientists will also argue that all scientific progress would come to a halt if we suggest that biological life may have been designed. But there are scientists who have PhDs in biology and do groundbreaking research – *and yet they do NOT believe that micro-evolution can explain descent from a common ancestor!* (See the list of books at the end of this appendix)

In fact, some of these scientists do not even believe in descent from a common ancestor. They believe common design is a better way to interpret the data. But their belief in common design as an explanation for the origin of species does not stop them from doing empirical research nor does it keep them from learning more about the functions (and limits!) of micro-evolution!

In fact, one could argue that the true threat to scientific progress is the refusal to consider any paradigm other than the one currently held by the majority. Scientific progress takes place when one asks questions and thinks outside the box. Scientific progress is held back when one holds to dogmatic assertions and refuses to consider other possibilities.

How Do We *Know* What We *Know* ?

At this point I would like to confess that I believe in a young earth (around 10,000 years) and that the universe and all life were created by God in six normal days. How do I *know* this to be the case? **Not by empirical science!** Instead, I have another way of *knowing* about the origin of the universe and life. Simply put, I believe the Creation versus Evolution debate really comes down to the issue of *epistemology* – that is, how do we *know* what we *know*?

A young person once said to me: *"I trust empirical science to give me all the information I need to know about life."* I then asked him if he believed that George Washington was our first president. He said, *"Of course I do!"* I then asked, *"But how do you know that? You can't go back in time and see him for yourself. How do you know that he even existed?"* He thought for a moment, and said: *"There are many artifacts that still exist that once belonged to him."* I then said, *"But how do you know for sure there is a direct correspondence between those items in the present and the person of George Washington who lived in the past?"* After a few moments he said, *"I trust the historical documents written by those who knew people who knew people who knew people who knew George Washington and were alive when he was our first president."* I then said, *"So, you trust the word of eyewitnesses who were alive at that time." "Yes,"* he said. I then added, *"You then most certainly do NOT rely on empirical science alone for all that you know. You also trust the word of reliable authorities for information about the past, and you are wise for doing so."*

What point am I trying to make? If we rely on empirical science alone for our knowledge about the origin and development of life in the *past*, there are many things we will never know for sure about that issue. We can use empirical science to examine the fossil record, comparative anatomy and DNA in the PRESENT – but our interpretation of what that data means for the origin and development of life in the PAST must be based on certain presuppositions that we can not know about for certain by using empirical science alone. In fact, there are some things that empirical science can not answer at all!

Therefore, even though I am very intrigued by the research being done by various Intelligent Design scientists, they will never be able to say much about their suggested "Designer" because this "Designer" is beyond the reach of empirical science – *and science is nothing more than an observational tool dependant upon our own limited reason and senses.*

Now, that doesn't mean we have no grounds for suggesting that a Designer is the best explanation for complex biological life. The point is that we can't use science to say anything of much significance about this Designer.

For example, let's say you go to a museum and see a painting on the wall. You would be wise to assume that this painting exists because of a painter! People would think you were a bit odd if you thought that the painting assembled itself by random chance processes over time.

However, unlike many paintings, this painting was not signed by the painter. In fact, no one knows who painted it. No one knows anything about the painter who produced this work of art. The painting is evidence of a painter – **but without any other information you will have no way of knowing anything more about the painter other than that the painter produced the painting.**

But what if a man walks up to you and introduces himself, and then says: *"How do you like my painting? I painted it 25 years ago. Do you want to know why I produced this work of art?"* As your conversation continues you are given information about the painter that you could never have known otherwise.

In Romans chapter 1 the Apostle Paul writes: **"...what may be known about God is plain ... because God has made it plain ... For since the creation of the world God's invisible qualities – his eternal power and divine nature – have been clearly seen, being understood from what has been made, so that men are without excuse."** Paul is here teaching us that the complexity and wonder of creation should be enough to convince anyone that there must be a Creator. Therefore, if people deny the existence of a Creator, they are without excuse.

In Psalm 19 we read: **"The heavens declare the glory of God; the skies proclaim the work of his hands ... Their voice goes into all the earth, their words to the ends of the world."** In Psalm 139 we read these words about God: **"For you created my inmost being; you knit me together in my mother's womb ... your works are wonderful, I know that full well."** Therefore, is it any wonder that Psalm 14:1 reads: **"The fool says in his heart, 'There is no God.'"** *Simply put, in Romans chapter 1 Paul makes it clear that the complexity of creation declares to every person that there is a Creator.*

However, the witness of creation is limited. Creation does not tell us much about the Creator other than that the Creator created all things. Creation does not give us any personal details about the Creator. Creation does not tell us what the Creator thinks of us. Does the Creator love us? Does the Creator hate us? Does the Creator simply ignore us like we ignore the paramecium that lives in the swamp? Does the Creator have any plans for us? Creation simply can NOT give us this information.

In addition, observing creation itself does not tell me anything about HOW God created life in the first place – other than that God did it. Oh, I can examine creation and draw some conclusions – but I can only make an educated guess about generalities.

For example, by observing creation I could never come to the conclusion that God created all life in six days and that the first humans God created were two people, male and female, named Adam and Eve. Creation simply does not give me that information.

Finally, creation is not able to answer another curious question. Why did the Creator design a world filled with suffering, pain and death? Even though this present world is obvious evidence of a Creator, nevertheless, it seems as though God could have done a better job. The world appears to be broken!

For example, let's imagine you have a chance to see with your own eyes the ancient Greek statue known as the Venus De Milo. When you see this statue it will immediately be obvious that some artist fashioned it. Natural random processes could never produce such a work of art. Some great artist fashioned the Venus De Milo! That much is obvious!

However, if you then look at the Venus De Milo more closely you will notice that the arms are broken off. You will notice a scratch here and a chip there. You'll say: *"I wonder what happened to this work of art?"*

Let me take you back to William Paley for a moment. Paley was correct about his watchmaker argument. The creation certainly is evidence that there is a Creator. However, the one thing that Paley could not explain was why the Creator would make a world filled with suffering, pain and death.

When Charles Darwin was faced with the death of his daughter he eventually began to question the existence of God because he could not understand why the Creator would make a world filled with suffering, pain and death. Survival of the fittest seems to make more sense when suffering, pain and death are a natural part of a world where life arose by chance and where "might makes right."

However, there was some information that Darwin refused to consider. The Creator who made this world is not silent! The Creator has revealed Himself to us! The Creator has spoken to us!

In John chapter 1 we read: **"In the beginning was the Word, and the Word was with God, and the Word was God. He was with God in the beginning. Through him all things were made; without him nothing was made that has been made ... He was in the world, and though the world was made through him, the world did not recognize him ... The Word became flesh and made his dwelling among us."**

In 1st John chapter 1 we read: **"That which was from the beginning, which we have seen with our eyes, which we have looked at and our hands have touched – this we proclaim concerning the Word of life. The life appeared, we have seen it and testify to it, and we proclaim to you the eternal life, which was with the Father and has appeared to us."**

In Hebrews chapter 1 we read: **"In the past God spoke to our forefathers through the prophets at many times and in various ways, but in these last days he has spoken to us by his Son, whom**

appointed heir of all things and through whom he made the universe. The Son is the radiance of God's glory and the exact representation of his being, sustaining all things by his powerful word. After providing purification for sins, he sat down at the right hand of the Majesty in heaven."

The creation is obvious evidence that there is a Creator. But why did the Creator make a world filled with pain, suffering and death? The answer is: **"God did NOT make a world filled with pain, suffering and death!"** How do I *know* that? The Creator has told us Himself!

In Genesis chapters 1 & 2 we learn that God created the universe out of nothing! We can not come to that conclusion by observing the present creation. However, we know this to be true because God was there "In the beginning" and He has told us how it happened.

In Genesis chapter 1 we read: **"In the beginning God created the heavens and the earth … And God said, 'Let there be light,' and there was light."** If you read on in Genesis chapter 1 God explains how He gave form to this world and created all life in six 24-hour days. *(Later on in this appendix I will explain why the Hebrew text of Genesis makes it clear that the "days" of Genesis can be understood ONLY as normal 24-hour days.)*

The crown of God's creation was the humans He created "in His image." The "image of God" can imply various things, but it especially refers to the fact that God made Adam and Eve to live in loving fellowship with Him and with each other.

God's plan was that Adam and Eve – and all their descendants – would live in His love forever. When God finished His creative work at the end of the sixth day the text reads: **"God saw all that he had made, and it was very good."** *In God's very good creation there was no suffering, no pain, and no death.* Adam and Eve loved God and trusted His Word. But that was about to change.

Holy Scripture teaches us that the devil, a fallen angel, tempted Adam and Eve to reject God and His Word. He tempted them to decide for themselves what is good and evil. He tempted them to be their own gods. Even though God lovingly warned them that such a choice would result in death, they believed the devil's lie instead and turned their backs on God – and the rest is tragic history!

Why is there suffering, pain and death in this world? The answer is: "We sin against God! We don't love Him. We don't trust Him. We are sinners because we are descendants of Adam whose sinful nature we have inherited."

Paul explains this in Romans chapter 5 where he writes: **"...sin entered the world through one man, and death through sin, and in this way death came to all men, because all sinned – even over those who did not sin by breaking a command, as did Adam..."**

Simply put, even though we were not there in the Garden when Adam turned his back on God, Adam's sinful nature has been passed down to us. Therefore, we also make sinful choices and face death because of it. As Paul says at the end of Romans chapter 6: **"The wages of sin is death..."**

We must understand that the suffering, pain and death in this world is God's way of showing us that something is wrong. His very good creation is broken, and we're to blame. In Romans chapter 8 Paul writes: **"For the creation was subjected to frustration, not by its own choice, but by the will of the one who subjected it, in hope that the creation itself will be liberated from its bondage to decay and brought into the glorious freedom of the children of God."** *Romans chapter 8 gives us both BAD news and GOOD news.*

The BAD news is that God's very good world is in bondage to decay because of our sin against Him. This broken world is God's sign that we need a Savior. Of course, the GOOD news is that God has given us such a Savior! (See Romans 8:28-39)

In addition, in 2nd Corinthians chapter 4 Paul gives us this GOOD news: **"For God, who said, 'Let light shine out of darkness,' made his light shine in our hearts to give us the light of the knowledge of the glory of God in the face of Christ."**

Paul then gives us more GOOD news in the next chapter. In 2nd Corinthians chapter 5 Paul writes: **"...if anyone is in Christ, he is a new creation; the old has gone, the new has come! All this is from God, who reconciled us to himself through Christ and gave us the ministry of reconciliation: that God was reconciling the world to himself in Christ, not counting men's sins against them. And he has committed to us the message of reconciliation. We are therefore Christ's ambassadors, as though God were making his appeal through us. We implore you on Christ's behalf: Be reconciled to God. God made him who had no sin to be sin for us, so that in him we might become the righteousness of God."**

The God who created this world sent His One and Only Son to save this world through His death on the cross where He took upon Himself the sin and guilt of every child of Adam and suffered the damnation we deserve that we might have the hope of a New Creation.

In fact, just as God finished His very good work of creation at the end of the sixth day. In the same way, God finished His very good work of saving us at the end of the sixth day when Jesus cried out from the cross: **"It is finished!"**

God's New Creation begins in ***our*** lives when the Holy Spirit works through the Good News to bring us to faith in Jesus, our Lord and Savior. God shows us our sin and guilt so that we will repent and trust in Jesus through whom we NOW have complete forgiveness of sins through His blood shed for us.

Those who trust in Christ as their Savior do not have to fear death. Just as Christ died and then rose from the dead and lives forever, we who believe in Him can face death knowing that when Christ returns He will then raise our bodies from the dust of death – sinless and glorified – and we will live with God forever in the New Creation He will give us on that Day. When Christ returns this broken creation will be liberated from its bondage to decay. When Christ returns He will create a new heavens and a new earth!

The Apostle Peter writes the following in 2nd Peter chapter 3: **"Dear friends, this is now my second letter to you. I have written both of them as reminders to stimulate you to wholesome thinking. I want you to recall the words spoken in the past by the holy prophets and the command given by our Lord and Savior through your apostles. First of all, you must understand that in the last days scoffers will come, scoffing and following their own evil desires. They will say, 'Where is this 'coming' he promised? Ever since our fathers died, everything goes on as it has since the beginning of creation.' But they deliberately forget that long ago by God's word the heavens existed and the earth was formed out of water and by water. By these waters also the world of that time was deluged and destroyed. By the same word the present heavens and earth are reserved for fire, being kept for the day of judgment and destruction of ungodly men. But do not forget this one thing, dear friends: With the Lord a day is like a thousand years, and a thousand years are like a day. The Lord is not slow in keeping his promise, as some understand slowness. He is patient with you, not wanting anyone to perish, but everyone to come to repentance. But the day of the Lord will come like a thief. The heavens will**

disappear with a roar; the elements will be destroyed by fire, and the earth and everything in it will be laid bare. Since everything will be destroyed in this way, what kind of people ought you to be? You ought to live holy and godly lives as you look forward to the day of God and speed its coming. That day will bring about the destruction of the heavens by fire, and the elements will melt in the heat. But in keeping with his promise we are looking forward to a new heaven and a new earth, the home of righteousness."

At this point I would like to go back to Genesis chapters 1 and 2 and briefly explain why many Christians throughout history have understood the creation account in Genesis as literal history – *and why this view is necessary for preserving the Good News of Jesus and His work on the cross for us.*

You may know that there are some who try to accommodate Darwinian macro-evolution with belief in God. Now, I do not deny that God could have used macro-evolution to create all life if that is what He had chosen to do. But if we take God's Word in Holy Scripture seriously, we must then conclude that He did NOT create life using macro-evolution. In fact, we will learn that such a view conflicts with what Scripture teaches about the existence of death and the purpose of the cross!

I will now give you some information that will explain why the days of Genesis chapter 1 are normal 24-hour days, and why Adam and Eve were real people who rebelled against God at a real point in history after which God set into motion a real plan of salvation that would take place in real history for us and our salvation.

Some of the content in the following section of this appendix is based on information I received from a lecture given by Dr. David Adams, professor of Old Testament at Concordia Seminary in St. Louis, Missouri.

The meaning of "day" in Genesis chapter 1

(The Hebrew word for "day" is ***yom***)

- The Hebrew word *yom* almost always means a normal 24-hour day. The Hebrew word *yom* is used 2317 times in the Old

Testament. Numerous uses of words similar to *yom* in languages related to Hebrew provide overwhelming evidence that a 24-hour day is the most common meaning of *yom* .

- In a few cases the Hebrew word *yom* does have other meanings derived from its common meaning of a 24-day: **1)** A period of light, as opposed to a period of darkness (see Genesis 1:5a, 18); **2)** A point in time that something occurred (the Hebrew word *beth* + *yom* means "in the day" or "when" – see Genesis 2:4 and 3:5); **3)** A year – especially when used in the plural form (see 1st Samuel 27:7 and Exodus 13:10); **4)** When *yom* is used with the definite article ("the") it means "today" (see Genesis 4:14); **5)** When *yom* is used with the Hebrew preposition *beth* it may mean a period of time, especially when used in the plural form (see Genesis 5:4).

- There is a general principle followed by most biblical scholars: "Do not view a word or text in a figurative sense (for example, "day" means "millions of years") unless the immediate and/or wider context indicates that you should." The Hebrew text of Genesis chapters 1 and 2 is <u>historical narrative</u>. Jesus Himself speaks of Adam and Eve in a literal manner in Matthew 19:4-6! Also, in Acts 17:24-26 Paul teaches that the common ancestor of all humanity was the historical man, Adam!

- In Genesis chapter 1 there is nothing to indicate that an extended or figurative meaning is implied: **1) The use of the words "evening and morning" throughout Genesis chapter 1 strongly implies that *yom* means a 24-hour day.** Some attempt to refute this fact by pointing out that in Genesis 2:4 *yom* refers to the whole six days of creation and so it may not mean 24-day in Genesis chapter 1. However, in Genesis 2:4 *yom* is used with the preposition *beth* (see above) which means "when" and not a 24-day. Since *yom* is used with the preposition *beth* in Genesis 2:4 it can not be compared to the use of *yom* <u>without</u> *beth* in Genesis chapter 1. Another way some try to refute the fact that the use of "evening and morning" in Genesis chapter 1 proves that *yom* refers to a 24-hour day is that they will point to the New Testament where it says that Jesus was in the tomb "three days and three nights" which actually means "over the course of three days" and not three full 24-hour days. However, even though *yom* can be used in this way, this argument actually refutes those who want *yom* to mean "millions of years." When the New Testament teaches that Jesus was in the tomb "over the course of three days" it means that He was in the tomb for LESS than three full days. If Genesis chapter 1 were to mean that God created the world "over the course of six days" this would mean that He created the world in LESS than six full days and NOT over the course of millions of years; **2) The Hebrew word *echad* ("one") in Genesis 1:5 is a cardinal number and so does NOT refer to the first day in a sequence of days (that would be an ordinal number). Instead, the Hebrew word *echad* when used with *yom* could actually be translated "one day" – and this would refer back to Genesis 1:3-4 where "one day" is defined as a period of darkness and light (that is, "evening and morning"). Therefore, Genesis 1:3-5 clearly teaches that *yom* is intended to be understood as a 24-hour day in Genesis chapter 1!**

- In Exodus 20:11 God says that His people should work six days (normal 24-hour days) and rest on the seventh day (a normal 24-hour day). God bases this pattern on the seven day creation week in Genesis 1:1-2:3. This strongly suggests that *yom* must be understood as a normal 24-hour day in Genesis chapter 1.

Various Interpretations of *yom* in Genesis chapter 1

- **Almost all the early Church fathers (and most other Christian leaders throughout history) taught that Genesis was literal history and that *yom* meant a 24-hour day.**[322] The few exceptions to this (for example, the early Church fathers Augustine and Origen) used philosophical presuppositions about how God *had to create* to impose a foreign interpretation upon the Hebrew text by saying that *yom* was not a normal day. However, their purpose was NOT to teach that the days of Genesis could have been billions of years. Instead, their purpose was to teach that God created the universe and all life in one instantaneous moment! In other words, they believed that God created in LESS than six 24-

[322] See *Refuting Compromise* by Jonathan Sarfati, 67-140. Also see *Could God Really Have Created Everything in Six Days?* by Ken Ham in *The New Answers Book* edited by Ken Ham, 88-112.

hour days. But later biblical scholars rebuked such an interpretation. For example, Martin Luther (in his commentary on Genesis) rebukes Augustine for allowing his philosophical presuppositions about how God *had to create things* to influence the clear reading of the text. In fact, Augustine did not know any Hebrew and only a little Greek. Augustine did not even read the Hebrew text of Genesis! Therefore, he was not able to understand the proper meaning of *yom* as a normal 24-hour day in Genesis chapter 1.

- **Most liberal biblical scholars admit that *yom* means a normal 24-hour day in Genesis chapter 1.** However, they do not believe that Scripture is the inspired and inerrant Word of God. Instead, they believe that whoever wrote Genesis chapter 1 was simply giving his subjective opinion about how God created the world. Nevertheless, these liberal scholars agree that a proper reading of the Hebrew in Genesis chapter 1 leads us to conclude that *yom* must mean a normal 24-hour day. For example, a highly respected liberal scholar, Hermann Gunkel, writes: "Naturally, the 'days' are days and nothing else … the application of the days of creation to … periods or the like is, thus, a very capricious corruption…" Also, Dr. James Barr (professor of Hebrew at Oxford University) once wrote a letter to David Watson on this issue: "So far as I know, there is no professor of Hebrew or Old Testament at any world-class university who does not believe that the writer(s) of Gen. 1-11 intended to convey to their readers … that creation took place in a series of six days which were the same as the days of 24 hours we now experience…" Simply put, respected liberal scholars agree that the Hebrew word *yom* in Genesis chapter 1 should be understood as a normal 24-hour day! They just do not believe it is actually God's revelation to us about true events in history.

- **Those who want to try to reconcile Genesis chapter 1 with modern scientific theories about the age of the earth and the origin of life have come up with various ways to reinterpret the meaning of Genesis chapter 1 to fit in with modern science:**

1) ***The Gap theory*** suggests that there is a very long gap of time (possibly billions of years) between Genesis 1:1 and

Genesis 1:2. This theory teaches that Genesis 1:1 describes the creation of the universe. Then, supposedly billions of years later, the earth was ruined by some sort of catastrophe (gap theorists usually associate this catastrophe with the casting out of the devil from heaven). Therefore, according to the gap theory Genesis 1:2 describes the ruined earth which was billions of years old at the time. Then, according to the gap theory, Genesis 1:3-2:3 describe God's restoration of the earth and all life within the span of six normal 24-hour days. Even though gap theorists do NOT believe in the scientific conclusions of those who hold to Darwinian macro-evolution to explain the origin of life. The fact is that gap theorists DO believe the scientific conclusions of those who believe that the earth must be billions of years old. Therefore, instead of reading Genesis 1:2 in its natural sense (which teaches that the earth was not yet fully formed on the first day of creation), gap theorists impose the modern scientific view of the age of the earth upon the text of Genesis. The problem with the gap theory is that there is no evidence for their view anywhere in Holy Scripture. Also, their interpretation of Genesis 1:1-2 is not based on the reading of the text itself. Instead, they allow modern scientific assumptions about the age of the earth to influence their reading of the Hebrew text.

2) ***The Progressive Creation theory*** also attempts to harmonize the text of Genesis chapter 1 with modern scientific assumptions that the earth must be billions of years old. They do this by suggesting, in conflict with all the evidence, that the Hebrew word *yom* can mean millions or even billions of years. However, those who hold to this theory do NOT agree with modern scientists who assert the theory of Darwinian macro-evolution as the explanation of the origin of life. Instead, those who hold to progressive creation believe that God created all life forms *ex nihilo* ("out of nothing") at various stages throughout the millions and billions of years supposedly suggested by the Hebrew word *yom* . Again, as with the gap theory, the problem with progressive creation is that such people allow modern scientific assumptions about the age of the earth to influence their reading of the Hebrew text in Genesis. In addition, in contrast with the gap theory, progressive

creation allows for death in God's very good world BEFORE Adam and Eve rebelled against God. This suggests that death is natural and not a consequence of Adam's sin. This has tragic consequences for the biblical teaching about the relationship between sin and death and the need for Christ's atoning work.

3) ***Theistic Evolution*** attempts to harmonize the text of Genesis chapter 1 not only with modern scientific assumptions about the age of the earth but also with modern scientific assumptions about the origin of life – namely, Darwinian macro-evolution! Simply put, those who hold to theistic evolution suggest that God used Darwinian macro-evolution to create life on this planet. The problem with theistic evolution is obvious. Not only does theistic evolution force us to completely deny the historicity of the creation account as well as the clear meaning of the Hebrew text of Genesis chapter 1. In addition, theistic evolution forces us to believe that God used a process to create life that requires "chance, mutation and death" – and all this as part of God's very good creation BEFORE Adam and Eve rebelled against God! Theistic evolution ultimately leads to a denial of the authority of Scripture and its teaching about original sin as well as the need for Christ's atoning work on the cross.

Simply put, the problem with these various theories described above is not only that they distort the clear reading of the Hebrew text of Genesis 1. Worst of all, progressive creation and theistic evolution teach that suffering and death were a natural part of God's very good creation. In other words, suffering and death were part of God's creative process and NOT the result of our sin against God! In fact, theistic evolution ends up denying the historicity of Adam and his sin with the result that the doctrine of original sin is also denied and, along with it, the necessity for the atoning work of Christ! *No wonder some theologians who promote these theories are now also questioning whether the teaching of Christ's atoning work should even be part of the Christian Faith!*

For example, in chapter three of this book I quoted from *The Sins of Scripture* where Bishop John Shelby Spong writes: **"Let me state boldly and succinctly: Jesus did not die for your sins or my sins. That proclamation is theological nonsense ... We are not fallen,**

sinful people who deserve to be punished. We are frightened, insecure people who have achieved the enormous breakthrough into self-consciousness that marks no other creature that has yet emerged from the evolutionary cycle. We must not denigrate the human being who ate of the tree of knowledge in the Genesis story. We must learn rather to celebrate the creative leap into a higher humanity. Our sense of separation and aloneness is not a mark of our sin. It is a symbol of our glory. Our struggle to survive, which manifests itself in radical self-centeredness, is not the result of original sin. It is a sign of emerging consciousness. It should not be a source of guilt. It is a source of blessing ... Jesus did not die for our sins ... That is a god-image that must be broken; but when it is, the traditional way we have told the Jesus story will surely die with it. I believe it *must.* When it does, I think it will be good riddance."

What is really at stake?

The various approaches that compromise Scripture in order to accommodate scientific views may appeal to human reason, but there is no real middle ground here. What is at stake is not only the question of how God created the world, but also the questions of the nature of Scripture as divine revelation, of the nature of God and His relationship with nature, and of the reliability of the Christian Faith.

Always in the background in the argument over creation is the nature of the Bible. Historic Christianity has viewed (and continues to view) the Bible as revelation from God. But modern liberal Christianity views the Bible as a collection of religious documents expressing nothing more than the subjective spiritual opinions of ancient people.

In other words, liberal Christianity does NOT view Scripture as revelation from God that gives us a true of account of His actions in history. In contrast, Scripture itself teaches that it is inspired by God and therefore is a factual account of God's activities in history (see Matthew 19:1-6, Luke 3:23-38 & 24:44, John 5:39-46 & 10:34-36, Acts 7:2-53 & 17:1-12, Romans 1:1-4 & 15:1-4, 1st Corinthians 4:6 & 15:1-4, 2nd Timothy 3:14-17, Hebrews 1:1-3, 1st Peter 1:10-12, 2nd Peter 1:19-21 & 3:14-18).

We must understand that Christianity is not merely one subjective human opinion about God among many alternatives. Nor is Christianity a "moral religion" in the sense that it merely gives us rules for living in this world. Instead, the Christian Faith is about <u>God's</u>

saving actions ***in history*** to rescue His creation from the slavery into which it sold itself through disobedience and unbelief. The Christian Faith is based on the claim that certain events ***really did happen within space and time*** -- the Creation, the Fall, the Exodus, the Incarnation, the Crucifixion, and the bodily Resurrection of Jesus Christ. If these things did not actually happen in history, then Christianity is a false Faith (see 1st Corinthians 15:12-19).

The title of this appendix is: **"Creation versus Evolution: Whose Word Do We Trust?"** Early in this appendix I suggested that the debate between Creation versus Evolution really comes down to a matter of *epistemology*, that is: "How do we *know* what we *know*?" Scientific assumptions about the PAST based on observations of data in the PRESENT are one way of knowing information about the age of the earth and the origin of life – *but this is a very limited way of knowing this information!* However, if we believe that Scripture is the inspired and inerrant Word of God who has revealed to us His actions in the PAST as well as the purpose of those actions, then we have another ***and much more reliable way*** of knowing about the age of the earth and the origin of life as well as the purpose behind it all!

Science deals only with what can be evaluated by the senses. Not only is science limited in what it can know about data in the PRESENT. Science is even more limited regarding what it can know about events in the PAST. Science is God's gift for helping us have dominion over the realm of creation. Science, like all human knowledge, is finite, and cannot therefore evaluate questions that transcend the realm of nature – *such as whether God created the world and all life forms in six 24-hour days!*

Only a reliable witness from the PAST could give us certain information about the creation of the world and the origin of life. Thanks be to God! We have such a reliable Witness! God Himself was there "In the beginning" and He has revealed to us HOW and WHY He created us! I'm not suggesting that Scripture answers all our questions about the phenomena we witness in the PRESENT day creation. What I am suggesting is that Scripture gives us the answers we need to know. Even more, Scripture teaches us how to ask the right kind of questions!

There is no conflict between science and Christianity as long as each realm speaks to its own issues. For example, we should NOT use Scripture to figure how to construct a microwave oven or how to destroy cancer cells. Scripture does not address these issues. In the same way, we should not wrongly assume that science is the only or even best way of knowing about events in the PAST such as the age of the earth and the origin of life – especially since Scripture **does** clearly address those issues! Most importantly, we should not use the knowledge we gain from science to lead us to doubt the clear teachings of Holy Scripture – *especially on those issues that empirical science can not even begin to address with any certainty!*

If we use science to attempt to critique what the Bible says about creation, this would lead inevitably to the denial of all miracles – such as the virgin birth of Christ, Christ's resurrection, the resurrection of OUR bodies, and the creation of the New Heavens and New Earth on the Final Day. All of these (and other similar acts of God), by definition, are no more able to be confirmed by science than God's having created the world in six 24-hour days.

The Bible gives one epistemological principle for Christians with questions about the age of the earth and the origin of life: *Faith* in God's Word! So, whose word do we trust? Hebrews 11:3 reads: **"By faith we understand that the universe was formed at God's command, so that what is seen was not made out of what was visible."**

SUGGESTED READING LIST

In this appendix I did not attempt to address all the scientific opinions surrounding the Creation versus Evolution debate. However, you need to know that not all modern scientists agree with what most scientists teach about the age of the earth or especially the theory of Darwinian macro-evolution.

The following books in this reading list do not agree with each other on all points – but they DO all question macro-evolution via purely naturalistic causes. Most of these authors are respected PhD scientists in their field. The books with a (ID) next to the title take an Intelligent Design approach. Those with a (C) next to the title take an Young Earth Creation approach.

(ID) *Belief in God in an Age of Science* – John Polkinghorne

(ID) *Billions of Missing Links* - by Geoffrey Simmons

(C) *Coming to Grips with Genesis* – by Terry Mortenson

(ID) *Darwin's Black Box* – by Michael Behe

(ID) *Darwin's Proof: The Triumph of Religion Over Science* – by Cornelius Hunter

(ID) *Darwin on Trial* – by Philip Johnson

(ID) *Defeating Darwinism by Opening Minds* – by Phillip Johnson

(C) *Evolution Exposed: Biology* – by Roger Patterson

(C) *Footprints in the Ash* – by John Morris and Steve Austin **(a study of Mt. St. Helens)**

(ID) *Genetic Entropy and The Mystery of the Genome* – by John Sanford

(ID) *God's Undertaker. Has Science Buried God?* – by John Lennox

(ID) *How Blind is the Watchmaker?* – by Neil Broom

(C) *How Could a Loving God ... ?* - by Ken Ham

(ID) *Icons of Evolution* – by Jonathan Wells

(C) *In Search of the Genesis World* – by Eric Von Fange

(C) *In Six Days* - edited by John Ashton **(50 PhD Scientists who believe in Creation)**

(ID) *Mere Creation* – edited by William Dembski **(essays by various scientists)**

(ID) *Modern Cosmology and Philosophy* – by John Leslie

(ID) *Of Pandas and People* – by Percival Davis & Dean Kenyon

(C) *On the Seventh Day* – edited by John Ashton **(essays by 42 PhD Scientists)**

(C) *One Blood* – by Ken Ham

(ID) *Origins* – by Robert Shapiro

(ID) *Quarks, Chaos and Christianity* – John Polkinghorne

(ID) *Questions of Truth* – by John Polkinghorne and Nicholas Beale

(ID) *Quantum Physics and Theology* – by John Polkinghorne

(C) *Radioisotopes and the Age of the Earth: Vol. 1 & 2* - by Eugene Chaffin, Andrew Snelling, Larry Vardiman

(ID) *Reason in the Balance* – by Phillip Johnson
(C) *Refuting Compromise* – by Jonathan Sarfati
(C) *Refuting Evolution* – by Jonathan Sarfati
(C) *Refuting Evolution 2* - by Jonathan Sarfati
(ID) *Science's Blind Spot* – by Cornelius Hunter
(ID) *Seeking God in Science* – by Bradley John Monton
(ID) *Signature in the Cell* by Stephen C. Meyer
(ID) *Signature of Controversy* by David Klinghoffer, Stephen Meyer and David Berlinski
(ID) *The Cell's Design* by Fazale Rana

(ID) *The Politically Incorrect Guide to Darwinism and ID* – by Jonathan Wells
(C) *The Mythology of Modern Dating Methods* – by John Woodmorappe
(ID) *The Design Revolution* – by William Dembski
(C) *The New Answers Book: Volumes 1, 2 & 3* - Ken Ham **(essays by various scientists)**
(ID) *The Biotic Message* – by Walter ReMine
(C) *The Battle for the Beginning* – by John MacArthur
(ID) *The Privileged Planet* – by Guillermo Gonzalez
(C) *Thousands ... not Billions* – by Don DeYoung
(C) *Ultimate Proof of Creation* – by Jason Lisle
(ID) *Uncommon Dissent* – edited by William Dembski **(essays by various scientists)**
(ID) *What Darwin Didn't Know* – by Geoffrey Simmons

(C) Web page: **www.answersingenesis.org**
(ID) Web page: **www.arn.org**

╬ *APPENDIX IV* ╬

Testimonies from LCMS Pastors

Several months ago I was giving a radio interview on the program **Issuesetc** *. We were discussing what Scripture teaches about homosexual behavior, and how Christians can speak God's Truth in love to those who are burdened by this.*

At one point during the interview we took a phone call from a man who did not like what we had to say. After he said some negative things about Holy Scripture, he then asserted that no man who had a homosexual orientation would want to be a member of the LCMS - much less a pastor in the LCMS.

I responded by saying that I know of laypeople who are proud and faithful members of the LCMS who also bear the burden of homosexual desire. But, by God's grace, they strive to live sexually pure lives.

In addition, I also added that I know of pastors in the LCMS who bear the burden of homosexual desire. But, by God's grace, they strive to live sexually pure lives.

Yes, you read the above paragraph correctly! There are pastors in the LCMS who bear the burden of homosexual desire. They also rejoice in the pure teaching of God's Word in the LCMS which sets them free from their bondage and gives them peace with God. ***I have asked some of these brothers to write down their testimonies. They wish to remain anonymous, and so their actual names will not be used. Prepare to be blessed by their witness to Christ!***

My life of struggle and my life in Christ - **by "William"**

As I take a morning walk around the nearby city park, ear buds connecting me to my local public radio station so I can catch up on world news, a guy runs by. Not just any guy, but in my estimation an extraordinarily handsome man. Shirtless, muscled, he runs along seemingly without a care in the world. But me? The reaction is instantaneous. A painful pang physically grips my heart. I look away. I look back as he speeds away into the distance. I try to walk with my eyes closed. I'm not like him. Oh, how I want to be like him. I want to know what it feels like to be in his skin, with that body. He is more masculine than me. I wonder if he would ever be my friend. Nah, I'm not good looking enough, not masculine enough, not man enough.

And so begins another "chew-through-concrete" day. If that guy were on the other side of a poured concrete wall I would dig, claw, seriously chew through the cement to be with him. At times it is all-consuming, and I hate it. I despise every moment that I'm attracted to men. It is not who I am as a baptized child of God. It is not who I am as a new creature in Christ. It is not who I am as a Lutheran pastor.

There. I said it. I'm a pastor in the confessional, conservative, Word-and-Sacrament shaped Jesus-Christ-and-His-cross centered Lutheran Church-Missouri Synod and I struggle with same gender attraction.

What I wrote above is what goes on in the head of many guys struggling with same gender attraction. At least that's what goes on in my head. But what do I call this? "Gay" is a word I refuse to describe myself. It is politicized; it is often times used by people who have given up and given themselves over to the dishonoring of their bodies with dishonorable passions (Romans 1:24, 26). "Sexually broken" perhaps gets closer to the mark in that the gift of sexuality ends up bent, not used according to God's original intentions. But if something is "broken," then it can be "fixed," right? Many well-meaning people and some organizations and Christian counselors have approached the struggle of homosexuality as if it is something that can be easily repaired, like changing a tire or rebuilding an engine or transmission. Just stop acting out. Get married and it will all be different. Pray harder. Read God's Word more. Although all of those things are in and of themselves honorable and good things for Christians to do, even when pointing someone to the Gospel gifts of Jesus these are heard as Law. The reality needs to be faced that the flesh isn't budging very easy on this one. More later about the help I found, or better, was graciously shown to me.

Most people think of the physical aspect of homosexuality. They are repulsed by it, and rightly so. Yes, homosexuality is against God's order of creation, His complementary design of men and women. It is illogical to argue otherwise. But what many people don't realize is that same gender attraction is much more mental than it is physical. Homosexuality is much more nurture than nature. You will note that I have used the words "same gender" and "same sex" attraction. In my estimation and experience this most accurately describes with what the Christian man or woman struggles. It avoids the baggage which has been attached to the popular words "gay" and "homosexual," though I realize the Hebrew and Greek words of Scripture are translated "homosexual." This is not to avoid the word but rather to foster the discussion and pastoral and parishioner care of those who are hurting. The reality is there are many Lutheran men and women who struggle with same gender attraction. Thanks be to God they have not given themselves over to the darkness of sin and evil but rather seek to live in the light of Christ.

What I now share with you is what same gender attraction looks like in the life of cradle-to-not-yet-grave pastor in the Lutheran Church-Missouri Synod.

Childhood

I was not born "gay." The realization that I was attracted to the same gender was a gradual one. Having grown up on a farm, isolated from other neighborhood boys and born into family where male cousins were either older or younger than me, the opportunities for interaction with men of any age were sparse. My father worked two jobs, and even though I knew he loved me, he just wasn't around much in those early years of my life. On Sundays, though, he made sure we worshipped as a family. I delighted in learning the liturgy. I was enamored with Sunday school and the Bible stories imparted to me. Little did I know that these would become some of my greatest comforts later in life. God bless the pastors who preached Jesus and His cross into my heart and ears and the Sunday school teachers who taught me of Jesus and His great and unconditional love for me. Little do they know that they probably saved my life, both physical and spiritual.

My main source of interaction was with my mother. As life went on, it seemed quite natural and comfortable for me to play with girls on the playground. But this opened me up to teasing and name calling. For me the lives and ways of men were a curiosity. I didn't understand their actions, their thinking, their way of interacting. I was jealous and terribly wanted to be like them.

Grade school

Already in kindergarten I had a hard time. Having grown up unintentionally isolated I had a difficult time connecting with boys my own age. I didn't know what to say, what to do. I was clueless to the rough-and-tumble world of the playground. Even then I was the kid with my nose buried in a book or standing on the edge of the playground or jumping rope with the girls. Oh, if only I had known boxers also jump rope, maybe I could have redeemed that activity.

I was eleven years old when I went to Lutheran summer camp for the third time. Each time was a lonely experience in terms of fitting in with the guys in the cabin. I especially hated the sports part and my lack of skill and confidence. Even the ability to just laugh off a missed ball made me the target of name calling. But that particular summer the kid who had the lower bunk actually paid attention to me. He liked to joke around, something which was entirely foreign to me. It felt good. I relished the idea of having a friend. He lived in a town over from me. Our fathers actually worked in the same industry and knew one another.

A couple of months later, during the autumn, an invitation came from him through his father to mine asking if I wanted to spend the night at his house. I'm sure my parents breathed a sigh of relief that I was finally going to get out of my shell. I went and spent the night. We went up town for a fall celebration. We walked around the dark streets. When we returned to his house he asked me to push a piece of heavy furniture in front of his bedroom door in order to keep out his pesky sisters, or so he said. Then he sexually abused me the entire night. I had no escape until my father came to get me. When morning came and breakfast was announced and the door was unbarred, I locked myself in the bathroom feeling numb and dirty. I'm sure my one syllable replies to my father's questions about the sleep over were frustrating and puzzling to him. In some ways that experience closed the deal on my same sex attraction. Supposed friendship and sex, shame and the feeling of dirtiness enshrouded me in darkness and confused me even further.

Junior High

Though my parents stated many good reasons for me to attend a Lutheran school I have often wondered if they, at least as best as they could and for a limited time, also did so in order to protect me from the teasing and ostracizing which was beginning to increase as grade school progressed. My father signed me up for a sport in the public junior high. I did it solely to please him, but it did not go well for me. I was terrified and just plain socially unprepared for the life of sports or junior high boys.

But in my Lutheran school I was insulated and somewhat protected for a time. What had begun in baptism and continued through the teaching in Sunday school was expanded in daily religious education. I memorized hymn stanzas and Bible verses. Like a sponge I soaked up the foundational theological education which became a part of my daily life. A Gospel pattern began to shape my life. Except for Saturdays I heard and learned God's Word. I wanted to do this forever. I excelled in confirmation, acing every memory assignment and quiz. Even then I wanted to be a pastor. My confirmation pastor encouraged me to become one. Surely I was well prepared for the world before me.

High School

But how wrong I was. I'll be blunt and say that I hated most every day of high school. Coming out of an excellent parochial education I was little prepared for the larger world of high school. What I experienced then would today be called "bullying," though naming it and reacting to what happened would have changed nothing. Most meals in the cafeteria I ate alone and as fast as I could. One day while eating, a female—not male, but female—classmate stood up in front of my 130-some fellow students and loudly announced, "William is a fag." First there was dead silence and then laughter broke out. What had I done or said? I was a quiet person. I kept to myself. Was my struggle so obvious that my peers could see it written on my face? At that moment I remembered the words of my father, "Never let them see they've gotten to you." I stared at my tray. I went back to reading a book. My face burned hot and red.

Perhaps what hurt most of all that day, though, was that my thirty-some fellow Lutheran confirmands from a couple of years ago said nothing, not a word. They comprised about one fourth of everyone in that lunch room. No one came to my defense, publicly or privately. My fellow brothers and sisters in Christ gave no assurance or comfort. Now, it may be a lot to ask of Lutheran high school sophomores to keep the Eighth Commandment and to defend one's neighbor, to "speak well of him, and explain everything in the kindest way." But we pastors can certainly make this a part of our ongoing teaching of our youth, to do just that, to defend those who are vulnerable to mocking and derision, the mentally challenged, the stutterers, the awkward kids, the shy, the sexually uncertain kids. If only our youth were taught that if even five of them had approached this girl, they could have made a huge difference. "You have crossed the line. You have embarrassed yourself. What you have said is not true. He is our dear brother in Christ and you will not act that way again. Christ and we forgive you. You know the right thing to do. A public apology is now in order."

The ripple effect of that day continued for months afterward. In the locker room during P.E. and in the classroom whispers and comments made under classmates' breath reached my ears and ripped at my heart.

Years ago I read a collection of stories about animals who had protected people. One of the stories was about a farmer in a barn yard. While in the cattle pen a bull, unprovoked, attacked the farmer from behind. He began to inflict serious damage upon the farmer. Then the cows stepped in. They encircled the farmer and protected him. The farmer began to crawl toward the fence. They continued to follow him, deflecting the rampage of the bull until the farmer was safe. Though this may be difficult for us Lutherans to hear, surely we can do better than cattle.

Whereas the words openly spoken inflicted a deep wound, the ensuing silence was even worse. And there begins one of the insidious parts of same gender attraction—the issue of self-fulfilling prophecy. If they can see it, then it must be true. I really must be a fag. Then the self-loathing and self-hatred increases exponentially. If only I were different. If only I was like *them*—the jocks, the cool guys, the confident guys, the guys not made fun of. Finally, I did find my niche by pursuing various clubs and activities which seemed to be safe and fit my interest. I became president of all the groups. I would create for myself positions of respect. On the outside I finally appeared to fit in — sort of — but on the inside there was still a huge disconnect. I continually looked over my shoulder, waiting for the next attack. Yet on the inside, like a cannon ball sent by the Road Runner straight through Wile E. Coyote, I had a perfect black hole needing to be filled.

College

I chose a LCMS college many hours away from my home town. You can now see why. I wanted a new start. No way was I going to attend a state university where even one of my high school classmates could be found. I desperately wanted a new beginning. Even there at times I was publicly called names, usually by athletes. Again, no one countered their public words of derision. Again my fellow Lutherans were silent.

Nine years after being sexually abused the cycle of depression hit an all time new low during my junior year. I couldn't sleep at night, increasingly tormented by the memory of the sexual abuse. I broke up with a girl friend. I withdrew from friendships. My grades began to suffer. My parents became concerned about my physical appearance and well-being. I had learned of private confession and absolution. Perhaps that was a place I could go, before the face of God and into the ears of a pastor and speak aloud all of the darkness. But the campus pastor was simply an untrustworthy man. Students began to speak of things which had been told to him in confidence and which he had shared with others. If the first pastor had no respect for the seal of the confessional, how could I trust my off campus pastor?

So, I decided to take a different approach. I made an appointment with a secular counseling office with which the college had contracted. The counselor asked what had brought me to him. I told him I couldn't sleep. He scheduled me for an evaluation. I went and took a battery of tests. I was assigned a female grad student working on her MSW. I showed up for the unveiling of the results. My IQ was above average. My talents and abilities showed I was suited to pursue the pastoral ministry. Almost as a side note the counselor informed me that I was a "latent homosexual." She told me that in her opinion I would not act upon this. But that was exactly what I wanted to do, and yet I did not even have the vocabulary or guts to verbalize what was really going on in my head. Within the limited number of sessions allowed by the contract with the college the counselor taught me some relaxation techniques and that was it. She didn't get original sin. She didn't get actual sin. Nor did she get the forgiveness of sin in Jesus. I had pursued a dead-end path of help.

Seminary

I vividly remember driving on I-64 in St. Louis and seeing the green sign which directed me to the exit leading to Concordia Seminary. My thought was this, "What have I gotten myself into now?" But I was excited about seminary. Again, this would be a new beginning, a fresh start.

Not long before I started seminary a couple of deadly events occurred in the life the seminary, one involving a recent graduate and one a student. Parishioners in the synod began to question why the seminaries were not catching these problems before they escalated to disastrous ends. Our seminaries decided it was time to administer an emotional and mental health screening in order to detect any serious problems which needed immediate attention. We first-year seminarians were given the assessment and we were given a deadline by which to return it. So, I'm assuming, most of us did. I did. I thought then, "Now they're going to find out. I don't know if I can hide this." Many weeks passed and curiosity got the best of me. I asked the person responsible for administering the inventory whatever became of them. He informed me that the inventories had not been properly administered and so they had been thrown into the trash. I breathed a sigh of relief all the while desperately wanting to finally address this same sex attraction tormenting.

Seminary was finally different, though. My classmates (and remember, this is an all-male group) were more mature than any others I had been surrounded by. I enjoyed the theological debates. The non-judgmental friendships which formed became very precious to me, though I still kept men at arm's length all the while wanting to be on the "inside" of the friendships and activities going on around me. With great hesitancy and much fear I joined an intramural team. I started to gain some confidence. Maybe this time the struggle of same gender attraction would go away. As in college, I attended daily chapel services, hearing God's Word and having it soak into a shame-filled, sin-starved heart.

Dating and Marriage

Though I had dated girls during high school and college, these relationships were really deep friendships. There was no physical attraction beyond common interests and a protection against loneliness. Most importantly to me at the time was to put up a smokescreen so as to not give the impression I wasn't interested in women.

Then, out of the roughly three billion women in the world, a subset of whom were of marriageable age, and in the most surprising and unanticipated way, I fell in love with the one woman to whom I was attracted and still am! Surely, I thought, now that I'm married all the same gender attraction would fade away. The first month was great. The first year was pretty good, though the temptations started to slowly creep back. The next several years were mixed.

Parish life

Newly graduated, newly married, certainly this again would be a new start. Finally, in my mind, the time had come to put the old away and really, truly put on Christ.

Let me describe three moments in parish life, one during seminary and two after graduation from seminary.

The first scene was on a summer internship. The struggle had become fierce. My body shook at the fight that was going on in me. I went into the un-air conditioned summer heated sanctuary, locked the doors and stood before the most holy altar of God and started screaming at Him. Why was this happening to me? Why wouldn't He—the omnipotent, omniscient, omnipresent God—cure me of this single sinful stranglehold on my soul? Physically and emotionally spent I fell upon the communion rail. Would it ever end? Would it never end?

The second scene happened a few years into ministry. A non-Lutheran friend in whom I had hesitantly confided my struggles suggested that a twelve-step group might help. I took a risk and drove the two hours to get to the meeting. Having never been to one before, I watched and listened. People were polite. They were honest, sometimes painfully honest, more so than I had ever heard people speak in the church. During the late night drive home I began to think about the abuse which had happened. The details of the abuse were vivid in my mind. They tormented me just about every night. But it had always bothered me that I couldn't remember the date when it happened. I've always been good at remembering dates, birthdays, anniversaries, saints' days, you name it. But this I could not remember. I knew the month and the year, but not the date. As I drove the two hours back home I racked my brain, searching for the missing piece of that puzzle. To many this may seem like an insignificant bit of information, but it was important for me. After so many miles, as I turned the corner to go down my street, I remembered. I finally remembered some twenty years later. But the effect on me was not what I expected. I anticipated the remembering to be the acquisition of just another small piece of objective information to be filed in a more accessible part of my brain. But this was not so. I pulled into the drive way. I put the car in park. I turned off the ignition and then I began beating my head against the steering wheel and started screaming. Starting from the top of my head through the middle of my body it was as if fingers had dug into my scalp and I was being ripped in half. This incident was one of the most terrifying moments in my life. I am only glad that my wife didn't witness what I went through. The screaming was absorbed by the interior of the car; the scene acted out in the dark of night. Emotionally and physically spent, I finally stumbled into the house and fell into bed, only to begin another day of internal torture.

The gay world will talk about the "nurture" part of homosexuality, the deficient relationships with fathers and the overly emotionally entanglement with needy mothers. The gay world will try to make a lot of hay out of the "nature" part, that is, genetic causes. "God made me this way." "I've always been this way." "Hey, it's just part of the evolutionary process. Some of us just go a different route." But what the gay community rarely talks about is the sexual abuse which has taken place in the lives of so many young people. The abuses brought to light in the Roman Catholic Church have shed some light on this, but the deeply hurtful memories and pain get buried in the talk of law suits and monetary awards. In the secular world the Canadian hockey player Sheldon Kennedy finally broke the silence of the abuse which happened to him by his coach. My own informal survey has centered around this one question, "When did you first experience something sexual?" Most often the answer has to do with an older boy, teen or an adult who preyed upon a younger, vulnerable boy.

But invariably the boys who were abused don't start dealing with the violence enacted upon their own bodies, minds and souls until they are men in their 30s or 40s. By that point the weight becomes too great. They snap. They have to talk. Without proper pastoral care and careful, healing attention to their emotional and mental needs, they give up and give themselves over to a world in which they were never meant to be. They keep doing what was done to them in the hopes that the next time it will feel right. They end up lonely old men, robbed by the sin acted upon them, enticed by misdirected sexual needs lying outside the blessings of heterosexual marriage. Some completely despair of all hope and help and forgiveness—they commit suicide. Surely the Church-at-large—and certainly the Lutheran Church-Missouri Synod—can do better than being virtually silent to the tormented world of same sex attraction. With her great understanding of Law and Gospel, we Lutherans have the best to bring to those within our synod and to those outside. Pray that we have the courage to be so bold in the face of such sin and hurt and pain, bringing Christ who took on our human flesh and who through His divine nature has defeated the enticements and entrapments of evil.

And finally the third scene I now describe for you was the breaking point when I was finally reduced to nothing. It was the beginning of healing, though at the time I really thought I was done for.

My family was out of town, attending a larger family event. I had stayed behind to carrying on ministry. I was having a pretty good weekend. The spring weather was great; the to-do list was getting shorter. And then Sunday early evening temptation hit me like it had never hit me before. I struggled. I ignored what sainted Martin Luther had encouraged us all to do, that when Satan is tempting us, to find Christians friends and not be alone. I thought I could do it myself. I couldn't. ***I fell and I fell hard.*** I was now at the end of my rope. I could no longer live a double life.

I had just enough strength to call a non-Lutheran friend. He heard the distress in my voice and at great inconvenience to himself, he spent many hours with me to make sure that I was out of danger. As my friend was leaving he gave me the name and phone number of a Christian counselor. My friend made me promise I would make that phone call the next morning. I did. The mental health resources of our insurance plan were helpful enough, though I commend Concordia Plan Services for their increased financial support to the mental health of church workers. I began making five hour round trip visits to a dear, wise Christian counselor who specialized in a very specific form of therapy, one which deals with post traumatic stress disorder. After almost three decades I could finally go to sleep without the tormented memory of the sexual abuse. The abuse had become manageable; the abuser became forgivable. This counselor helped me unravel the tangled web of father issues, abandonment issues, sexual issues and the many other events which are described above. Though not Lutheran (notice a pattern here of who made themselves available, my dear Lutheran brothers and sisters), this counselor understood Law and Gospel, sin and forgiveness, and the hope and healing which is ours through Christ's suffering, death and resurrection. I have for him the greatest respect and owe him the deepest thanks possible for giving me once more hope in Christ.

I finally was able to tell my wife about the sexual abuse, and then a few months later, the hidden struggle I have had these so many years. Yes, this was a severe blow to her, bringing anger, sadness and fear on her part. There was fear and shame on mine. She spent time with my therapist in order to hear from him what all of this meant and the path of healing it would take for me to have some semblance of peace.

Solomon wrote, "*And though a man might prevail against one who is alone, two will withstand him—a threefold cord is not quickly broken.* (Ecclesiastes 4:12) The third cord in our marriage—our Savior Jesus Christ—did not break or fail us. Forgiveness prevailed. My wife's enormous ability to love and forgive and her amazing stubbornness to not give up on our marriage was a gift I could not have imagined. The rest is her story for her to tell, and so I won't try to interpret her own thoughts or feelings.

And now . . .

The past seven years have been hard. I won't sugar coat it. To undo so many years of thinking and behaving is a daunting task. After a break in therapy I now see another non-Lutheran but Christian counselor who brings a different set of skills. Now I am working on reprogramming my thought patterns through cognitive therapy.

In this I am confident: I am God's child. I was born a heterosexual male. That was God's original and good plan for me. I did not choose my parents. I did not choose to be sexually abused. I did not choose to be made fun of. But that's my history and I have had to take ownership of it. I still don't understand why things have happened to me except that I live in a sinful world. I have sinful flesh. I am pestered daily by Satan who delights in sin. I know you fight against the same enemies, though your personal struggles may be entirely different.

And I have found enormous comfort in these words of St. Paul, "*And we know that for those who love God all things work together for good, for those who are called according to his purpose.* (Romans 8:15) The things that happened to me and the things I myself have done were not and are not good. I continually flee back to my Savior Jesus to hear my sins forgiven and to lean on His strengthening and forgiving body and blood. But, in the above words of St. Paul, God in Christ Jesus has turned this to good. Do not misunderstand me. There is a danger here where someone might choose to tempt God and say, "Here. I'm going to do this sin. Give it Your best shot, God, and see what You can do with it." But this I can say: God has been able to turn even what

I have already described into good. I pray that God will continue to work my life for the good of many and to the glory of His name.

To quote St. Paul from Second Corinthians, *"So we do not lose heart. Though our outer nature is wasting away, our inner nature is being renewed day by day. For this slight momentary affliction is preparing us for an eternal weight of glory beyond all comparison, as we look not to the things that are seen but to the things that are unseen. For the things that are seen are transient, but the things that are unseen are eternal"* (2 Cor. 4:16-18). I pray that you, too, do not lose heart. The abundant grace of Jesus will sustain you in ways you can't even imagine.

And what of Jesus?

As you have read my story I pray that the golden thread of the Gospel has been clear even in the midst of great darkness, disappointment and despair. Were it not for my Savior Jesus I would not be writing this now. I shudder to think where this all could have led, for any path but the narrow path of Christ's gracious way leads only to destruction and death.

From a month old until this very day my life has been buried with Christ in the waters of baptism. It took me a long time to learn and believe that my true identity is found in the death and resurrection of Christ Jesus which became mine when the water and the Word of God washed me clean—and still does! My baptism, yes, *my* baptism, which is a gift from God, has sustained me day in and day out, even when I didn't remember my baptism, even when I couldn't remember my baptism.

Private confession for those struggling with same gender attraction is a precious gift. To speak into a pastor's ears what has been so darkly and wrongly done to others needs the clear and sharp scalpel of the Law and what has so shamefully been done by others needs the strong, loving medicine of the Gospel. A refreshing breath of air blows through the soul which has given to Jesus what has weighed on the heart so heavily. Such is my practice. I would not give up private confession and absolution for anything.

And we dare never underestimate the forgiveness of sins and the strength received from the body and blood of Jesus for and in our own sinful flesh and blood. A predecessor in my parish turned away from the Lord's Table a Lutheran man struggling with his sexual identity. As one who stands in both shoes, it distresses me that what the man asked for and needed so much that day was refused him because of the title "homosexual" assigned to him. I am a firm believer and practitioner of closed communion and the tough church discipline questions which are laid upon the pastor who distributes the gifts of Christ to those who come to the table of the Lord. But to refuse a hurting man letting it be known what his struggles and sins were? I'll let you ponder your own response to such a situation. Yes, there is a place for forgiveness in the repentant life of those who struggle with same gender attraction.

But wait, there's more!

What brought me to write this so that you could read it? While listening to the nationally syndicated radio program Issues, Etc, I heard Pastor Tom Eckstein address the topic of homosexuality. Obviously I would be interested in the topic. As I listened I quickly appreciated Pastor Eckstein's calm, caring and compassionate approach to the topic. He spoke pastorally about those who had come to him for God's grace and healing. I literally had to pull the car over, though, when I heard him speak one sentence concerning clergy in the Lutheran Church-Missouri Synod struggling with same gender attraction. Had I heard Pastor Eckstein correctly? I listened to the program again to make sure he had really said it. He had. So with great hesitation I sent him an anonymous email thanking Pastor Eckstein for addressing the topic of homosexuality in general and especially the painful reality of LCMS clergy struggling with what so many in the pew struggle with too. He graciously responded to my email and offered his pastoral confidentiality and care to me. I took the leap and a very deep breath and wrote him back with my name signed to the bottom of the email. Since then Pastor Eckstein has continued to be a great gift of God to my personal life. He asked if I would be bold enough to share my story. So here you have it.

And what about you?

If you are a heterosexual person who is so inclined to consider helping those who struggle with same gender attraction, may I commend to you the following words from St. Paul, "*Put on then, as God's chosen ones, holy and beloved, compassionate hearts, kindness, humility, meekness, and patience, bearing with one another . . .*" (Colossians 3:12-13a).

For a moment imagine your congregation on a Sunday morning. See the faces of the people who are there Sunday in, Sunday out. What does your pre- or post-service coffee and Bible class group look like? On any given Sunday a fellow member could say, "Last night at my AA meeting we . . . ." You would think nothing of that comment. You might put your hand on that person's shoulder and say, "Is there anything I can do for you? Hang in there. I'll pray for you."

But what if that person struggled with same gender attraction? Could you put your arm around him or her and say, "I'm glad you're here. I'll pray for you. Is there anything I can do? Would you like to go out with us for Sunday lunch? What are your plans for Thanksgiving?"

And so a word to the heterosexual, straight Lutheran men in my church body: You got to step up to the plate, guys. Perhaps you do not realize the very simple gift you possess in helping someone with same gender attraction. You can model and you can teach.

Is there a more gracious and loving group of Lutheran men among us who are mature in their faith and express a deep desire for bringing Christ to the nations, which includes the population of same gender attraction strugglers, then the International Lutheran Laymen's League? The LLL groups of congregations should be safe and accepting groups for men struggling with same gender attraction. Be not afraid. The men who might be brought into your midst already are fearful enough. Express to them the love of Christ and the brotherhood which is so precious to us.

Though my comments have focused on the struggles of male same gender attraction, what I have just said about the LLL can also be said of the Lutheran Women's Missionary League. Is there a more wonderful group of women who overflow with the love of Jesus and have the same heart for missions that the LLL shows? True femininity and womanhood exude from these ladies. They have much to offer to women hurting from same gender attraction. May God open the hearts and societies of the LWML to receive such a challenge. May they express Christ's love in the way only the LWML can to hurting, struggling sisters.

In your strong but caring way you can encourage a struggling man to participate in the male activities of the church. Take him to the ball field over lunch and practice hitting a few balls. Set him up with a fishing pole and cast a few. Invite him to a local sporting event. Ask him to go out for a drink after the mid-week service. Be ready for hesitancy. Be ready for lame excuses. Guys, he's scared and hurting.

But go for it. Use your best Christ-centered gifts and encouragement to him so that he may grow more confident in his masculinity and as a fellow brother in Christ.

If I could encourage parents, parishioners and pastors alike, it would be to not dismiss mood changes, symptoms of withdrawal, even posture changes as hormonal or being typical of the teenage years. With great care pastors need to articulate the Law and Gospel of homosexuality when teaching the sixth commandment in confirmation class, letting the Gospel predominate and offering hope to those silently sitting there who may be struggling. It's about building trusting relationships and communicating that the door to the office, the door to the confessional is always open. Lutheran laymen who are confident in their heterosexuality and masculinity need to step up to the plate and encourage pre-teens and teens who may not have good role models at home or in the family. And finally, we need to get over being offended by the Gospel. Consider these two final Scripture passages, both from Hebrews:

For because He Himself [Jesus] has suffered when tempted, He is able to help those who are being tempted. (Hebrews 2:18)

For we do not have a high priest who is unable to sympathize with our weaknesses, but One [Jesus] who in every respect has been tempted as we are, yet without sin. Let us then with confidence draw near to the throne of grace ,that we may receive mercy and find grace to help in time of need. (Hebrews 4:15-16)

According to God's Holy Word in Hebrews, Jesus was tempted in every way, which includes the temptation of homosexuality. The Lord Jesus knows exactly what it feels like, and yet for our sake He did not sin and, in fact, died for that very sin, too, so that lives and souls and bodies may be clean in and by His precious, saving blood. May all glory and praise be to God alone.

- "William" –

A Testimony from "Martin"

January of 1976, pet rocks and mood rings were the fads of the previous fall and holiday season, although, in the cold of Wyoming winters mood rings were usually black no matter whether you were happy or sad. The country was about to turn two hundred and I had turned fourteen the previous October.

It was just after Christmas break. I was walking down the hall of the Junior High and I saw ahead of me a fellow student who, from the back, could have been either a boy or a girl. His/her medium length blond hair was a style that was popular with both boys and girls that year. He/she held his/her body straight and exhibited an energy as he/she walked that I found very intriguing. I found myself being attracted in a way that was new to me and rather exciting as I wondered whether it was a boy or a girl I was watching. As I looked and wondered who this student was, she turned around and it was obvious she had breasts. She was a girl. And with the answer to my curiosity came a sense of great disappointment. The moment I realized I had been watching a girl all sense of attraction left me. And in the next moment I felt a sense of tremendous fear and guilt. I had been attracted when I thought that other student might be a boy. I had very much wanted it to be a boy. My attraction fled the moment I knew she was a girl. And if I was attracted to someone only when I thought they were another boy then, my teenage mind drew the obvious conclusion.....I probably was homosexual.

This was not a new concept to me. For some reason Christians have closed their ears to statements by homosexuals like, "I have always been gay." In reading statements on the internet from parents who have just learned of their teen's homosexuality it is obvious that many Christian parents believe homosexuality to be a choice their children have made in response to society's openness toward the gay lifestyle. But the roots of homosexuality really do go back much farther than pastors, parents and youth leaders often realize. Most homosexuals will tell you they felt different from the time they were very small. Certainly for me that was the case.

From second grade on I had always preferred playing dolls with the girls over football and baseball with the boys. Starting in third grade, I was often called fag, fairy or queer. I think it was in fourth grade I convinced my parents that I was too old for a birthday party. I told them I would rather just have dinner and cake with the family. The truth is I didn't know any boys I wanted to invite and all the girls would be going to the party of a girl whose birthday fell on the same day as mine. By fifth grade I had been beaten up at least twice for being a "sissy."

I don't want to give the impression that all the boys in school made fun of me. It was probably no more than half a dozen who determined to make my life miserable. I suspect that if you were to ask people who grew up with me what I was like they would say I was a quiet, nerdy kid who was pleasant to be around and willing to help them with homework when asked. Perhaps, had I the courage to reach out, I would have had quite a few friends. But I let my own sense of being different and the teasing of a few scare me away from trusting anyone enough to make close friends.

As grade school ended, I hoped and prayed that whatever made me different would go away, that I would grow out of it somehow. But standing in the hall that January of my 8th grade year, I realized the boys who had teased me and called me names were right, I was a queer.

I think I still held some vain hope that I might grow out of it but over the next few years that hope grew fainter and fainter and by 17 I figured I was homosexual for life.

This was especially hard for me to face because I had also gown up in a strong Lutheran family. Almost all my favorite memories of childhood involved church. I loved VBS. I enjoyed Sunday School. My earliest memories are of the Bible stories my mother read to me. I loved sitting in the kitchen while she prepared dinner and we talked together about God and the bible. Next to home, church was my favorite spot on earth.

In fact, I had wanted to be a pastor from the time I was in kindergarten. I used to set up a card table as an alter and use a little metal cereal bowl as an offering plate as I played "church" with my teddy bears as a congregation. I loved worship and still do. For some reason I found the Te Deum Laudamus especially moving, even in grade school. I loved weekday school in which we learned about the liturgy and the life of Martin Luther. I even enjoyed confirmation class although the number of doodles in my small catechism testify that I did not always pay attention.

Upon realizing I was homosexual, therefore, the answer seemed clear to me. I just needed to pray more, read the Bible more and dedicate myself to God even more firmly. None of it worked. My attraction to other males simply grew stronger as adolescence progressed.

Here too I see church workers and parents confused about the dynamics of homosexuality. From the outside they see a kid who was active in youth group and faithful in worship suddenly declare himself gay and seem to throw away the faith in which he was raised to live in a way that is a disappointment to his parents. Looking at the influences in his life at that moment, they often say things that indicate they believe pro-gay influences at his high school or college have lured him away from the training of his youth. I generally find this is not the case. What looks like rebellion from the outside is, on the inside, hopelessness. The young man has usually tried everything the church and his parents have told him to do but still finds himself attracted to other men. Finally, he determines that the Church has no answers for him, gives up on fighting a hopeless battle and enters the gay lifestyle.

For this I will always thank God, through the Church, Christ did give me an answer. It was not the answer I was expecting or looking for. I had hoped that if I was faithful enough God would change me. Instead, the answer I received was that God's love and salvation do not depend on me at all.

It was toward the end of 8th grade confirmation class. I asked my pastor "how can we say that good works do not take us to heaven when the Bible says we need to have faith. Isn't faith a 'good work'?" He gave me a good Lutheran answer that faith is not something we do but something God works in us through the Word and the Sacraments. Later we each had a private interview with the pastor before confirmation day. He asked me, "If God were to ask you why He should let you into heaven, what would you say?" I said, "because I have faith that Christ died for my sins." Pastor answered, "close, God is not obligated to take you to heaven because of your faith. He will take you to heaven because Christ died for you. So point to Christ's work on the cross, not your own faith."

The implications of both those answers took years to fully sink in. But as they did I also began to realize that I did not need to become heterosexual for God to love or forgive me. Just as the ability to change my orientation was beyond my power, so was my ability to do anything to influence God's love for me. I began to realize my overwhelming helplessness in the face of sin and God's overwhelming power to love in spite of sin for the sake of Christ.

When Pastor Tom Eckstein asked me to write a testimony it put me in somewhat of a quandary as my life has none of the elements that one expects from a testimony. On the one hand I never delved deeper into the gay lifestyle than some minor experimentation around the edges during my college years. In fact, what experimentation I did was so mild most would probably still consider me a virgin. So I have no titillating details of being pulled from the midst of depravity that would lend an aura of excitement to my testimony. On the other hand, neither has God seen fit to change my sexual orientation so I have no tale of miraculous divine intervention to share.

All I can say is that I live where we all do in this sinful world, in the tension of being both saint and sinner at the same time.

As sinner I know that homosexual love can not provide me with the answers I seek. Without being too graphic, what little experimentation I did have with homosexual behavior and what exposure I have occasionally had to gay pornography in my lifetime have demonstrated to me that two male bodies can not naturally nor comfortably join together in the kind of intimacy I desire. Perhaps, had I allowed myself to travel deeper on the road into the gay lifestyle, I would have learned to adjust and make do. But I could tell from the outset that homosexuality is ultimately unfulfilling and empty, that what it could provide was a lie and a mockery of the true closeness of marriage as God designed it.

And yet, how I still long for that connection, that intimacy with another man. How I yearn to have one person, a companion, to share with emotionally and physically. Even knowing how empty sin is and foreseeing it fruitless ending, the Old Adam cries out for that which would seem to satisfy now, for that which offers empty promises.

Is this not where we all are? Is this not where Peter was when he cried out, "Away from me, Lord, for I am a sinful man?" Is this not where Paul was when he mourned, "who will deliver me from the body of death?" Is this not where David was when he sighed, "my bones wasted away from my groaning?" Is this not why we stand before the altar and confess that we are sinful from birth, sinful in thought, word and deed?

In this sense, homosexuality has been a blessing for it never lets me forget that I am a sinner, helpless before my own sinful nature and that the only place I dare to live is before the throne of grace.

Yet, as a forgiven Saint I also know the wonder of the mercy of the Savior as a member of His body.

It seems that individualism is king in our world today. Religious propaganda tells us we need to have a personal relationship with Christ. We are told we need to make Him our personal Lord and Savior. We are told we must invite Him into our heart.

Yet, as a homosexually tempted member of Christ's body, that individualism is precisely what I do not need. Rather, I need to know that as a forgiven saint, I am a member of the family of God through the blood of Christ. I need to know that with Christ and through the forgiveness of Christ I have brothers and sisters who, though they may not understand, are related to me by ties deeper than human ancestry.

Once again, is this not where we all stand? Is this not why we say together the creed week after week, to rejoice in our shared confession of the work of God? Is this not why we join in the hymns of the angels and the shouts of the crowds in Jerusalem through the Sanctus? Is this not why we proclaim that we magnify God with angels, archangels and all the company of heaven?

In worship we weekly stand before the face of God, behold the Lamb of God in His Word and on the altar, are assured of a place at the family table through the mercy of Christ in communion and we are dismissed with ancient words of the benediction, assuring us that in leaving the place of worship we do not leave behind us the fellowship of Christ or our brothers and sisters.

The saint in me longs for and rejoices in this fellowship, this true spiritual intimacy that is deeper than any relationship in the world. This is the real connection. This is the answer the Church provides for homosexuality and all sin - that in the blood of Christ we have forgiveness, mercy, eternal life and a family in which we experience a love the world can neither comprehend nor know.

So I guess, in the end, my testimony is this. I am just like you. I am saint and sinner at the same time. And I am called to daily drown the old Adam, the sinner, through repentance while rejoicing in the New Man who lives and grows on the mercy of God and His Means of Grace.

This is the only answer the Church has - but what a powerful answer, to invite the powerless sinner to find forgiveness at the foot of the cross and to live as sinner saint until the day when Christ calls us home to Him. This, at the last, is all the answer that is necessary.

- “Martin” –

A Testimony from "John"

Romans 3:22-24 reads: "This righteousness from God comes through faith in Jesus Christ to all who believe. There is no difference, for all have sinned and fall short of the glory of God, and are justified freely by his grace through the redemption that came by Christ Jesus."

I was asked to write about my past struggle with same sex attraction. At first I was quite reticent to write about this. I was quite fearful for being hunted down and called out. But in the end, knowing that God would be glorified and be able to help those with similar temptations, I decided to write my testimony. I just want fellow saints and sinners to know that they are not alone, and that there is true hope and freedom in Christ Jesus. It might shock some to know that an LCMS pastor actually has had such temptations, yet if we take the Scriptures to be true, we know that we have all sinned and fallen short of the Glory of God. Just for clarification, I have not participated in any same-sex activity since becoming a pastor - and by the Grace of God I never will.

My earliest memories of having this struggle came about when I was a young child at my babysitter's home. She also babysat for a girl in my neighborhood and I remember being confused when it came time to play with toys. Admittedly she did not have a ton of boy's toys, but when she took out My Little Pony and Barbie, I really wanted to play with those items. I was reprimanded and told that those toys are for girls and not boys. On another occasion when I was younger, I was in a bookstore looking at some fantasy artwork in a Dungeons and Dragons book. I remember a picture of a woman being carried into a Viking hall surrounded by men, and I thought it was curious that I related more to the woman than the men in the drawing. I also found myself looking at men's bodybuilding books and finding it strange that I was attracted to the men in the book.

Later on in my preteen years, I was quite lonely as a child. Even though I was surrounded by kids in school, I was mixed in my emotions. Now, I can see that I was yearning for male companionship. I had an attraction for females, but it seemed like I was not attractive to anyone. So, in my loneliness I thought about my early childhood memories and thought that they were an indicator of whom or what my sexuality was based upon. I thought that maybe God meant for me to be a homosexual, but this was clearly against what the Word of God tells us. So, while I did find the girls in my high-school attractive, I decided to fantasize what it would be like to have a relation with guys. And the fantasies grew.

Later on in college, I still had mixed emotions and really started to wander away from the faith. I felt so ashamed and guilt ridden for having such thoughts and was frankly scared to tell anyone in the Church because of seeing how many fellow believers got angry when talking about homosexuals. I thought, "How in the world can one find freedom when it seemed like every other sin was forgiven, except this one." For long periods of time I would try and shove the feelings and emotions down within myself, deciding that this would be a sin that I could never confess and find forgiveness. All of the shame eventually became so great that I decided to try a homosexual experience. I came away with more guilt and became extremely depressed.

The turning point came in my young adult stage in life. I actually heard from my pastor about the issue of homosexuality. He told us that it was a sin, but that it was no different than those who have opposite sex relations. All sin before God was a cause for eternal condemnation. But, I also heard the sweetness of the Gospel. I heard that we all once were enemies of God, but through Christ and his death and resurrection, we have true freedom and forgiveness of my sins as we're told in Ephesians 5:8: "For you were once darkness, but now you are light in the Lord…" No one is beyond the reach of God's love, forgiveness, and healing. It was like my eyes were being opened for the first time, and I sought a private confession and absolution with my pastor.

After meeting with my pastor and receiving the forgiveness from Christ and the admonition to get help, I almost skipped out of the Church because of how happy I was. I left with a genuine Gospel-filled smile on my face. The weight from the guilt was literally taken off and I saw that I was indeed loved by God, even though I had these temptations and struggles. I now understood that having been set free, and with the help of the Holy Spirit, I could indeed resist. I was and am not alone.

However, I would be lying to you if I said that the occasional thought doesn't cross my mind – because it does. It happens once in a great while, but I immediately pray for the Lord to make the thorn pass and rely on His grace. And since my time with my home pastor, I enrolled with a Christian counselor who helped me to see that my feelings were actually for a strong and healthy male friendship that I lacked while growing up. He did not try and tell me that it was natural or that it was genetic. To this day I have continued to rely on God's love to help fulfill my desires and needs in this life.

Everyone needs compassion and forgiveness. There is no sin that cannot be forgiven by God. And our temptations won't end till we are called home to be with our Lord. But Christ and the Church has given me a true and real comfort and freedom in my trials. I urge those who are battling with the same issues to speak with their pastor. To describe the freedom that one has when they realize the true Graciousness and Goodness of God really cannot be totally conveyed, so I'll leave you with a Bible verse that has helped me throughout this struggle. John 8:36 reads: "So if the Son sets you free, you will be free indeed." Amen!

- "John" –

╬ *APPENDIX V* ╬

Recommended Resources

BOOKS

The Complete Guide to Understanding Homosexuality by Joe Dallas & Nancy Heche

Desires in Conflict by Joe Dallas

The Gay Gospel? by Joe Dallas

When Homosexuality Hits Home by Joe Dallas

The Same Sex Controversy by James White & Jeffrey Niell

Understanding Homosexuality by David Glesne

Straight & Narrow? by Thomas Schmidt

Welcoming But Not Affirming by Stanley Grenz

Scripture & Homosexuality by Marion Soards

A Christian Perspective on Homosexuality by Daniel Puls

The Bible and Homosexual Practice by Robert Gagnon

Homosexuality and the Bible: Two Views by Robert Gagnon & Dan Via

Homosexuality: The Use of Scientific Research in the Church's Moral Debate by Stanton Jones & Mark Yarhouse

Homosexuality and the Politics of Truth by Jeffrey Satinover

Counseling the Homosexual by Michael Saia

Someone I Love is Gay by Anita Worthen & Bob Davies

A Plan for Ministry to Homosexuals and Their Families (The Task Force on Ministry to Homosexuals and Their Families – LCMS)

ORGANIZATIONS & OTHER RESOURCES

Exodus International (web page: **www.exodusinternational.org**)

National Association for Research & Therapy of Homosexuality (web page: **www.narth.com**)

Parents and Friends of ExGays and Gays (web page: **www.pfox.org**)

Keys Ministry (web page: **www.keysministry.com**)

Regeneration (web page: **www.regenerationministries.org**)

First Light (web page: **www.firstlightstlouis.org**)

Mastering Life Ministries (web page: **www.masteringlife.org**)

Genesis Counseling (web page: **www.genesiscounseling.org**)

╬ BIBLIOGRAPHY ╬

A Plan for Ministry to Homosexuals and Their Families (The Task Force on Ministry to Homosexuals and Their Families / The Lutheran Church – Missouri Synod)

Anderson, Nancy and Wendell. *On Eagles Wings: Family Manual and Wives' Manual* (Nancy and Wendell Anderson, 1997)

Arndt, William; Hoerber, Robert and Roehrs, Walter. *Bible Difficulties and Seeming Contradictions* (Concordia Publishing House, 1987)

Arnold, William V. *Pastoral Responses to Sexual Issues* (John Knox Press, 1993)

Backus, William. *Telling the Truth to Troubled People* (Bethany, 1985)

Balch, David L. *Homosexuality, Science and the Plain Sense of Scripture* (Eerdmans, 2000)

Beck, James and Gundry, Stanley. *Two Views on Women in Ministry* (Zondervan, 2005)

Benner, David G. *Baker Encyclopedia of Psychology* (Baker, 1985)

Boswell, John. *Christianity, Social Tolerance, and Homosexuality* (University of Chicago Press, 1980)

Boswell, John. *Same-Sex Unions in Premodern Europe* (Random House, 1994)

Brawley, Robert L. *Biblical Ethics & Homosexuality* (Westminster John Knox Press, 1996)

Brooten, Bernadette J. *Love Between Women* (The University of Chicago Press, 1996)

Bruce, F. F. *The New International Commentary on the New Testament: The Book of Acts* (Eerdmans, 1984)

Butman, Richard E. and Jones, Stanton L. *Modern Psychotherapies* (IVP, 1991)

Cantarella, Eva. *Bisexuality in the Ancient World* (Yale University Press, 2002)

Carson, D. A. *Expositor's Bible Commentary: Matthew* (Zondervan, 1984)

Carson, D. A. and Woodbridge, John D. *Hermeneutics, Authority and Canon* (Zondervan Publishing House, 1986)

Chellew-Hodge, Candace. *Bulletproof Faith* (Jossey-Bass, 2008)

Chemnitz, Martin. *Examination of the Council of Trent: Part 1* translated by Fred Kramer (Concordia Publishing House, 1971)

Chilstrom, Herbert W. and Erdahl, Lowell O. *Sexual Fulfillment* (Augsburg, 2001)

Clinebell, Howard. *Basic Types of Pastoral Care and Counseling* (Abingdon, 1984)

Comstock, Gary D. *Gay Theology Without Apology* (Pilgrim Press, 1993)

Concordia: The Lutheran Confessions – A Readers Edition of the Book of Concord (Concordia Publishing House, 2005)

Countryman, William L. *Dirt, Greed & Sex* (Fortress Press, 1988)

Crompton, Louis. *Homosexuality and Civilization* (Harvard University Press, 2003)

Dallas, Joe. *Desires in Conflict* (Harvest House, 2003)

Dallas, Joe and Heche, Nancy. *The Complete Guide to Understanding Homosexuality* (Harvest House, 2010)

Dallas, Joe. *The Gay Gospel?* (Harvest House, 2007)

Dallas, Joe. *When Homosexuality Hits Home* (Harvest House, 2004)

Davies, Bod and Rentzel, Lori. *Coming Out Of Homosexuality* (IVP, 1993).

Davies, Bob and Rentzel, Lori. *Married and Gay* (Exodus International)

Davies, Bob and Worthen, Anita. *Someone I Love Is Gay* (IVP, 1996)

Dawn, Marva J. *Sexual Character* (Eerdmans, 1993)

De Youg, James B. *Homosexuality* (Kregel, 2000)

Delitzsch, F. *Commentary on the Old Testament: The Pentateuch* (Eerdmans, 1986)

Diamont, Louis and McAnulty, Richard D. *The Psychology of Sexual Orientation, Behavior, and Identity* (Greenwood Press, 1995)

Dover, K. J. *Greek Homosexuality* (Harvard University Press, 1989)

Downey, Jennifer I. and Friedman, Richard C. *Sexual Orientation and Psychoanalysis: Sexual Science and Clinical Practice* (Columbia University Press, 2002)

Duberman, Martin; Vicinus, Martha and Chauncey, George Jr. *Hidden From History: Reclaiming the Gay and Lesbian Past* (Meridian, 1989)

Dwyer, John F. *Those 7 References* (John F. Dwyer, 2007)

Edwards, George R. *Gay/Lesbian Liberation: A Biblical Perspective* (Pilgrim Press, 1984)

Foster, Kyle David. *Sexual Healing* (Regal, 2001)

Franzman, Martin H. *Romans* (Concordia Publishing House, 1968)

Franzman, Martin H. *The Word of the Lord Grows* (Concordia Publishing House, 1961)

Gagnon, Robert A. J. *The Bible and Homosexual Practice* (Abingdon, 2001)

Gagnon, Robert A. J. and Via, Dan O. *Homosexuality and the Bible: Two Views* (Fortress Press, 2003)

Garnets, Linda D. and Kimmel, Douglas C. *Psychological Perspectives on Lesbian, Gay and Bisexual Experiences* (Columbia University Press, 2003)

Glesne, David. *Understanding Homosexuality* (Kirk House Publishers, 2004)

Goss, Robert. *Jesus Acted Up: A Gay and Lesbian Manifesto* (Harper,1993)

Goss, Robert and West, Mona. *Take Back The Word: A Queer Reading of the Bible* (The Pilgrim Press, 2000)

Gould, Allan. *What Did They Say About Gays?* (ECW Press, 1995)

Grenz, Stanley J. *Welcoming But Not Affirming* (John Knox Press, 1998)

Grudem, Wayne and Piper, John. *Recovering Biblical Manhood & Womanhood* (Crossway Books, 1991)

Hall, Calvin S. and Nordby, Vernon J. *A Guide to Psychologists and Their Concepts* (Freeman and CO., 1974)

Ham, Ken; Wieland, Carl and Batten, Don. *One Blood* (Master Books, 1999)

Harrill, Albert J. *Slaves in the New Testament* (Fortress Press, 2006)

Harrison, Matt C. and Pless, John T. *Women Pastors? The Ordination of Women in Biblical Lutheran Perspective* (Concordia Publishing House, 2008).

Hasbury, Richard. *Homosexuality and Religion* (Harrington Park Press, 1989)

Heimbach, Daniel. *True Sexual Morality* (Crossway Books, 2004)

Helminiak, Daniel A. *What the Bible Really Says About Homosexuality* (Alamo Square Press, 2000)

Holben, L. R. *What Christians Think About Homosexuality* (Bible Press, 1999)

Horner, Tom. *Jonathan Loved David: Homosexuality in Biblical Times* (Westminster Press, 1978)

Horner, Tom. *Sex in the Bible* (Charles E. Tuttle Co., 1974)

Human Sexuality: A Theological Perspective (A Report of the Commission on Theology and Church Relations of the Lutheran Church – Missouri Synod, 1981)

Hummel, Horace D. *Concordia Commentary: Ezekiel 21-48* (Concordia Publishing House, 2007)

Hummel, Horace D. *The Word Becoming Flesh* (Concordia Publishing House, 1979)

Hunt, Morton. *The Story of Psychology* (Anchor Books, 1994)

Jeeves, Malcolm A. *Behavioral Sciences: A Christian Perspective* (IVP, 1984)

Johnson, Eric L. and Jones, Stanton L. *Psychology and Christianity* (IVP, 2000)

Jones, Stanton L. and Yarhouse, Mark A. *Homosexuality: The Use of Scientific Research in the Church's Moral Debate* (IVP, 2000)

Jordon, Mark D. *The Invention of Sodomy In Christian Theology* (The University of Chicago Press, 1997)

Journey Together Faithfully: The Church and Homosexuality (by the Task Force for ELCA Studies on Sexuality)

Kelly, J. N. D. *A Commentary on the Pastoral Epistles* (Baker Book House, 1978)

Kleinig, John W. *Concordia Commentary Series: Leviticus* (CPH, 2003)

Konrad, Jeff. *You Don't Have to Be Gay* (Pacific Publishing House, 1987)

Kostenberger, Andreas J.; Schreiner, Thomas R. and Baldwin, Scott H. *Women in the Church: A Fresh Analysis of 1 Timothy 2:9-15* (Baker Books, 1995)

Leahey, Thomas H. *A History of Psychology* (Prentice-Hall, Inc., 1980)

Lockwood, Gregory J. *Concordia Commentary Series: 1 Corinthians* (CPH, 2000)

Luther, Martin. Small Catechism (Concordia Publishing House, 1986).

Marin, Andrew. *Love Is an Orientation* (IVP, 2009)

Masaki, Naomichi. *Augsburg Confession XIV: Does It Answer Current Questions on the Holy Ministry* in Concordia Theological Quarterly, Vol. 70:2

McNeill, John J. *The Church and the Homosexual* (Beacon Press, 1993)

Meier, Scott T. *The Elements of Counseling* (Brooks/Cole Publishing, 1989)

Miner, Jeff and Connoley, John Tyler. *The Children are Free* (Jesus Metropolitan Community Church, 2002)

Mitchell, Christopher W. *Concordia Commentary: The Song of Songs* (Concordia Publishing House, 2003)

Nissinen, Martti. *Homoeroticism in the Biblical World* (Fortress Press, 1998)

Nordling, John G. *Concordia Commentary: Philemon* (Concordia Publishing House, 2004)

Okamoto, Joel P. *Office of the Holy Ministry* in Concordia Theological Quarterly, Vol. 70:2

Patterson, Linda J. *Hate Thy Neighbor* (Infinity Publishing, 2009)

Paulk, John and Anne. *Love Won Out* (Tyndale, 1999)

Piazza, Michael S. *Gay by God* (Sources of Hope Publishing, 2008)

Pronk, Pim. *Against Nature?* (Eerdmans, 1993)

Puls, Daniel W. *A Christian Perspective on Homosexuality* (CPH, 1996)

Rogers, Jack. *Jesus, the Bible and Homosexuality* (Westminster John Knox Press, 2009)

Saia, Michael R. *Counseling the Homosexual* (Bethany, 1988)

Sailhamer, John. *The Expositor's Bible Commentary: Genesis* (Zondervan, 1990)

Satinover, Jeffrey. *Homosexuality and the Politics of Truth* (Baker, 1996)

Scaer, David P. *The Office of the Holy Ministry According to the Gospels and the Augsburg Confession* in Concordia Theological Quarterly, Vol. 70:2

Schmidt, Thomas E. *Straight and Narrow?* (IVP, 1995)

Scroggs, Robin. *The New Testament and Homosexuality* (Fortress, 1983)

Sears, Alan and Osten, Craig. *The Homosexual Agenda* (Broadman & Holman, 2003)

Soards, Marion. *Scripture & Homosexuality* (Westminster John Knox Press, 1995)

Sonnenberg, Roger. *Human Sexuality: A Christian Perspective* (CPH, 1998)

Springett, Ronald M. *Homosexuality in History and the Scriptures* (Biblical Research Institute, 1988)

Spong, John Shelby. *The Sins of Scripture* (HarperCollins Publishers, 2005)

Stroup, Herbert W. and Wood, Norma Schweitzer. *Sexuality and the Counseling Pastor* (Fortress Press, 1974)

Stubrin, James P. *Sexualities and Homosexualities* (Karnac Books, 1994)

Swidler, Arlene. *Homosexuality and World Religions* (Trinity Press, 1993)

Switzer, David K. *Pastoral Care of Gays, Lesbians, and their Families* (Fortress Press, 1999)

Theological Implications of the 2009 ELCA Decisions (The Lutheran Church – Missouri Synod)

Thompson, Chad W. *Loving Homosexuals as Jesus Would* (Brazos Press, 2004)

Voelz, James W. *What Does This Mean?* (Concordia Publishing House, 1995)

Webb, William J. *Slaves, Women & Homosexuals* (IVP, 2001)

Wenz, Armin. *The Argument Over Women's Ordination in Lutheranism as a Paradigmatic Conflict of Dogma* in Concordia Theological Quarterly, Vol. 71:3/4

White, James R. and Niell, Jeffrey D. *The Same Sex Controversy* (Bethany, 2002)

White, Mel. *Stranger at the Gate* (Plume, 1994)

Willams, Craig A. *Roman Homosexuality* (Oxford University Press, 1999)

Willams, Patricia A. *Doing Without Adam and Eve* (Fortress Press, 2001)

Wink, Walter. *Homosexuality and Christian Faith* (Fortress Press, 1999)

Wold, Donald J. *Out of Order* (Cedar Leaf Press, 2009)

Women in the Church: Scriptural Principles and Ecclesial Practice (A Report of the Commission on Theology and Church Relations of the Lutheran Church – Missouri Synod, 1995)

Yamamoto, Isamu J. *The Crisis of Homosexuality* (Victor Books, 1990)

Galatians 6:1-2